A Harvey Cox Reader

A Harvey Cox Reader

Edited by

ROBERT ELLSBERG

ORBIS BOOKS

Maryknoll, New York 10545

ORBIS BOOKS
Maryknoll, New York 10545

Fathers and Brothers
MARYKNOLL
TOGETHER IN GOD'S MISSION OF MERCY

Founded in 1970, Orbis Books endeavors to publish works that enlighten the mind, nourish the spirit, and challenge the conscience. The publishing arm of the Maryknoll Fathers and Brothers, Orbis seeks to explore the global dimensions of the Christian faith and mission, to invite dialogue with diverse cultures and religious traditions, and to serve the cause of reconciliation and peace. The books published reflect the views of their authors and do not represent the official position of the Maryknoll Society. To learn more about Maryknoll and Orbis Books, please visit our website at www.maryknollsociety.org.

Library of Congress Cataloging-in-Publication Data

Names: Cox, Harvey, 1929- author. | Ellsberg, Robert, 1955- editor.
Title: A Harvey Cox reader / edited by Robert Ellsberg.
Description: Maryknoll : Orbis Books, 2016. | Includes index.
Identifiers: LCCN 2015042729 | ISBN 9781626981706 (pbk.)
Subjects: LCSH: Christianity. | Theology.
Classification: LCC BR50 .C63 2016 | DDC 230/.044—dc23 LC record available at
    http://lccn.loc.gov/2015042729

Contents

Preface

In 1965 Harvey Cox, a young Baptist theologian, published his first book. By any standard *The Secular City* was a phenomenal success—selling, all told, more than a million copies in over a dozen languages. For many Christians it became a kind of symbolic standard for the spiritual and cultural challenges of the 1960s. For its author, it established him as one of the most acute and interesting social observers on the American scene.

And yet, to achieve such early renown, as Cox would discover, can be a mixed blessing. In many ways he has continued to be known as the author of his famous book—often by people who have no memory of what it said, and even as his own work has taken him in many different directions. Still, it is a book that magazines and Cox himself have revisited at regular intervals—ten, twenty-five, and even fifty years later. It is, after all, a kind of landmark, in the truest sense—a marker held up from time to time to measure the distance that the world and Harvey Cox have traveled. This *Harvey Cox Reader,* compiled half a century after *The Secular City,* offers a different kind of perspective.

The Secular City was written at a time when many people were beginning to question the relevance of traditional institutional religion. "What I tried to say in that book," Cox has explained, "is that the God of the Bible is not confined to 'religion,'" that God was not dead but alive and well—not in some special "religious realm," but in ordinary human history. Rather than bemoan the waning of church attendance, Christians should be out cooperating with God's purposes in a passionate commitment to this world and its opportunities for greater justice, freedom, and humanity. The message struck a chord.

At the time Cox was deeply influenced by the work of Dietrich Bonhoeffer, the Lutheran theologian executed by the Nazis in 1945. In his prison letters Bonhoeffer had left behind suggestive outlines for what he called "religionless Christianity"—a gospel for a "world come of age." And yet if the task of the 1960s was to account for the rise of secularization and the decline of traditional religion, the challenge of subsequent decades seemed to be the extraordinary resurgence of religion. Whether in the rise of the Moral Majority in the 1980s, the role of the Polish Solidarity movement, the Islamic revolution in Iran, or the engagement of Christians in the revolutions of Latin America, there were signs throughout the world of a powerful religious revival.

Such developments didn't "disprove" the thesis of *The Secular City,* as some critics assumed. Cox had argued that the rise of secularization did not mean that God had disappeared from the world. By the same token, the various expressions of religious revival in subsequent decades did not mean that God had "returned." Indeed, developments in the world today seem to underscore the obvious fact that "the resurgence of religion is not everywhere and always a good thing." Sorting out the oppressive and liberating expressions of religion, in fact, has been an ongoing theme in his work.

In the 1970s and 80s such interests led Cox to enter deeply into the emerging liberation theology of Latin America, with its effort to reexamine and renew Christianity from the perspective of the poor. This flowed naturally from his constant interest in "people's religion"—focusing not just on the work of theologians but on what people really do and believe and how religion actually functions in their lives. Largely avoiding what he calls "the boardroom level of discourse," he has concentrated on the view from below—religion in its spontaneous, popular, indecorous, and sometimes seditious forms. Thus, his books are filled with glimpses of carnivals, pilgrimages, and exotic liturgies. He writes not just as a detached scholar, but as a participant-observer, a pilgrim, a friendly ambassador to realms of the spirit, at times a seeker engaged in his own quest for meaning. In *Turning East* he explored the attraction of the neo-oriental religious movements and described his own efforts "to grapple with the challenge of the Buddhist dharma to my mind and soul." In *Many Mansions* he described his forays into the field of interreligious dialogue. In the 1990s he explored the global rise of Pentecostalism. In *Common Prayers,* which drew on the experience of his own interfaith marriage, he offered an intimate journey through the Jewish year.

Cox's seeming knack for discovering "the next big thing," and his ability to write about theological issues for a wide popular audience, could prompt the charge of trendiness. And yet the selections in this volume make it clear how much his work has been guided by a set of remarkably consistent questions. Regardless of the context or the issue at hand, Cox has remained keenly attentive to what Pope John XXIII called the signs of the times, discerning how the Spirit is at work in the world, not only in expressions of faith, but also in expressions of doubt and questing. Both the faith and the questing spirit have deep roots in his own life.

Cox was born in 1929 in a small town in Pennsylvania. Growing up in the shadow of the Baptist church in Malvern, he has said that he can't remember a time when he didn't want to be a minister. After graduating from Yale Divinity School he was ordained to the American Baptist ministry in the chapel of Oberlin College, where he was serving as director of religious activities. In 1958 he went on to Harvard University, where he earned a PhD in the history and philosophy of religion in 1962. He then taught at Andover-Newton Theological School and served for a year as an ecumenical fraternal pastor in the divided city of Berlin. In 1965 he began to teach at Harvard Divinity School, where he remained for over fifty years, serving as the Hollis Professor of Divinity—the oldest endowed chair in the country. (Among the benefits of this post is the right to graze a cow in Harvard Yard—a privilege he exercised only once, on the occasion of his retirement in 2009.) At Harvard he has frequently crossed borders, engaging with scholars from the School of Government, the Business School, the School of Design, film studies, and other corners of the university. For many years his undergraduate course, "Jesus and the Moral Life," was one of the most popular courses on campus.

The social and political implications of the gospel have never been far from Cox's concerns. A friend of Martin Luther King, Jr., Cox was deeply engaged in the Civil Rights movement. He was a vocal critic of the Vietnam War and participated in the later anti-nuclear movement. In keeping with his work on liberation theology he taught off and on in seminaries in Mexico, Peru, and Nicaragua. Most recently he has studied the way that the market economy functions in our time as a kind of religious cult—with its own creed, rituals, and sacred texts. (On this theme he has been delighted to find agreement with Pope Francis.)

A fellow theologian has written of the "grave-merry man," who has mastered the art of "taking life seriously while playing, and of playing while taking life seriously." It is an apt description of Cox, who, after all, once proposed the image of the clown as the most real and relevant way to understand Christ today. His own spiritual life is nourished by prayer, the Bible, retreats at Trappist monasteries, and playing the tenor sax with a group called "The Morningside Jazz Ensemble."

With his many books and innumerable essays and lectures, spanning a career of over fifty years, it was a challenge to select the readings for this volume. One of the things that made it easier was Cox's tendency, in all his books, to start out with a general introduction that more or less summarizes his theme, along with a conclusion that points in the direction of wider questions. Fifty years after *The Secular City* Harvey Cox is still asking questions and searching for answers, still exploring the wider implications of the Gospel texts he discovered as a boy in Malvern, Pennsylvania. (His most recent book is entitled *How to Read the Bible.*)

Many years ago I had the opportunity to ask him what he would say if he could go back to the church in his hometown. He said: "Maybe I'd talk about the way the gift of the Spirit and Christian life can come to you through simple means, which it certainly did for me. The quality of the teaching in the church school there, the general level of preaching, to say nothing of the performance of the choir!—it was hardly at the highest level. But there was something authentic there, some reality that was undeniable. I guess I'd want to talk about the way the Spirit can reach you, even through ordinary means like that, and plant the seeds of a faith to last a lifetime."

Robert Ellsberg

Introduction

It is said that just before he sinks beneath the waves for the last time a man's whole life flashes before his eyes. I am a fairly good swimmer and don't expect to be caught in such a dire situation soon. But while reading through these excerpts from over fifty years of writing, something similar happened to me. I wrote the part on "The Tribal Village" in 1973, but perusing it carried me back to the beautiful corner of southeastern Pennsylvania where my earliest forebears, who were Quaker refugees from religious persecution, settled in the seventeenth century. I return there occasionally to visit the graves of my parents, grandparents, and great-grandparents. And I was reminded by Pope Francis in his eloquent address to Congress that all of us, even those whose ancestors arrived three hundred years ago, stem from immigrants.

My account of my time in the Merchant Marine in 1946 and 1947 described in "The Voyage of the *Robert Hart*" took me back to one of the most formative experiences of my life. Just turned seventeen, I was rudely exposed in Gdansk, where we delivered relief supplies, to the utter devastation war wreaks on innocent people. The ragged, dirty children who followed us through the streets begging and the pathetic teen-age prostitutes who sidled up to us as we walked through rows of devastated houses still linger in my mind. So there is a link between these two memories. My ancestors were Quakers (they called themselves simply "Friends") who refused to bear arms, and the ruined streets of Gdansk deepened my inherited opposition to war, and my suspicion of the military.

When I came to the section in this collection of my more theological writings I realized just how important it is to see them in context. After all, I marked the fiftieth anniversary of the publication of *The Secular City* in 2015; and one could think, well that was then but this is now. The astonishing success of that book took both me and the publisher by surprise. It eventually sold nearly a million copies, almost unheard of for a book on theology, then and now. And it was translated into a dozen languages including Catalan and Romanian. It was the bestselling original paperback in any field for the decade of the 1960s. Among other results, all this launched me into a temporary orbit of fame and publicity for which, then only in my thirties, I was unprepared and did not handle well. I began to take the recognition for granted. When Pope Paul VI told me in 1967 at the Vatican that he "had been reading" me, I did not think it all that unusual. Why wouldn't he be reading me? Everyone else (or so it seemed to me) was. Then, in the next five decades, when none of my books came even close to the readership gained by *The Secular City* (though some were quite widely read), I sometimes felt I was failing. Early success can be a plus, but it also carries a danger. Still, even though 1965 was *then*, a new fiftieth-anniversary edition was published by Princeton University Press in 2015. The book seems to have something to say not just then but now.

Readers of the section of this collection on *The Secular City* and the lively debate it kicked off will notice immediately that at that time I was hugely under the influence of the German pastor-theologian and anti-Nazi martyr, Dietrich Bonhoeffer. The theology of *The Secular City* is "Bonhoefferian." His placement of ethics at the heart of theology instead of its periphery, his deep desire to convey the gospel to the religiously "ungifted," and his embrace of a church divested of both the intellectual and the institutional trappings of Christendom struck me then, as they do now, as terribly important.

The other huge influence on my theological work was Paul Tillich. I had read some of his books as a seminarian at Yale in the mid-1950s, but I only studied with him during my doctoral work at Harvard. I was drawn to his interest in uncovering the religious dimension that lies just beneath the surface of "secular" culture and by his extensive enthusiasm for art, music, theater, and philosophy. I had read his work *The Courage to Be* when it first came out in 1950, and when Yale University Press asked me to write an introduction to the fiftieth anniversary edition in 2015 I accepted enthusiastically.

Tillich was not favorably disposed by Bonhoeffer, who—it might be recalled—wanted to develop a "non-religious" interpretation of the gospel. But for Tillich, religion was an indispensable dimension of human existence, and the substance of all cultural forms. I have never entirely reconciled my loyalties to these great thinkers, but I have also long since ceased to worry about it.

Part of the reason I had fallen under the spell of Bonhoeffer was that just before I wrote *The Secular City* I had spent a formative year of my life as an "Ecumenical Fraternal Worker" in the city of Berlin, where the bricks and barbed wire still divided the western from the eastern parts of the city. I resided with my young wife and two very young children in the western sector in an apartment on the Bundesalle in the Friedenau district, but my responsibility, teaching in a church-sponsored lay education program in what had been the Soviet occupied east but was now the German Democratic Republic, took me through Checkpoint Charlie three or four times a week. The teachers and faculty of the school, sponsored by the German Gossner Mission, were intensely interested in how to relate the Christian message to what they saw as an increasingly secular modern culture, one that in their case was undergirded by an officially atheistic regime. As a very recent Ph.D. this school gave me the opportunity to try out some of my ideas, in my limited but improving German, with largely sympathetic students. One young woman told me at the end of a semester that she had learned so much from me because I had to speak so slowly!

People are often amazed when they hear that the East German Communist regime allowed such a school to exist. What I have to explain is that the government there at the time gave the churches some elbow room as long as they did not take public stands against its policies. Of course we had Stasi informers in our classes, and we all knew it, but as the director of the school told me, with a wry smile, "they need to learn what we are teaching too, and we have nothing to hide." I was packing to leave Berlin in 1963 just as President John F. Kennedy delivered his "I am a Berliner" speech. I still love the city and visit it as often as I can.

Just after I returned home my own church, the American Baptists, invited me to give some talks at a national conference of Baptist students to be held at the denomination's assembly grounds on a beautiful lake in Green Lake, Wisconsin. This was just as the Civil Rights movement was moving toward its high point. The dogs and fire hoses of Birmingham had already been deployed, and I had participated in some demonstrations with our local chapter of Dr. King's Southern Christian Leadership Conference. Consequently I shaped my lectures at the student conference around Bonhoeffer, King, Berlin, and Birmingham. The talks were recorded but not published. Only after *The Secular City* made headlines did people at Judson Press (named for the famous Baptist missionary Adoniram Judson), which held the tapes, decide to transcribe and publish them. When they asked me what the title should be I suggested *God's Revolution and Man's Responsibility*. Readers should understand that although this little book was published *after The Secular City*, it was actually written *before*. Not that it matters much, but seeing the two in proper sequence conveys a better idea of the evolution of my thinking.

Many people were surprised when I published *The Feast of Fools* in

1969. It seemed to project a different tone than my previous books had, a lighter, some thought almost frivolous, one. But I did not see it that way. Always a close observer of cultural trends, and eager (à la Tillich) to examine them for any spiritual or theological dimensions, I saw in the upsurge of long hair, "be-ins," and balloons a vital dimension of the human spirit that had been almost doused by the obsession with efficiency and productivity in industrial civilization. This was also the period in my life when I was working together with Sister Corita Kent to stage upbeat protests against the Vietnam War. I learned a lot from Sister Corita, whom I had met when I gave a lecture at the College of the Immaculate Heart of Mary in Los Angeles. Her faith-inspired pop art, combining protest and spirituality with playful friskiness, seemed to me to hit just the right note. This period also coincided with my growing appreciation for what the Latin Americans call *religión popular*, the fiesta element in Christianity that my Protestant forebears looked upon with stern suspicion.

It is true that this element of human religiosity had been largely missing from *The Secular City*. But I was also aware of how cruelly this same element could be exploited and misused. This became the topic of *The Seduction of the Spirit*, which came out in 1973 just as I was also becoming aware of how many young people in America were becoming fascinated with religious movements arriving from Asia. Making use of the privilege I have as a professor to choose what courses I will teach, I announced a research seminar on these movements and encouraged students to visit, indeed to blend into, one of their expressions in the Boston-Cambridge area. They eagerly did so, showing up at gatherings of Tibetan Buddhists, Hare Krishnas, Vedantists, and Sufis. In order to accompany the students I did some of the same, and it was out of this participant-observer research that I wrote *Turning East* (1977), which, however, included an important chapter I called "Toward a Spirituality of the Secular" (Tillich and Bonhoeffer again). I continued to be interested in the significance of these so-called new religious movements (although some of them stemmed from traditions that predated my religion by a thousand years), and I became convinced that Christianity needed a strengthened and more nuanced theology of other faiths. I tried my hand at this task with *Many Mansions,* which takes its title from Jesus' assurance that in his father's house there are "many mansions," and "if it were not so I would have told you." As I pondered these questions I was significantly helped by the writing of the Cistercian monk Thomas Merton (who by the way had not liked *The Secular City*), whose mind had moved in the same direction.

No one who tries to follow my theological evolution can do so without understanding the enormous impact made on me by my experiences in Latin America. These began in the late 1960s when Father Gustavo Gutiérrez invited me to lecture at the Pontifical Catholic University of Lima in Peru. This Peruvian priest, who would soon become well-known as the "father" of liberation theology, had read some of my work and wanted me to speak at his university. It was a daunting challenge, but I went. In Peru I not only met Gustavo's students and colleagues, but I stayed with Maryknoll priests, accompanied them as they walked through the impoverished favelas and ministered to their people. After extending my trip to meet people Gustavo recommended in Chile, Argentina, and Brazil, I came back convinced that liberation theology, in one form or another, had to be the face of the future for all Christian theology.

Then in 1968 I accepted an invitation from Monsignor Ivan Illich to spend a summer with him in Cuernavaca, Mexico, at his Center for Inter-Cultural Formation. I liked Illich immensely, and that summer launched a friendship that was to last until his death in 2002. His photo hangs in my study among others who have influenced my life and thought. I continued to be drawn to the Catholic renewal he epitomized. But I was also saddened by the way Vatican officials opposed the movement, going so far as to "silence" Franciscan theologian Leonardo Boff. As a result of that I devoted many months of research in five languages to a book I called *The Silencing of Leonardo Boff* (1988). One can imagine how pleased I have been with the bold moves that Pope Francis, who is obviously inspired by liberation theology's "preferential option for the poor," has made in the three years of his pontificate. I was also thrilled to be asked to speak in June 2015 at a conference in Vitoria, Brazil, whose import was to get the liberation theology movement moving again now that there is a pope who supports it instead of trying to suppress it. Over five hundred people attended the conference, which attracted Catholics, Protestants, and Pentecostals. I was encouraged by the vivacity of the mostly young people who attended, all eager to take part. But perhaps my greatest joy on that occasion was that the other principal speaker was none other than Leonardo Boff, older and greyer than I remembered him (aren't we all?) but as forceful and eloquent as ever.

One of the biggest surprises for people who had been following my writing over many years was that in 1995 I published a book on Pentecostals entitled *Fire from Heaven*. What had gotten into me? Didn't this mark a radical departure from the author of *The Secular City*? Whatever one might say about these people who danced in the church aisles, claimed to "speak in tongues," and sometimes collapsed on the floor in ecstasy, Pentecostals seemed very un-secular.

My interest in so-called Spirit-filled Christians stems from my many years of living in and visiting in cities in many places in the world. Wherever I went—to Korea, Brazil, Italy, even Russia—they seemed to be there. And they seemed to be reaching people, especially the poor and the marginalized, that no one else was reaching. This was also true of the cities of America. My curiosity was piqued; they had to be doing something right. I began visiting their churches frequently, where I was always warmly received, and getting to know them personally. But I was sorry that so many "mainstream" Catholics and Protestants treated them so dismissively. I decided I wanted to write a book about them, designed to be read not by the Pentecostals themselves but by the people who, so it seemed to me, were treating them so haughtily.

To my great surprise it was not only these "outsiders" who read the book. Many Pentecostals also read it, and by and large were pleased—so they told me—that, although I included a couple harsh judgments, on the whole they found it fair. I began receiving invitations to speak at Pentecostal gatherings and institutions. This continued for many years until I began to feel like an honorary Pentecostal—though I never spoke in tongues!

But was this a reversal? I think not. Careful readers of my earlier work had noticed a genuine thread of continuity. From my earliest writing I had insisted all along that God was present not just in churches but in the everyday world (which in their own ways both Bonhoeffer and Tillich affirmed), and the Pentecostals I met as I was writing this book agreed. Genuine Trinitarians, they usually referred to God as the "Spirit," and their faith is so vibrant that in the merely one hundred years since their founding in Los Angeles in 1905, they have become by far the fastest growing segment of Christianity, spreading to every continent in the world. My friendship with Pentecostals reached a kind of peak in January 2015 when, in response to an invitation from Southeastern University in Florida, which was founded by the (Pentecostal) Assemblies of God, where I passed some happy weeks as a Guest Faculty Member. I taught classes, spoke in chapel, met with groups of faculty, and—not just incidentally—was happy to have escaped some of the glacial New England winter.

I have now completed fifty years of teaching at Harvard. I have lectured or taught in almost every division of the university including the Undergraduate College, the John F. Kennedy School of Government, the School of Education and during one semester several years ago at the School of Design (a course with the associate dean there on utopianism). For two decades I taught a course with very large enrollments at Harvard College called "Jesus and the Moral Life." My experience with that course fed into my book *When Jesus Came to Harvard,* in which I described how much I learned from the extremely diverse group of students, including Jews, Muslims, and Buddhists, as well as both Catholic and Protestant Christians.

I have also learned and profited from the rich range of colleagues with whom I have been surrounded. When one of my favorites, Professor Stephanie Paulsell, asked me to undertake a biblical commentary for Westminster Press I decided to do it, both because the prospect of working with her was inviting and because I never attempted such a thing before. The result was a single volume covering two biblical texts. Stephanie wrote the part on the Song of Songs while I wrote the section on the book of Lamentations. I had never plunged so deeply into a biblical book before, and I was alternately thrilled, exasperated, and discomfited. Lamentations is replete with murder, starvation, pillage, cannibalism, exile, a certain hopelessness. But through it all there is a continuing recognition that even if God seems to have abandoned us (a feeling everyone gets at one time or another), the Holy One who has been faithful in the past will be faithful again.

As the conclusion of my fiftieth year at Harvard Divinity School in 2015 coincided with the 200th anniversary of the founding of the institution, the dean asked me to deliver the annual Convocation address at the start of the school year. I focused on why some early nineteenth-century officials at Harvard College had called theology a "troublesome subject." I suggested that, yes, this is exactly what theology is supposed to be, that we should be in the business of preparing "troublemakers."

I hope my writing and teaching career still has a ways to go. As I write this I am preparing to spend some time at Arizona State University this winter (escaping the snow again), and I am writing a book for Harvard University Press that may be called *The Market God,* about the formative role consumer capitalism plays in our lives, to the point of having become a pseudo religion.

In rereading what I have written above, I fear that some readers may get the impression that all I do is read and teach and write books. That is hardly the case. I love to preach and do so whenever I am invited, often in my own Baptist congregation here in Cambridge. I am the father of eight grandchildren, each one more brilliant than the last.

I have been jailed while working with Dr. King and briefly incarcerated at the United States Air Force Academy in Colorado Springs (with three other Protestant ministers and a group of young women who were Catholic religious novices) for protesting the Vietnam War by handing out St. Francis's Peace Prayer. I continue to play tenor sax in a jazz ensemble. With my wife, Nina, a professor of history, especially of Russia, we travel all over the world, often as "study leaders" on Harvard Alumni Travel journeys. Last summer we visited Greece, Croatia, Montenegro, Italy, and other places on the Adriatic Sea. Next spring we will travel to Japan. I am thankful to God for the life he has given me, for my health, which remains good, and for the marvelous bevy of friends and family that surrounds me.

Harvey Cox
Cambridge, MA

October 2015

1

The Tribal Village (1973)

This chapter is taken from The Seduction of the Spirit: The Use and Misuse of People's Religion *(New York: Simon & Schuster, 1973), 23-46, 51-52.*

Just as I am, without one plea
But that thy blood was shed for me
And that bid'st me come to thee
O Lamb of God, I come, I come.
　　　　　　　　—Hymn by Charlotte Elliot (1789–1871)

In 1935, when I was six years old, the town of Malvern, Pennsylvania (Chester County), listed a population of 1,555. Apart from this fairly modest demographic aggregate, it had little else to boast of, at least as measured by this fallen world's avaricious calculus. Even in 1935 the world seemed to have left Malvern behind. Like a line drawn by a steel scalpel, the four-track "mainline" of the Pennsylvania Railroad bisected the town into "this side" and "across the bridge." But the trains didn't stop. Like arrogant, preoccupied strangers, they screamed through on their way east to Paoli or west to Harrisburg, bypassing Malvern. There was a persistently whispered rumor that the PRR had once offered to build its passenger depot at Malvern but that the conservative Quaker town fathers on the borough council had turned it down, so the depot was built two miles east in Paoli. Whether this oral tradition is true or not, today Paoli is blessed not only with the passenger depot but with a four-lane highway for its main street, plus more supermarkets, shopping plazas, parking lots, and specialty shops than Malvern could ever dream of. Richard Nixon spoke in Paoli during his unsuccessful Presidential campaign against John F. Kennedy in 1960. He bypassed Malvern on his way to his next stop, which was, I think, Downingtown. No Presidential candidate has ever visited Malvern, the constantly cold-shouldered little borough of my birth. I feel sure none ever will.

Even the highway bypassed Malvern. Up until the New Deal, a curving macadam road, then called the Lincoln Highway, ran through Malvern a quarter of a mile on the "other side" of the tracks in the section where most of the few blacks and all of the very few Italians in Malvern then lived, separated from each other by the highway. But during the 1930s a new concrete four-lane highway was constructed to link Philadelphia to Harrisburg via Paoli, Downingtown, and Coatesville. Malvern was bypassed. The old Lincoln Highway deteriorated and became neglected, in places even unused. Children played ball on it, and alfalfa shoots poked through the cracked tar. The tunnel it had run through, under the Pennsylvania Railroad tracks, was filled in with shale and dirt, creating a puzzling dead end for later generations of drivers unfamiliar with local history, and a relatively unpoliced nighttime parking area for couples intent on lust.

Industry had also bypassed Malvern. There was a small steel-tubing factory where a lot of people in town worked. But part of the sorry psychological history of the town was its rebuff and abandonment by the Hires root beer people. It seems to have been a case of downright desertion, and during most of the years of my childhood an ugly daily reminder of the humiliation stood on the corner of King and Bridge streets, at the very center of town. It was the large red-brick building once used by the Hires company but now empty and falling apart. Its windows broken, doors bashed in, walls collapsing, the building was finally decreed a safety hazard and razed. But for reasons I've never learned, even the razing was never finished. Maybe the money ran out, maybe the company lost interest. For whatever reasons, it was to remain for decades a half-destroyed, hence even more perilous, ruin. I can still remember a large glob of brick and cement, as tall as a man and three times as thick, hanging by a strand of cable from a half-exposed third-floor girder, like a grotesque sword of Damocles. I had been solemnly warned time and again by my parents never to play around the wrecked building. I'm sure they were right. It was not only unsafe, it was an open shame, and the bypassed people of Malvern would just as soon have forgotten it.

Still, the presence of the old Hires ruin provided the one occasion in my childhood memory when Malvern was not bypassed. During World War II, when the Civil Defense authorities of the neighboring towns wanted to stage a realistic air-raid drill, they selected Malvern as the site. Although it seemed at the time like an honor, in retrospect I wonder: Malvern was picked for the affair because, more than any other town anyone knew of, it looked like one of those bombed-out cities we saw pictures of in *Life*. Obviously Malvern was good for *something*.

Well, the Civil Defense drill was a great success, staged with theatrical realism and gusto. People came from miles away to watch, and the old Hires wreck served as a perfect smashed and twisted backdrop. Smoke bombs transformed it into a nearly believable Coventry. Sirens wailed. Once the crowd gasped as a dummy was thrown off the top of the ruin near the Damocles sword and into a fireman's net. Civil Defense wardens, aides, and anybody who could somehow obtain an armband rushed to and fro shouting orders and caring for the wounded, whose injuries, typed out on sheets of paper, were safety-pinned to their chests. I was selected as one of the victims. I still remember a youngish Dr. Jacob Sherson, who years later attended my father while he was dying of cancer, pretending to take care of the fictional injuries described on my paper. He was young, new in town, the only Jew anybody in Malvern knew; and he was obviously trying to do his bit. I remember well because I was embarrassed that my injuries ("bruises and contusions") were not nearly as serious as those of the girl next to me. She had a broken neck and internal bleeding. Some people have all the luck. Anyway, it was a great day for Malvern, even if the reasons our town was selected were a little ambiguous. At least once we had not been bypassed.

I know that nowadays towns *like* to be bypassed. Perhaps the somewhat isolationist decision of our curmudgeonly town fathers to let Paoli have the honor, noise, and congestion of the train depot might be viewed today as progressive, even ecologically sound. I know too that city officials today *try* to get highways out of the center of town and to move factories off Main Street, though I doubt that today Hires or anyone else could get away with leaving a teetering eyesore and fire-trap in its wake. But in those days, especially for the kids, it seemed that Malvern was a place the whole world had left behind. Unlike our great-grandparents, many of whom had lived in or near Malvern, we were constantly reminded of the big world outside by radio shows and magazines. But that world was somewhere else, or so we thought. We had to leave town to see a movie, board a train, visit someone in the hospital or even (after ninth grade) to go to school. Since the world had bypassed Malvern, it seemed to many of us, or at least to me, that a kid would have to leave Malvern to find the world.

I'm not so sure about that today. When I wrote *The Secular City* nearly ten years ago, I was still living in the heady ecstasy of escape from Malvern, the gossip-ridden small-town "fish bowl," where everybody knew everybody else. I even constructed an improbable typology of tribe-town-technopolis, ostensibly to make sense of the course of recent world history, but more probably to make sense of my own autobiography. Recently it has seemed to me that tribe, town, and technopolis are *not* stages in the maturation of the species at all, even though they did appear historically in that order. Rather, they are different ways of being in the world, each with its own richness and value, each with its faults and limitations. At this stage, there is a little of each in me.

Malvern, for me, represents tribe more than town. It is my ancestral taproot, my *axis mundi,* the cosmic navel, the sacred grove where I first discovered sex and work and death and love. It is where I first felt the unbearable cold that attacks your toes when you trudge home and pull off icy wet stockings after a day of sledding. It is where I first tasted the blood from my own lip, bashed into my irregular teeth by a big kid everyone called Ikey. That must have been in 1936, because he had caught me a block from home wearing my Landon sunflower, a gift from my grandmother, our family's most successful politician. (Politics in the 1930s had also bypassed Malvern, which had remained serenely Republican, at least on "this side" of the tracks, without interruption since the founding of the GOP in 1856.) It is where I first discovered myself alone in the woods on my stomach during an autumn game of hide-and-seek and heard the beat of my own heart against the earth and found that the soil has a dense, dark smell and that under every rotting branch there lives a whole sub-universe of scurrying midges who show little regard for passenger depots and four-lane highways. And Malvern is where I first learned about God. For if the world had bypassed Malvern, He certainly had not.

Even in the 1930s you didn't have to leave Malvern to find God. For a town with fewer than 2,000 souls we were more than amply blessed with churches. We had more churches than filling stations, more churches than saloons, more churches than restaurants. In fact, if I count correctly, there were more churches than all of those things put together. Which is cheating a little, because in those days we didn't have any restaurants. We did have two saloons and three gasoline stations. We had, however, eight churches. God had not only not bypassed Malvern, He had also generously provided a rich, if somewhat bewildering, variety of ways to approach Him. The tribe had several clans, and although there was sometimes suspicion and sniping among them, there was never intratribal war. Maybe that is why I've always been a pluralist. When you grow up in a town where on a warm Sunday with all the church windows open you can hear gospel hymns being sung and the Mass being chanted at the same moment, pluralism comes easily.

The churches of Malvern during the 1930s reflected, of course, what my scholarly mentors have since taught me to recognize as "class and ethnic lines." To start at the top of the pecking order, there was a lovely limestone meeting house, with nearby antique stables. It was used by the diminishing but stubborn band of Quakers. Inside were hard wooden benches, appropriate, I always thought, to the parsimony and severity of the Quakers I knew. I only saw those benches through the windows, however. Although the meeting house stood only a block from where I lived, and I often cut across its lawn on my way to my grandparents' house, I never once entered it. That seems strange to me now, especially as I remember being in all but one of the other churches at least once. Maybe it's because the congregation was so small and the meetings took place, I think, only once a month. Maybe it's because they never held youth meetings, community Christmas services or even weddings—which provided the occasions for my visiting other churches. More likely I absorbed from my parents a feeling that the Quakers, who had founded Malvern after all and represented the closest thing we had to a nobility, were a cold and inhospitable lot. They had some personal reasons too. My paternal grandfather, John Foreman Cox, had been "separated from meeting"—that is, excommunicated—in 1898 for "marrying out of meeting"—that is, taking a non-Quaker girl to wife. Grandfather immediately became a not particularly devout Baptist and hated the Quakers ever after. Grudges among the clans do last a long time in bypassed villages, even unto the children's children.

Well, to slide down one notch on the scale, we also had a small Presbyterian church in Malvern. During the whole period of my boyhood its congregation persevered patiently under the preaching of a pleasantly intense and lively man cursed with the most rasping, abrasive voice I have ever heard and given to forty-five minute sermons. Why, I often wondered, did they stay? I think I know now: They had no place to go. The Presbyterian church provided the niche for that minuscule stratum of the upper-middle who were not "birthright Quakers" (and surely no one *else* would attend meeting) but who would have felt miserably uncomfortable with the altar calls and teary revivals at the Methodist and Baptist churches. Far better the predictable drone of dependable moralisms that you could cope with, at least, in your pew than to be asked to "come forward" or to testify. John Calvin would have been mildly pleased to see that his God cared for the elect even in Malvern. You had to leave town during the 1930s to be an Episcopalian. The closest Episcopal church, the Church of the Good Samaritan, was in Paoli, two miles away. The only family I knew in Malvern who went there was that of the president of the town's only bank. No, there was also my Uncle Frank, the town's only undertaker. A marvelously genial man, he was, however, seen by some people, including my parents, as something of a social climber. He was the one person we knew who belonged to a golf club and drove a Cadillac. When he retired from his mortuary business a few years ago, he also became a bank president.

We all admired and liked Uncle Harry despite his upward mobility. Maybe it was the way he did it. Although the Episcopal church smacked to me in those days of the society pages, coming-out parties and people who wore red coats and rode horses after foxes and dogs—a very distant world indeed—Uncle Harry had been a poor up-country Episcopalian from a very pious family *before* he got rich, so he never got snooty about it. Maybe because he saw so many dead bodies he seemed to have a kind of jocular contempt for worldly rank and privilege. He made it big, but he never forgot old friends or kissed anybody's ass. And he was a vestryman at the Church of the Good Shepherd, Episcopal.

There were two churches for blacks, or "colored people," as every well-mannered kid was taught to say in those days before Malcolm X and Stokely Carmichael. On "this side" there was an African Methodist Episcopal (A.M.E.) congregation housed in a tiny brick building on an unpaved street in a section of town where, to this day and in seeming disregard for the changing tides of racial integration, separation and the rest, black and white families live cheek by jowl. My Grandmother Cox often took me to church suppers at the A.M.E. church. It never occurred to me then that the black townspeople at the suppers, enjoying that savory ham, corn on the cob and fried chicken, were also voters, and that her being there might have helped her to get re-elected year after year to almost any office she wanted, or that she went there for that reason. I don't honestly think it occurred to her either. For Maud Cox it was one way to get away from cooking dinner and to chat for two hours with willing listeners.

The other black church remains a mystery to me even today. It stood across the bridge, not much more than a shack clinging to a corner of land near the abandoned section of the old Lincoln Highway. It housed a Baptist congregation made up mostly of the poor, mainly darker-skinned, black people who lived nearby. It represented then, I suppose, the end of the class-ethnic spectrum opposite the Quaker meeting.

Maybe that's why it is the only other church in Malvern I have never been inside. But I still feel sad and cheated about that. I went to school and played and fought with kids who went to that church, but not until I was in my teens did I see anything odd about their having completely separate ways to God. I sometimes wonder now if that strangeness ever struck them.

St. Patrick's Roman Catholic Church, a large stone Romanesque structure, stood next door to the rambling brick-and-frame double house I lived in. On the other side of the house stood the large brown Baptist church where I belonged. When people find out today that I spent the first seventeen years of my life living in the only house standing *between* the Baptist and the Catholic churches of Malvern, they often make some quip to the effect that I was fated or predestined to become an ecumenical theologian. I'm not so sure about that. I am sure, however, that the location has a lot to do with the way I felt about the Catholic Church. The way I felt, and still feel, expressed in a few words, is "close, but outside."

During the 1930s Vatican II, the ecumenical movement and all that could hardly have been anticipated in anyone's wildest fantasies. Catholics were busy building up the separate school system so many of them would now like to unload. In Malvern the parochial school was a tiny affair, housed in an old residence across the street from the church. The pupils, always clothed in black and white uniforms, played during recess on a gravel lot next to our side yard. They were pretty noisy during their games but got very quiet amazingly fast, I thought, when the nun rang a large silver bell. I grew up thinking there was *something*—I was never really sure what it was—*different*, either about me or about them. In the 1930s there were probably more reasons for the Catholics to feel different from me than vice versa. The bitter memory of Al Smith's defeat in 1928 still rankled. Catholics and Protestants lived in overlapping but still somewhat separated worlds and heard piles of rumors and nonsense about each other, some of which is still there in our heads. Most of it we just forgot as soon as we heard it, but the impression of a real difference persisted.

Many years later, in 1959, when I was a graduate student at Harvard, I helped organize a group in which Catholics and Protestants could meet to discuss theology and politics. How daring the idea seemed in 1959! Since then I have taught Catholic (as well as Jewish, Buddhist, Mormon, Muslim, and atheist) students; lectured at the Pontifical Catholic University of Peru in Lima (the first non-Catholic theologian to do so); been personally received (and mildly condemned) by Pope

Paul VI; preached in Catholic churches; celebrated communion jointly with priests; been arrested in peace demonstrations with priests and nuns. Together with one Catholic priest, Nicolas Spagnola, I officiated at one of the first ecumenical wedding services ever held in Boston, the marriage of my youngest brother, Phil Cox, to Mary Ellen, née de Stefano. It took place at the Sacred Heart Church in Newton. I suspect that at least as many Catholics as all other people put together read my books.

But despite all this welcome ecumenical thaw, and despite our natural desire to emphasize similarities, we are now at the stage, I think, where we can not only admit to but celebrate our differences. They make the stew more succulent. A lot of those differences, I am discovering, have to do not with doctrine but with feeling. And a lot of them root in our childhood.

My own childhood impression about Catholics was that they were just that: different. Not that they had guns in their church basements or were going to take over the country, but that their religion seemed like an unnecessarily elaborate caricature of what I had been taught was quite simple and that the rules they followed, like not eating meat on Friday, were not only very strict but pointless. It really wasn't the Friday abstinence I minded, it was the impression they conveyed, usually subtly, but often explicitly, that somehow they were closer to God because they devoutly ate tuna fish while I ate salami. What bothered me, I guess, was not the difference itself but that they seemed very sure they were right and, at times, even arrogant about it. By high school it was a commonplace among the rest of us that it was just plain useless to argue with Catholics about religion, because no matter what you said, they *knew* they were right, or at least they seemed to know.

I don't think all that would have irked me so much except that I harbored a secret suspicion from a very early age that they just might be right. Sometime very early on, just after I had learned to read, I noticed one day that their church had engraved on its cornerstone an inscription stating that it had been founded by Jesus Christ Himself. Himself! The comparable stone in our church said "Founded in 1846," which even as a small kid I knew was considerably *later* than Jesus Christ's time. Besides, when men walked by the Catholic church some of them took off their hats. They didn't do that in front of ours. And whenever I peeked in the half-open doors of St. Patrick's while on my way to Stackhouse's grocery store or the post office, I'd catch a glimpse of a mysterious darkness broken only by an even more mysterious flickering red lamp. Catholic playmates assured me in hushed tones that

Jesus Christ Himself was up there on the altar. We didn't even *have* an altar, let alone one with Christ Himself on it. Many times I would like to have ventured into the dim recesses of St. Patrick's, but I was scared. It seemed so foreboding, so dark and awesome. I wondered to myself sometimes how it would feel to be inside that fearsome place, not to be viewed as an outsider, how it would feel to be at home there, protected by those uncannily powerful mysteries instead of threatened by them.

I never got into the main section of that Catholic church until my cousin Phyllis married a Catholic man when I was in my late teens. The closest I got were those occasional peeks plus attending musicals in the church basement. Again it makes me a little sad to think about that. I had cousins and playmates right on my street who were Catholics. They wore medals, crossed themselves now and then, went to confession on Saturday afternoons and, of course, didn't eat hamburger on Friday. But we never once visited each other's churches. They had been taught, at least they told me then, that it would be a sin for them so much as to *enter* our church. There was even some question, I remember, about whether they would be endangering their souls to come into the social hall of our church for a covered dish supper on Wednesday night. Naturally I could not help wondering what it was about our church that posed such a terrible threat.

All the same, I was secretly a little relieved that they were not allowed to come in, because I was afraid they'd see right away that there wasn't much to it. We had no little red lamp, no rose windows, no exotic darkness. Our windows were plain glass. I wasn't exactly ashamed. I just didn't think they'd understand what was important to me about my church, and I knew I couldn't tell them. So they might get even more smug. Better they shouldn't know.

No one ever told me I'd go to hell if I went inside the Catholic church. I did get the clear impression, however, from both sides, that my presence was not sought and that I would not be very welcome. I still remember a dream I once had as a child in which I found myself sitting and trying to appear unobvious in the last row of the Catholic church— very dark and terrifying in the dream—during a Mass. Suddenly I was being singled out by the priest and commanded in a sepulchral echo-chamber voice to kneel. When, years later, I read Kafka's *The Trial*, I was astonished to find a very similar theme there, K.'s strange experience in the cathedral of Prague. Maybe it's an archetype.

In any case, archetype or no, I grew up with the feeling that Catholics either knew something I didn't know or thought they did. And I really wanted to know which it was. I think I still do. Though I hated to admit it, it often seemed to me that our Baptist church, which with an average Sunday attendance of fewer than a hundred people was still the most "successful" non-Catholic church in town, nevertheless looked somehow amateurish, precarious, and insecure when compared to the Catholic one. That would have been all right too, I guess, but what really hurt was that my Catholic playmates always seemed so sure. They seemed to have no doubts whatever, and I had had doubts ever since I could remember. Was there *really* a God, or were people just wishing? Did we really go somewhere better after Uncle Harry had drained our blood and we'd been put in a satin-lined casket, lowered into a grave and covered with dirt, or did we lie there forever and ever, the worms devouring our flesh? I lay awake many sleepless nights over those questions, even at nine and ten—and I still sometimes lose sleep over similar questions today. Maybe my Catholic friends and cousins had doubts too after all. Or maybe they didn't. In any case, they *talked* and *acted* as though they didn't, and that's what bothered me most about them.

Today, decades later, when I talk honestly to Catholics, I get the feeling that, although they belong to the Catholic Church, they know now how I felt then. For now, even on the inside of their church, that serene assurance is gone. So is that secure conviction that it all goes back directly to God Himself. Catholics too now know that awful sense of precariousness. The flickering red light is still there, at least in some parishes, but doubts and uncertainties inhabit the darkness around it. The Catholic Church I knew from the outside, and they from the inside during those now long-gone days, just doesn't exist any more. In that sense we are all "outside" now, and our task is to learn how to live with it.

There was also a Methodist church in Malvern, quite small, where the people sang a little louder and took revival a little more seriously than we Baptists did. They sang hymns that might have seemed a little too emotionally explicit to the more dignified pillars of our church. On a warm Sunday evening, from two blocks away, you could hear the Methodists singing:

> What a wonderful change in my life has been wrought,
> Since Jesus came into my heart!
> Floods of joy o'er my soul like the sea billows roll,
> Since Jesus came into my heart.

It was one of their favorites. They would sing the verse and then hold the word "since" a long, long time, coming down and then bouncing ahead on the word "Jesus." Their singing was often accompanied by a trumpet or even a trombone. In our church, musical instruments other than the organ were generally used only for solos. I have since learned that the 1930s and 1940s were a period of great emphasis on social action in American Methodism. Somehow that emphasis never seemed to reach Malvern. But I don't really mind that very much. It was a happy, warm church where nobody looked at you funny if you really poured the volume into a gut-busting hymn: "*Since . . .* Jesus came into my heart. . . ."

My own family belonged, more or less, to the Baptist church next door. My parents, during my boyhood, rarely attended, although later on, after I went to divinity school, they went more often. But they were never very regular churchgoers. Still, all through the 1930s they did send us to Sunday school, where my excommunicated ex-Quaker grandfather took the class roll and counted the nickels and pennies in the collection. But that was about all the religion he could take. He left the church building after his Sunday school treasurer's duties were done and sat on his front porch reading the Sunday edition of the Philadelphia *Inquirer* and smoking a cigar. He never once attended church services, so far as I remember, during his entire life. My grandmother never missed. A large handsome woman reputed to have been a famous beauty in her youth, she was kind, jolly, easygoing, and totally untheological. For her the Baptist Church, the Fire Company Women's Auxiliary, and the Women's Republican Club were all overlapping tents in the same big county fair, and she loved to be in the center of it all. Although she was at times a member of various county and even state Republican committees, her politics was as nonideological as her religion was nontheological. She hated cooking, rarely cleaned house, dressed haphazardly and spent most of the day wandering the streets of Malvern conversing cheerfully with everyone she met. She never lost any election she ran in, and she died of a heart attack in her seventies one blistering July afternoon while buying the rolls and hot dogs for the annual volunteer fire company fair.

My own recollections of the First Baptist Church of Malvern are a mixture of warmth, boredom, awe, guilt, and fascination. We sang hymns about crosses and blood and pilgrims and diadems. We heard time and again stories about David and Goliath, Saul and David, Adam and Eve, Cain and Abel, Jesus and Judas. At unforgettable moments other people, and eventually myself, would be immersed in the sloshing waters of the baptismal pool, with the congregation singing "Just as I Am." I remember especially the second verse of that hymn:

Just as I am, though tossed about
With many a conflict, many a doubt

> Fightings and fears within, without,
> O Lamb of God, I come, I come.

That was just how I felt, and it seemed good to be able to sing it. I was at home in church since before I can remember.

I know, probably better than most people, how narrow and mossy Baptist churches, maybe all churches, can be—how intolerant, ignorant and all the rest. When I went to college I was sometimes embarrassed when people would ask about what they usually referred to as my "religious background." It seemed to be assumed that having something like that in your childhood, though unfortunate, could be outgrown. But since I've gotten beyond that sophomore intellectual stage, I have never wanted to disavow that so-called "background," because when all is said and done, it remains the way I met the holy, and I've never been able to shake that off. I doubt that I'll ever want to.

I got baptized myself when I was ten, going on eleven. That seems a little young, and in retrospect I can scarcely claim to have reached the age of consent. I can't say that I'd had a deeply emotional salvation experience beforehand or anything like that. I had not. I hardly knew what was happening.

One Sunday our minister, Mr. Kriebel, visited our boys' Sunday school class and asked how many were now ready to follow Jesus into the waters of baptism. We all liked Mr. Kriebel immensely. A youngish man at the time, he was a somewhat uninspiring preacher but an incomparable small-town pastor. He was always on the spot when people were down with flu or stomach trouble or when someone died. Besides, he took us swimming in his rattling 1935 Ford and both coached and pitched for the church's softball team. He had a way of standing stiffly in his tight Sunday clerical clothes which made you think he would be more comfortable in a cotton pullover and sneakers. He read a lot though, especially biography, and peppered his sermons with stories from the lives of great painters, explorers, and composers. Mr. Kriebel in 1939 made $1,600 per year plus use of parsonage and car expenses. We boys all admired him, and it seemed important to him that Sunday that we be ready to follow Jesus. So we all said we were. It sounded like a small thing to do.

There were only six of us in the class, so Mr. Kriebel had us all come over to his parsonage for three or four weeks for a baptismal class where, mainly, we learned what we were to say when the deacons examined us and how to respond to the questions the minister himself would put to us in the baptismal pool. Our preparation, however, was not very adequate, since it did not include instructions on how to handle the situation that would arise if one of us got the giggles during the prayer part of the deacons' meeting, which is exactly what happened. Our examination by the deacons was a disaster, but they were not of a mind to turn down candidates for baptism, I guess. So they accepted us.

I was baptized not in a white robe as the pictures of old-time baptisms show but in a pair of worn white slacks and a loose white shirt. The minister wore a black robe, weighted at the bottom seam to keep it from floating up, and hip boots. At baptisms that I'd seen before I knew about those boots. I was always astonished at how quickly he could reappear in the pulpit, perfectly dry, after conducting a baptism, to dismiss the congregation. The baptismal pool itself, as in most Baptist churches, was located behind the pulpit and built in such a way that you could both enter and leave it from its sides without having to walk through the congregation. I've been told that in old Baptist churches this architectural concession to the modesty of candidates for baptism was not the custom, that the pools were often built near the center and that when you came up dripping and sputtering from the waters you could not disappear discreetly into a wing but had to make your way, with lots of help of course, right through the waiting congregation to wherever you got dried and reclothed. Of course in the really old days baptisms occurred in rivers. By 1940, however, in the First Baptist Church of Malvern, they had become considerably more decorous.

I entered the pool that Sunday with very little sense of what I was doing or why. The choir and congregation sang very softly, "Just as I am, without one plea." The water came up to just above Mr. Kriebel's waist. It came up to my armpits. He stood facing the congregation over the edge of the pool and read something from the Bible. I think it was about the baptism of Jesus by John the Baptist in the River Jordan. I stood with my side to the congregation on his right. When he finished the reading, he closed the Bible and asked me in quiet serious tones whether I accepted Jesus as my personal savior. I said I did. He then said, in a somewhat more public voice, that he was baptizing me in the name of the Father, Son and Holy Spirit, placed one hand behind my back and lowered me backwards into the water while I held a white handkerchief over my nose and mouth, as we'd been taught, to keep the water out. He held me under only for a second, then pulled me back up, turned me around and handed me to the deacons who were waiting in the wings to help me dry off and return to the main section of the church to be welcomed into the congregation as a full participant.

I tried to be as nonchalant as possible about my baptism, even to joke about it as soon as I could. I even remember quipping lamely to the elderly deacon who helped dry me that I wouldn't need a bath that night. But I just couldn't pass it off as glibly as I wanted to. It made a telling impression on me. I'd be very sorry if in some future ecumenical version of Christianity that terribly primitive rite, so archaic and so incontrovertibly "out of date," were to disappear. I say that even though I was baptized long before I should have been. My real religious crisis, when I agonized over whether I was saved, going to hell, and all the rest, came during my late adolescence. I even resented at that time that the minister and deacons had allowed us to get baptized, maybe even pushed us into it before we were ready. I don't resent it now. They were doing the best they could. They probably wanted to get us all into the church before we dropped out of Sunday school, which a lot of boys did in their teens. And with me, it worked. I did drop out of Sunday school soon after I was baptized, but I hardly ever missed church. I went, not because I had to, but because I wanted to. I don't know why for sure. Somehow it just seemed important.

My resentment at being baptized at ten before I was ready, and then having no ritual available to mark my adolescent religious crisis, may help explain some of my current interest in ritual. I believe that as a culture we are ritually out of phase. We are dragooned into rituals that mean little or nothing to us—saluting flags, national anthems, commencements, even bar mitzvahs and confirmations—yet when we need the symbolic deepening of an important experience, we somehow lack the necessary gestures and images.

Nothing is easier to make fun of than the sloppy, improbable form of baptism I experienced at ten, the awkward effort, complete with hip boots and warmed waters, to keep something of the primitive in a modern hygienic setting.

But maybe we laugh too soon. Remember *your* emotional state at thirteen or thereabouts? Remember your need to deal all at once with anxiety and awkwardness, identity and faith, finding your way out of childhood, facing your own death, finding something to live for? Is it any wonder that nearly every culture in the world has devised rites of passage—initiation and puberty rituals—to deepen and resolve this perennial crisis? The Cheyenne lad goes out to the forested hills alone, sleeps on the ground, lives without food, suffers cold and loneliness, sees a vision and then returns to the tribal circle to become a brave and to receive a new name. He has endured his ordeal and is now an adult.

Today in America we have few if any puberty rites. Children pass awkwardly and without ritual through sprouting pubic hair, menstruating, changing voice, having wet dreams, getting hold of the family car keys. No wonder we undergo "identity crises" until we die. Rituals should mark and celebrate the transition from one phase of life to the next. But our lives are phaseless, like an automatically geared car shifting noiselessly from one speed to another. And the result is that we never know for sure what gear we're in now. Children try to act like adults and adults like children.

For me, despite its being too early and only fully appreciated much later, my baptism was what some young people today might call a "real trip." There were all the symbols of blood and suffering (sharing the death of Jesus), the physical act of going under the water, the facing of embarrassment, fear, the triumphant emergence, the feeling that I'd been through something and was starting a new phase.

The word "trip" here is not accidental. I wonder sometimes how much drug trips have begun to take the place of our culture's forgotten or abandoned puberty rites. The experience is similar in many ways. You expose yourself to danger and death. You make a break from the world of childhood. You see visions. You may suffer pain. You come back, usually, and are received into a new phase of life by those who have undergone the ordeal before you. You may even feel you've seen God or have found a way of life.

I don't believe for a minute that all those terrifying "drug education" spots on TV will scare kids out of trying drugs. In fact, they may have the opposite effect. Everyone longs, sometimes secretly, to experience altered states of consciousness. Adolescents are intrigued by death and danger, *not* repulsed. How can people lure them *into* movies with the same symbols they somehow think will *repel* them from drugs? Our drug epidemic may or may not be a serious one. But I believe it is the symptom of a deeper cultural disease—the disappearance of legitimate occasions for ecstasy, trance, emotion and feeling, and the erosion of traditional rituals. When I was a kid, people got "high" at revivals and during other religious events. Everyone needs to experience that special kind of mental elation now and then. If we don't do it one way we will do it another. We won't outgrow drug abuse until those needs too, not just our needs for bread and housing, are cared for. Man does not live by bread alone.

In recent years I've become much more interested in this issue of "ritual" (a word I usually define as "symbolic action," in contrast to myth, which is symbolic thought. The two go closely together and are seldom discovered in isolation from each other). I forget just when the word "ritual" ceased having a negative, sticky sanctimonious connotation for me and began serving as a pivot around which I could organize a lot of the loose ends not only in my thinking but in my life. Maybe it happened in the middle 1960s when I first fell in with the "radical Catholics" like Corita Kent, Dan Berrigan, Ivan Illich, and the people from Emmaus House. Maybe it happened during that period of the anti-war movement when the immolation of draft cards in altar-candle flames was going on. In any case, the power of symbolic acts, "the politics of gestures," certainly became a central concern for me by the time the peace movement began using rituals like coffins, mock burials, fasts, sanctuary vigils, and the rest. After participating myself in many of these rites, and seeing the impact they had on all kinds of people, I couldn't really go on claiming that man is leaving behind his "religious stage," including ritual and myth. I just could not believe that idea any more after, for example, watching dozens of young men come forward and solemnly burn draft cards at the altar of the Arlington Street Church. It was all there again—puberty rite, sacred flame, ordeal, risk, the symbolic act of cutting oneself off from one community and becoming part of another, the choosing of a new way of life. The boy becomes a man with a new name. As those draft cards crackled in the candle flames, I could see in the smoke the shadows of rites that reached back to the infancy of the species. I became convinced at that moment that although modern urban man was certainly not religious in most conventional senses of the word, neither was he secular in the way I had once thought. I could see that ritual and religion were not going to wither away, and that the real issue now was whether they would be used for man's liberation or to keep him in bondage.

The Berrigans and many others had seen all that and felt it long before I did. They knew the potency of gestures. They acted on it in the blood pouring and the burning of draft records. In their melding together of ritual and revolution, the politics of symbolic gesture again began to play a decisive role in the American consciousness. I'm convinced now that man never "outgrows" rituals, although he certainly uses them for vastly different purposes and relates to them in ever-changing ways.

Until quite recently I was deeply confused about the sources of my interest in ritual. Hadn't I come from a notoriously "anti-liturgical" and "non-ritualistic" church? Was I regressing into a primitive stage of my own, and maybe even mankind's religious development? Was it a loss of nerve?

I think the answer to all those questions is no. I grew up in a church which I was told time and again by those inside it and outside it was "anti-ritualistic." But it is no such thing. It holds at the core of its life one of the most powerful rituals anyone has ever undergone—identification with the burial and resurrection of the God through a deathlike total immersion in water. It fairly *crawls* with archetypes, and however much Baptist preachers may inveigh against "ritualism," and I've heard it inveighed against hundreds of times, people who, like me, have gone through the waters at an impressionable age can never honestly deny the uncanny power of that experience, even if they have junked all the doctrinal interpretation long since. Archetypes touch you at a level far deeper than doctrines.

What I am saying is that I no longer view my recent increased interest in ritual and myth as a deviation from my "background" but as a rediscovery of its essential quality. Mircea Eliade says somewhere that initiation is the most pervasive and perennial of all forms of ritual. I think he is right. Even more importantly, an initiation rite like the one I experienced, even when shorn of its particular denominational interpretation, still creates a life paradigm of enormous potency. Plunging under the water says that life is made up of one risk after another, that maturation requires the continuous surrender of familiar securities, that I can't breathe free unless I have taken the leap.

But church was not just terror and purgation for me. It was also a groove: taking up the collection in wooden plates with green felt bottoms and discreetly trying not to notice who put how much in; thumping out the bass line in choir anthems like "Jerusalem" and "The Stranger of Galilee" after my voice changed; consuming enormous amounts of baked ham, candied sweet potatoes and lemon meringue pie at potluck suppers. But, more than anything else, what got to me about church was the ministers.

The ministers who came to our little congregation for what was usually a short pastorate, probably because they were paid so poorly, were a varied, eccentric and completely unstereotyped lot. They could hardly have been cum laude seminary graduates to find themselves in what must have been an unprestigious outpost even in its own denomination. Still they were always larger-than-life figures to me. Their black suits and booming voices set them apart from other mere mortals. Their sheer knowledge seemed amazing to me and their confidence and poise unbounded. But at the same time they were invariably friendly and accessible. They even *wanted* to know me. They were a little like God. Although ministers obviously commanded respect and even deference, they also weeded their tomatoes, had sickly wives and squawking children, and sometimes seemed discouraged or angry. Besides, they had huge collections of books, were actually *paid* to read them and to prepare sermons. They knew, it seemed to me, almost everything, and they didn't seem to be afraid to die. How else were they able to talk about it when nobody else did? I can't remember when I didn't want to be a minister when I grew up.

When I think back, there were obviously other things about the ministers that attracted me. For one thing, they were never completely at home in Malvern. Most people in our town were born there or close by and lived there until they died, although even in the 1930s they were beginning to leave town to die in the hospital in the county seat seven miles away. But the minister always came from somewhere else, stayed a few years, then left. He was always something of an outsider, without cousins and uncles in town. He was *in*, but not *of*, our world, to paraphrase St. Paul. His coming and his going reminded me of that vast larger cosmos in which little Malvern was located. The preacher, even if he stayed five years, was always to some extent a stranger in a strange land. Maybe that gave him a little of the aura of transcendence or at least of the "otherness" the representative of God must always signify, whether he likes it or not.

The fact that ministers came and went or, as it was always put, were "called" and "went on to larger fields of service" also made its impact on the congregation. We knew the church was not his but ours in a special, rather disquieting way. We knew we couldn't ultimately depend on someone else to solve our problems. Because Baptists have a congregational form of church government, we came to sense very sharply, especially during the times of preacher transition, that our choices were real and important. This was true even among the kids, since anyone who had been baptized could vote in a church election. It was one of the few things we did not giggle about. No one *sent* a pastor, as happens in Catholic and Methodist churches. We had to "call" him, and this meant appointing a pulpit committee that would go around interviewing prospective candidates, listen to them preach, and then recommend one, or sometimes two, for a vote by the full congregation. I know all this well because my first real experience in participatory democracy came when I was thirteen. That year, because I was a little precocious and president of the youth group, I became a full voting member of one of these periodically necessary pulpit committees.

When the preacher left we were on our own, abandoned in a sense like Christ on the cross by what classical theologians call the *deus absconditus*. We had to take things into our own hands and start over.

It was sobering to sit with all those adults, some of them sixty years older than I, and to know that my thirteen-year-old vote would help determine who would lead our church for the next few years. But I also felt a heady tingle of power. No mere student council or Boy Scout election this. We were charged with the awesome task of choosing the man to represent God in our midst. And we did it. Ever since then I've been less apprehensive about sharing power with nonspecialists, letting the people themselves make decisions. I've been more skeptical of a god who does everything for us or to us and more willing to imagine a divine–human partnership than many theologies allow. Maybe that's why I'm more intrigued by people's religion and popular culture. I can honestly say that as a kid I absorbed more about God and man from participating in congregational life than I did from the worship and preaching.

There was even a kind of paradox between the preaching and the practice that set up a tension I have felt ever since. The preaching tended to be vaguely Calvinistic, spiced with generous doses of pietistic flavoring. Basically, however, we were told that God saved man by grace, that grace was unmerited and that there was nothing at all we needed to do to earn it, just accept it. The analogy of a gift versus a purchase was used all the time by the preachers, and people giving testimonies would frequently repeat the idea that they had tried to do this or that with no satisfaction and had finally been saved only when they realized that God's love was absolutely free, that Christ had already died for our sins and that all we had to do was to "open our hearts and receive Him." But in contrast to this God-does-it-all preaching there was the evident fact that *we* had to keep the church going, organize its programs, select its leaders, pay its bills and paint and repair the building. God did not do that, we did; though when we were finished we always thanked God for what He had done. The ancient riddle of faith and works, activity and acquiescence was built into my consciousness from the start.

It is an eternal riddle. In various guises it has charmed and pursued me throughout my life. I am intrigued by the multiple ways people form and are formed by their cultures. It is not only true, as Churchill once said, that we first shape our buildings and then are shaped by them. It is also true, I believe, of our symbols, our institutions, our culture and our religion. My fascination with this unending interactive process goes back, I am sure, to that portentous experience of power and weakness, of selecting preachers and then being taught by them, of molding and being molded by a religious community—all of which took place with such a vivid quality in the life of a small religious congregation like the First Baptist Church of Malvern.

* * *

I left in 1946 to get out to see the world that had bypassed Malvern. I did it by spending a few months on the horse and cattle ships being run after the war by UNRRA and the U.S. Merchant Marine. During those months I sailed to England, Germany, Poland, and Belgium, first on a dilapidated Liberty ship called the *Robert Hart*, named for the captain of a previous vessel who, in defiance of a new regulation, had insisted on going down with his ship instead of abandoning it; and then on a newer ship called the *Pass Christian Victory*, named after a small Gulf port in Mississippi. Malvern seemed very far away, but everywhere we tied up I visited churches, many of them still in ruins. I never told my shipmates about my boyhood hope to someday become a minister. I felt they wouldn't have understood, and besides in those days I often wondered about it myself.

I came back to Malvern for a short while before I went away to college at the University of Pennsylvania in 1947. But after I'd crossed the ocean a few times Malvern didn't seem the same. No one in my family had ever crossed an ocean. Most had rarely ventured outside Chester County. Before I left I had wanted to get away from Malvern. Now I'd been away, but I didn't really want to come back. Besides, everything was changed. Ministers had come and gone in the Baptist church. The old brown coloration I remembered, somber and serious, was gone. It was now painted white and had a new "religious education" wing. Later on, after I'd graduated from divinity school, my father died and my mother sold our old brick and frame house to the Catholic church next door. It is now occupied by the Sisters of St. Joseph. The last time I was in town I noticed that the old Hires ruin had been removed, and a small clean plastics factory stands on that once shameful spot. An independent fundamentalist group has bought the limestone Quaker meetinghouse. The trains still bypass Malvern, but now that everybody drives cars the townspeople feel more mobile, if not as involved with one another. A couple of housing developments have added five hundred souls to the population, so it is now actually possible to see someone in the post office no one knows. Even Malvern has edged over the line and is now almost a *suburb*, no longer the tribe or, more accurately, the *village* where I grew up. The tribe is gone, at least physically, especially for the people who still live there. But for me, Malvern will never change. The tribal village is eternal. The old Malvern which is gone forever is more real for me than the new one that now exists. It molded impulses and instincts that still move me every day. It aroused obsessions that still haunt me. It kindled longings I will feel until I die. Malvern was the place where, as I might once have said, and can still say in another way, "Jesus came into my heart," where the awful sense of the fathomless mystery and utter transiency of life first dawned on me, and where I discovered that in the midst of all that terror and nothingness I was loved. What more could anyone's tribal village do for him?

2

The Voyage of the *Robert Hart* (1983)

This chapter is taken from Just as I Am *(Nashville: Abingdon Press, 1983), 31-41.*

In 1946, when I was seventeen like nearly every seventeen-year-old I have ever known (including three of my own) I wanted to get AWAY. I was a high school student during the Second World War. I watched older friends and cousins disappear from town and return after basic training in blue or khaki uniforms. I watched some of them leave and not come back ever again, ever. Despite my Quaker roots, along with everyone else in Malvern, I was caught up in the "Win-the-war-against-the Germans-and-the Japs" enthusiasm of the last popular war America fought. But in a secret place in my heart I did *not* want the war to be over, not until I had been in it.

It did end, however, in 1945, with two mushroom clouds over Hiroshima and Nagasaki. With my high school friends I celebrated V.E. Day and V.J. Day by blowing noisemakers and riding around on fire engines with the sirens screaming. But inwardly I was crestfallen. History had, it seemed, passed me by.

But not completely. The following spring, when I was still a junior in high school, I read that the United Nations Relief and Rehabilitation Administration was shipping livestock to Europe to replenish the devastated herds and that young men were needed on the cattle boats. Still inebriated with adolescent wanderlust and the residue of the going-into-the service élan, I decided to sign up. I announced my intention to my parents and, to my astonishment, they agreed. Looking back, I am still astonished. Maybe their reluctance was lessened by the fact that the Church of the Brethen Service committee, which had carried on a private project of sending heifers to war-ravaged Europe, had been commissioned by UNRRA to recruit and train the seagoing cowboys. In any case, within a few weeks, just after the last day of classes in 1946

I arrived in Baltimore, Maryland, to ship out on an antiquated, rusting Liberty ship called the *Robert Hart* with a cargo of foaled mares and cows. Our destination was Gdansk, Poland, known more recently for the historic strike in the Lenin shipyard and the beginning of the Solidarity movement in Poland.

Herman Melville has written somewhere that the ship he first sailed on was his "Yale and Harvard." Although I later attended both those institutions, I know what he meant. I learned more and grew up more during those weeks on the *Robert Hart* than during any other period of my life. The faculty of Robert Hart University consisted of the ship's crew and officers, my fellow "cowboys," and especially the "supervisor," the martinet who was in charge of the cowboy crew. A diminutive Simon Legree with a colossal ego and a rasping foghorn bass voice, he obviously knew what we greenhorns whispered to one another in our minuscule sleeping quarters on the ship's fantail: that in the pantheon of the *Robert Hart*, the captain was God Almighty and he was Jesus Christ. My image of Jesus, nurtured by Sallman's *Head of Christ* and pictures in Sunday school books, was a different one. Still, he was a man I decided not to cross if I could possibly avoid it. I knew I was at his mercy and that his idea of mercy was not that of gentle Jesus meek and mild.

Maybe I tried a little too hard. In any case one day, about a thousand miles out of Baltimore, he saw me trying to slip by him unnoticed. He stopped me and ordered me to descend to the lower 'tween deck and to hold onto the end of a bulky hawser, the other end of which was being used to hoist a canvas ventilator to siphon fresh air down to the horses. He told me to hold onto it with all my might, insinuating that I did not have much, while he supervised the rigging. He warned me not to let go of it or climb back out until he told me to.

I obeyed. Although I was supposed to be watering the horses on another deck at the time and had been on my way to that assignment, something told me that if I had not said, "Yes, sir!" I could expect anything from the cat-o-nine-tails to keelhauling. I had probably read too many sea stories. Jack London's *Sea Wolf* and Richard Henry Dana's *Two Years Before the Mast* had been my favorites as a fourteen-year-old. Up until then the supervisor had not seemed to notice me, and I had considered myself lucky, but now he had issued a direct command. I climbed down the ladder with the rope and, so as not to be pulled into the hatch opening by the tugging I could feel from above, planted myself a few yards back in a position where I could not see out and braced myself against the girder.

I had seen canvas ventilators hoisted before and I knew the whole operation took only about five minutes. Although the pressure on my arms felt like it was pulling them out of the sockets I was determined (a) to prove to the supervisor that I was not the weakling he implied I was, and (b) not do or fail to do anything that would arouse his ire. Ten minutes passed, then fifteen, then twenty. My arms and neck and back ached, but every time I eased my weight on the hawser it began slipping up, dragged by the force of the stiff north Atlantic winds. When my watch showed that a half hour has passed I began to panic. I could not hold on much longer. What to do? If I let go, I imagined the vent flying off the rigging into the ocean. If I tied the hawser around my waist and climbed back out I would have disobeyed the deity. Frantic, I looked at the horses who munched nonchalantly on their hay and offered no advice or succor. I began to wonder why I had not stayed in Malvern and taken that job in Aunt Mary's drugstore. I also began to understand what it might have felt like when the inquisitors stretched Joan of Arc on the rack.

Finally I could take it no longer. Tying the hawser around my waist as best I could I tried to climb up the steel ladder only to find that my arms were too exhausted to cling to the rungs. Slowly and laboriously I made my way up, throwing my whole arm over each step so I would not drop three decks, the hawser still around my waist. After ten minutes of agonized ascent I crawled onto the deck. The supervisor was nowhere in sight. The line had been looped over a crane and the ventilator lay folded on the deck. I had been tricked. Humiliated. And not by one of my fellow cowboys, but by a man who had the legitimate authority to tell me what to do.

Now the inner pain began to exceed the aches in my arms. I quickly made my way to my own hold and started watering the horses with my mates who asked me in less-than-friendly tones where the hell I had been. I avoided their eyes and mumbled that I had been "doing a job for the supervisor." When I saw the little despot later in the day he glanced at me slyly but I did not ask him what happened. I had had enough abasement for one day.

That night I lay on my bunk unable to sleep because of the pains in my arms and the rage that wracked my stomach and chest. Occasionally I would nod off only to wake up in a minute or two with my shoulders screaming and my saliva turned to acid. For the first time in my life I savored the taste of pure loathing. I *hated* the supervisor. I wanted to kill him, smash his head in with one of the pitchforks, kick him down an open hatch cover, watch him die in piles of reeking manure. What troubled me most, as I winced and tossed, was that this petty pasha had *legitimate* authority over me. He *was* my boss. Although I was sure there were some legal limits on what he could do to me, I also knew that in the midst of the ocean there was no one around (except maybe God the captain who dwelt in his own celestial realm and had other things to do) to supervise the supervisor. I could go nowhere to get away from him. That thought stopped my breathing for a moment. Nowhere to go. No court of appeal. I was stuck on a ship with a tyrant whose power over me was not only arbitrary but in some crazy way also legitimate.

I did not lead a mutiny against the supervisor. I chose the coward's path—avoidance, deference, waiting it out. If I saw him on the port side, I would cross to the starboard. I kept out of his range. But ever since that day I carry—in a way that only pain and humiliation can teach—a recognition of why people rebel against tyrants, even those with a legitimate claim to authority. It was not just that single incident with the supervisor and the ventilator line that gave me a feeling for the underdog, the person being cheated, misused, debased. That prejudice probably came to me from many sources. But the will to fight back against domination needs the energy of anger to keep it alive, and often when I imagine myself in the place of any oppressed person anywhere and try to sense what is sustaining them, I remember the supervisor and feel the stitch in my shoulders. Then I know. There is not only "that of God" in every person, there is also that which can only take so much before it fights back. And that too, I believe is of God. In any case, whoever he was, I decided that night as the *Robert Hart* plowed toward Europe, that the supervisor definitely was *not* Jesus Christ.

If the faculty of Robert Hart University was the crew, its laboratory was the horses and cows. My deck had horses. Foaled mares, bred just before our departure presumably to double the delivery load, they were touchy and irritable. Being stuck in a dark hold for three weeks, never exercised, tossed by the motion of the ship, they constantly stomped and whinnied. Nearly a hundred of the eight hundred we started with died before we reached Europe. Each day we hoisted the dead horses out of the hold with cranes and dropped them into the sea and sharks tore them up as soon as they hit the water.

The horses were not in a good mood and their mood got worse by the day. Two weeks out of Baltimore (remember this was the *Robert Hart,* not the *Queen Mary*; she made eleven knots at full speed) a particularly nervous black mare reached out and bit me on my left shoulder, still sore from the time of testing with the Antichrist. The bite punctured and lacerated the skin and I had to be treated by the ship's purser, the only medical aide on board, whose skills were limited to aspirin, tincture of iodine, and Scotch. He did not know much about stitching people up so I was repaired with gauze and adhesive tape. Thirty-five years later I still carry a tiny stigmata from that bite. Every time I shower or swim I have a chance to remember the *Robert Hart*, the black mare, the supervisor.

But it was all worth it. Every day at sea I leaped out of bed when the bell rang at five; I was thousands of miles from Malvern; I was doing something important; I was becoming an adult. Every day I made a short entry in a log, still imagining at times that I was Richard Henry Dana in the days of the clipper ships. I keep that log in my closet, and when I feel nostalgic after a dull faculty meeting, I thumb through it. Reading it always brings back sights and smells. For example, on July 13, 1946, while we were making our way through the North Sea where leftover mines were still bobbing around I made the following entry:

> The captain didn't make an inspection today having been awake all night taking us through the mine fields. Passed two floating mines on the portside about 7:00 P.M. only 50 yards away, a little too close. We put empty feed bags soaked in DDT around the hold since the flies are really bad. Slept with my life jacket at the foot of my bed.

The words sound flat and reportorial when I read them today. I don't sound scared. Was I? In those days, a year after the war, ships still ran into mines that had broken from their moorings and were floating loose. I'm sure I knew even then that the *Robert Hart* was not invincible and that I could die at seventeen, which was not in my life plan. But was I frightened? Did I pray? I don't think so. I considered myself a Christian, having been baptized a few years earlier at our local Baptist church. I remember taking a Bible with me in my blue seaman's bag. But in 1946 I still must have had that innocent, late-adolescent omnipotence we float on at seventeen. If the ship itself was not invincible, I somehow assumed *I was*. If it were blown out of the water, I would swim courageously in my life jacket until a rescue vessel came. Then, face coated with oil, like the courageous merchant seamen in the war movies I had seen, I would be hauled aboard, given hot coffee, wrapped in blankets, photographed by the newspapers. Later I would come home with stories that matched anything the war veterans (those who actually came home) told. At seventeen, for me, death was something that happened to other people. I think this is true for most seventeen-year-olds. Maybe that is why the military likes to recruit "teenagers." Millions of them have died in older men's wars over the centuries, probably believing until the last moment that they were indestructible.

The ship did not sink. On a warm July day in 1946 it crept into Novyport, the harbor area of Gdansk. That evening we were given shore passes, and I spent the next four hours walking the dim streets with two shipmates. For blocks in every direction Gdansk was rubble. It smelled of rotting garbage and acrid smoke. The proud Hanseatic port and "free city" of Danzig before the war, celebrated more recently by Günter Grass in his novel *The Tin Drum*, had been bombed and shelled by both sides. Bands of children, grime worn into their faces and arms, many wearing the jagged remains of adult castoff clothes, followed us everywhere we went asking for candy, money, and cigarettes. Oily pimps sidled up to us with offers of "my sister" or "my daughter," whistling the way they had heard sailors do at women, describing the voluptuous shape of their ladies-for-sale with hand motions and gestures.

I felt sick and returned to the ship early. Was this the Europe I had looked forward to seeing? Charred wreckage, hungry children, sadness and chaos? The next morning, when my friends wanted to go ashore again, I pretended to be ill. I think I told them I "had a hangover," which always passed as a manlier alibi. I lay on my mattress and stared at the bottom of the bunk above me. So, this was the world outside Malvern, the historic Europe of cathedrals and boulevards and museums I had heard about. Of course I had seen pictures of war rubble. I suppose I knew I would see some. But *this?* Suddenly I wanted to be home again. I wanted to sit on the porch with my father in the twilight while he smoked his pipe and talk about his work, what was happening in town, county politics. I thought of my own little sister, who was then ten, out on the streets at midnight begging for chocolate bars, or being offered for a night of "fucky, fucky" for five dollars. I felt tears welling up but I could not cry. I only clenched my teeth, and for the first time in my life, sensed a cold anger at any God who would let something like this happen.

Later in the day I got hungry and pulled myself out of bed to go to the ship's galley. No one was there, so I opened the big crew refrigerator and made a spam and cheese sandwich. I poured a cup of coffee. But I could not eat. Feeling miserable and lonely I wandered out on deck. The horses and cows were being unloaded by Polish stevedores using flying stalls rigged on the ship's cranes. I sat on a hatch and watched.

A few minutes later a Polish dockworker who seemed to be in charge asked me for a cigarette. I gave him a whole pack. He did not light one (they never did—the cigarettes were for the black market) but instead signaled his men to take a break and sat down near me. He spoke a little English, asked me where I was from, how old I was, what I thought of Gdansk.

When I obviously could not answer the last question he said, "Too bad you could not have seen this"—gesturing toward the miles of twisted metal frames and shattered brick—"before the war." I listened. He reminded me of my father somehow. He talked about Danzig in the days before the Nazis, then the Russians had come. He told me about his home, now destroyed, his family, now nearly all dead, the evening band concerts, the school he had attended. All "before the war."

The war. The war. Slowly I began to realize something. The war I had seen from the secure perspective of high school, and had secretly hoped would last long enough so that I could be in it, had done all this to Gdansk, to him, to the thin children in their oversize, discarded battle jackets and lacerated sweaters. During the next days, as the ship remained tied up in port and I began to venture back down the gangway and into the town, I sensed a new object of my disgust and revulsion: the war. The war had done this. Of course it had been the Germans and the Russians who had actually fired the cannons and dropped the bombs. I knew that. But something clicked. Had the people who had started, fought, won, lost the war ever considered that it would transform little children the age of my sister into packs of thieving scavengers roaming the alleys? Somehow I did not think about the millions of dead, the incalculable property damage, all the other horrendous costs. I was obsessed with the children. I knew not only that the supervisor was not Jesus Christ but that if there was any God at all, anywhere in the universe, *that* God could not have wanted this to happen.

The voyage home was uneventful. Without the horses and cows to feed there was little for the cowboy crew to do after we had shoveled tons of manure into cargo nets and dumped it into the North Atlantic. I slept in the sun on the hatch cover, read, and thought. I thought a lot. I could not get the memory of those knobby-kneed Polish children out of my mind. As the long, empty days passed, I became aware of a conviction growing inside me that there could not be another war. It just was not worth it.

The voyage of the *Robert Hart* took place many years ago. Like Melville, however, I can say that antiquated old vessel was "my Yale and Harvard." More. It took me to a place where, even without a shot being fired at me, I found out something about who I was and what my life was meant to be. Decades later, standing on the steps of the chapel at the U.S. Air Force Academy in Colorado with Sister Mary Luke Tobin, a group of novice nuns from the religious order she headed, and a small group of church people from Denver, I thought momentarily about that voyage. We were handing out copies of St. Francis's prayer for peace to the Air Force cadets as they entered the chapel for Sunday worship. We were also giving them the latest reports on the current bombing of Vietnam and asking them to think and pray about what they were being trained to do. The security police of the academy first asked us politely to stop it, then ordered us sternly to leave. But this order, unlike the hawser-holding order I had heard from the supervisor, I quietly disobeyed. So did all the nuns. A few minutes later a military police van appeared. We all knelt in prayer on the steps. One by one we were escorted to the van and then to the base prison.

We were only detained for a few hours. Then the air police drove us to the base exit with a personal letter from the commander forbidding us ever to enter the academy grounds again. While we were locked up, however, we talked with one another about where we had first picked up our common revulsion for war, and I heard myself talking about the *Robert Hart,* the streets of Gdansk, the children. I noticed, to my surprise, that I could still remember some of their faces. My voice broke as I spoke, and I even found a New Testament text coming to mind. It was one I had at times thought unduly harsh but in this case seemed appropriate beyond measure: "If anyone should harm one of these little ones, let a millstone be tied about his neck and let him be cast into the midst of the sea" (paraphrased). Yes, into the *sea,* with dead horses, the sharks, the manure, I thought silently, knowing that the sisters would not appreciate the connection that existed in my mind.

I am sure the *Robert Hart* was sold for scrap soon after the voyage to Gdansk. Liberty ships had been constructed to make only two or three voyages, and it had already made several. But I still have a photograph of the *Robert Hart* taken as our motor launch sped away from it when we disembarked the last time in Baltimore. I am fonder of that picture than of those I have of the college buildings I studied in, some of them ivy-covered and venerable.

Recently I began to wonder what happened to those children. Did they survive the hunger and cold of the following winter in Gdansk? Did any of them grow up to become workers in the Lenin shipyards? Was one of them Lech Walesa or one of his associates? I will never know. What I do know is that one travel-entranced American teenager was never the same again after his voyage to Gdansk. A youthful adventure, sparked by adolescent restiveness, the reading of sea yarns, and a romantic lust for travel, had unexpectedly become a faith journey. There would be more.

3

The Secular City and Its Debate

The Secular City, published by Macmillan in 1965, became a surprise best-seller, translated into many languages, and stirring widespread debate. The following selection is from an introduction to the twenty-fifth anniversary edition of the book published in 1990.

The Secular City Twenty-five Years Later (1990)

I wrote *The Secular City* after having lived for a year in Berlin, where I taught in a church-sponsored adult education program with branches on both sides of the barbed wire. The wall was constructed a few months before I arrived, so I had to commute back and forth through Checkpoint Charlie, whose familiar wooden shack and warning sign—"You are leaving the American sector"—have now been placed in a museum. Berlin had been the home of Dietrich Bonhoeffer, and many of his friends and co-workers were still there. So we talked a lot about Bonhoeffer that year, especially about the musings he set down during the last months of his life about the hiddenness of God and the coming of a "post-religious" age in human history. In the tense and tired Berlin of the early 1960s that made a lot of sense.

In retrospect, of course, it is easy to see that human religiosity is a much more persistent quality than Bonhoeffer thought it was. Nearly everywhere we look in the world today we witness an unanticipated resurgence of traditional religion. The renaissance of Islamic culture and politics, the rebirth of Shinto in Japan, the appearance of powerful Jewish, Hindu, and Christian "fundamentalisms" in Israel, India, and the U.S.—all these have raised important questions about the allegedly ineluctable process of secularization. But where does that leave us?

If anything, I believe these developments make the central thesis of *The Secular City* even more credible. I argued then that secularization—if it is not permitted to calcify into an ideology (which I called "secularism")—is not everywhere and always an evil. It prevents powerful religions from acting on their theocratic pretensions. It allows people to choose among a wider range of worldviews. Today, in parallel fashion, it seems obvious that the resurgence of religion in the world is not everywhere and always a good thing. Do the long-suffering people of Iran believe that after the removal of their ruthless shah, the installation of a quasi-theocratic Islamic republic has turned out to be a wholly positive move? Do those Israelis and Palestinians who yearn for a peaceful settlement of the West Bank bloodletting believe that either the Jewish or the Muslim religious parties are helping? How do the citizens of Beirut and Belfast feel about the continuing vitality of religion?

The truth is that both religious revival and secularization are morally ambiguous processes. Both heal and destroy. We still desperately need a way of welcoming diversity that does not deteriorate into nihilism, and a sober recognition that neither religious nor secular movements are good or bad as such. Both can become either the bearers of emancipation or the avatars of misery, or some of each. Wouldn't a modest sprinkling of secularization, a de-religionizing of the issues, come as a welcome relief in Ulster, and help resolve the murderous tensions in Kashmir and the Gaza strip? . . .

The thesis of *The Secular City* was that God is first the Lord of history and only then the Head of the Church. This means that God can be just as present in the secular as in the religious realms of life, and we unduly cramp the divine presence by confining it to some specially delineated spiritual or ecclesial sector. This idea has two implications. First, it suggests that people of faith need not flee from the allegedly godless contemporary world. God came *into* this world, and that is where we belong as well. But second, it also means that not all that is "spiritual" is good for the spirit. These ideas were not particularly new. Indeed, the presence of the holy within the profane is suggested by the doctrine of the incarnation—not a recent innovation. As for suspicion toward religion, both Jesus and the Hebrew prophets lashed out at much of the religion they saw around them. But some simple truths need restating time and again. And today is surely no exception.

In rereading *The Secular City* after a quarter of a century I smiled occasionally at its audacity, the way a father might chuckle at the shenanigans of a rambunctious child. Its argument is nothing if not sweeping. By page 12 of the introduction the reader has been wafted through a dizzying tour of nothing less than the whole of human history, from tribe to technopolis, from Sophocles to Lewis Mumford, from the Stone Age to Max Weber. And all of this before chapter one. Then comes the theological portrait of the "coming" of the secular city in which Barth and Tillich and Camus and John F. Kennedy jostle each other in what might have seemed to all of them a somewhat unfamiliar proximity. The next part of the book is devoted to what I called "revolutionary technology," a phrase that, at least in those days, struck people as a world-class oxymoron. It is followed by an attack on *Playboy* magazine, which I called "antisexual," that drew me into a furious (at first) and later tedious debate with that magazine's publisher. A lot of territory to cover in a 244-page book.

The final section is a polemic against the so-called "death of God" theologians who were *au courant* at the time. I portrayed them, correctly I think, as remaining obsessed—albeit negatively—with the classical god of metaphysical theism, while I was talking about Someone Else, the mysterious and elusive Other of the prophets and Jesus, who—like Jacques Brel—was very much alive although living in unexpected quarters. I have never been able to understand why, after having unleashed this *guerre de plume* against the death-of-godders, some critics persisted in including me among them.

In any case, the death-of-god theology had an unusually short half-life, whereas the issue I tried in my youthful enthusiasm to tackle—the significance of the ongoing battle between religion and seculariza-tion—rightly continues to stoke debate and analysis. To illustrate the dilemma from my own Christian tradition, how many Mother Teresas and Oscar Romeros does it take to balance a Jim and Tammy Bakker? And how do we measure Pope John II's courageous vision of a "Europe without borders" against his worldwide crusade against contraception? So much good and so much mischief is done—as it always has been—in the name of God. Perhaps the suggestion I made at the end of *The Secular City*, which sounded radical to some readers then, is still a good one: we should learn something from the ancient Jewish tradition of not pronouncing the name of the Holy One, live through a period of reverent reticence in religious language, and wait for the spirit to make known a new vocabulary that is not so tarnished by trivialization and misuse.

I actually said a little more than that, and the final paragraph of the book may be worth recalling because it prepared the way for the theological movement that was to pick up where *The Secular City* left off. On that last page I speculated on the significance of the puzzling fact that, according to the book of Exodus, when Moses asked for the name of the One who told him to lead the Israelite slaves from their Egyptian captivity, the Voice from the burning bush refused to give it. Moses was to get about the business of liberating his people. "Tell them

'I will do what I will do' has sent you," the Voice said. That, apparently, was enough. The name would come in God's good time. Reflecting in 1965 on the astonishing episode, I wrote:

> The Exodus marked for the Jews a turning point of such elemental power that a new divine name was needed to replace the titles that had grown out of their previous experience. Our transition today . . . will be no less shaking. Rather than clinging stubbornly to antiquated appellations or anxiously synthesizing new ones, perhaps, like Moses, we must simply take up the work of liberating the captives, confident that we will be granted a new name by events of the future.

Although I was only dimly aware of it at the time, in this paragraph I was actually proposing an agenda for the next stage of theology, one which was taken up with a brilliance and daring far beyond my hopes, first by Latin American theologians and then by others throughout the world. For between these concluding lines, which crystallized the thrust of the entire book, can be detected what were to become the two basic premises of liberation theology.

The first premise is that for us, as for Moses, an act of engagement for justice in the world, not a pause for theological reflection, should be the first "moment" of an appropriate response to God. First hear the Voice, then get to work freeing the captives. The "name" will come later. Theology is important, but it comes after, not before, the commitment to doing, to what some still call "discipleship."

This inverts the established Western assumption that right action must derive from previously clarified ideas. Liberation theology's insistence that thought—including theological thought—is imbedded in the grittiness of real life is one of its most salutary contributions.

The second premise of liberation theology is that "accompanying" the poor and the captives in their pilgrimage is not only an ethical responsibility, but that it provides the most promising context for theological reflection. Not just "history" in general, but the effort of excluded and marginalized people to claim God's promise is the preferred "locus theologicus." As the Catholic bishops of Latin America put it in their influential statement of 1968, one must think theologically from the perspective of a "preferential option for the poor." It is not hard to see now, although I was scarcely able to see it then, that the next logical step after *The Secular City* was liberation theology. But the link between the two was neither simple nor direct.

At first I was puzzled at how much attention the Spanish translation of my book, *La Ciudad Secular,* received from Latin American theologians. They criticized it vociferously, but they also built on it. They invited me to Peru and Mexico and Brazil to debate it. But as I listened to their criticisms I became convinced that they understood it better than anyone else, maybe even better than I did myself. Still, they made use of it in a way I had not anticipated. Gustavo Gutiérrez, whose controversial book *The Theology of Liberation* appeared a few years after mine, clarifies the connection best. In the economically developed capitalist countries, he explains, secularization tends to take a cultural form. It challenges the hegemony of traditional religious worldviews, calls human beings to assume their rightful role in shaping history, and opens the door to a pluralism of symbolic universes. In the poor countries, however, secularization assumes quite a different expression. It challenges the misuse of religion by ruling elites to sacralize their privileges, and it enlists the powerful symbols of faith into the conflict with despotism. In the Third World, as Gutiérrez puts it in one of his best-known formulations, the theologian's conversation partner is not "the nonbeliever" but rather "the nonperson." This means that among the tarpaper shantytowns of Lima and São Paulo the interlocutor of theology is not some skeptical "modern man" who thinks religion stifles thought; rather, it is the faceless people whose lives as well as faith are threatened because tyrannies grounded in some religious or nonreligious mythology strangle them into an early death. The distinction Gutiérrez makes shows that he is applying the same praxis-oriented approach to theology I advocated in a different religious and political environment. Liberation theology is the legitimate, though unanticipated, heir of *The Secular City.* . . .

There is much continuity. But there are also many important contemporary theological currents for which I can find little foreshadowing in *The Secular City.* For starters, in reading the book again in 1990 I winced every time I saw the word "man" blatantly wielded to refer to anybody and everybody. The first page of the introduction: "The world has become man's task and a man's responsibility. Contemporary man has become the cosmopolitan." And so on. I would feel better if I could claim that it was, after all, only a matter of blunderbuss pronouns, that today my language would be gender inclusive. But I know it cuts deeper than that. The truth is that *The Secular City* was written without the benefit of the two decades of feminist theological scholarship that was to begin shortly after it was published. What difference would it have made?

A lot. In fact, knowing what I know now, I would have had to recast virtually every chapter. How could I rely so heavily on the themes of disenchantment and desacralization, as I did in the opening section, without coping with the obvious fact that these historical processes— which I saw in a positive light—suggest a certain patriarchal domination of the natural world with which women have been so closely identi- fied in Hebrew and Christian religious symbolization? More basically, I have learned since 1965, often from my own students, that we can no longer read the Bible without recognizing that it comes to us already severely tampered with, expurgated, and perhaps even edited with an eye to perpetuating the authority of men. I have learned that many of the classical sources I was taught to rely on so heavily, from Augustine to Tillich, sound very different when they are read with women's ques- tions in mind. And my last chapter, "To Speak in a Secular Fashion of God," would have had to take into consideration that employing exclu- sively male language for the deity has contributed to the marginaliza- tion of half the people of the world. . . .

There is another important theological current that at first seems strangely missing from *The Secular City* but whose absence, in retro- spect, one can understand if not forgive. The American city is the principal locus of African-American theology. It was not until a few years after the publication of my book, however, that black theologians began making that fact evident to the wider theological community. It is all the more surprising that I overlooked African-American religion in 1965 since I was personally caught up in the civil rights movement. I had first met Martin Luther King, Jr., in 1956, during the summer of the Montgomery bus boycott. At the time I was chaplain at Oberlin College in Ohio and I invited him to come speak. He flew in a few months later and we started a friendship that was to last until his death in 1968. As a member of his Southern Christian Leadership Confer- ence I marched and demonstrated in both the North and the South. I responded to the call to come to Selma, was arrested and jailed briefly in Williamstown, North Carolina, and took some of the responsibility in organizing the SCLC's effort to desegregate St. Augustine, Florida. All through these years my family and I lived in Roxbury, the predomi- nantly African-American section of Boston.

Still, it was only later, with the advent of the Black Power movement and the coming of black theology, that I began to take seriously what the modern American city meant to African-Americans. Again, if I had thought about this very carefully at the time I could have foreseen some of the reservations black theologians voiced about *The Secular City*. Its controlling metaphors of "the man at the giant switchboard" and "the man in the cloverleaf," which were meant to symbolize the communication grid and the mobility network of the modern metropolis, seemed implausible to people who had been denied both mobility and communication, and for whom the city was often not a place of expanded freedom but the site of more sophisticated humiliations. It became clear to me only as the years passed that *The Secular City* reflects the perspective of a relatively privileged urbanite. The city, secular or otherwise, feels quite different to those for whom its promise turns out to be a cruel deception.

In the years that have passed since *The Secular City* was published much has happened to the cities of the world, including American cities, and most of it has not been good. Instead of contributing to the liberative process, many cities have become sprawling concentrations of human misery, wracked with racial, religious, and class animosity. The names Beirut, Calcutta, South Bronx, and Belfast conjure images of violence, neglect, and death. Ironically, the cities of the world have often become the victims of their own self-promotion and the failure of the rural environs to sustain life. Millions of people, both hopeful and desperate, stream into them to escape the unbearable existence they must endure in the devastated countryside, but what do they find?

If Mexico City spells the future of the city, then the future looks grim. Lewis Mumford, who began his life as a celebrant of the possibility of truly urban life, became disillusioned before his death in 1990. He once wrote that when the city becomes the whole world the city no longer exists. That prediction now seems increasingly possible. By the year 2000 Mexico City will have nearly 32 million residents, of whom 15 million will eke out a marginal existence in its smoggy slums. Calcutta, Rio de Janeiro, Jakarta, Manila, and Lima will not be far behind, all with populations between 10 and 20 million, with half the people in each city locked into ghettos of poverty. Indeed, in some African cities such as Addis Ababa and Ibadan, somewhere between 75 and 90 percent of the population will live in shantytown squalor.

In the cities of the U.S. we have not fared much better. Real estate values gyrate, making millions for a select few, while homeless people, now including increased numbers of women with children, crowd into church basements and temporary shelters. The already marvelous cultural mix of our cities, spiced by the recent arrival of increasing numbers of Asians and Latin Americans, could enable us to prove to the world that ethnic diversity is a plus. Instead, in some cities at least, we hover on the edge of a technicolor war of all against all: white against black against yellow against brown. And the whole picture is worsened by the diminution of the middle class and the increasing chasm between those with too much and those with too little. One is sometimes tempted simply to give up on the city.

We should not. One of my main purposes in writing *The Secular City* was to challenge the anti-urban bias that infects American religion (at least white church life). How many times did I hear, as a child, that "God made the country, but man made the city"? This is a gravely deficient doctrine of God. We need a spirituality that can discern the presence of God not just "In the Garden" as the old Protestant hymn put it, but also, as a better hymn says, "Where cross the crowded ways of life,/Where sound the cries of race and clan. . . ."

The Bible portrays a God who is present in the jagged reality of conflict and dislocation, calling the faithful into the crowded ways, not away from them. Nothing is further removed from this biblical God than the inward-oriented serenity cults and get-rich-now salvation schemes that inundate the airwaves and pollute the religious atmosphere. Here Bonhoeffer had it exactly right. From behind bars he wrote that we are summoned as human beings to "share the suffering of God in the world." If the divine mystery is present in a special way among the poorest and most misused of his or her children, as the biblical images and stories—from the slaves in Egypt to the official lynching of Jesus—constantly remind us, then allegedly religious people who insulate themselves from the city are putting themselves at considerable risk. By removing ourselves from the despised and the outcast we are at the same time insulating ourselves from God, and it is in the cities that these, "the least of them," are to be found.

I have no intention of rewriting *The Secular City* with benefit of nearly three decades of hindsight. I cannot. Even if I could, it would be pointless. After it was published I experienced what literary critics often point out, that any work of art—a poem, a painting, even a book of theology—quickly escapes its creator's hand and takes on a life of its own. Within a few months of its modest first printing (10,000 copies), and even though it was scarcely noticed by reviewers, the book began to sell so briskly the publisher moved to multiple printings. Soon it appeared on bestseller lists—unheard of at the time for a book on theology. Sales moved into hundreds of thousands. The publisher was astonished, as was I. . . . Within a couple of years the book's sales, in all editions and translations, were approaching a million.

What did I learn from all this? For one thing, that most theologians and most publishers had severely underestimated the number of people who were willing to spend good money on serious books about religion. *The Secular City* may well have marked the end of the unchallenged reign of clerical and academic elitism in theology. Laypeople were obviously ready to get into the discussion. In fact, they were demanding to be part of it and were unwilling to allow theologians to continue to write books just for each other. Whatever one may think about the ideas in *The Secular City*, they are neither simple nor obvious. The book cannot be read with the television on. I do not take credit for having called forth the vociferous and critical laity we now seem to have in every church, and perhaps especially the Catholic Church, who make so much marvelous trouble for ecclesiastical leaders. But I like to think that *The Secular City* helped create the climate that forced church leaders and theologians to come down from their balconies and out of their studies and talk seriously with the ordinary people who constitute 99 percent of the churches of the world.

Of course, there are things I would do differently today, not only in how I would write *The Secular City*, but in virtually every other area of my life. "We get too soon old," as the Pennsylvania Dutch aphorism puts it, "and too late smart." Knowing what I do now about the Jewish religious tradition, I would not counterpose law and gospel as captivity to the past versus openness to the future, as Rudolf Bultmann and a whole tradition of German theologians taught me to do. The law too, I have come to see, is a gift of grace. I would also try not to base my theological reading of current world history so narrowly in my own Christian tradition, but would try to draw on the insights of other traditions, as we must all increasingly do at a time when the world religions elbow each other in unprecedented closeness. After all, Muslims and Buddhists and Hindus had already created cosmopolitan world cities when Western Christendom still consisted of backwater villages. We may have something to learn from them about transforming our urban battlefields into communities that nurture life instead of throttling it. We need all the help we can get if Mumford's dystopian nightmare—a planet transformed into a vast urban non-city—is to be avoided.

Was *The Secular City* a harbinger of postmodernism, as one writer recently suggested? The word itself did not exist then, and I am not sure I know what it means today. But if it suggests a willingness to live with a certain pragmatism and provisionality, a suspicion of all-encompassing schemes, a readiness to risk a little more disorder instead of a little too much *Ordnung,* then I think the book qualifies. Nearly ten years after *The Secular City* Jonathan Raban published a book titled *Soft City: The Art of Cosmopolitan Living.* It is sometimes cited as the first clearly postmodernist text. If it is, it may be significant that when I read it, a few years after its publication, I immediately felt I had found a compatriot. Raban says:

> ... the city and the book are opposed forms: to force the city's spread, contingency, and aimless motion into the tight progression of a narrative is to risk a total falsehood. There is no single point of view from which we can grasp the city as a whole. That indeed is the distinction between the city and the small town. . . . A good working definition of metropolitan life would center on its intrinsic illegibility.

This "illegibility" is part of what I was getting at. It is one of the principal features of the new secular world-city we are called to live in today, bereft of the inclusive images and all-embracing world-pictures that sustained our ancestors. We will always need those orienting and value-sustaining symbols. But today we must learn to appreciate them in a new way because we know in our bones that no one of them, and not even all of them together, can provide a point of view by which the totality can be grasped. In short, living in the city should be the school of living in the postmodern, "illegible" world. It should be a continuous lesion in "citizenship," in how to live in the world-city. But we still have not learned. As Raban says,

> we live in cities badly; we have built them up in culpable innocence and now fret helplessly in a synthetic wilderness of our own construction. We need . . . to make a serious, imaginative assessment of that special relationship between the self and the city; its unique plasticity, its privacy and its freedom.

It's true: "we live in cities badly." But we *must* learn to live in cities or we will not survive. We are missing our big chance, an opportunity that God or destiny has provided us and which, if we muff it, may never come up again.

Tucked away on page 177 of *The Secular City* comes a little-noticed paragraph that perhaps I should have used as an epigraph for this essay, or maybe it should be put in italics. Secularization, I wrote, "is not the Messiah. But neither is it anti-Christ. It is rather a dangerous liberation." It "raises the stakes," vastly increasing the range both of human freedom and of human responsibility. It poses risks "of a larger order than those it displaces. But the promise exceeds the peril, or at least makes it worth taking the risk."

All I could add today is that we really have no choice about whether

we take the risk. We already live in the world-city and there is no
return. God has placed us in this urban exile, and is teaching us a
more mature faith, for it is a quality of unfaith to have to flee from
complexity and disruption, or to scurry around trying to relate every
segment of experience to some comforting inclusive whole, as though
the universe might implode unless we hold it together with our own
conceptualizations. God is teaching us to approach life in the illegible
city without feeling the need for a Big Key.

This does not mean we have to become nihilists. Far from it. Several years ago a friend told me he thought the implicit concept underlying *The Secular City* is the good old Calvinist doctrine of providence.
At first I balked, but I have come to believe he is right. We live today
without the maps or timetables in which our ancestors invested such
confidence. To live well instead of badly we need a certain strange confidence that, despite our fragmented and discontinuous experience,
somehow it all eventually makes sense. But *we* don't need to know the
how. There is Someone Else, even in *The Secular City*, who sees to that.

The Epoch of the Secular City (1965)

This selection is from the original Introduction to The Secular City: Secularization
and Urbanization in Theological Perspective *(New York: Macmillan Company,
1965), 1-12.*

The rise of urban civilization and the collapse of traditional religion are the two main hallmarks of our era and are closely related
movements. Urbanization constitutes a massive change in the way
men live together, and became possible in its contemporary form only
with the scientific and technological advances which sprang from
the wreckage of traditional world views. Secularization, an equally
epochal movement, marks a change in the way men grasp and understand their life together, and it occurred only when the cosmopolitan
confrontations of city living exposed the relativity of the myths men
once thought were unquestionable. The way men live their common
life affects mightily the way they understand the meaning of that life,
and vice versa. Villages and cities are laid out to reflect the pattern of
the heavenly city, the abode of the gods. But once laid out, the pattern
of the polis influences the way that succeeding generations experience
life and visualize the gods. Societies and the symbols they live by influence each other. In our day the secular metropolis stands as both the

pattern of our life together and the symbol of our view of the world. If the Greeks perceived the cosmos as an immensely expanded polis, and medieval man saw it as the feudal manor enlarged to infinity, we experience the universe as the city of man. It is a field of human exploration and endeavor from which the gods have fled. The world has become man's task and man's responsibility. Contemporary man has become the cosmopolitan. The world has become his city and his city has reached out to include the world. The name for the process by which this has come about is *secularization*.

What is secularization? The Dutch theologian C. A. van Peursen says it is the deliverance of man "first from religious and then from metaphysical control over his reason and his language."[1] It is the loosing of the world from religious and quasi-religious understandings of itself, the dispelling of all closed worldviews, the breaking of all supernatural myths and sacred symbols. It represents "defatalization of history," the discovery by man that he has been left with the world on his hands, that he can no longer blame fortune or the furies for what he does with it. Secularization occurs when man turns his attention away from worlds beyond and toward this world and this time (*saeculum* = "the present age"). It is what Dietrich Bonhoeffer in 1944 called "man's coming of age."[2]

To some, Bonhoeffer's words still sound shocking, but they really should not. He was merely venturing a tardy theological interpretation of what had already been noticed by poets and novelists, sociologists and philosophers for decades. The era of the secular city is not one of anticlericalism or feverish antireligious fanaticism. The anti-Christian zealot is something of an anachronism today, a fact which explains why Bertrand Russell's books often seem quaint rather than daring and why the antireligious propaganda of the Communists sometimes appears intent on dispelling belief in a "God out there" who has long since been laid to rest.

The forces of secularization have no serious interest in persecuting religion. Secularization simply bypasses and undercuts religion and goes on to other things. It has relativized religious world views and thus rendered them innocuous. Religion has been privatized. It

---

1. Professor C. A. van Peursen's remark is quoted from a mimeographed report assembled by Professor Charles West on a conference held at the Ecumenical Institute of Bossey, Switzerland, September 1959; it is included in Section I of the Appendices. For more on van Peursen's work, see Chap. 3.

2. Dietrich Bonhoeffer's statements will be found in his *Ethics* (New York: Macmillan, 1959) and his *Letters and Papers from Prison* (New York: Macmillan, 1962; London: SCM Press, 1953).

has been accepted as the peculiar prerogative and point of view of a particular person or group. Secularization has accomplished what fire and chain could not: It has convinced the believer that he *could* be wrong, and persuaded the devotee that there are more important things than dying for the faith. The gods of traditional religions live on as private fetishes or the patrons of congenial groups, but they play no significant role in the public life of the secular metropolis.

Of course there are events and movements which momentarily raise questions about whether secularization is really succeeding in unseating the gods of traditional religion. The self-immolation of a Buddhist monk, the rise of fanatic sects such as Soka Gakkai in Japan, the appearance of the Black Muslims in America, even the new vigor of Roman Catholicism—all seem to suggest that the published obituaries of religion have been premature. But a more careful look will reveal that these phenomena cannot be understood apart from certain swift-flowing secular currents in the modern world. These currents either express themselves in quasi-religious form or else elicit adjustments in religious systems which alter them so radically that they pose no real threat to the secularization process. Thus the revival of ancient Oriental religions gives voice to the nationalistic political aspirations of peoples who preserve antiquated symbols but use them for utterly novel purposes. Pluralism and tolerance are the children of secularization. They represent a society's unwillingness to enforce any particular world view on its citizens. Movements within the Roman Catholic Church culminating in the Second Vatican Council indicate Catholicism's growing readiness to be open to truth from all sides. Pluralism is asserting itself where once a closed symbol stood.

This is the age of the secular city. Through supersonic travel and instantaneous communications its ethos is spreading into every corner of the globe. The world looks less and less to religious rules and rituals for its morality or its meanings. For some, religion provides a hobby, for others a mark of national or ethnic identification, for still others an esthetic delight. For fewer and fewer does it provide an inclusive and commanding system of personal cosmic values and explanations. True, there are some people who claim that our modern age has its secular religions, it political saints, and its profane temples. They are right in a manner of speaking; but to call, for example, Nazism or communism "religions" overlooks a very significant difference between them and traditional religions. It obscures the fact that Nazism was a throwback to a lost tribalism and that every day communism becomes more "secularized" and hence less "religious."

The Secular City and Its Debate 43

The effort to force secular and political movements of our time to be "religious" so that we can feel justified in clinging to *our* religion is, in the end, a losing battle. Secularization rolls on, and if we are to understand and communicate with our present age we must learn to love it in its unremitting secularity. We must learn, as Bonhoeffer said, to speak of God in a secular fashion and find a nonreligious interpretation of biblical concepts. It will do no good to cling to our religious and metaphysical versions of Christianity in the idle hope that one day religion or metaphysics will once again regain their centrality. They will become even more peripheral and that means we can now let go and immerse ourselves in the new world of the secular city. The first step in such an immersion is learning something about its peculiar characteristics. But before we do we must ask more precisely about the other key term we have used in describing the ethos of our time, *urbanization*.

If secularization designates the content of man's coming of age, urbanization describes the context in which it is occurring. It is the "shape" of the new society which supports its peculiar cultural style. In trying to define the term *urbanization*, however, we are confronted with the fact that social scientists themselves are not entirely agreed about what it means. It is clear, however, that urbanization is not just a quantitative term. It does not refer to population size or density, to geographic extent or to a particular form of government. Admittedly some of the character of modern urban life would not be possible without giant populations concentrated on enormous contiguous land masses. But urbanization is not something that refers only to the city. As Vidich and Bensman have shown in *Small Town in Mass Society*,[3] high mobility, economic concentration, and mass communications have drawn even rural villages into the web of urbanization.

Urbanization means a structure of common life in which the diversity and the disintegration of tradition are paramount. It means an impersonality in which functional relationships multiply. It means that a degree of tolerance and anonymity replace traditional moral sanctions and long-term acquaintanceships. The urban center is the place of human control, of rational planning, of bureaucratic organization— and the urban center is not just in Washington, London, New York, and Peking. It is everywhere. The technological metropolis provides the indispensable social setting for a world where the grip of traditional religion is loosened, for what we have called a secular style.

The age of the secular, technological city, like all preceding ages,

---

3. Arthur J. Vidich and Joseph Bensman, *Small Town in Mass Society* (Garden City, N.Y.: Anchor Books, 1958).

does have its own characteristic *style*—its peculiar way of understanding and expressing itself, its distinctive character, coloring all aspects of its life. Just as the poets and architects, the theologians and the lovers of the thirteenth century all partook of a common cultural substance, so in our time we all share a fund of unspoken perspectives. Just as the straight aisles and evenly clipped hedges of the eighteenth-century formal garden exhibited a style found also in deist theology and in neoclassic verse, so our secular urban culture makes itself felt in all our intellectual projects, artistic visions, and technical accomplishments.

The French philosopher Maurice Merleau-Ponty (1908-1961) means the same thing when he speaks of a particular *manière d'être*. He says:

> If indeed philosophy and the film agree, if reflection and techniques of work participate in a common meaning, it is because the philosopher and the film maker have in common a certain manner of being (*manière d'être*), a certain view of the world which is that of a generation.[4]

For purposes of convenience we shall divide the *manière de d'être* of the secular city into its *shape* (the social component) and its *style* (the cultural aspect) and shall deal with these ideas in Chapters 2 and 3, respectively.

We must now describe more fully what we mean by the *secular epoch*, and in order to do so it may be helpful to contrast it with two other cultural epochs which expressed different patterns of human community. For purposes of comparison we shall make use of a somewhat contrived word, *technopolis*. It will be used here to signify the fusion of technological and political components into the base on which a new cultural style has appeared. Although the term is an artificial one, it reminds us that the contemporary secular metropolis was not possible before modern technology. Modern Rome and modern London are *more than* larger versions of their Augustinian or Chaucerian forebears. There comes a point at which quantitative development releases qualitative change, and that point was reached in urban development only after the modern Western scientific revolution. Manhattan is inconceivable without structural steel and the electric elevator. Technopolis represents a new species of human community. The fact that it is a neologism will remind us that it is not yet fully realized.

By way of contrast to technopolis, let us arbitrarily designate the pre-

---

4. Maurice Merleau-Ponty, *Sens et non-sens* (Paris: Nagel, 1948), p. 309. My translation.

ceding epochal styles, according to their characteristic social forms, the *tribe* and the *town*.

The styles or periods of the tribe, the town, and the technopolis are in no sense merely successive. Nor are they mutually exclusive. If modern Paris is not simply a larger version of medieval Paris, neither should its discontinuity be exaggerated. As Lewis Mumford has shown, the roots of the modern city reach back into the Stone Age.[5] Our modern metropolis became possible only after technical advances had solved some of the problems which had heretofore placed iron limits on the size of cities; but the technical metropolis in a sense simply actualized in steel and glass, in pace and personality, what had already been present embryonically in Athens and Alexandria. Nor is tribalism merely a historical category. Even today we can find people in Africa and the South Pacific who still live a tribal existence, and we find residents of New York City with tribal mentality. Town culture, representing a kind of transition from tribe to technopolis, still persists within and around the urban centers; its residue influences the viewpoint of everyone whose youth was marked by small town and rural values—and whose was not?

We are all tribal, town, and technopolitan to some degree, but technopolitan culture is the wave of the future. With this caution let us look at the characteristics of these three epochal styles.

When man appears in history he is already a social animal living in a collective group. Whatever purposes were served by the various social-contract theories of Rousseau or Locke in advancing personal rights, they can now be seen as sheer fiction, as social myths with little grounding whatever in history. The tribe is the setting where man becomes man. It represents an extension of blood and kinship ties, and tribal man celebrates this familiar solidarity by singing songs of the common ancestors of all his people. Thus among African pygmies, Australian bushmen, American Indians, wherever remnants of tribal structure have been preserved, the venerable ancestors who are often semi-divine beings are ritually conjured in wine, dance, and ballad.

Tribal societies and primitive peoples have supplied one of the recurrent fascinations of modern man. It began perhaps with curiosity about the beginnings of human societies, especially among the French philosophers who wanted to develop a rational rather than a theological version of man's origins. This interest was fed by the discovery and investigation of the allegedly less civilized peoples of North America

---

5. Lewis Mumford, *The City in History* (New York: Harcourt, Brace, & World, 1961; London: Secker & Warburg), see especially Chaps. 1-3.

and the South Pacific. The romantic myth of the Noble Savage marks an enthusiastic stage of this fascination. More recently it has evolved into the science of cultural anthropology.

By *tribal society* we have in mind a stage in human social development which has been described variously as totemic, preliterate, primitive, and even savage or pre-logical. The variousness of the terms illustrates the problem, since they include descriptive and pejorative labels as well as terms designed to illuminate different aspects in the lives of peoples who seem increasingly remote from us in the modern technopolis. No one word, not even *tribal*, describes them accurately. One thinks, for instance, of Clyde Kluckhohn's Navaho,[6] of W. Lloyd Warner's black Australian Murngin,[7] of Bronislaw Malinowski's Trobriand Islanders.[8] These peoples, all in some sense "primitive," differ widely from one another.

In addition, it has become increasingly clear since the early studies of Frazer, Taylor, and Durkheim not only that primitive societies vary widely from each other, but that even within these societies one can discover greater disparities among personalities than scholars had originally supposed. Paul Radin has reminded a later generation that in any society, for example, one can find some people who take its religion more seriously than others. As he says, there is always the simple pragmatist who wants his religion to "work," as well as the "priest-thinker" who systematizes and orders beliefs.[9]

But one consensus has clearly emerged from modern anthropological studies. It is that the religion and culture of a society cannot be studied apart from its economic and social context. Religion is embedded in behavior and institutions before it is consciously codified, and the alteration of social and economic patterns always entails religious change. As Paul Radin puts it, "No correlation is more definite or more constant than that between a given economic level of society and the nature of the supernatural beings postulated by the tribe at large or by the religious individual in particular."[10]

When man changes his tools and his techniques, his ways of producing and distributing the goods of life, he also changes his gods. Tribal,

---

6. Clyde Kluckhohn has written a number of books and articles on Navaho culture; see his *The Navaho*, with Dorothea Leighton (Cambridge, MA: Harvard University Press, 1946).

7. W. Lloyd Warner, *A Black Civilization* (New York: Harper & Row, 1958).

8. Bronislaw Malinowski, *Magic, Science and Religion and Other Essays* (Garden City, N.Y.: Doubleday, 1954).

9. Paul Radin (ed.), *Primitive Religion* (New York: Dover, 1957).

10. Ibid. p. 192.

town, and technopolitan existence represent first of all different forms of social, economic, and political community. As such they symbolize different religions or belief systems.

For this reason, tribal societies, despite their idiosyncrasies, do exhibit certain common features.

Tribal life grows out of kinship ties. It is really an expanded family, a group in which tradition prescribes the proper relationship with any person one is likely to meet during a normal lifetime. Tribal societies are compact and enclosed. Prolonged contact with the outside world is bound to be disruptive, but such disruption catches up with every tribe sooner or later. There are no hiding places left on our shrunken globe for the Noble Savage. Oil wells dot our Indian reservations and industrialism is on the march in Africa. Ours may be the last generation to be able to study primitive peoples directly.

So tribal life has to be studied as a process, not as a static category. The tribe represents that stage during which man moves from a belief in ghosts and demons to a belief in gods, from spells and incantations to prayers, from shamans and sorcerers to priests and teachers, from myth and magic to religion and theology. All of this happens only when the economic structure of the society allows for a group of self-conscious religious specialists to emerge. There is no time for codification if everyone's energy is spent in simply keeping alive. There is no need for a definition of the relationships between the mythical heroes and divinities until questions are raised or other tribes with other divinities are encountered. As the tribe moves toward a more settled life, the camp, the village, and the town begin to appear.

The transition from tribe to town represents one of the decisive breakthroughs of human history. It is best epitomized by the emergence of the Greek *polis*. The polis appeared when bellicose clans and rival houses met here and there to form a new type of community, loyalty to whose laws and gods replaced the more elemental kinship ties which had previously held force. The gods of the tribes were demoted and a new religion arose, often centering on a common divine ancestor. As the nineteenth-century French scholar Fustel de Coulanges asserts in his classic study *The Ancient City*,[11] the founding of the polis was a religious act. A new cultus was formed whose gods were higher than those of the constituting clans. To be a citizen of the city was to be a member of the new cultus, often centered around a semi-divine founder such as Aeneas.

---

11. Numa Denis Fustel de Coulanges, *The Ancient City* (Garden City, N.Y.: Doubleday, 1956; London: Mayflower Books), Book Three, Chaps. 3-5.

But the conflict of loyalties between family custom and the law of the town, between blood ties and the more impersonal justice of the polis, deeply disturbed the soul of the ancient Greek. Sophocles' tragedy *Antigone* projects this conflict onto the stage. In *Antigone* we watch a struggle between the needs of the arising polis for order and equality, symbolized by King Creon, and the deeper bonds of blood, represented by Antigone. Antigone feels she must bury her brother, Polynices, who has fallen in a revolt against the polis. Creon has decreed that as a traitor Polynices must lie unburied, to be devoured by the dogs and the birds. Caught in the fatal contradiction between family and polis, Antigone and Creon collide, with catastrophic results for both. Though the play is often interpreted and directed as a portrait of religion and the laws of God (Antigone) versus the tyranny and the laws of men (Creon), the Athenians who first witnessed it knew better. They realized that they were watching a reproduction of the anguished struggle going on within our own breasts, a struggle in which gods and values were ranged on both sides. *Antigone* signals the painful transition of a culture from tribe to town, a metamorphosis whose fearful scope and psyche-threatening uncertainty can be matched only by the present transition from town to technopolis.

The tribe was a family writ large. Its roots reached back to a common mythological past, and its members were locked together in lines of consanguinity. It bestowed on all its members an unquestioned place and a secure identity. It answered most of the great questions of human existence—marriage, occupation, life goals—almost before they were raised. Tribal tradition gave the answers. Tradition, whether danced, chanted, or carved into masks or figurines, provided a rich, complex, and utterly complete catalog of images, identities, and values.

Tribal man is hardly a personal "self" in our modern sense of the word. He does not so much live in a tribe; the tribe lives in him. He is the tribe's subjective expression. He grasps himself within a closed system of compact meanings in which there is no room for any transcendent point of view or critical detachment.[12] Man and nature, the animals and the gods, all form one continuous life process whose meaning courses through it just below the surface and can erupt anywhere in a transparent moment of magical or religious power.

The appearance of currency and the development of the alphabet supply two essential ingredients in the shattering step from tribe

---

12. For a discussion of the contrast between "compact" and "differentiated" symbol system, see Eric Voegelin, *Order and History,* Vol. I: *Israel and Revelation* (Baton Rouge: Louisiana State University, 2000).

to town. Both devices tend to free individuals from traditionally prescribed relationships and to expand enormously the possible occasions for human contact. A man with a sheep to barter for bread must find a person who both has bread and wants wool or lamb stew. The range of possibilities is small and will tend to be directed by tradition. Sheep raising and bread baking will be passed on from father to son. Economic contacts and familial patterns will not be distinguishable. But the man who can sell a sheep and buy bread with the money is at once a more mobile and a more independent operator. The jingle of coins tolls the end of tribal existence and signals the beginning of a more impersonal, more rationalized way of living together.

In the same way, as writing develops, man's dependence on the person of the shaman or the oracle is undercut. Now he can begin to examine documents himself. Books and parchments can circulate and be perused outside the dim circle of the sacred fire where one had to cling to the storyteller's every syllable and defer to his traditional role in order to find out about the world. Writing depersonalizes man's access to information.

Once again the economic framework is crucial. Writing began as a tool of commerce, but quickly became a way to acquire knowledge and therefore power. Thus it had political and religious consequences. Contact with the "outside," with ideas and possibilities not accessible within the tribe, provided one key to the development of town culture. It was difficult, but not impossible, for strangers to become a part of the town. As Lewis Mumford has correctly seen, one became part of the tribe solely by accident of birth or blood, whereas the town provides a place where strangers can become fellow citizens.[13]

This transformation of "strangers and outsiders" into "fellow citizens and members of one another" recalls, of course, an expression close to the heart of the New Testament message (see Ephesians 2). It suggests one good reason why the early church, from its outset a detribalizing movement in which there was "no longer Jew nor Greek," spread most quickly in the towns and cities. We shall return to this later on, but here it does raise the interesting question of why even the storied Greek polis never realized in full the ideals of town life. It never became fully open or fully universal. It always remained partly a tribe. Athens and Rome felt it necessary to preserve the fiction that all their citizens had sprung from the loins of a common ancestor. Both failed to see that universal citizenship could not be reconciled with slavery and imperialism. There are in fact two reasons why Athens never

---

13. Lewis Mumford, *op. cit.,* p. 151.

became a city or a metropolis in the modern sense of the word, why it
never achieved the population size, the complexity, the anonymity, or
the uncanny vastness of the modern urban area. The first is that these
elements were just not possible until modern scientific technology had
set the stage. But the second is that the universality and radical openness of Christianity were not yet present to dispel the remnants of tribalism. Fustel de Coulanges believes that what was missing from the
Greek and Roman "cities" was the universal God of Christianity. The
ancients, he says, "never represented God to themselves as a unique
being exercising his action upon the universe. . . . Religion was entirely
local . . . special to each city."[14] It was the lack of that totally inclusive
claim of the Gospel that kept the ancients' towns to some extent tribal.
Only after the beginning of the Christian era was the *idea* of an inclusive metropolis conceivable, and even then it took nearly two millennia
to realize it. "Christianity," Fustel de Coulanges goes on, ". . . was not
the domestic religion of any family, the national religion of any city
or of a race. It belonged neither to a caste nor to a corporation. From
its first appearance it called to itself the whole human race."[15]

Antigone is the tragic figure who symbolizes the painful transition
from tribe to town, from kinship to civil loyalties. In a sense Socrates
represents a comparable tragedy in the transition from polis to cos-
mopolis, from the gods of the city to the universal community of mankind. He did not reject the "gods of the city" as his accusers claimed he
did. Rather he simply refused to take them with unqualified seriousness. He saw that they have a place, but only a limited and provisional
place. His execution marks Athens' refusal to develop from a provincial polis to a universal metropolis.[16]

Perhaps what we have called the "town" will eventually be recognized as itself merely a transitional stage between the tribe and the
technopolis, between two forms of communal-collective existence,
between the preliterate man of the cave painting and the post-literate
man of the electronic image. There are indeed striking analogies
between tribal and technopolitan life. In fact, for Marxist theory, the
"bourgeois" period (which usually means "the age of the town dweller")
constitutes nothing more than a long, conflict-ridden transition from
primitive communism to Socialist communism.

But for most of us town culture cannot be dismissed as merely tran-

---

14. Fustel de Coulanges, *op. cit.*, p. 151.
15. Ibid., p. 391.
16. Maurice Merleau-Ponty, *Eloge de la Philosophie* (Paris: Gallimard, 1953), pp.
48-57.

sition. It is part of us. The age of the towns gave us printing and books, rational theology, the scientific revolution, investment capitalism, and bureaucracy. It gave us many other things as well, but these are the ones which relate closely to what Max Weber, in characterizing the age, has called "rationalization."[17] Especially in the Calvinist Puritanism which was in many ways the prototypical religion of the period, Weber saw a classical instance of what he termed the "routinization of charisma." These are also the aspects which provide the most evident contrast with both tribe and technopolis. The shaman is the symbol of tribal man. He dances and chants his religion. The Puritan or maybe even the Yankee is his town-culture counterpart. Town man meditates on the word and hears it preached. Tribal man merges with his daemon and his group. Town man is a discreet individual who reads *Robinson Crusoe*. Tribal man's gods whirl with him in the night of sensual ecstasy. Town man's God calls him from an infinite distance to work soberly in the daylight of self-discipline. This comparison may make town man sound spare and astringent, but we should not deal with him too harshly, first because he rarely lived up to the image we have painted of him, and secondly because he was preparing the way for technopolitan civilization. Without him it could never have begun.

To Speak in a Secular Fashion about God (1965)

This selection is excerpted from Chapter 11 of The Secular City, *251-53.*

On 30 April 1944, Dietrich Bonhoeffer wrote to one of his friends from his prison cell words that have both tempted and tormented theologians ever since. "We are proceeding towards a time," he wrote, "of no religion at all. . . . How do we speak of God without religion. . . . How do we speak in a secular fashion of God?"[18]

No wonder Bonhoeffer's question bothers us. It reminds us of two incontrovertible facts. The first is that the biblical faith, unlike Buddhism, for example, must *speak* of God. It cannot withdraw into silence or cryptic aphorisms. A God to whom human words cannot point is not the God of the Bible. Bonhoeffer's question also reminds us, however, that the word *God* bewilders or confuses modern secular man.

17. Max Weber, *The Protestant Ethic and the Spirit of Capitalism* (New York: Scribner, 1958; London: Allen & Unwin).
18. Dietrich Bonhoeffer, *Prisoner for God* (New York: Macmillan, 1959), p. 123.

His mental world and his way of using language is such that the word *God* has become more and more problematical for him. This reveals the impasse: if man cannot speak of God in the secular city, then all we have said about secularization and the biblical faith is nonsense and the whole thesis of this book is erroneous. We must deal with this painful question of Bonhoeffer satisfactorily or all that we have said so far becomes implausible.

Significantly, Bonhoeffer himself supplies a much-needed clue for where to start in seeking to answer his question. Many years before his imprisonment he wrote this paragraph in his commentary on the Second Commandment:

> "God" is not for us a common concept by which we designate that which is the highest, holiest and mightiest thinkable, but "God" is a name. It is something entirely different when the heathen say "God" as when we, to whom God himself has spoken say "God" . . . "God" is a name. . . . The word means absolutely nothing, the name "God" is everything.[19]

Here Bonhoeffer drops an invaluable hint about how we should proceed. He reminds us that in the biblical tradition, we do not speak "about God" at all, either "in a secular fashion" or in any other. When we use the word *God* in the biblical sense, we are not speaking about, but we are "naming," and that is an entirely different matter. To name is to point, to confess, to locate something in terms of our history. We can name something only by using the fund of memories and meanings we carry with us as individuals and as a species. This makes the act of naming, whether naming God or anything else, more than merely a theological or linguistic problem. Theologies and languages grow out of a sociocultural milieu. They spring from one or another epochal *manière d'être*. This makes the problem of "speaking in a secular fashion about God" in part at least a sociological problem.[20]

But speaking about God in a secular fashion is not just a sociological problem. Since we live in a period when our view of the world is being politicized, in which, as we shall see in a moment, the political is replacing the metaphysical as the characteristic mode of grasping reality, "naming" today becomes in part also a political issue. It becomes a question of where, in the push and pull of human conflict, those cur-

---

19. Dietrich Bonhoeffer, *Gesammelte Schriften*, IV, p. 606. Author's translation.

20. For a brilliant discussion of naming by an extremely influential but little-known thinker, see Eugene Rosenstock-Heussey, *Die Sprache des Menschengeschlechts* (Heidelberg: Verlag Lambert Schneider, 1963).

rents can be detected which continue the liberating activity we witness, in the Exodus and in Easter. Speaking of God in a secular fashion is also a political issue.

But the sociological and political considerations in no sense exhaust the depth of Bonhoeffer's riddle. Despite the efforts of some modern theologians to sidestep it, whether God exists or not *is* a desperately serious issue. All the palaver about the terms *existence* and *being* and all the sophisticated in-group bickering about non-objectifying language cannot obscure the fact that there remains an indissoluble question after all the conceptualizations have been clarified. It is the question the Spanish philosopher Miguel Unamuno rightly felt overshadows all other questions man asks: Is man alone in the universe or not?

So Bonhoeffer's query has three parts. It is first of all a *sociological problem.* We say problem because it can be answered at that level with relatively little difficulty. It is also a *political issue.* An issue is a somewhat more demanding challenge. It requires us to take some risks and make some choices, to take sides. It necessitates our indicating where the same reality whom the Hebrews called Yahweh, whom the disciples saw in Jesus, is breaking in today. But finally, Bonhoeffer presents us with what is a *theological question.* He makes us answer for ourselves whether the God of the Bible is real or is just a rich and imaginative way man has fashioned to talk about himself. No amount of verbal clarification can set this disagreement aside. In the last analysis it is not a matter of clear thinking at all but a matter of personal decision. Luther was right: deciding on this question is a matter which, like dying, every man must do for himself.

The Secular City Debate (1966)

This selection is taken from an Afterword to The Secular City Debate, *edited by Daniel Callahan (New York: Macmillan Company, 1966), 179-80, 190, 192-203.*

One of my reasons for writing *The Secular City* was to challenge a popular misconception about the relation of theological reflection to practical life. I had noticed that many serious people in the heady and demanding world of day-to-day decision making in our urban civilization suspect that theology is something for the cloister or for the groves of academe. They think of it as a highly esoteric specialty with no relevance whatever to the issues they face. Oddly enough, I found that many theologians shared this prejudice. Jealous of their prerogatives as specialists and often insecure among both the *hommes d'affaires* and the poor people, they had convinced themselves that theology probably had, in fact, little interest to anyone but theologians.

I strongly differ with this view of the place and purpose of theology. I recognize that theological work demands a degree of training and skill equivalent to that of any other discipline. But I also believe that the *reason* for theology's existence is the critical nurture of the whole historical community whose symbols and practices theologians investigate. My own theological perspective leads me to discount any supernatural "overhead" or "God-out-there." Thus, for me, the theological enterprise seeks to grasp the problems man faces in this historic present in the light of his past and his future, that is in light of faith and hope. Without the stimulus and prodding of theology, in this sense of the word, life becomes unreflective, ahistorical, and provincial. It can degenerate into a kind of moral and spiritual astigmatism, or more accurately, a near-sightedness in which nothing is seen in any real perspective. But without a continual conversation with the real world, theology itself also suffers. It becomes effete, trivial, and precious. Thus *The Secular City* was written in an attempt to get theologians to open their eyes to the secular world and to get those who inhabit this secular world to understand it and themselves in a historical-theological perspective. . . .

* * *

When I turn to those parts of *The Secular City* I would affirm even more emphatically today, the first would be the basically positive evaluation of the process of secularization. Today I feel more strongly than ever that the secularization should not be viewed as an example of massive and catastrophic cultural backsliding but as a product of the impact of the biblical faith itself on world civilization. . . .

Still, the process of secularization is not an unqualified good. I wish to affirm a direction in history, even a process of evolutionary differentiation in the history of religion. But I want to avoid a simple "progress view." Here the image of the crap game, which I originally borrowed from Archie Hargreaves and which drew numberless comments, both positive and negative, will help. I would argue that secularization "raises the stakes" of the game. It puts man in a position where he can do more harm than good, where his mistakes will be costlier and his virtues will be more salutary than ever before. Secularization means increased control by man over his physical environment, deepened knowledge of his own inner workings, mightier weapons, more powerful medicines, higher aspirations, the need for more account-ability. The secularization of the world is a summons to man to grow up. He can still refuse. But his refusal in our time would be incompa-rably more catastrophic than in any previous period.

Another point at which I would not only decline to retreat but might even wish to sharpen the question has to do with those criticisms of my willingness to identify certain movements and events in our time with the breaking in of the Kingdom of God. I would want to reiter-ate my insistence that in the secular city itself we can discern certain provisional elements of the promised Kingdom. Some reviewers have sniffed occasionally about my "sectarian" bias, or my propensity to overlook bad things that are there in the city, like the loneliness which accompanies anonymity, of the alienation which results from too much mobility. . . .

True, sectarians have sometimes made the mistake of identifying marks of the Kingdom too quickly. They have often been wrong in their confession. But we have just come through a period of theologi-cal ethics in which our error lay in quite the opposite direction. Chas-tised rightly by Reinhold Niebuhr for putting too much hope in mere political solutions, for being too sentimentally impressed by idealistic schemes, we learned to put great emphasis on the complexity and dif-ficulty of all moral issues. We saw the Kingdom of God as an "impos-sible possibility," as a transcendent standard of judgment by which the pretensions of our petty human plans could be exposed.

But perhaps we learned our lesson too well. In trying to avoid moral oversimplifications we saw more ambiguity than anyone else. In guard-ing the Kingdom of God from ideological perversion, we rendered it politically irrelevant. To say that the Kingdom of God is not of this earth is true—but only half true. It is also "in the midst of us." It is among us like mustard seed and yeast. Its first fruits can be tasted even now. It not only empowers us to say no to the pride and pretense of man; it also allows us to say yes where the Messianic era breaks in on the darkened world. It requires us to be specific not only in our con-demnations but in what we support. Though this can produce mistakes and will require constant repentance and reexamination, nothing is so morally wrong as phrasing one's moral concerns in general terms when the situation requires the specific.

I appreciate more than I can say the attention which thoughtful crit-ics have lavished on *The Secular City*. Their comments, even when most negative, flattered and pleased me. They often helped me to strengthen my argument here and there. But as for the basic thesis of the book, that secularization should be welcomed as an occasion requiring maturity in man, here I still stand; I can take no other.

* * *

Finally, I come to the issue which has fascinated me most since the publication of *The Secular City*. It is the one dealt with in the final chapter, entitled "To Speak in a Secular Fashion of God." I concede that this chapter does not fully accomplish its purpose. My only defense is that the failure is not wholly mine but is shared by the entire theological community. For years the doctrine of God in theology has become more and more problematical. We have ignored or passed over it, but our sloth has now returned to haunt us. It serves us right, I think, that our shirking the work we should have done on the problem of God has now produced the widely celebrated "death-of-God" movement in theology which, if it makes no constructive contribution toward extricating us from the quagmire, dramatizes with chilling cogency the bankruptcy of the categories we have been trying to use.

The "death of God" means different things to different theologians. For some it means the final disappearance of that divinity which had been perched at the fulcrum of our classical metaphysical systems. Insofar as we have confused this abstract deity with watered-down versions of the biblical Yahweh, often welding the two together, it signals his demise too. For others, the "death of God" denotes the disappearance of those familiar and culturally prescribed ways of encountering the numinous which touched our forefathers but no longer reach us. Modes of religious experience are shaped by cultural patterns, and when social change shakes and jars the patterns, conventional ways of experiencing the holy disappear too. When an individuated urban culture replaces the thickly clotted symbol system of a pre-urban society, modalities of religious experience shift. If this happens over a long period of time, religious systems often develop apace. When social change happens swiftly, the cultural symbols may lag behind. But eventually the people experience the death of its gods. Hence the experience of the "death of God" correlates with a rapid dissolution of traditional cultural patterns and is a frequent characteristic of societies in abrupt transition.

The death-of-god syndrome, whether experienced as a collapse of the symbol system or as an evaporation of the experience of the sacred, can only occur where the controlling symbols of the culture had been more or less uncritically fused with the transcendent god. When a civilization collapses and its gods topple, theological speculation sometimes moves either toward a God whose life center lies outside of culture (Augustine, Barth) or to a thoroughgoing skepticism which can take the form of the "death of God." In our own period, marked by man's historical consciousness' reaching out and encompassing everything in sight, the previous nooks and crannies reserved for the transcendent have all been made immanent. As we shall argue later, only a god of the "not-yet" still transcends history while touching it, the traditional marks of the biblical God, he who though "beyond history" still influences it. Pluralism and radical historicism have become our permanent companions. We know that all doctrines, ideals, institutions, and formulations—whether religious or secular—arise within history and must be understood in terms of their historical milieu. How then do we speak of a God who is "in but not of" secular history, who is somehow present in history yet not exhausted in His total being by the historical horizon? How, in short, do we maintain an affirmation of transcendence in a culture whose mood is radical and relentlessly immanentist? . . .

I have no answer. I can only indicate how I am grappling with this conundrum and where I now hope some new hint of an opening can be found. I am now pursuing the hints, perhaps misleading, of two vagabonds on the periphery of theology, Pierre Teilhard de Chardin and Ernst Bloch. Both men are to some extent pariahs. Chardin was a Jesuit paleontologist whose speculations on the place of man in the cosmos have elicited stern warnings from the Holy See. Ernst Bloch is the eighty-year-old Marxist Revisionist whose irrepressible originality ended in his departure from Communist East Germany. Both of these men represent the outskirts, or the frontiers, of theology. Neither belongs to the club. But if our present crisis teaches us anything, it is that the club is probably finished unless it begins to listen to the outsiders.

For all its wooliness and lack of scientific precision, the thought of Pierre Teilhard de Chardin, with its passion for assigning man a significant place in the vastness of the cosmos and its dynamically immanentist doctrine of God, attracts me. I am not really impressed by those earnest souls who point out the gaps in Teilhard's scientific accuracy, because I do not think Teilhard's case necessarily rests on the empirical accuracy of his paleontological data. His scientific research really provides Teilhard with little more than a platform from which to launch his singularly biblical vision of man's place in the cosmos. Teilhard's theology is essentially poetic and only accidently scientific, in the narrow sense. It is really a Christian cosmology, the first we have had for some time that has really engaged the imagination of modern man.

"Since Galileo," writes Teilhard in the newest translation of his works,

The Appearance of Man (New York: Harper and Row, 1966), "in the eyes of science man has continually lost, one after another, the privileges that made him consider himself unique in the world. Astronomically . . . biologically . . . psychologically. . . . Now paradoxically, this same man is in the process of re-emerging from his return to the crucible, more than ever *at the head of nature*; since by his very melting back into the general current of convergent cosmogenesis, he is acquiring in our eyes the possibility and power of forming in the heart of space and time, *a single point of humanization for the very stuff of the world.*"

What Teilhard has understood with superb clarity is that the question of God comes to us today "in, with and under" the question of man. The two are inextricable, as we might have imagined had we taken the significance of Jesus seriously. It is for this reason that the contemporary theological rediscovery of the parturient if puzzling thought of Ernst Bloch interests me too, perhaps even more than the work of Teilhard.

Though there are many differences, both Teilhard and Bloch discuss transcendence in terms of the pressure exerted by the future on the present. They both see that his future is the key to man's being, and they recognize that an authentically open future is only possible where there is a *creature* who can orient himself toward the future and relate himself to reality in terms of this orientation—in short, *a creature who can hope.*

Both Teilhard the maverick Catholic and Bloch the renegade Marxist saw reality as a radically open-ended process. Teilhard detected in the logic of evolution an ever-deepening humanization of man and hominization of the universe. Bloch concerned himself with "Man-as-Promise" and mapped out what he called "the ontology of the not yet." Teilhard roamed through the aeons of geological time and the breathtakingly massive universe and focused on the appearance within them of the phenomenon of man, that point where the cosmos begins to think and to steer itself. Bloch's stage for philosophizing is human history, exhumed from its imprisonment in timelessness and launched on a journey into the future. The hope which makes this future possible, Bloch contends, was introduced into the world by biblical faith. Both Bloch and Teilhard saw what the Germans now call the "*Impuls der Erwartung.*" One examined the way cosmic space and time seem to dwarf man, the other the way history seems to buffet him. But then both moved on to emphasize man's growing capacity to apply science and critical reflection in the shaping of his own destiny. Both saw the future not just as that for which man is responsible, but as that for which he now *knows* he is responsible.

My present inclination in response to the provocation of the "death-of-God" theology and the urgent need for a no-nonsense "leveling" in theological discourse is to think that if we can affirm anything which both defines and transcends history it will be the *future* as it lives in man's imagination, nurtured by his memory and actualized by his responsibility. . . .

Bloch considers himself an atheist, as does Heidegger. But just as many theologians, such as Bultmann and Ott, have found significant clues for a doctrine of God in Heidegger, there are even more suggestive hints in Bloch. Bloch postulates, for example, a *correspondence* between *man* (as that being who hopes, dreams and is open to history) and the *developing world* itself. He sees this *Entsprechung* (correspondence) between "the subjective content of hope" and the "objectively possible," and tries, often unsuccessfully, to describe it. It is a correspondence, he says, between "subjective" and "objective" hope, and it raises the question in Bloch's mind of an "identity" between man-who-hopes and a structure of reality which supports and nourishes such hope.

At this point the Christian naturally thinks of qualities sometimes attributed to God in theology. Bloch is in no sense unaware of the similarity. He holds that this identity between subjective spontaneity and historical possibility is the "demythologized content of that which Christians have revered as God." So he insists that atheism is the only acceptable stance today in view of the fact that the Christian God has been imprisoned in the stable categories of a static ontology. . . .

But Bloch's main theses cannot be easily dismissed, at least from my perspective. Along with Teilhard, he offers the only exit from the theological dead end signaled by the death-of-God theologians. Thus I agree with Wolf-Dieter Marsch when he gingerly suggests that so long as Christians cling to the static *is* as the normative predicate for God, such thinkers as Bloch must rightly continue to regard themselves as atheists. But if theology can leave behind the God who *is* and begin its work with the God who *will be*, or, in biblical parlance, *"He who cometh,"* an exciting new epoch in theology could begin, one in which Ernst Bloch's work would be extraordinarily important. If the present wake is for the God who "is" (and now "was"), this may clear the decks for the God who *will be*. I cannot say for sure that this path will lead anywhere, but it would require a thorough reworking of our major theological categories. We would see Jesus, for example, not as a visitor on earth from some supraterrestrial heaven, but as the one in whom precisely this two-story dualism is abolished for good and who becomes the pioneer and first sign of the coming New Age. We could see the community of faith as those *on the way* to this promised reality, "forgetting what is behind and reaching out for that which lies ahead" (Phil. 3:14). The doctrine of God would become theology's answer to the irrefutable fact that the only way history can be kept open is by "anchoring" that openness somewhere outside history itself, in this case not "above," but ahead.

Still, I would be the worst of imposters if I pretended that in the God of Hope we can immediately affirm the one who will appear when the corpse of the dead God of metaphysical theism is finally interred. He may not appear even after we have buried the God of theism. The whole attempt to work out a new and viable doctrine of God for our time may be fated to fail from the beginning. But I am not yet ready to throw in the towel. Before any of us do, I hope we will exercise the terrible freedom made possible to us by the present *Götterdämmerung* of the divinities of Christendom to think as candidly and rigorously as possible about where we go from here.

This then is where I now find myself on those fiendishly difficult questions raised by my final chapter. I still believe that the problem of speaking in a secular fashion of God has important sociological and political aspects. But I believe it has theological dimensions far more baffling than those indicated in *The Secular City.* Though my critics have not given me much help in solving this problem, they have dislodged me from the ground on which I once stood, and for that I am grateful. They have pushed me along the most promising path I could find. The have turned my face toward the future, where if man meets God again, that encounter must take place.

Beyond Bonhoeffer? (1966)

This selection is taken from "Beyond Bonhoeffer? The Future of Religionless Christianity," an Appendix to The Secular City Debate, *206, 211-14.*

Dietrich Bonhoeffer, the martyr-theologian of the German Resistance—despite the fact that he has become an enigma, a fad, a saint and in some cases an embarrassment in the two decades since his execution by the SS—had his finger on the very issues which continue to torment us. We must be careful not to tear Bonhoeffer out of his context and apply his somewhat fragmentary insights in a wholly different setting. All the same we cannot yet "move beyond" him because we have not yet faced his challenge seriously. His uncanny capacity to uncover the hidden skeletons in the closets of theology and to see issues coming around the corner means that we have not shaken him. It may be embarrassing to assign readings from someone who has already been written up on a photo essay by *Life*, but as one American theologian put it, "We have to continue studying Bonhoeffer even though he is a fad."

The recent publication in English of extended excerpts from Bonhoeffer's early writings, under the title *No Rusty Swords,* gives us a new opportunity to assess where we now stand on the issues Bonhoeffer raised and how his astonishing theological intelligence might still help us. . . .

Surely the most difficult part of Bonhoeffer's work for most people to grasp is his talk about a "nonreligious" interpretation of the Gospel, his suggestion that for the "man come of age" we must find a way to speak of God "in a secular fashion." To some readers this still sounds like sheer nonsense. Religionless Christianity seems to be a *contradictio in adjecto.* But this is just where Bonhoeffer makes his most incisive contribution. If he is misunderstood here, then all he says about the style of church life, about political obedience and about ethics will be lost.

Why do we need a nonreligious interpretation of the Gospel? We have seen that Bonhoeffer believed that the church comes into existence at the edge of paganism. It is shaped both by the thrust of the Gospel and by the changing cultural topography of the world. This is just why we need a nonreligious interpretation. It is necessitated, Bonhoeffer believed, both by the requirements of the Gospel and by the needs of the twentieth-century world.

The Gospel, Bonhoeffer insisted, is the good news of grace. It calls for no moral or intellectual preconditions on the part of the bearer. Nor does it demand any religious precondition. Bonhoeffer used the early Christian debate on circumcision to make this point. The apostles decided quite early that they could not require circumcision of new Christians and still be true to the free grace of God. Likewise today, Bonhoeffer argued, no precondition must be exacted as the price of grace. "Being religious" is the modern equivalent of being circumcised. It must not be made into a precondition of grace, since God's grace has already been lavished on man and is free. Also, as a student of Karl Barth, Bonhoeffer had learned that religion is not always a good thing, that it can become man's way to escape God as easily as it becomes man's way to serve Him. In short, his first reason for dereli-gionizing the Gospel was strictly theological.

But Bonhoeffer also argued for a religionless Christianity because of the ethos of the modern world. He saw in the process of secular-ization, which he dated from about the time of the Renaissance, not some seasonal tempest which would soon blow over, but a coming to fruition of much that Christianity had planted in the soil of Western civilization. In this respect Bonhoeffer stands closer to some Catholic humanists, to the traditional Catholic admiration for *urbanitas*, than he does to many Protestants. As an astute observer of his fellow men, he thought he detected the appearance in our time of a new type of per-son later termed by Helmut Gollwitzer as the "areligious personality." Also, unlike so many theologians, Catholic and Protestant, Bonhoef-fer affirmed much of the impact of the Enlightenment. He admired and celebrated man's growing power over nature, his aesthetic genius, his capacity to generate values. He pleaded with fellow theologians to begin fashioning theologies which would speak to man not in his weak-ness, sickness and death, but in his maturity, strength and responsibil-ity. He did not feel that to acclaim man's stature somehow detracted from the glory of God.

To the very end Bonhoeffer lived with joy on the edge of paganism. In his final days he exchanged ideas with a Communist cellmate, the nephew of Molotov. Bonhoeffer loved and admired the atheists and agnostics with whom he lived his last hours. No doubt they deepened his determination to find a nonreligious interpretation of the Gospel. Standing on that difficult border between church and world, he had an unshakable certainty that the God of grace could speak even to the nonreligious man. True both to earth and Heaven, both to God and man, he saw with rare clarity that such a stance would necessitate far-reaching changes in future theology.

In short, Bonhoeffer wanted us to believe in man and his possibili-ties, and he did not feel that this should weaken our faith in God. This is obviously another point where we would be arrogant to claim that we are "beyond Bonhoeffer." The enormous and somewhat unmerited attention now being lavished on Teilhard de Chardin surely shows that many people today wish to acknowledge man's crucial place in the cos-mos while still affirming God's encompassing sovereignty. They turn to Chardin, whose thought is often far less than intellectually precise, mainly because few other theologians have dared to strike out in this direction. Chardin also wanted to celebrate man in his strength.

But need this man be "nonreligious"? Since for Bonhoeffer religion implied an element of dependency, a weakness which must be matched by a strength from elsewhere, a need for answers not to be found by man himself, on his terms, the "man come of age" would *not* be religious. There will be those today, of course, contending with some justification that religion need not mean all these things and that therefore Bonhoeffer's nonreligious interpretation would not be as radical as it first sounds. Perhaps they are right. Perhaps the meaning of the word "religion" can be so radically redefined that Bonhoeffer's challenge will evaporate. But I doubt it. For the vast majority of people today, especially in America, "religion" still means very much what he had in mind.

Bonhoeffer was utterly serious. He emphasized time and time again that God had founded his church "beyond religion," that to be a Christian was "not to be religious in a particular sense, but to be a man." He meant that we should not deplore, but greet the appearance of the areligious personality. He meant that Christians should not be trapped into some crusade to defend "religion" of whatever sort against the threat of "atheism" or of "secularism." After all, certain types of atheism are closer to biblical faith than are certain types of religion. Pompey was shocked when he pushed his way into the inner court of the Jewish Temple after conquering Jerusalem and found no statue. He became convinced that the Jews were really atheists, which as far as his gods were concerned they probably were. The early Christians were maimed and murdered not principally because they believed in Jesus, but because they did *not* believe in Caesar. They were the forerunners, Bonhoeffer would argue, of the areligious personalities of our age.

But how *shall* we speak of God to the secular man? Bonhoeffer gave no answer. Still, from the very issues to which he devoted his life, we may get some hint. Gathering up those interests, we could speculate as follows:

1. A divided church will not speak to the man come of age. Mired in its own provincialisms, obsessed with defenses of its partial truths, it elicits hardly more than a yawn from the people Bonhoeffer wished to address. If reconciliation and authentic community constitute God's gift to the world, then a dismembered church contravenes its own message. Unity is not something for Christians to enjoy among themselves. It is a prerequisite of mission.

2. A church which eschews politics, or worse still, uses politics to shore up its own position in the world, will never speak to secular man. Ministers and nuns on picket lines for racial justice today

are not just signs of the church's "social concern." They are evangelists, telling modern man what the Gospel says. The church which remains securely within the "spiritual realm" will annoy no one and convince no one, for secular man is a political animal *par excellence,* and that indispensable dimension of the Gospel which goes "beyond politics" begins after, not before, the political obedience of Christians.

3. A church whose ethical pronouncements remain generic and abstract will never speak to the secular man. He does not live "in general." He lives his life in a particular place, doing a certain job, faced with specific issues. Vague moral advice does not interest him. Specific ethical demands may infuriate him, stimulate him, or encourage him. But at least he will hear them, which is all the church can ever succeed in accomplishing. Whether he believes or obeys is not, in the final analysis, determined by the church but by the Spirit of God at work within him.

Thus the answer to the fourth issue raised by Bonhoeffer, how to speak of God to the secular man, will only be given to us as we grapple faithfully with the previous three. Of course Bonhoeffer has been misunderstood and misused. He will be again. Of course theological fads are always dangerous. But we are in no sense finished with Bonhoeffer. Nor do I believe we can move "beyond" him until we begin to be the kind of church he knew we must be, a church which lives on the border of unbelief, which speaks with pointed specificity to its age, which shapes its message and mission not for its own comfort but for the health and renewal of the world.

4

God's Revolutionary World

This chapter is taken from God's Revolution and Man's Responsibility *(Valley Forge, PA: The Judson Press, 1965), 15-36.*

It is time that we Christians move our focus from the renewal of church to the renewal of world. M. M. Thomas, one of the leaders of the ecumenical movement and a great Indian Christian, said recently that the World Council of Churches, since its inception in 1948, has been far too obsessed with discussions about the church. His criticism applies to all of us. We have talked about the unity of the church, the mission of the church, the renewal of the church. We have talked far too much about the church, but not enough about God's world. This does not mean that we must devise some kind of nonchurch Christianity, but it does mean that we can correct our ecclesiastical over-emphasis. As D. T. Niles, another Asian Christian, once put it, if we want to speak with God, then we had better find out something about the world because that is the only subject in which God is interested.

Let us take a look at the meaning of this world from a biblical perspective. Our starting point would be the opening words of the Bible: "In the beginning God created the heavens and the earth." We begin there because our thinking should start with what God has done and is doing in the world. Only then can we discover how through the church we respond to what he is calling us to be and to do in the world.

The New Testament uses several terms to refer to the world. It uses the word *kosmos* (orderly arrangement), for example, from which we get the words "cosmic," "cosmonaut," and even "cosmetic." It also uses the word *aiōn*, from which we have our word "eon," designating a long period of time. When we read through the New Testament, we are often confused by alternating negative and positive statements about the world. "Do not be conformed to the world," we hear; then we read on another page that "God so loved the world." We should be very careful, as we read the New Testament, to notice that one English word, "world," is used to translate two or three different Greek words. When the world is referred to positively, the word *kosmos* is most often used. When it is referred to negatively, either *aiōn* is used or an adjective such as "fallen" is placed before *kosmos*. The word *aiōn* could also be translated "world spirit" or "fallen age" rather than "world." The Bible has nothing against "the world."

When the Hebrew people talked about the "world," they didn't mean simply the stage on which the drama of human enterprise is played out—not just the rocks and hills. They meant the cast of this drama, too:

> The earth is the Lord's and the fullness thereof,
>   the world and those who dwell therein. . . .

What the Hebrews had in mind here was not simply a physical entity. They meant a "lived world," the world of human decisions and dependencies, the interlocking spheres of hope and frustrations, the social world, the cultural world; what we might call the human world. They meant the *kosmos*, insofar as it became the sphere of man's aspirations and man's meaning. This is the world as the Bible sees it.

Let me illustrate this meaning further from contemporary usage. We often talk about the "business world" or the "world of entertainment," referring not just to the physical properties of these worlds, but to their human reality. Likewise, when we speak of "the campus," we don't mean simply the green turf but rather the human life which is lived in this community called the campus. I think this comparison helps us to understand what the Bible means when it says "world." It means the entire constellation of all these interrelated human worlds.

What does the Bible say about this world? I would like to list four assertions the Bible makes about the world.

First assertion: The world is created, sustained, and judged by God. It is his creation. It belongs to him. "The pillars of the earth are the Lord's," says Hannah in 1 Samuel, "and on them has he set the world." We should make clear at the outset that this is not a statement about the physical origin of the solar system. It is not something intended to rival some geological or astronomical theory about where the Milky Way or the planet Earth came from. Rather, this is a statement of the Hebrew community's faith that the world belongs to God, that he is the continuing source of our very life itself—of our common life—and that he stands as its ground, sustaining it and making it possible. It is a confession by the Hebrew people of the same thing that we mean when we sing "He's Got the Whole World in His Hands." It is a confession that all we have and all we are and all we can ever be comes to us from somewhere else, from someone else. It is a confession that there is no such thing as a self-made man. When Zampano in Federico Fellini's unforgettable film, *La Strada,* says, "All I want is to be left alone; I don't need anyone," he is denying the very basis of life. The breath that we breathe, the bodies that are ours, the very name that we bear, the language that we speak, all of these are given to us by others. There is no self-made man. We all stand in daily need of the God who is as near to us as the nearest thou, because it is through the nearest thou that God bestows life on us daily.

The creation story is also a confession that the world is good. God made it and saw that it was good—except for one thing: There were no women. So God finished making it good by creating a woman: "It is not good that the man should be alone." When we say that God created the world, we are affirming that it is good that he has placed us in a relationship of interdependency on one another as men and women, as human beings who can't get along without each other. Our first assertion, then, is that the world is created, sustained, and judged, and lies in the hands of God.

The second biblical assertion about the world is that the world is the object of God's love and concern. "God so loved the world that he gave his only son . . . not to condemn the world, but that the world might be saved through him." God loved the world, not the church. Jesus came and lived and taught and died in the world. He came into this human world of interdependency and reciprocity, a world characterized by human beings' need for each other. He became involved in this world, dependent on other human beings, subject to rejection, hatred, inattention, frustration. It is *this* world that God reconciled to himself. God was in Christ reconciling the *world* to himself, not the church. This world is the object of God's love and concern; God wants man to love this world, not to reject it. He wants man to have dominion over the world, to take care of it responsibly, to celebrate the astonishing fact that it is here, to thank God for it, to participate joyfully in it.

Let us look again at the story of God's creation of the world and his creation of Adam, "the man." It is hardly necessary to say the Adam was, of course, not the first Cro-Magnon who crawled up to the level of *Homo sapiens.* "Adam" is you and I, those whom God creates and to whom he assigns responsibility. God says to this Adam, in effect: "Have dominion over the world, tend the garden, cultivate it, be responsible in your care and concern for this world, love it, celebrate it."

He also tells Adam to name the animals. It is both fascinating and significant that God did not name the creatures himself. A name denotes meaning and purpose. God does not give names to the objects of our physical universe, to the things that we find around us. It is to man that God has assigned this responsibility. So God brought the giraffe, the pterodactyl, and the microorganism to Adam, for he wanted to see what man would name them. The Bible says that "whatever the man called every living creature, that was its name." God did not have any secret names he was getting ready to give these animals, which he put in the mind of man. He gave man the responsibility. It continues to be our responsibility to give meaning and significance to the things that we find in our universe. Nowadays we find a lot more of them than our forefathers did. We find whole world systems, whole microcosmic and macrocosmic systems that we have to name, and to which we have to give purpose. This naming is a much larger task, perhaps, than our forefathers had, but it is the same task—to love and to give significance and direction to the world in which we are placed. We are to make a joyful noise, to clap our hands, say the Psalmists, because we as men are given this world to love, to nourish, and to cultivate.

Another way to express the same idea is to say that for God the world is a life-and-death matter. He is willing to die for it, and our assignment is to have the same love for the world that he has. "As thou didst send me into the world," said Jesus, "so I have sent them into thy world." As God comes to the world, so does his church go to the world to love it, to be ultimately concerned about it in life-and-death terms. Our second assertion, then, is that the world is God's life-and-death concern, the object of his love and of his renewing activity.

The third assertion is that the world (by this I mean the political and secular world) is the sphere of God's liberating and renewing activity. The world is the theater of God's being with man. The God of the Bible, in rather sharp distinction to the other so-called gods and deities of the ancient Near East, was characterized precisely by the fact that he worked in and through political events. He would not share his deity with the stars, nor the sun, nor the moon. These bodies were merely things that God had created, not divine beings. The God of the Hebrews was the God who revealed himself in the exodus, in the conquest, in the exile, in the defeat of the kingdom. He revealed himself in political events, in the liberation of the people from economic serfdom and political slavery, in the military conquest of the land, in the defeat at the hands of a world power. Thus he used political and military events to get the things done in history that he wanted done. He was perfectly willing to use people who denied him, people who had never heard about him, and even people who defied him, to do his work. The forty-fifth chapter of Isaiah illustrates how the biblical God uses those who deny him. Here God is depicted as speaking to Cyrus, the king of the Persians. Cyrus was certainly not a Christian, not even a Jew, but a pagan conqueror, a worshiper of false gods. So perhaps wherever the world "Cyrus" is used in the passage you might, to make it contemporary, substitute the name Mao Tse-tung or Castro.

> Thus says the Lord to his anointed, to Cyrus,
>   whose right hand I have grasped,
> to subdue nations before him and ungird the loins of kings,
> to open doors before him
>   that gates may not be closed:
> ". . . I am the Lord, and there is no other,
>   besides me there is no God;
>   I gird you, though you do not know me,
> that men may know, from the rising of the sun
>   and from the west, that there is none beside me;
>   I am the Lord, and there is no other. . . ."

God used people who did not know him. He anointed them. The word "anoint" is the same word we use of "ordained." He set them aside and had them do his work. He used them, furthermore, through political events. The God of the Bible was and is a God who is only secondarily interested in nature. He is first and foremost interested in political events. The story of God's creating the heaven and the earth, the hills and the streams, came later in the development of the Hebrew faith than the first assertion that he was the God who "brought us out of Egypt, from the house of bondage." In order to read our Bibles correctly, we ought to read Exodus first and then Genesis, because this is the order in which the Hebrews came to their understandings. This primacy is very important, because when we speak about God's presence in the sacraments we must notice that we are not talking about the presence of God in some kind of natural element—in bread, or wine, or grape juice. We are talking about the way God makes himself present in an *action,* in the *breaking* and *distributing* of the good things of the earth, in making available to all men something to quench their thirst and to satisfy their hunger. This is where God is present, and we are immediately on the wrong track if we start off identifying God primarily with natural phenomena, whether it is sunsets or beautiful lakes.

God is first of all present in political events, in revolutions, upheavals, invasions, defeats. When the Bible speaks of God, it is almost always in political language. It talks about a covenant, which means a "treaty." It talks about judges, kings, and the Messiah—one who brought in a new kingdom, a kind of revolutionary. All these titles, unfortunately, have been falsely spiritualized and religionized over the years of Christian history. But, except very peripherally, there are *no* "religious words" used to describe God in the Old Testament. The word used for the "service of God" in the Old Testament is also used to refer to the service of a soldier or a citizen in the army of the king. Unfortunately this word has been translated as "worship," which has a cultic and spiritual significance for us that it did not have in the Hebrew. The other biblical term referring to worship really relates to a symbolic act of allegiance something like our military salute, by which a subject of the king or a soldier in the army symbolized his allegiance and willingness to obey. Unfortunately this word is also translated as "worship."

Perhaps it is our task as Christians in the twentieth century, at the end of what Bonhoeffer calls the "religious era," to begin now to despiritualize all of these words, to give them back their gritty, earthy, political significance. This, then, is the third assertion: It is the world, the political world and not the church, which is the arena of God's renewing and liberating activity. The church participates in this liberation only insofar as it participates in the world. To turn our back on the world is to turn our back on the place where God is at work.

The fourth assertion is simply a kind of logical conclusion of the first three: The world is the proper location of the Christian life. It is where the Christian is called to be a Christian. It is where his discipline and devotion, his defeats and victories occur. The world is the place of Adam's assignment, the place of Jesus' ministry, the place of the church's mission. The Gospel writers tell us that Jesus spent his time with people called the *Am ha-Aretz*, those beyond the pale of morality and law, including drunkards, winebibbers, and shady characters. He turned his back on the accepted moral and religious leaders of the day and spent his time in what we would call the seamy side of the world. Here were the people with whom and through whom he carried out his ministry. His career was climaxed in a clash with the urban power structures. He was executed on a public dump, and the sign over his gibbet was written in three languages. The crucifixion occurred at a crossroads of the world. This is where it *continues* to occur, where languages and cultures clash, where the urban power structures in their injustices are challenged, where people are willing to turn their backs on the accepted religious and moral standards of the day in order to stand with God in what he is doing for the world.

The world is a place into which Christians have been sent: "Go into all the world." Jesus says in his final prayer, "I do not pray that thou shouldst keep them from the evil one." The evil one is always tempting us to turn our back on the world, to take the "religious" way out, to preserve ourselves, to strive for our own sanctification at the expense of the renewal of the world. When Jesus prays that we not be taken out of the world, he means as Christians we have no special entrée to what is happening in the world. It means that we work alongside non-Christians and live with them, because this is the only way to be present in the world. We have no private entrance.

Let us sum up. God has the whole world; it is in his hands. This world, not the church, is the object of God's life-and-death concern. He works through the world, not just through the church, to accomplish his purposes. Later on we shall say something about the church, about how the church participates in God's activities in the world, but first of all we have to clear the stage of our obsessive talk about the church so that we can begin to talk about the world. . . .

Two dangers have crept into our thinking as Christians and have tended to distort the biblical understanding of the world:

The first, as we have just said, is that there is entirely too much talk about the church—the mission of the church, the nature of the church, the renewal of the church, and so on. This fault is present even in the Student Christian movement, which unfortunately in the last fifteen or twenty years has become progressively more clericalized. In the "good old days" the student movement wasn't so interested in ecclesiastical talk. It is good that we are getting back to some of the "holy worldliness" which characterized those earlier days. The first task of the church is to discern the presence and the activity of God in the world and to follow him there, where he *is*.

God has been doing things in the world in the past fifteen or twenty years, far in advance of the church. Professional baseball, and not the church in your community, took the first step integrating the races. We are very late in this whole business. We must run to catch up to what God is already doing in this world.

Those who were present on August 28, 1963, between the Washington Monument and the Lincoln Memorial for the March on Washington can testify to the quiet but firm determination of a large group of our citizens who will not wait any longer for the church to decide whether it wants to take the lead in integration. Eugene Carson Blake, of the United Presbyterian Church, was right when he said there:

> And it is partially because the churches of America have failed to put their own houses in order that 100 years after the Emancipation Proclamation, 175 years after the adoption of the Constitution, 173 years after the adoption of the Bill of Rights, the United States of America still faces a racial crisis.
>
> We do not, therefore, come to this Lincoln Memorial in any arrogant spirit of moral or spiritual superiority to "set the nation straight" or to judge or to denounce the American people in whole or in part.
>
> Rather we come—late, late we come—in the reconciling and repentant spirit in which Abraham Lincoln of Illinois once replied to a delegation of morally arrogant churchmen. He said, "Never say God is on our side, rather pray that we may be found on God's side."

This is the situation in which we find ourselves as Christians now—racing to catch up and once again be found on God's side—because he is way ahead of us. He is using forces and movements quite apart from the Christian church, as he has always done, to accomplish his purposes in the world.

The other way in which we have distorted the biblical picture of God's world is by an overspiritualization of the meaning of the Christian life. This is the most sinister distortion of the Bible abroad today. The spiritualizers always try to banish God from the earth and to distort the pictures of how he gets his work done in his world. Spiritualization is the characteristic heresy of the twentieth century, especially among American Protestants. The biblical faith has been transformed into a gaseous chimera.

The task of Christians in our generation is to restore the Old Testament earthliness and solidity to the wispy language of Christianity. This is not a new battle; it has been fought all through the years of Christian history, and not always with success. The language of traditional theology fails us at many points. If a Hebrew twenty-five hundred years ago had been asked to tell something about his God, it would never have occurred to him to say "omnipotent," "omnipresent," or other words which we have inherited from our theological tradition. His answer would have been specific and unpolished: "He is the God of Abraham, Isaac, and Jacob. His is the God who brought us up out of the house of bondage." This is a political god, a relational god, and yet also the god and father of our Lord Jesus Christ. He is no discarnate wrath. Our faith is centered on events as tangible as nails, as substantial as thorns, and as human as the cry of pain.

In fact, the Bible simply does not know any spiritual realm, any religious realm separate from the carnal realm. The spirit in the Bible is precisely that which enlivens and directs bodily activity. Very early in the Bible, God tips us off to his method of working in the world. He frees the captive people from economic and political bondage. He does not free these people to some kind of inner forbearance or of spiritual liberty; they *don't* say with Richard Lovelace,

> If I have freedom in my love,
>   And in my soul am free,
> Angels alone, that soar above,
>   Enjoy such liberty.

No, he frees them to a new economic and political existence in the world; they are no longer slaves to Pharaoh. The biblical God recognizes no inner freedom apart from external conditions of freedom. He is not simply concerned with "nice feelings" between races, for example, but with the structural necessities which make racial reconciliation possible—integrated schools, open employment, unrestricted housing. These are the settings in which human beings once again become brothers. The world as God made it is an integrated world, but segregation of any sort is a rickety artifice made by man. Theologians need to engage not so much in demythologizing as in despiritualizing the Bible. The best way to do this is to stand with one foot in the Old Testament and one foot in the political struggles of our world today. From this dual standpoint, one can examine what God is saying to modern man in the New Testament. Any other position, I think, distorts what he is saying.

Of course, we have to add that the world as God makes it, as he gives it to us, and as he places us in it, is not the world as we have taken it from him. We have dislocated and distorted God's world. We created our own cardboard world in which we prefer to live rather than in God's world. God gave man and still gives him dominion over the forces of the world, we decide to give the world dominion over us. Take, for example, money, political power, sex, work, play—all the things that go into this wonderful world that God has given us, the things he has given us to enjoy and to have in reciprocity with each other. We have made them our little tin masters and ourselves their slaves. Rather than utilizing these things as the God-given means of creating community between man and his fellowman, man and woman, labor and management, nation and nation, we have used them to beat down and to misuse those other human beings through whom God would come to us—the God who is as near to us as the nearest thou. We have rejected the world that God makes and that God gives us. We have fabricated our own little world around our family, our nation, our race, or our class. In so doing we deny the very principle of life as God makes it—interdependence—or we try as hard as we can to squeeze God into something called the "religious area" of life.

There is always one section of *Time* magazine each week devoted to religion. I am sure this is the last section that God reads, if in fact he reads *Time* magazine. God is much more interested in the world than he is in religion. Archbishop Temple once said that God is probably not interested in religion at all. Don't for a moment believe that religion is the sure road from man to God or even that it is the road from God to man. The great theological service performed by Karl Barth for our generation was his warning that religion is often the last battleground on which man fights against God and tries to make God something less than the sovereign of all of life.

God has created a world, and we have messed it up. God has given us a world, and we have refused it and made our own—but our own world is a phony, ramshackle one and God's world is the real world. No matter how we try to avoid this real world that God is constantly creating and making anew, it is always breaking in on us, and sometimes God uses a Cyrus to do the breaking-in.

> Thus says the Lord to his anointed, to Cyrus,
>   whose right hand I have grasped . . .
> to open doors before him
>   that gates may not be closed.
> ". . . I will break in pieces the doors of bronze
>   and cut asunder the bars of iron. . . ."

As children we have all seen the famous picture of Jesus standing outside the door and have been told by Sunday School teachers to notice that there was no knob on the outside of this door. The only way God can open it, we were told, is for us to open it from the inside. But, if we had read the forty-fifth chapter of Isaiah, we would recognize that when we don't want to open the door, God sometimes finds a Cyrus and smashes the door down. God is continuing to find Cyruses now to bash down the doors that we do not feel we are quite ready to open. He doesn't always wait for the church to be willing and ready. He finds a Cyrus so that, while we are satisfying ourselves with our flimsy caricature world, God is breaking in upon us with his real world again.

This breaking-in by God is what is happening in our present world revolutions. We must use the plural because there are several revolutions going on simultaneously, and it is sometimes very hard to separate them. There is an anticolonial revolution which has reached a fantastic speed and pace in the last decade. There is a scientific revolution in which man is once again assuming dominion over the earth and exercising the privilege of naming the animals. There is a revolution for racial freedom in which the people in this world who don't have white skin have determined they will no longer play second fiddle to the white minority. There is a peace revolution going on, and we find ourselves with an economy geared to a cold war. God is in all those revolutions.

There is a secular revolution going on, too—a secular revolution in which the dominance of ecclesiastical powers is being challenged, in which a real pluralism is emerging in America and the ancient stranglehold of feudal and aristocratic churches in Europe and in South America is being broken down. God is in this revolution too, although it is harder to see him there. No doubt it is hard for us to concede that God works through secularization, the revolution against the remnants of religious world views. But he does. Jesus of Nazareth was the first person to challenge the unquestionable authority of the religious world view. The clue to all of Jesus' teachings, perhaps, is in his recurring words, "You have heard that it was said to men of old . . . But I say to you. . . ." No inherited religious or moral teaching, regardless of its weight of ancestral authority, can now go unchallenged.

God is breaking the bar on the door of our rickety shack, the creation which we put up in the face of his creation. He is coming in to us. He is renewing and recreating his world, and he wants us to be a part of his reconstructing activity. This is the call of evangelism. This is the invitation to be a Christian, to come from where we are and to be a part of what God is doing in this world. Man is once again being given his dominion over the created order. We are once again discovering our interdependence. Women, colored peoples, colonies, all the persons we have used as objects are asserting now that they too have dignity and personhood. Equally significant is the fact that in our own nation religious escapism is disappearing. William Stringfellow on the first page of his book, *A Private and Public Faith*, says that the religious revival in America is dead and that this is the best thing that could have happened to the gospel of Jesus Christ. Stringfellow is right. Since

God works in the world, and religion is often a way of escaping from the world, the demise of the "religious revival" is in fact a very good thing.

There may be some who will be troubled by these statements. Is this reaction really very new? Who was it about whom the writer of Acts said, "These men who have turned the world upside down have come here also"? They weren't Communists. Who were they? Paul L. Stagg writes about rapid social change in Latin America in this way: "Constructive change is not a threat to order or stability, except to an *unjust* order, but rather a prelude to an authentic order. God's order (the peace of justice) is not on this side of change, but on the other side. The more fixed and inflexible a society becomes the more dehumanized it becomes." Continuing, he quotes from Richard Shaull, who has been working for twenty years with the students of South America as a missionary: "Change is the way the God of justice shatters an unjust order and opens up the way of God's will for justice." Not only is change willed by God, but it is God who brings about change. He is on the move, and if we want to be related to him we must be on the move also.

God's activity in the world today is a call to us to become the kind of Christians whose witness and discipline are relevant to what he is doing in our century. To respond to this call requires discipline. It has been accurately reported that we as free churchmen have lost the sense of discipline. But the discipline we must recover in order to participate in God's reconstruction of the world is different from the discipline our grandfathers had. Arthur Koestler says that what we need today is a mixture of the saint and the revolutionary. What he is calling for is a blend of the humility and passion of the classical saint with the political realism and the "engagement" of the revolutionary.

It is curious, isn't it, that so much of our best biblical and other Christian literature has been written behind bars. Why do you suppose that is? Is it because Christians are called to be God's avant-garde, *already* living in the new era, *already* living in the kingdom of justice, brotherhood, and peace that God is bringing in? This citizenship of the future kingdom as it already becomes present often involves us in conflict with the custodians of the past. The passage from Isaiah which I have quoted was obviously written by a prophet in captivity. Paul's epistle to the Philippians was written in a jail. More recently another saint-revolutionary has written not from a Babylonian or Philippian jail, but from a Birmingham jail and his words say something about the call of Christians to catch up with God in what he is doing in his world. Writes Martin Luther King:

There was a time when the church was very powerful—in the time when the early Christians rejoiced at being deemed worthy to suffer for what they believed. In those days the church was not merely a thermometer that recorded the ideas and principles of popular opinion; it was a thermostat that transformed the mores of society. Whenever the early Christians entered a town the power structure immediately sought to convict them for being "disturbers of the peace" and "outside agitators." But the Christians pressed on, in the conviction that they were "a colony of heaven" called to obey God rather than man. . . . But the judgment of God is upon the church as never before.

In Fellini's film, *La Strada*, the clown tells the girl Gelsomina to stay with the unlovable Zampano. "If you don't love him and stay with him," he asks, "who else will?" This is a parable of our calling in God's revolutionary world. We are called to love this world and "stay with it," to take upon our shoulders the responsibility for its reconstruction and renewal. This is the assignment that God has given us, and he will give us the strength to fulfill it.

5

The Feast of Fools (1969)

The following selections are taken from Feast of Fools: A Theological Essay on Festivity and Fantasy *(New York: Harper & Row, 1969), 3-6, 7-10, 16-18, 82-84, 86-97, 161-62.*

OVERTURE

During the medieval era there flourished in parts of Europe a holiday known as the Feast of Fools. On that colorful occasion, usually celebrated about January first, even ordinarily pious priests and serious townsfolk donned bawdy masks, sang outrageous ditties, and generally kept the whole world awake with revelry and satire. Minor clerics painted their faces, strutted about in the robes of their superiors, and mocked the stately rituals of church and court. Sometimes a Lord of Misrule, a Mock King, or a Boy Bishop was elected to preside over the events. In some places the Boy Bishop even celebrated a parody mass. During the Feast of Fools, no custom or convention was immune to ridicule and even the highest personages of the realm could expect to be lampooned.

The Feast of Fools was never popular with the higher-ups. It was constantly condemned and criticized. But despite the efforts of fidgety ecclesiastics and an outright condemnation by the Council of Basel in 1431, the Feast of Fools survived until the sixteenth century. Then in the age of Reformation and Counter-Reformation it gradually died out. Its faint shade still persists in the pranks and revelry of Halloween and New Year's Eve.

Chroniclers of Western history seldom lament the passing of the Feast of Fools. There are reasons why they do not. Often it did degenerate into debauchery and lewd buffoonery. Still, its death was a loss. The Feast of Fools had demonstrated that a culture could periodically make sport of its most sacred royal and religious practices. It could imagine, at least once in a while, a wholly different kind of world—one where the last was first, accepted values were inverted, fools became kings, and choirboys were prelates. The demise of the Feast of Fools signaled a significant change in the Western cultural mood: an enfeeblement of our civilization's capacity for festivity and fantasy. Its demise showed that people were beginning to see their social roles and sacred conventions through eyes that could not permit such strident satire, that they no longer had the time or the heart for such trenchant social parody.

Why did the Feast of Fools disappear? The question is part of a much larger one that scholars have debated for years. Are the religious patterns of postmedieval Europe the cause or the effect of the new social and economic practices that culminated in capitalism and the industrial revolution? Why did the virtues of sobriety, thrift, industry, and ambition gain such prominence at the expense of other values? Why did mirth, play, and festivity come in for such scathing criticism during the Protestant era?

I do not wish to join in that debate here. This is not a historical treatise and I recall the Feast of Fools only as a symbol of the subject of this book. It is important to notice however that festivity and fantasy do play a less central role among us now than they did in the days of holy fools, mystical visionaries, and a calendar full of festivals. And we are the poorer for it.

There are those who would claim that we still have festivity and fantasy, but that they take a different form. We celebrate at office parties, football games, and cocktail gatherings. Our fantasies glitter in the celluloid world of the cinema and on the pages of *Playboy*. Science fiction still conjures up fanciful worlds. Perhaps. But my contention in this book is that whatever forms of festivity and fantasy remain to us are shrunken and insulated. Our celebrations do not relate us, as they once did, to the parade of cosmic history or to the great stories of man's spiritual quest. Our fantasies tend to be cautious, eccentric, and secretive. When they do occasionally soar, they are appreciated only by an elite. Our feasting is sporadic or obsessive, our fantasies predictable and politically impotent. Neither provides the inspiration for genuine social transformation.

At least all of this has been true until quite recently. Now, however, we are witnessing a rebirth of the spirit of festivity and fantasy. Though we have no annual Feast of Fools, the life affirmation and playful irreverence once incarnated in that day are bubbling up again in our time. As expected, the bishops and the bosses are not happy about it, but it is happening anyway. This incipient renaissance of fantasy and festivity is a good sign. It shows that our period may be rediscovering the value of two components of culture both of which were once seen in the Feast of Fools. The first is the feast or festival itself: important because it puts work in its place. It suggests that work, however rewarding, is not the highest end of life but must contribute to personal human fulfillment. We need stated times for nonwork to remind us that not even an astronomical gross national product and total employment can bring a people salvation. On feast days we stop working and enjoy those traditional gestures and moments of human conviviality without which life would not be human. Festivity, like play, contemplation, and making love, is an end in itself. It is not instrumental.

The other important cultural component of the Feast of Fools is fantasy and social criticism. Unmasking the pretense of the powerful always makes their power seem less irresistible. That is why tyrants tremble before fools and dictators ban political cabarets. Though a stated occasion for political persiflage can be exploited by the powerful to trivialize criticism, it need not be. From the oppressor's point of view satire can always get out of hand or give people ideas, so it is better not to have it at all.

The Feast of Fools thus had an implicitly radical dimension. It exposed the arbitrary quality of social rank and enabled people to see that things need not always be as they are. Maybe that is why it made the power-wielders uncomfortable and eventually had to go. The divine right of kings, papal infallibility, and the modern totalitarian state all flowered after the Feast of Fools disappeared.

Today in the late twentieth century we need the spirit represented by the Feast of Fools. In a success- and money-oriented society, we need a rebirth of patently unproductive festivity and expressive celebration. In an age that has quarantined parody and separated politics from imagination we need more social fantasy. We need for our time and in our own cultural idiom a rediscovery of what was right and good about the Feast of Fools. We need a renaissance of the spirit, and there are signs that it is coming.

* * *

INTRODUCTION

I know nothing, except what everyone knows—
if there when Grace dances, I should dance.
                    —W. H. Auden, "Whitsunday in Kirchstetten"

Mankind has paid a frightful price for the present opulence of Western industrial society. Part of the price is exacted daily from the poor nations of the world whose fields and forests garnish our tables while we push their people further into poverty. Part is paid by the plundered poor who dwell within the gates of the rich nations without sharing in the plenty. But part of the price has been paid by affluent Western man himself. While gaining the whole world he has been losing his own soul. He has purchased prosperity at the cost of a staggering impoverishment of the vital elements of his life. These elements are *festivity*–the capacity for genuine revelry and joyous celebration, and *fantasy*–the faculty for envisioning radically alternative life situations.

Festivity and fantasy are not only worthwhile in themselves, they are absolutely vital to human life. They enable man to relate himself to the past and the future in ways that seem impossible for animals. The *festival*, the special time when ordinary chores are set aside while man celebrates some event, affirms the sheer goodness of what is, or observes the memory of a god or hero, is a distinctly human activity. It arises from man's peculiar power to incorporate into his own life the joys of other people and the experience of previous generations. Porpoises and chimpanzees may play. Only man celebrates. Festivity is a human form of play through which man appropriates an extended area of life, including the past, into his own experience.

Fantasy is also uniquely human. A hungry lion may dream about a zebra dinner but only man can mentally invent wholly new ways of living his life as an individual and as a species. If festivity enables man to enlarge his experience by reliving events of the past, fantasy is a form of play that extends the frontiers of the future.

Festivity, of course, does not focus solely on the past any more than fantasy reaches only toward the future. We also sometimes celebrate *coming* events, and our minds often recreate bygone experiences. But despite this obvious overlap, festivity is more closely related to memory, and fantasy is more akin to hope. Together they help make man a creature who sees himself with an origin and a destiny, not just as an ephemeral bubble.

Both our enjoyment of festivity and our capacity for fantasy have deteriorated in modern times. We still celebrate but our feasts and parties often lack real verve or feeling. Take for example a typical American New Year's Eve. It is a celebration, but there is something undeniably vacuous and frenetic about it. People seem anxiously, even obsessively determined to have a good time. Not to have a date for New Year's Eve is the ultimate adolescent tragedy. Even adults usually hate to spend the evening alone. On New Year's Eve we bring out the champagne and hurl paper streamers. But under the surface of Dionysiac carousing we feel something is missing. The next day we often wonder why we bothered.

Our mixed feelings about New Year's Eve reveal two things about us. First, we are still essentially festive and ritual creatures. Second, our contemporary feasts and rites are in a dismal state. The reason New Year's Eve is important is that it so vividly energizes both memory and hope. As hoping and remembering creatures, we rightly sense something of unusual symbolic significance about that peculiar magical time when the old year disappears forever and the new one begins. We personify the occasion with a bearded old man and a pink baby. We take a cup of kindness for the past (for "old acquaintance"), we kiss, we toast the future. The New Year's Eve party demonstrates the vestigial survival of forgotten feasts and rituals.

But the vaguely desperate air lurking behind the noisemakers and funny hats is also significant. We dimly sense on New Year's Eve and sometimes on other occasions a whole world of empyrean ecstasy and fantastic hope, a world with which we seem to have lost touch. Our sentimentality and wistfulness arise from the fact that we have so few festivals left, and the ones we have are so stunted in their ritual and celebrative power.

Still, we are not wholly lost, and the fact that we still do ring out the old and ring in the new reminds us that celebration, however weakened, is not yet dead.

While festivity languishes, our fantasy life has also become anemic. Once effulgent, it now ekes out a sparse and timid existence. Our night dreams are quickly forgotten. Our daydreams are stealthy, clandestine, and unshared. Unable to conjure up fantasy images on our own, we have given over the field to mass production. Walt Disney and his imitators have populated it with virtuous mice and friendly skunks. Low-grade cinema and formula-TV producers have added banal symbols and predictable situations. But the enfeeblement of fantasy cannot be blamed on the mass media. It is the symptom of a much larger cultural debility. Indeed, the sportive inventiveness of today's best filmmakers proves both that it is not the technology which is at fault and that human fantasy still survives in a dreary, fact-ridden world.

What are the reasons for the long, slow decay of festivity and fantasy in the West? The sources of our sickness are complex. During the epoch of industrialization we grew more sober and industrious, less playful and imaginative. Work schedules squeezed festivity to a minimum. The habits formed are still so much with us that we use our new technologically provided leisure either to "moonlight," or to plan sober consultations on the "problem of leisure," or to wonder why we are not enjoying our "free time" the way we should.

The age of science and technology has also been hard on fantasy. We have J. R. R. Tolkien's hobbits and the visions of science fiction. But our fact-obsessed era has taught us to be cautious: always check impulsive visions against the hard data. Secularism erodes the religious metaphors within which fantasy can roam. Scientific method directs our attention away from the realm of fantasy and toward the manageable and the feasible. True, we are now discovering that science without hunches or visions gets nowhere, but we still live in a culture where fantasy is tolerated, not encouraged. Part of the blame belongs to secularism. There was a time when visionaries were canonized, and mystics were admired. Now they are studied, smiled at, perhaps even committed. All in all, fantasy is viewed with distrust in our time.

But why should we care if festivity and fantasy now play a smaller role in human life? Why not simply turn the world over to sobriety and rational calculation? Is anything significant lost? . . .

It is important to emphasize that among other things man in his very essence is *homo festivus* and *homo fantasia*. Celebrating and imagining are integral parts of his humanity. But Western industrial man in the past few centuries has begun to lose his capacity for festivity and fantasy, and this loss is calamitous for three reasons: (1) it deforms man by depriving him of an essential ingredient in human existence, (2) it endangers his very survival as a species by rendering him provincial and less adaptive, and (3) it robs him of a crucial means of sensing his important place in fulfilling the destiny of the cosmos. The loss is personal, social, and religious.

The picture, however, is not quite as bleak as I have painted it so far. Despite the long-term erosion, it is also true that in very recent years, industrial man has begun to rediscover the festive and the fanciful dimensions of life. A centuries-long process may be reversing itself. Our recent increased exposure both to non-Western cultures and to those sectors of our own civilization that have escaped complete integration into the industrialization process have made us aware that we are missing something. Technologically produced leisure has forced us to ask ourselves some hard questions about our traditional worship of work. Young people in industrial societies everywhere are demonstrating that expressive play and artistic creation belong in the center of life, not at its far periphery. A theatre of the body replete with mime, dance, and acrobatics is upstaging our inherited theatre of the mind. Street festivals, once disappearing as fast as the whooping crane, are

coming back. Psychiatrists and educators are beginning to reject their
traditional roles as the punishers of fantasy. Some are even searching
for ways to encourage it. The awakened interest of white people in the
black experience has enhanced our appreciation for a more festive and
feeling-oriented approach to life. We call it "soul." Films, novels, and
plays explore the world of dreams and even some philosophers are
rediscovering the significance of fantasy. Even in the churches, dance,
color, movement, and new kinds of music dramatize the recovery of
celebration. In short we may be witnessing the overture to a sweeping
cultural renaissance, a revolution of human sensibilities in which the
faculties we have starved and repressed during the centuries of industrialization will be nourished and appreciated again.

But it could turn out differently. What we take as the evidence of
a cultural rebirth in our midst may be a deceptive flush on the cheek
of a dying age. Or, an equally grim prospect, the hesitant beginnings
of a festive resurrection in our time could be smashed or spoiled. Still
worse, the present rebirth of spontaneous celebration and unfettered
imagining could veer off into destructive excess or vacuous frivolity.

Which of these things will happen? We do not know. In fact the fate
of our embryonic cultural revolution is still open and undecided. What
will happen to it is largely up to us. I do not labor under the delusion
that theology can either spark or stave off a cultural revolution in our
time. It may play a role in the eventual outcome but its role will probably be a minor one. Nevertheless, theology has a deep stake in the
outcome of our crisis not just because it is committed to man but also
because the crisis is in part a religious one. If twentieth-century man
finally succumbs and does lose the last remnants of his faculties for
festivity and fantasy, the result will be disastrous. The heart of the religious view of man and the cosmos, especially in its Christian version,
will be torn out. Correspondingly, if the battle for man's humanity is
to be won at all, a religious vision will have to play an important role
in that victory.

Ironically, the contemporary religious views of man, whether that
of Teilhard de Chardin, of Martin Buber, or of Jürgen Moltmann, now
face a criticism that is nearly the opposite of the one theologians faced
two centuries ago. At that time the typical enlightened critique alleged
that Christianity belittled man, called him a "despicable worm" or a
"worthless sinner," when it was clear, at least to the critics, that man
was really a noble and elevated being. A certain type of humanism
emerged in conscious opposition to Christianity. Today the shoe is
often on the other foot. Secular critics of Christianity find religion

unreasonably affirmative in its estimate of man's place. Against what seems to be Christianity's groundlessly grandiose view of human destiny, the secularist frequently reminds us that we are, after all, only a transient eczema on a small planet in a third-rate galaxy. Its critics now often deride Christianity not for making man paranoid but for giving him what seem to be illusions of grandeur.

The fact that the continuing debate between religious and nonreligious intellectuals has recently taken this turn is a significant one. It means that the stature and significance of man rather than the existence of the deity is now the main focus of discussion. It also suggests that religion's stake in the rebirth of festivity and fantasy is even deeper than we had at first supposed. Festival occasions enlarge enormously the scope and intensity of man's relation to the past. They elevate his sense of personal worth by making him a part of an epic. Fantasy offers an endless range of future permutations. It inevitably escalates man's sense of his powers and possibilities. Therefore, the cultivation of celebration and imagination is crucial to religion and to man himself, if the biblical estimate of his status ("a little lower than the angels") has any validity. Perhaps this is why observance and revelry, ritual and myth have nearly always been central to religion, and why they seem to be making a comeback today.

* * *

FANTASY AND UTOPIA

Utopia has long been a name for the unreal and the impossible. We have set utopia over against the world. As a matter of fact, it is our utopias that make the world tolerable to us: the cities and mansions that people dream of are those in which they finally live.
        —Lewis Mumford, The Story of Utopias

The rebirth of fantasy as well as of festivity is essential to the survival of our civilization, including its political institutions. But fantasy can never be fully yoked to a particular political program. To subject the creative spirit to the fetters of ideology kills it. When art, religion, and imagination become ideological tools they shrivel into caged birds and toothless tigers. However, this does not mean that fantasy has no political significance. Its significance is enormous. This is just why ideologues always try to keep it in harness. When fantasy is neither tamed by ideological leashes nor rendered irrelevant by idiosyncrasy, it can inspire new civilizations and bring empires to their knees.

How? It does so through that particular form of fantasy we might call "utopian thought," social vision, or perhaps simply "political fantasy." Political fantasy goes beyond the mere political imagination. It is not content to dream up interesting twists within existing societal patterns. It envisions new forms of social existence and it operates without first asking whether they are "possible." Utopian thinking is to the *polis,* the corporate human community, what fantasy is to the individual person. It provides the images by which existing societies can be cracked open and recreated. It prevents societies, like thought systems, from becoming "closed and ossified." It can be dangerous if it tempts people away from dealing with the real issues. There are societies that have gone mad in this sense. But a society without the capacity for social fantasy faces equally serious dangers. It will die of sclerosis instead of schizophrenia, a much less interesting way to go.

Like individual fantasy, which needs an open "language" and a vehicle for embodiment if it is not to be lost, political fantasy also requires a symbolism that will stimulate it without constricting it, and a social means both for nourishing it and for feeding its potency back into the polis. Without such a symbolic and structural nexus, political fantasy, like the erratic private visions of individuals, will become incoherent even to its own visionaries, and will soon evaporate into the ozone.

On the other hand political fantasy must never be trapped into those definitions of the possible, the feasible, or the practical that inform any given polis. Like "reality," the term "possibility" is not a very precise one. History has a way of surprising us by confounding our most assured convictions about what is possible. We should not even be too sure about death and taxes. The charge that some idea lacks "realism" can become a spear in the arsenal of reactionaries, hurled testily at anyone whose vision might upset existing privilege and power. Therefore, the powers that be must never hold the mortgage of the house of political fantasy. Its social location must be "in but not of" the existing order. And this is not easy to manage.

In the past a certain type of political fantasy often flourished as what we now call "utopian thought." We find it in the books of Sir Thomas More, Edward Bellamy, Tommaso Campanella, and many others. These venturesome social fantasizers never merely tinkered with rearranging the furniture. They struck out toward a whole new social structure, which they sometimes described in considerable detail. Though some of the contents of their utopias may now strike us as a bit bizarre, their main contribution was to show that man could think out wholesome new social forms. Their influence on the polis has been considerable.

But something has happened to this traditional utopian thinking. It has been declining for two hundred years and by now our society has almost completely lost the capacity for utopian thought. Our images of the future tend to be drawn as extensions of the present. Our social imagination has atrophied. Unlike previous generations whose visions of the society exceeded their means of accomplishing them, we suffer from a surplus of means and a shortage of visions. In this sense we have lost the capacity for fantasy and cannot escape the present. The multihued maps of urban planners rarely include any ideas that are not quantitative extensions of existing cities. Planning institutes project futures that seem woefully similar to the present in most of their characteristics. Even in that bedlam of future speculation, science fiction, the asteroid ages depicted often seem to be marked mainly by vastly expanded and refined technologies. Space travel, telecommunication, robotry, and weapons systems have all been "improved," but rarely does anything significantly new in political terms enter the picture. The most widely read portraits of the future in recent years, *1984* and *Brave New World,* are not utopias at all but "dystopias," warnings to us of how awful things will be if we continue on our present course.

The problem is a serious one. When we run out of images of the future polis that are radically at variance with what we now have, we limit the possible range of changes. We initiate a self-fulfilling prophecy and end up with more of the same. This process soon ends in social and cultural stagnation. It produces the inert society. . . .

* * *

In the past the spinning of visions was one of the functions performed by seers, prophets, and holy men. Of course, religion also thwarted visions as Joan of Arc and many others discovered. The same is true today. Religion often simply legitimates existing institutions, personal styles, and patterns of power distribution. This is religion as the "opiate of the masses." But as Marx rightly saw, religion is not only an *expression* of injustice and suffering; it is also a form of *protest* against it. Often this protest expresses itself in the vision of a new epoch. The political fantasy of a "messianic era," a new age in which the relations of men with each other and with nature are fundamentally transformed, arose quite early in the history of Israel. There are parallels though not equivalents in other religious traditions.

In Christianity this vision of the Kingdom of God or the New Jerusalem has had a rich and stormy career. Sometimes it has acted as a catalyst stimulating the culture to transcend itself and its current values. At other times it has braked and deterred change. It is useful to examine the conditions under which religion operates in these different ways.

The power of the vision of a new world to spark change and innovation is undercut in at least three ways. One is to *postpone* the vision to an epoch beyond time and history. We merely wait for it, and patience becomes a primary virtue. Another way to destroy the catalytic power of a social vision is to *reduce* it to more "realistic" or "feasible" dimensions. We settle for less than we envision because anything more would be utopian. The tension is relaxed. A third is to *spiritualize* or *individualize* the radical hope so much that it becomes trivial, or at least socially inconsequential. The immortality of *my* soul takes the place of a new heaven and a new earth.

All three approaches undermine the political impact of religiously inspired social fantasy. If the new epoch is found only in heaven, in a concordat of compromise, or within my own inner spirit, then social transcendence, at least as inspired by religion, is lost.

How does religion contribute to a society's capacity for self-transcendence? It does so by symbolizing an ideal toward which to strive, and by doing so with enough emotional magnetism to provide a powerful source of motivation. This requires, however, an element of enactment and demonstration—the missing element in most of the classical utopian writers.

There is, however, another utopian tradition in addition to that of More and Campanella. It is the tradition of those who *tried out* new forms of community life and personal human style instead of just writing about them. These are the people who founded Brook Farm and the Oneida Community, people who actually constructed, on a small scale, schools, factories, communities, cities, and regions as a concrete expression of their inspired hopes. They *embodied* political fantasy. And the models they created, though some were bizarre and many were short-lived, often had a powerful influence on the larger body politic.

Today, again, we are beginning to see an outbreak of experiments in new types of human community. Communes and co-ops are appearing all over the country. This new quest is the present form of man's perennial search for the transcendent, the new era, the blessed community. So those who today are patiently groping for new forms of human community, in school, slum, home, and among nations, stand in a long tradition. I do not mean here the tradition of the refugee colonies and immigrant bands who from earliest history have left the larger tribe behind and for one reason or another have split off on their own. There are groups like these. But the ones I mean belong to the ancient company of those who though they are deeply discontented with the state of the society and withdraw at least in part from "the world" to fashion a new communal fabric, never abdicate their responsibility for the whole. They are searching for models that others may learn from.

One important historical example of the conscious reformation of communal life is the Christian monastic movement. It was and is a complex affair and we can make few generalizations about it. However, in a period such as ours, turning again to intentional communities and conscious experimentation with alternative institutional patterns, we might do well to lay aside some of our prejudices about monasticism and look again at its history as a possible source of images for us today.

Let us first dismiss that extremely provincial criticism of monastic life which once sprang from our post-Victorian preoccupation with sexual expression. Because most monks have been celibate we used to dismiss their life styles as unnatural and unattractive. However, only a society trapped in the backlash against nineteenth-century sexual hypocrisy could reduce its judgment of monasticism to these proportions. Already a younger generation of "post-post-Victorians" is appearing for whom sex is not such an issue. The artist Van Gogh perhaps put it best when he said that the sex life of an artist must either be that of a monk or that of a soldier. Anything in between distracts him from his vision. The fact that the monks chose the former should not distract us from their vision.

Monasticism was actually an immense and multifarious series of experiments in alternative community life styles. The monks prayed and meditated (directed fantasy), sang, read, composed music, copied and illuminated manuscripts, studied every classical language and discipline, developed new agricultural techniques, provided solace and hospitality, worked, ate, and drank together in thousands of different communal patterns. Nor were they wholly "withdrawn" from the everyday world. They interacted with it at a hundred different levels. They served, taught, nursed, prayed for, and contributed to the life of the commonweal. The different monastic orders embodied numberless fantasies of how human beings could live together in love and mutuality.

The monks understood their relation to the rest of Christendom within a theological worldview that seems implausible to us today, at least on the surface. They were praying for the people who had less time to pray because they fought, ruled, or toiled in the fields. The monks lived out a longing for spiritual perfection that was hardly possible for all men. Their communities, in other words, were contribut-

ing in their own distinctive way to the future everyone in Christendom
expected or at least hoped for, a blissful reward in heaven after death.

Though this theology eludes us today, the monks were really more
accurate than we often think. They were in fact contributing to the
future of the whole civilization, though not quite in the way they understood. The seeds of the Renaissance and the Reformation were culti-
vated in the monasteries. Luther and Mendel were both monks. The
Benedictines practiced participatory democracy centuries before it
became a political issue. The idea of a disciplined work schedule and of
work as service to God began with the monks, and without it the whole
Industrial Revolution could never have occurred. Max Weber was right
when he said that during the Reformation "every man became a monk
and the whole world a monastery." Life styles, discipline, and communal patterns that had been born, nourished, and refined in small communities now supplied the pattern for a whole civilization.

Many monasteries were closed during the Reformation. But the tradition of model human communities acting out their visions of human
life did not die. Utopian communities began to spring up and the practice continues down to our day. During the sixteenth century whole
cities such as Geneva and Münster became the sites of model communities. Often property was shared, as the monks had done it, and in
some places so were wives and children. In general, the more visionary
of these experiments, now grouped by scholars under the term "radical Reformation," were uprooted and destroyed by Lutheran, Catholic,
and Calvinist authorities. The ideas lived on, however, and American
history is studded with examples of communitarian utopias, from
Oneida to California's new rural communes.

Today we are witnessing a rebirth of the monastic, utopian tradition. It is good that we are. A society needs seedplots and models. It
needs a variety of experimental tryouts of new institutions, life patterns, values, symbols, and rituals. Not all of these will survive and only
a few will ever see their visions incorporated by the larger *polis*. The
medieval period saw the birth of hundreds of monastic movements
that split, expired, or disappeared, but others survived to enrich the
entire epoch.

The new monasticism we need will, of course, differ from the old
in a number of ways. It can hardly be built around vows of celibacy,
although it must be said that these vows did serve a real purpose once.
So many later utopian communities have foundered on sex we are
forced to concede that the ability of some monasteries to survive for
centuries may have had something to do with the "monk's solution" to

this perennial problem. The Oneida group tried out a form of group marriage. Present utopian communities are evolving still newer ways of dealing with sex, children, and family structure. It is good that they are. We cannot merely assume that the present urban nuclear family will continue forever.

Also, model communities must find some way to grasp and symbolize their relation to the whole that avoids both the arrogant abdication of "humaner than thou" withdrawal as well as the servility of the research team that strays only as far as the corporation allows it. Here, the monastic model, in which the oneness of Christendom still operated as a unifying theme, is more helpful than the extreme Protestant sectarian idea in which sometimes each schismatic group claimed that it alone was *vera ecclesia christi*. We need a theology of political fantasy that will undergird conflict, unflinching criticism, radically variant values, and very disparate corporate patterns since eventually all these will be salutary for the whole. This perspective must be shared in some measure by the highly variegated experimental communities themselves and by the "straight" civilization of which they are still a part.

Finally, in our time, it will be necessary for utopian experimentation to innovate in only one aspect of a society's whole life. Some people, of course, may still be able to enter fully into total subsocieties where education, worship, work, and play are all included. Most, however, will live part of their lives in the "straight" world of facts and feasibility, and will be involved in the continuous embodiment of political fantasy in only one or two aspects of life—in their leisure, residence, politics, schooling, worship, or work. This requirement stems from the multiplex structure of our urban society. We are sorted out into such a variety of functional relations—at school, club, office, home—that we are able to experiment, perhaps even quite radically, with one without needing to wait until the others are ready to come along. This enables visionaries to project and act out their fantasies in one sector without feeling they must transform everything at once. A person can participate in a wholly new kind of educational, familial, or housing concept without breaking his relation to the electric company or even the city government.

Johannes Metz, a Roman Catholic theologian, has rightly insisted that there is a valid place for ascetic discipline and monasticism today, even for a "flight from the world." However, this flight must be, he says, a "Flucht nach vorn," a conscious movement *ahead,* into the future. It must grow out of an ascetical refusal to be bound by today's societal standards, a bold attempt to shape the future of human community by stepping toward that future before it engulfs us.

Rabelais, in his *Gargantua and Pantagruel,* draws a fetching portrait of the fictional Abbey of Theleme where under the escutcheon "Do As You Please," people gathered away from the diversions of the world to pursue enjoyment in single-minded devotion. Historians of the utopian movement believe the idea of the Abbey of Theleme was an enormously important one for the model communities men hatched later. The exotic fantasy of Rabelais had succeeded by using a traditional form, the abbey, to convey a different content. Again structure facilitated both fantasy and its feedback.

The Abbey of Theleme can hardly serve as our model now. Nor can Münster or Brook Farm. But here and there all over the world today venturesome people are beginning to experiment with brazen new forms of human interaction. The search for "transcendence" is not dead today. It takes the form of the quest for livelier, more just, more satisfying, and gentler forms of human community. It continues that seeking after the ever future Kingdom that Jesus commended. What these various experiments need is not a common ideology, but a way to understand each other, a stimulus to keep going and a circuiting through which the energy they generate can vitalize the rest of us.

In the medieval period the genius of a universal church managed to include both model communities and the larger society in one catholic family. After the Reformation, though the institutional unity was broken, schismatic sectarians and orthodox churchmen at least shared the common symbols of Christianity. Even people intent on burning each other were tuned in on the same symbolic signal.

Today, however, we have no common wave length to keep us in touch. Nor do we have an institution that somehow makes St. Francis understandable to the Emperor, and allows peasants, priests, monks, and knights all to see some sense in the calling of the other. Today our conscious community experimenters are out of touch, symbolically and institutionally, not only with the *polis* but with each other.

We cannot return to the medieval wave length, nor should we desire to. That period paid a high price for its unity and its capacity for communication. The vitalities of history finally cracked it open. What we can ask, however, is whether we today can have a structure that will both energize and legitimate social fantasy, and which will permit a playback of fantasy without imposing preconceived limits on what is to be dreamed.

* * *

We live at a time when all our inherited institutions from the family and the university to the nation state and the system of international trade are under question. There is not a single institution that we take for granted. Not only that, but the authority structures of all institutions are caving in. Vertical bureaucracies are collapsing. Inherited privilege cuts very little ice. Increasingly people exert authority only because they can make a contribution to some shared purpose.

But just because our inherited institutions are cracking and splintering does not mean we have new ones ready to take their places. Maybe we should not. Maybe the patterns that emerge from the disintegration of existing institutions will differ so markedly from our present ones that we should not even call them "institutions." That question remains open.

Whatever happens, however, people will continue to dream up new and different ways of living together. They will have to. The pace of change always reveals the inadequacy of existing ways, and that pace is accelerating. People will not only dream up new patterns and be criticized for doing so. They will try them out on a small scale, refine them, discard some, keep others. If their activity ever ceases human society will rumble to a stop, rust, and disintegrate. Just as individuals need a fantasy life to keep alive, societies need fantasy to survive. Political fantasy, the fantasy of the *polis,* is not a luxury but a necessity.

But political fantasy cannot proceed in a vacuum. It requires a "field," a symbolic and structural context. It needs a special form of flexible institution in order to live and to interact creatively with the political world. This must be an institution that has the form of an ordinary institution, but that differs because it exists not for itself but to link the two worlds of fact and fantasy. Let us call it a "meta-institution." This "meta-institution" must have a number of characteristics. In order to animate fantasy it must cultivate the symbols that opened men to new levels of awareness in the past. It must be in effective touch with the most advanced artistic movement of the day and with historical and transhistorical images of the future. It must teach men to celebrate and fantasize. But above all it must provide a fertile field where new symbols can appear. Since man is body and heart as well as brain, it must include affective and ritual components. Finally, it must be a part of the culture in which it lives but sufficiently free so that its fantasies are not pinioned and hamstrung by present expectations.

To move to traditional theological language for a moment, this meta-institution must be one in which the lives of the prophets and saints of old are commemorated, in which the hope for the New Humanity is celebrated and in which "new truths" are "ever breaking forth from God's holy word." It must be a polis within the polis, living within the political community but neither identical with it nor slavishly loyal to it. It must be a pilgrim band that has no earthly home, but seeks "another city," whose king is not Caesar.

This, of course, is language traditionally used about the church. Can this needed meta-institution be the church? The very idea sounds preposterous, and is. But the fact that we so quickly reject the notion is a dismal commentary on how far the institutional church has strayed from its historical calling. The church more often than not uses the memories of the saints not to encourage us in creativity but to bludgeon us into conformity. It has emptied the gestures of celebration until they have become barren and joyless. It has discouraged radical fantasy as a possible threat to its hard-won place in Caesar's society. It cannot take the risk of putting its ultimate loyalty in the "world to come" (the tomorrow of embodied fantasy), because it has too deep a stake in the world of yesterday and today.

The sad truth is that the church *cannot* be the meta-institution our world needs to instruct us in festivity, to open us to fantasy, to call us to tomorrow, or to enlarge our petty definitions of reality. It cannot for only one reason: the church is not the church. That is, what we now call "churches" have departed so markedly from their vocation as agents and advocates of Christian faith that only a residue of that historic calling remains. Dim echoes of it are still heard in its preaching and pale shadows of it appear in its liturgy. But the substance has been thinned and the spirit dulled.

The breach between what the churches were meant to be and what they have become is almost as wide as the chasm between what they now are and the saving remnant our world needs. For this reason that familiar question, "Can our present churches be renewed so that they can assume their real task?" is not the basic one.

The question we should be asking should run like this: Given the fact that our polis, the human community, needs a company of dreamers, seers, servants, and jesters in its midst, where shall this company come from? Given the fact that biblical imagery—Jesus, Job, Jeremiah—has produced prophets and revolutionaries in the past, how can we keep telling these stories? Given the fact that in festive ritual man's fantasy life is both fed and kept in touch with the earth, how can we eat the bread and toast the hope in ways that ring true? How can we keep restating the vision of the New Age so that the poor and the persecuted continue to push and the princes and potentates never feel secure?

When we ask these questions we are no closer to satisfying answers, perhaps. But at least we have stopped restricting our vision. Worrying about what might be possible in the existing churches is fruitless. By changing the question we have moved from mere ecclesiastical imagination to the level of true fantasy. We have left behind the tired and useless task of "renewing the church" and are now concerned with the recreation of the world.

Then, surprisingly perhaps, when we are no longer fixated on their "renewal," we may begin to notice aspects of the churches that can contribute to that coming meta-institution of festivity and fantasy we need and want. We can detect life beneath the crust and embers in the ashes. Here and there a small flame may even break through. Nevertheless, the new church we look for need not come entirely from the churches of today. It certainly will not. It will come, if it comes at all, as a new congeries of elements, some from the churches, some from outside, some from those fertile interstices between. And it will assume a shape we can hardly predict, though we can sometimes see its outlines—in fantasy.

* * *

CODA

The Feast of Fools flourished during a period when people had a well-developed capacity for festivity and fantasy. We need to develop that capacity again today. We cannot and should not try to resuscitate the jesters and gargoyles of the Middle Ages. But neither need we exclude medieval man entirely from our consciousness. We can benefit from the experience of that time to enrich and vitalize our own, just as we can learn from other historical epochs and other civilizations.

What the medieval period had was a kind of festivity which related men to history and bound them to each other in a single community. Neither national holidays nor periodic but empty "long weekends" had yet appeared to divide and trivialize human celebration. Today we need a rebirth of festivity that will make us part of a larger history than they knew and will link us to an immensely expanded world community. Our survival as a species may depend in part on whether such authentically worldwide festivals, with their symbols of a single global community, emerge among us.

The Middle Ages also displayed a capacity for fantasy that, although it became more constricted during the industrial centuries, may now be staging a comeback. Medieval man, for all his limitations, placed a higher value on imagination than we do. He could make believe more easily. His saints and holy people did things we would not permit. Would St. Francis and St. Theresa escape incarceration, at least for purposes of observation, in the modern world? We need fantasy today. Can we make a more secure place for it in our cognitively overdeveloped schools? Can we mold a universal symbolism within which we can both fantasize and still communicate? Can we become less doctrinaire about what constitutes "mental health" and encourage a much more generous range of life styles? A rebirth of fantasy need not result in the death of rational thought. Both belong in any healthy culture.

Will we make it? Will we move into this world of revitalized celebration and creative imagination? Or will we destroy ourselves with nuclear bombs or man-made plagues? Or will we survive as a precarious planet where a small affluent elite perches fearfully on the top of three continents of hungry peons? Or will we all end up in a subhuman world of efficiently lobotomized robots?

The world symbolized by the Feast of Fools is neither *Walden Two* nor *1984*. It is much more heterogeneous, messier, more sensuous, more variegated, more venturesome, more playful. It is a world for which a fiesta or even a love-in is a better symbol than a computer or a rocket. Technology need not be the enemy of the spirit in the modern world. But it should be a means to man's human fulfillment, not the symbol or goal of that fulfillment itself.

When we honestly ask ourselves whether we can have such a life-affirming world, we must move beyond mere optimism or pessimism, for the empirical evidence is either mixed or unfavorable. But we can hope. Hope in the religious sense rests in part on nonempirical grounds. Christian hope suggests that man is destined for a City. It is not just any city, however. If we take the Gospel images as well as the symbols of the book of Revelation into consideration, it is not only a City where injustice is abolished and there is no more crying. It is a City in which a delightful wedding feast is in progress, where the laughter rings out, the dance has just begun, and the best wine is still to be served.

6

The Seduction of the Spirit (1973)

The following selections are taken from The Seduction of the Spirit: The Use and Misuse of People's Religion *(New York: Simon & Schuster, 1973), 9-18, 318-29.*

RELIGION AS STORY AND SIGNAL

All human beings have an innate need to tell and hear stories and to have a story to live by.

Whatever else it has done, religion has provided one of the main ways of meeting this abiding need. Most religions begin as clusters of stories, embedded in song and saga, rite and rehearsal. Go back as far as the bloody Babylonian epic of Gilgamesh or to Homer's accounts of the gods and heroes of Hellas. Or read the tales told by Bantu priests, Cheyenne holy men or Eskimo shamans. They are all, in their own way, stories. The Hebrew Scriptures are largely stories; so is the New Testament. Rabbis, saints, Zen masters and gurus of every persuasion convey their holy teachings by jokes, *kōans,* parables, allegories, anecdotes and fables. There has never been a better raconteur than Jesus of Nazareth himself.

There are two kinds of stories that are especially important as vehicles for religious expression. The first is *autobiography*, or "testimony," the first-person account of the teller's struggle with the gods and the demons. It begins inside the speaker and says, "This is what happened to me." Recently neglected, testimony deserves reinstatement as a primary mode of religious discourse. It is a genre which celebrates the unique, the eccentric and the concrete. I suspect its decline in recent years is related to our industrial society's emphasis on interchangeable units, both human and mechanical, and its consequent suspicion of the particular and the irregular. But that is just what is valuable about autobiography. It reclaims personal uniqueness in an era of interchangeability. In an age of externality it uncovers what the classical mystics once described as "interiority." Autobiography is *my* story.

The second religiously significant mode of storytelling is what I call "people's religion." It is the collective story of a whole people. Like popular music and folk medicine, people's religion is usually mixed with superstition, custom and kitsch. Specialists and professionals view it with suspicion. But along with autobiography, it is an essential form of storytelling, a kind of corporate testimony. People's religion includes both the folk religion of ordinary people in its unsophisticated form and the popular religion that occurs outside formal ecclesiastical institutions and ad hoc rituals and do-it-yourself liturgies. I call both folk and pop varieties "people's religion" because they are both variant expressions of genuine collective interiority. People's religion is *our* story.

There is a third type of religion which is neither testimony nor folk expression but which also serves an important purpose. It is the religion that is coded, systematized, controlled and distributed by specialists. Religion in this form, though it still bears certain marks of a story, has actually become a system of what I call "signals." Most of the great religions of the world are a mixture of story and signal.

The distinction between story and signal is important, not only for understanding the various forms of religion but for grasping the very nature of contemporary societies. Stories reflect those forms of human association which blend emotion, value and history into a binding fabric. Signals, on the other hand, make possible large-scale and complex types of human association where such binding would not be possible. Stories amplify. They elicit emendations and embellishments from their bearers and often tell us more about the narrator than about the plot. Signals specify. They cue a single patterned act and tell us nothing about the signaler. Stories enrich the fund of common recollection and stimulate shared imagination. Signals permit people to move around in systems that would grind to a halt if all communication had to be deep and personal. Stories depend for their zest on eccentricity, hyperbole and local color. Signals must be clear, and their clarity requires the paring away of all extrinsic data. Jokes are stories. They convey multiple layers of information all at once and can be told and interpreted in several different ways. Traffic lights are signals. They transmit one unequivocal message and discourage all but one response. Both jokes and flashing yellow lights have a place. Jokes do much more than merely make us laugh, and signals not only prevent cars from crashing into each other, they also serve a thousand other indispensable functions.

All societies need both stories and signals. Large societies like ours especially need both the autonomous activities people engage in without anyone else's planning these activities and also the impersonal procedures that make possible the constant flow of ideas, goods and persons. Religions also serve their purpose best when they include both the spontaneous personal aspect and the inclusive consensus on value and vision that makes whole civilizations possible. The problem, however, is one of proportion, and what has happened in most modern societies in recent decades represents an ugly distortion of the symmetry that should obtain between story and signal, between people's faith and clerical religion. We have contracted the cultural and religious equivalent of leukemia. In leukemia, the balance between white and red blood cells is lost. The white cells first outnumber, then begin to cannibalize the red ones. In time the victim invariably dies. Similarly in our social body, institutionally programmed forms of activity which should be balanced with random, capricious and inwardly initiated forms of human action now threaten instead to devour them. This is happening in everything from travel to education and from religion to making love. Organized sports replace play. Prefabrication makes building something become obsolete. Tourism takes the place of travel. Religious faith is channeled into the institutional expansion of churches. No human impulse seems safe from the omnivorous onslaught of programming.

The swamping of stories by signals concerns me because I think something fundamental is at stake. Although signals multiply in dense, bureaucratically organized cultures, they are actually a less human form of communication. Animal language consists almost entirely of signals—the screech, the bark, the howl—but human beings are storytellers, and without stories we would not be human. Through our stories we assemble our pasts, place ourselves in a present and cast a hope for the future. Without stories we would be bereft of memory or anticipation. We know we are something more than mere hairless bipeds, because of our parables, jokes, sagas, fairy tales, myths, fables, epics and yarns. Not only have we created innumerable stories, we have also found endless ways to recount them. We dance them, draw them, mime them with masks and carve them on rocks. We sing them around tables stacked with the cold remains of a dinner. We whisper them in the ears of sleepy children in darkened bedrooms. We stammer them out to confessors and therapists. We inscribe them in letters and diaries. We act them out in the clothes we wear, the places we go, the friends we cherish. As soon as our young can comprehend our words we begin to tell them stories, and the hope we harbor for our elders is that we will be able to hear their full story before they go.

Religion should be the seedbed and spawning ground of stories. But today religion is not fulfilling its storytelling role. Like the society it inhabits, it has become top-heavy with signals and systems. Meanwhile the stories, without which there would be nothing to systematize, grow fainter. This is true at both the individual and the corporate level. It is time for a rebirth not just of testimony but also of people's religion.

I realize that the use of the word "religion" to describe the content of network TV and popular magazines may seem confusing. We think that the mass media inform or entertain us, and in the modern world we have gotten used to making sharp distinctions between "religion" on the one hand and news, entertainment or advertising on the other. But these distinctions have already outlived their usefulness. True, the "church religion" of our modern Western society is usually distinguishable from our commercial, artistic and political institutions. But ours is a highly unusual pattern. Preliterate peoples and traditional societies rarely have a separable set of "religious" activities. For the ancient Hebrew or the contemporary Eskimo, such distinctions are meaningless. In most cultures, religion is not separable. It is an integral part of healing, planting, learning, hunting, dying and giving birth. Only in the modern industrial West have we delimited the term "religion" to describing what goes on in and around churches, synagogues and mosques. But even that habit is now changing. Scholars are beginning to recognize that "religion" can no more be equated with what goes on in churches than "education" can be reduced to what happens in schools or "health care" restricted to what doctors do to patients in clinics. The vast majority of healing and learning goes on among parents and children and families and friends, far from the portals of any school or hospital. The same is true for religion. It is going on around us all the time.

Religion is larger and more pervasive than churches. . . . "Religion" is that cluster of memories and myths, hopes and images, rites and customs that pulls together the life of a person or group into a meaningful whole. The cluster need not be very systematic, although theologians spend a lot of time trying to make it so. A religion can be creative or demonic, theistic or nontheistic, consciously held or only dimly recognized, static or mercurial, spontaneous or imposed, story or signal. Whichever it is, it lends coherence to life, furnishes a fund of meanings, gives unity to human events and guides people in making decisions. Religion, as its Latin root suggests, is what "binds" things together.

Any religion, whether story or signal, has three identifiable components. First, it tells us *where* we came from and in connection with that often tells us what is wrong with us and how we got that way. Theologians call this part of religion its "myths of *origin, creation and fall.*" Second, religions hold up some *ideal* possibility for humankind. They project the blessed condition of salvation or satori or nirvana. They portray what it would mean to be fully saved or liberated, and sometimes this ideal is personified in saints and holy people. Third, a religion tells us *how* to get from our present state (sick, alienated, lost, in captivity) to what we can be or ought to be or already are if we only knew it. This is the "means of grace."

With this definition in mind, it now becomes easier to see why I think the signal clusters of the mass media can also be understood of religion. TV shows and magazine ads seethe with myths and heroes. They guide decisions, inform perception, provide examples of conduct. Does that make our mass-media culture "religious"? I do not think we can explain its grip on people in any other way. Its preachers tell us what our transgression is: our armpits are damp, our breath is foul, our wash is gray, our car is inadequate. They hold up models of saintly excellence before our eyes: happy, robust, sexually appreciated people who are free, adventurous, competent, attractive. These blessed ones have obviously been saved or are well on the way. And the sacramental means of grace that have lifted them from perdition are available to you and me—soaps, deodorants, clothes, pills, cars. If, despite our devoted attendance at the sacraments, we never seem to attain the promised bliss, well, salvation can be the quest of a lifetime. Mass-media culture is a religion, and we rarely get out of its temple.

Some critics complain that this broader use of the term "religion" only confuses people by violating the usage of ordinary language. They point out that we normally use the word "religion" to designate what people do in churches, or to describe belief in a supernatural being. To broaden the usage, they argue, merely sows confusion.

But surely this narrow usage of "religion" confuses people even more. It blinds us to the fact that we live today in the midst of *competing* religions and value systems and that we are being pressed by this warfare of the gods into making choices we would rather avoid. If we exempt mass-media images from religious definition and evaluation, we allow them to influence us unconsciously, while we continue to dismiss them as trivial. We fail to notice that the behavior models they promulgate often directly contradict the life goals Christianity celebrates. By assigning "religion" and "mass media" to separate spheres we think we are avoiding painful choices, but the fact is that the two are competing for the same loyalties. We should see the mass media instead, I believe, as disguised forms of religion. When we do, we become aware that life is a never-ending series of choices among conflicting values and disparate beliefs, and that when we do not make those choices ourselves, someone is always ready to make them for us.

* * *

So far I have touched on the three forms of religion this book is about—testimony, people's religion and the value patterns promulgated by the mass media. I have argued that religions serve the human spirit best when they nurture a lively mixture of stories and signals, but that our society is suffering from a lethal overload of signals. There is still another distortion in the relationship between story and signal, however, one that damages the fabric of the human community even worse than disbalance does. It appears when signals begin to *pose* as stories, when control cues pretend to be something other than what they are. This is what I call the "seduction of the spirit."

The term "seduction" as I use it here is not intended to conjure boudoir scenes. To seduce means to mislead or to deceive, and although the word has been used most often to refer to affairs of the heart, most of the so-called seductions that occur between men and women are probably not seductions at all. With rare exceptions, both people are usually fully aware of what is going on. What interests me about the idea of seduction as applied to the spirit, however, is that the great seducers of history all had one thing in common: they could use the natural needs and instincts of another person for their own selfish ends. Seducers employ the language and gesture of dialogue, trust, intimacy and personal rapport with consummate skill. They do it, however, not to develop personal intimacy but to subvert it, not to nourish human community but to undermine it. Seduction is the most callous form of exploitation because it tricks the victim into becoming an unwitting accomplice in his own deception.

The seducer is a signaler wearing the garb of a storyteller. What he tells sounds like a story and has all the marks of a story, but it is really a "line" or a spiel or what is not called a "cover." In this book I use the word "seduction" to refer not to the misuse of romance but to the misuse of religion, not to sex but to the spirit. The seduction of the spirit, in short, is the calculated twisting of people's natural and healthy religious instincts for purposes of control and domination. It is the cruelest abuse of religion because it slyly enlists people in their own manipulation.

When we look at the religious situation of the late twentieth century in the light of a broadened view of what religion is and how it is used and misused, it turns out to be a complex picture indeed. After centuries of enlightenment and skepticism modern man is now evangelized, catechized and proselytized more than ever; but he does not perceive the process as a religious one, so he fails to see what is happening. There are some people who are zealously critical of "religion" in the narrow sense, but they remain vulnerable to religions they do not recognize as such. Meanwhile another irony has appeared. To many skeptics' surprise, "religious" practices and ideas they had thought were long since discarded or outgrown have begun to reappear, often quite noisily, on the streets of our secular cities. From astrology to Zen, from mysticism to Pentecostal healing, from ecstatic dance to chanting—a massive rebirth of spiritual energy is occurring, albeit mostly outside the walls of the institutional churches. Organized religious groups seem bewildered by this unforeseen turn of events. In their justifiable attempts to infuse some moral content into the massive signaling structures of our civilization they have themselves become signal-heavy bureaucracies, cut off from the freshening sources without which both religion and culture die. Understandably they seem startled and frightened by the spiritual outbursts of recent years. When churches are stunned by a revival of piety, and TV commercials take over the indoctrinating once handled by priests, no wonder the picture is confusing.

The situation will become less perplexing, however, if we stop trying to understand it as a battle *between* faith and reason, emotion and intelligence, religion and science. We will make sense of our scene only if we begin to view it as a rebellion by story and symbol against a culture which had gone much too far in the direction of cues and signals. What we are witnessing is a reassertion of the small-scale, the spontaneous, the particular in response to a surfeit of the large-scale, the programmed and the prepackaged. When these terms become clear, religion can no longer be cast as hero or as culprit. It can be both, neither, or a little of each. Healthy religion, like healthy culture, requires a balance of energy and form, of spirit and structure, of story and signal. In an era like ours, where the balance is dangerously wrong, religion can either worsen the disease or help contribute to a recovery.

This is the only sound basis on which religious movements, new or old, established or exotic, overt or covert, can be judged.

What role would religion play in a healthy culture? It would spawn both visionaries and codifiers, both prophets and priests. It would be a source of energy and a basis for moral consensus. It would celebrate both heart and head. When the personal, small group and civilizational levels are feeding one another properly, a robust interdependence appears. Stories and symbols enrich memory and conjure new fantasies; prayers and rituals nourish alternative forms of consciousness; signals and structures solidify past gains and provide the necessary stability. Religion as personal testimony, group ritual and civilizational self-image nourishes the spirit at every level.

The problem is that despite the current renaissance, our culture still remains grotesquely out of balance, so consequently religion must play a different role. It must become corrective and critic. If the freeing of persons or groups from the intrusive control of their lives by outside forces is what our benumbed era needs more than anything else, then in our time we must reclaim testimony and people's religion, if necessary at the expense of organized and coded religious systems. Let the apostate, the miscreant and the dissenter thrive! Just as important, we should expose those forms of religion which, posing as entertainment, education or something else, nonetheless stupefy our psyches with vacuum tube demigods, consumer panaceas and mock-up visions of supernal bliss. The actual stories of men and women and the shared memories of living groups could be silenced forever by seductive signals; so we must become partisans instead of onlookers. People's religion is in danger and testimony is discouraged. But without these forms of storytelling we would cease to be human. Therefore religion in our time can best restore balance by being partisan, by supporting the storytellers against the signalers.

* * *

THE FUTURE OF THEOLOGY: A POETIC POSTSCRIPT

The foregoing pages are in part a defense of the extravagant variety of forms religious expression takes against those who would like to tailor the spirit to precut patterns—a defense, if you will, of schism, heresy and heterodoxy. It is also a defense of the reality of religion against those who dismiss it as delusion, superstition or opiate.

In my saner moments I doubt very much that such defenses are actually needed. The human spirit will undoubtedly continue to spawn myths and weave symbolic meanings, without much regard either to intellectual attacks or to zealous defenses, as long as the species exists. Though in the short run the spirit is catastrophically subject to trickery, coercion and exploitation, in the long run it can neither be exterminated nor domesticated. It is, as St. Paul says, "Persecuted but not forsaken, cast down, but not destroyed." But if my role *as advocatus spiritis* has helped even a little bit, I am glad.

The future of theology, however, does not seem as secure as the future of the spirit. The religious evolution of humankind began millennia before theology appeared and will presumably continue long after theology disappears. True, as long as human beings continue to be both religious creatures and thinking creatures they will inevitably think about their religion. But the question is what *form* human thought, about religion or anything else, might take. I doubt that such thought will be "theological" in the present sense of the word. Theology, after all, is the expression of a particular form of thought—reflective, analytical, objective—that has arisen only in recent centuries and will probably not last forever. Sciences, mental forms and modes of thinking come and go, but the creativity of the spirit continues. We can be thankful that the future of the spirit and of the race does not depend on the eternal survival of theology. What then, in the light of all that has gone before, should the future of theology be?

The theology of the future should be a kind of play . . . I mean play in three senses of the word: play as "making fun of," play as "making believe" and play as "useless" or non-productive activity. The case for such a harlequinesque theology runs something like this:

(1) As "making fun of," theology is a satirizing activity which debunks destructive myths. It criticizes the cramping symbols that keep people busy turning the wheels of grandiloquent institutions and bowing down before bloated cultural and political tetrarchs. The theologian's job is to be a persistent muckraker of spurious mystiques. He is the "demythologizer," the exposer of fraudulent meanings and pasted-on values. He is the theologian as jester or holy fool, the one who pricks pretenses and shouts out for everyone to hear that the king has no clothes. I call this "making fun of" because I believe lampoon is one of the most effective forms of cultural demythologizing. Denying the powerful their mystique destroys the fear they must nurture in the souls of the powerless. Dismantling and deflating auras, halos and nimbuses is part of any theology devoted to human liberation.

History abounds with precedents for this debunking role of the religious critic. There are many stories of Zen masters who burn statues of the Buddha to shock their followers out of their blind awe. The Hebrew prophets spoofed the claims of the kings, and the early Christians punctured the sacred legends that sacralized the Roman emperor. The Russian holy fools parodied bishops and czars in public. Luther told bawdy stories about the pope. All "critical" theology is an attempt to advance the freeing of the human species by undercutting the magical authority of sacred texts and the spurious legitimacy of proud rulers. This does not mean that religious traditions or secular states are divested of all claims to loyalty, but it does mean they cannot base their claim on ignorant deference, obfuscation or deception.

We should never doubt that the jester's job is a "serious" one. . . . "Making fun of" may not be fun for the one who does it, but it is an integral part of the theologian's calling. And insofar as every thoughtful man or woman of faith is also to some extent "a theologian" (I do not believe theology should remain forever the province of an elite), this risky fun making is the calling of all.

(2) Theology is play not just as making fun of but also as "making believe," as fantasizing, pretending or imagining. Theologians should be transmuting old symbols, exploring alternative metaphors, juxtaposing unlikely concepts, playing with new and improbable images of man and woman, God and world, earth and sky. The great theologians of the past have not merely examined and systematized existing religious patterns. They have ventured new ones. They have invented new pictures, woven new connections, spun new ideas. Admittedly constructive, imaginative theology has been neglected for a long time. This is partly due to the century-long reign of critical theology. Consequently theologians today would sometimes prefer to use another word for the fanciful side of their activity—maybe "theo-poetics." Some purists argue that the "ology" part of the word "theology" makes it a science in which imagination and fantasy would naturally be out of place.

But I disagree. The "ology" part of "theology" (as in "biology" and "geology") comes from the Greek *logos* ("word," "meaning," "significance"). To banish the imaginative side of life to the illogical insignificant or meaning-less is to accept a crippling restriction on what counts as meaning or on what is "logical." I believe, on the contrary, that play, pretending and imagining are alive with meaning and significance. Only a prosaic definition of what is "logical" could deny that play is "logical." Our whole age is bogged down by just such restrictive nomenclature. Happily the condition may be temporary. Some of the best thinkers in modern science are beginning to notice again how essential the imaginative component is in any science. . . .

It is both sad and ironic that just as some biologists and physicists are beginning to welcome the place of play in the disciplines, theologians, who have labored so arduously for decades to have theology accepted as a "science," now cling to a rigid no-nonsense view of theological method. It is sad because it so badly constricts the scope and style of theology. It is ironic because theology in the past has often made its most decisive contributions in the writings of people who were not afraid to admix metaphysics, autobiography and fantasy. A history of theology purged of its prayers, confessions, visions, imaginary dialogues, improbable puns and wild speculations would be a dull and misleading one. . . .

When children "make believe" they often pretend they are someone else. This suggests another significant job that theology as "making believe" has to do: exploring and relating to one another the various alternative forms of human consciousness.

More and more frequently nowadays theologians are urged to get to work and build a twentieth-century *Summa Theologica,* a new medieval synthesis which this time would have to integrate not only Christ and Aristotle, as St. Thomas' *Summa* did, but all the major non-Western traditions plus kundalini yoga, Sufism, bio-energetics, Tarot cards, the nature mysticism of the Dakota Indians, and, if possible, the *I-Ching.* This hope for an updated version of the thirteenth-century synthesis is more frequently voiced by imaginative moderns like William Irwin Thompson who feel the pain of the present spiritual fragmentation and long for a new civilizational faith in which each altar will have its place. My view, however, is that it is not only impossible now to construct a new comprehensive religious metaphysic but that even the attempt to do so represents an early medieval answer to a late postmodern question. Admittedly system construction can also be a form of play, as anyone who has toyed with an erector set or built a sand castle knows. But the devising of a new synthesis is still mainly a job of intellectual planning and joining, and at this pivotal stage in the evolution of religious consciousness what is most needed is not a neatly carpentered system. What we need rather is to learn how to experience one another's spiritual traditions from the inside. What we suffer from most is not a poverty of intellectual competence in theology but an erosion of experience and a failure of imagination. Few people who consider themselves "non-religious" today reject faith because it seems unreasonable. They reject it, or rather ignore it, because it does not seem to touch or intersect their own experience. The blame for this lies not so much with religion as it does with the numbing and anesthetizing of the psyche which is the price our civilization has paid for industrial affluence and the technical mastery of the world. People who are taught from their earliest years to stifle and distrust all feelings that are not "useful" or "productive" soon grow incapable of experiencing most of what the religious traditions of history are all about. A population that has been trained to compete and accumulate will inevitably become blind and insensitive to vast ranges of experience still available to people who have not been so hardened. One cannot, as Jesus said, serve both God and Mammon.

The theological problem is twofold. Some people feel alienated from their own religious tradition and intrigued only by exotic import models, but incapable of experiencing them at any depth. Other people feel equally estranged from any religious experience at all: God is a cipher, mystics and saints are harmless psychotics, and religious celebration is a dangerous surrender to impulse and irrationality. For either group even the most brilliant and persuasive new theological synthesis would elicit only another jaded yawn.

"Make-believe" involves setting aside for a brief period the role, self-image, identity and world view within which one operates most of the time and trying out another way of being. Children do this quite easily. People who for one reason or another have escaped the standard industrial form of consciousness and can still experience transport, ecstasy and trance do it too. But most adults in highly organized bureaucratic societies find it virtually impossible to do. They go through life with an antenna tuned to one or two wavelengths when there are hundreds or maybe even thousands available. What is the future theologian's responsibility to such lost sheep as these?

It is not, in the first instance, I believe, to elaborate a new comprehensive system. Even a system which somehow integrated the thousand wavelengths would remain opaque to people whose receivers are turned off. No, the first job theologians have is to learn from the shamans and the gurus how to help people encounter and experience the vast solar systems of reality they are now missing. And this means that the "complete theologian" must first learn, as every guru must, how to travel these worlds of meaning himself. Only then can he learn how to guide others. Like a vaudeville trouper or a repertory player, he must master the technique of moving in and out of different religious traditions without losing his own psyche in the process. Such a course will be perilous, but without this personal exploration of the terrain, any *Summa* he might eventually assemble would turn out to be an airy mental vehicle, as fragile as a floating soap bubble, just as lovely perhaps but also just as evanescent. There can be no short cut. Tomorrow's theology must move from experience to exposition, from testimony to text, from *Confession* to *Summa*. It cannot move the other way and still be the theology we need at this historical moment.

This still does not solve, of course, the conundrum of the one and the many or the danger of nihilism, which is always posed by radical pluralism. William James confronted that issue by serenely assuring us that since we live in a pluralistic universe we need not bust our heads over how it all goes together. I suspect that James may have been right, but whether he was or not, I suspect also that the way we will cope with the radical diversity of meaning-worlds in the coming epoch will *not* be to assign each a place in some large whole. Rather, we will cope with it by evolving a form of human consciousness which can move from one world to another without panicking or falling to pieces. Thus the next *Summa* might consist not of a thousand chapters but of a thousand alternative states of being, held together not by a glued binding but by the fact that all thousand are equally real.

Imagine what kind of world it would be if instead of merely tolerating or studying them, one could actually *be,* temporarily at least, a Sioux brave seeing an ordeal vision, a neolithic hunter prostrate before the sacred fire, a Krishna lovingly ravishing a woodsful of goat girls, a sixteenth-century Carmelite nun caught up in ecstatic prayer, a prophet touched by flame to go release a captive people. One need not be a follower of Carl Jung and believe that all these figures are already present in our archetypal unconscious waiting to be awakened, though that might very well be true. Even if it is not, we still have enough records, cave scrawlings, memoirs, amulets and oral reports to help us find our way into these people's lives, if we would let ourselves. And we still have, in however precarious condition, people's religions, the infinitely valuable unabsorbed traces of forms of consciousness that are older, richer and more complex than ours.

Admittedly the trek from our present infinitesimal range of consciousness and our ingrained terror of unknown psychic states to the pluriform future I have just described will be an arduous one. And the only place I know to begin is with our nearly forgotten childhood capacity to make believe we are someone else. But that, after all, should not come as a total surprise. Someone did say once, "Except ye become as little children, ye can in no wise enter the Kingdom of Heaven."

(3) Theology can become play in a third sense, namely as non-instrumental, non-productive, "useless" activity. As an enterprise which, like play, serves no goal beyond itself, theology rightly defies the modern prejudice which decrees that only useful things have a right to exist.

I first became aware of the invaluable uselessness of theology when a few years ago I attended a five-day conference sponsored by the World Council of Churches on the ethical problems posed for the modern world by scientific technology. We heard papers and reports; discussed and debated; listened to technical experts, political advocates and theological interpreters. There were many eloquent pleas for the churches to become "relevant," to say a significant word to the technical society, to learn to speak in the idiom of the industrial-technological world. Everyone seemed earnest, serious and determined.

All through the conference there sat just in front of me a venerable bishop of the ancient Ukrainian Orthodox Church, vested in flowing robe and long beard, trying manfully to listen to the thousands of words pouring into his headphones from the simultaneous interpreter in the glass booth at the side of the hall. He never said a word throughout the whole five days. At the end of the conference, when all our heads were buzzing with ideas, arguments, charts, trends and graphs, someone apparently thought it would be a nice idea to ask him to pronounce the benediction. When he had listened to the translation of the request and was sure he knew what was expected, he rose to his full height, smoothed his robe, beard and long flowing locks and strode to the front of the hall, his bishop's miter in hand. He stood facing the assembly, an icon of the Mother of God swinging from a golden chain around his neck, and blessed us all with a sweepingly expansive sign of the cross. Then, holding his hand high, he began to pray in a language I had never heard. Apparently few others had ever heard it either, because the simultaneous translating receivers went dead. People at first switched frantically from channel to channel, then stopped. The interpreters in the glass booths looked at one another in panic, shook their heads and then sat silently. The bishop's prayer swelled and receded like ocean waves. After several minutes it stopped. I later found out the language in which the bishop had prayed was Old Slavonic, the archaic liturgical language of his church. Not only did the Russian interpreters not know it but I was told that even in the Ukraine very few people know it. No wonder the earphones had gone silent in defeated exasperation. With another wide sign of the cross, the bishop then walked—"recessed" is the proper word—back to his document-cluttered desk. There were embarrassed coughs and throat clearings. The well-known "irrelevancy" of the Eastern Orthodox Church and the equally notorious irrelevancy of prayer had once again been irrefutably documented in our midst.

Or had they? I felt, on the contrary, that we had just witnessed the most significant episode of the conference. I went immediately to the bishop and thanked him for his prayer. He seemed surprised but grateful. He even gave me a special individual blessing then and there, making the sign of the cross that was a shade smaller than the one he had bestowed on the multitude. For some reason I felt closer to the bishop at that moment than I did to any of the other participants. Only later did I come to know why.

Unwittingly, I am sure, the Ukrainian Orthodox bishop had demonstrated that one of religion's most important features is its intractable irrelevance, its eccentricity, its downright inconvenience. Religion is an antique settee on the freeway, an almost indecipherable old song disturbing the bleep of the computers. Try as anyone will to doll it up, it is never fully "up to date," and to my mind it should not be, which is why I've never liked the word *aggiornamento* ("bringing up to date") to describe what the church allegedly needs.

The greatest danger posed by the technological world we were discussing at that conference is precisely that it infects our language and our images. It gets into our heads and our words. It levels down our cultural quirks and our religious peculiarities. It produces an increasingly uniform world with less and less place for oddness, transcendence or deviancy. It dismisses as "irrelevant" those impulses and idioms that cannot be tailored to its Procrustean couch of efficiency. It defines what is "useful" and then makes usefulness the ultimate test of value and validity.

I often think of that bearded old patriarch with his timeless icon of the Theotokos dangling on his midriff. He had said a wholly irrelevant, and therefore gloriously "relevant" word. Though he was probably unaware of it, he had reminded us that there are areas of the human life which are simply not reducible to technological or even political relevancy. He had spoken to us in the idiom of the spirit, and those who were attuned to it knew what he was saying even though the words never came through the transistor headsets. He had said his piece in a language of costume, gait, gesture and sign that keeps alive a dimension of human spirit now fatally threatened by the very technical reality to which some people wanted him to be "relevant."

Theology is play in the sense that it is not just useful, relevant or productive in the way those words are understood in societies organized around efficiency and getting results. It represents a stubborn holdout among the "sciences," and when it accepts the industrial-technical closure of the world of human meaning, or tries to blend into the one-dimensional flatland, it betrays itself. As a holdout, theology has, paradoxically, something important to say to technopolis. It has an eschatological word, a kind of summons to mankind to decide about its future. The paradox is that something which seems so *out* of date, so strangely held over from such a remote past, may be in the only possible position to postulate a radically alternative future. The technical mentality deprives us of a sense of the past. But when a person or a society is robbed of its past, it has that much less chance to bring any critical perspective to bear on the present.

Of course it does not necessarily work that way. A church (or anything else) that lives wholly in the past may be so insulated from the present that its memory does not create any friction.

Still, one purpose of memory is to remind us that the present moment is not all there is, and to provide a source of alternative images of the future. Without memory there would be no discontent, no awareness of oppression, no hope for a changed future. The marvel of play is that it reminds us that productive work is not the ultimate end of man. Man was made not just to shape the world but to delight in it, not just to glorify God but "to enjoy Him forever." Play, among other things, is something we do for its own sake, with no extrinsic goal in mind. It is something we do just for the hell of it, and so is theology. It is not only, as St. Thomas said, the intellectual love of God, it is also a kind of intellectual delighting in Him, and in His world, forever. My hope is that, in this sense, theology will always be a little useless.

7

Turning East (1977)

The following selections are taken from Turning East: The Promise and Peril of the New Orientalism *(New York: Simon & Schuster, 1977), 7-21, 157-75.*

NEVER THE TWAIN

The idea for this book began on the day Harry, Denise and Michael knocked on my front door. It was a quiet Sunday afternoon, and when I opened the door, two young men and a young woman asked if they could come in and talk to me about Krishna. Both the men had shaved their heads, except for a small ponytail at the back. They wore bright saffron robes, simple bead necklaces and sandals. One wore a loose-fitting white shirt-blouse lined with intricate brown-and-blue patterning. Both carried tubular drums encased in woven baskets and ribbons and slung around their necks with broad sashes. The men had two white lines painted on their faces, beginning at the bridge on the nose and running up into their scalps. They told me later this was the sign of *tilaka*, a symbol of the dedication of their bodies to Krishna. All in all they might have looked downright menacing if they had not been smiling. The woman had blue eyes and wore a pale sari, a light shawl and sandals. Her hair was long. She carried finger cymbals and a shoulder pouch stuffed with books and pamphlets. Only later on did I learn that their names were Harry, Denise and Michael. They introduced themselves as Bhārgava dāsa, Krishna Kumari, and Caityaguru dāsa. They were all members of the International Society for Krishna Consciousness, better known as the Hare Krishna movement, and I asked them to come in.

"East is East and West is West," Rudyard Kipling once declared in an often-quoted line, "and never the twain shall meet." But as I sat that day and listened to Harry (Bhārgava dāsa), Denise (Krishna Kumari), and Michael (Caityaguru dāsa), I wondered. Harry, it turned out, had been brought up in a liberal Protestant family in Orange, New Jersey. His family, he said, attended church only episodically. They had, however, transmitted to him a "certain feeling for morality" but no very distinct idea of God. Denise had been born into a Jewish family in Brooklyn, had gone to Hebrew school and had recently returned home to attend a younger brother's bar mitzvah. Michael came from a Boston Irish Catholic family, had attended parochial schools for years and had once briefly considered becoming a priest. We talked for an hour, and as we did, my two younger children crept in, stared and then listened attentively as Bhārgava dāsa, Krishna Kumari and Caityaguru dāsa each told about the path that had brought them from the spiritual traditions of their families into the Hare Krishna movement. As they spoke, Krishna Kumari took some *prasada*—cookies which have first been offered to Krishna—and handed them to the children, who munched them appreciatively. Later, as they arose to leave, the guests offered to give me (though a contribution would of course not be refused) a lushly illustrated English version of the Bhagavad Gita, the Song of God, one of the best known Hindu scriptures, as translated by the founder of their movement, A. C. Bhaktivedanta Swami Prabupada. I accepted, and as the visitors wended their way further down the street, drumming, clinking the cymbals and chanting "Hare Krishna," I noticed my children eagerly poring through the pages of the Bhagavad Gita and staring at the pictures of sky-blue Krishna and the dark-eyed cowmaidens of Vrindaban.

The unexpected Sunday visit puzzled me. Who were these strange visitors from so near and yet so far away? Were they purblind fanatics, confused adolescents, the brainwashed victims of some hypnotic cult leader? As we talked, they had not seemed like any of these. What were they, then? Was this the meeting of East and West that Kipling thought would not take place until both eventually stood at "God's great judgment seat"?

As a child I had scarcely heard of religions other than Christianity and Judaism. I had certainly never met any adherents of them. My initial encounter with the Bhagavad Gita came in a college sophomore comparative religion course. Now all that seemed to be changing. The Orient, or at least some of its Western representatives, was now literally knocking on my door, and the Gita lay open on the living-room floor. East and West were beginning to intersect in ways that neither Rudyard Kipling nor I had anticipated.

The Hare Krishna devotees themselves represented only a small group, but they are a part of something larger and much more significant—a wave of interest among Americans in Oriental spirituality whose scope and intensity is unprecedented in the history of American religion. True, a degree of fascination with the East has existed in America since at least the early nineteenth century. Ralph Waldo Emerson and Walt Whitman both read the Gita. Emerson published a Hindu-inspired poem called "Brahma," and his transcendentalist philosophy includes elements that sound distinctively Hindu, such as the idea of the "Oversoul." This early nineteenth-century wave of Indian thought not only influenced transcendentalists; it also created movements like Theosophy and the Unity School of Christianity. In the latter part of the century, a second wave of influence occurred. The famous Swami Vivekananda arrived in 1893 from India and founded the Vedanta Society, which still exists today. The influence of Oriental spirituality in the West is hardly something new.

But there is something new about the present situation. In previous decades, interest in Oriental philosophy was confined mostly to intellectuals and was centered largely on ideas, not on devotional practices. There is no evidence that Emerson ever sat in a full lotus. Today, on the other hand, not only are large numbers of people who are in no sense "intellectuals" involved, but they appear more interested in actual religious practices than in doctrinal ideas. The recent wave of interest in Oriental forms of spirituality seems both broader and deeper than the ones that preceded it.

As I began to look into this remarkable new development in American religious history, and to ask myself what it meant, I quickly noticed something else: the town I live in provides an extraordinarily fertile field for pursuing an inquiry into neo-Oriental religious movements. Cambridge, Massachusetts, was blessed by its English colonial founders with a name derived from their old university, and designed to suggest civility and higher learning. It is the home of Harvard, the oldest university in America. But in recent years Cambridge has also become something its Calvinistic founders could hardly have foreseen. It is one of the four or five most thriving American centers of the neo-Oriental religious surge. This should not be surprising, since Cambridge is full of just the kind of people to whom these movements appeal—mainly young, usually white, and almost always of middle-class background. An acquaintance of mine, recently returned from Benares, the Holy City of India, where millions come to bathe in the sacred waters of the Ganges, took a look around Cambridge last year and promptly rechristened it, "Benares-on-the-Charles."

The analogy is an apt one. Within twenty blocks of the intersection of Massachusetts Avenue and Boylston Street, forty or fifty different neo-Oriental religious movements thrive. A few blocks west stands the Zen center, furnished with black silk cushions, bells, an appropriately wizened and wise-looking resident master, and a visiting Zen sword-play instructor. In the other direction, in the basement of a hospitable Episcopal church, the Sufi dancers meet twice a week to twist and turn like the legendary whirling dervishes in a ritual circle dance, chanting verses from the Koran, the Muslim holy book, in atonal Arabic. A few blocks to the northeast is the Ananda Marga center, located in a large gray frame house on a maple-lined residential street, and specializing in a combination of meditation and community action. If one is ready for a deep plunge into imported odors and colors, one seeks out a few blocks to the south the headquarters of my Sunday visitors, the Hare Krishnas, officially known as the International Society for Krishna Consciousness. There the devotees hold a weekly feast of savory Indian food and a somewhat less piquant introductory lecture on the myster-ies of the Krishna devotion. The cleanshaven followers of the young guru Maharaj Ji's Divine Light Mission have a meeting place ten blocks southeast, near Central Square. Recently a group of self-styled Sikhs, immaculately clad in white robes, turbans and wrist daggers, have opened a vegetarian restaurant near the shore of the Charles, called the Golden Temple of Conscious Cookery. One should not overlook the nearby International Student Meditation Center, founded several years ago by the Maharishi Mahesh Yoga, the best known of the swamis of the late sixties, where one can go to be initiated into the mysteries of TM. More recently, the followers of Sri Chinmoy, the former postal clerk guru who lives in Queens, have begun to be more in evidence. There is also Dharma House, eleven blocks north, founded recently by Chogyam Trungpa Rinpoche, the Tibetan Buddhist lama. And there are dozens of smaller, less stable groups, countless Yoga centers, Tai Chi exhibits and sitar concerts. When one adds them all together, the picture of Cambridge as an intellectually prim university town fades as the image of a hive of neo-Oriental religious fervor begins to take its place.

What has provoked this Oriental religious revival? Who are the people who find themselves caught up in it? Why have they left either some more conventional Christian or Jewish form of religious life—or no religious life at all—to become seekers or adherents in these new spiritual movements? What does it all mean for American culture and for Christianity?

When these questions began to puzzle me after the visit of the Krishna disciples, I decided to devote some of my own energy and to enlist my students into looking for the answers. Eventually, I thought, I might even write a book on the subject. Some of the students were already involved in one or another neo-Oriental practice and were eager to learn more. Most were just curious about what the movements meant to their adherents, why they had joined, what they were looking for. Consequently they were ready to visit, observe, participate in meetings and rituals, talk with devotees, and then pool their findings with the experiences of fellow students.

There was still a problem, however. I recognized that even though my home town provided a marvelous field of inquiry into the new Orientalism, and my students were eager to help, one very formidable obstacle remained. The obstacle was me. I could not afford to overlook the fact that, ever since my late teens, I have had a standing suspicion of excessively "inward" and socially passive religions. Especially since my college years, when I left a pietistic student religious organization because of its members' sanctimonious Toryism, I have steered clear of any religion that seemed to give people an excuse for withdrawing from the pain and confusion of the world. I had been intellectually converted from my own fundamentalism in my junior year in college by reading Reinhold Niebuhr's *Moral Man and Immoral Society* with its withering exposure of pietistic individualism. In my years of graduate study, I developed an admiration for Paul Tillich, who always considered himself a "religious socialist," and for Walter Rauschenbusch, the prophet of the American social gospel. Later I came to admire the Reverend Martin Luther King, Jr., and still later I became acquainted with the various schools of "liberation theology," including those emanating from the Catholic left of Latin America. This personal history made me very suspicious, at least initially, of the neo-Oriental wave, and I knew that, no matter how hard I tried to maintain scholarly objectivity, my inner distrust for all "opiates of the people," East or West, might continue to influence me, if mainly on the unconscious level. Even in my own judgment I did not seem to be the right person to carry out a fair and impartial study of something which many people saw as a massive retreat from the social activism of the previous decade.

After giving the problem of my own possible bias a lot of thought, I decided to do the study anyway. I was just too curious about the new movements to ignore them, and I desperately wanted to answer the questions they raised in my mind. Also, although my prejudice against some of the movements was undeniable, I was at least fully aware of it and could take it into consideration in any judgments I would make. Furthermore, as one colleague assured me when I asked for advice on this issue, anybody who is interested enough in anything to spend time learning about it inevitably has some feelings about it. Consequently, after I spent some preliminary weeks along with my students scouting out the turf, we screwed up our collective courage and plunged into our "field," the Benares-on-the-Charles.

During the first several weeks of the study we all had a marvelous time. Together and separately we attended dozens of meditation sessions, feasts, satsangs, introductory lectures, inquirers' meetings, worship services and study circles. We asked questions, read mounds of tracts and pamphlets, watched, listened and filled up countless tape cartridges. The students enjoyed the enterprise, and so did I. For once we were getting some things straight from the source instead of from the textbooks. And the groups we visited were invariably hospitable and open to our questions. What I would later refer to as Phase One, of three distinct phases of the study, was well under way.

As our work continued, we began to collate the answers people gave to our questions about why they had begun to participate in such movements. Many of the people we spoke with expressed a need for friendship or community, some antidote to loneliness. They seemed to have found in their fellow practitioners a degree of companionship they had not found elsewhere. Others told us they had wanted to learn a discipline or practice—chanting, meditating, bodily exercise—which they claimed had brought them into immediate touch with God or spiritual reality, or themselves, or something from which they had previously felt separated. Still others told us they had turned East because of their dissatisfaction with one or another aspect of Western religion, or because they simply needed a clear spiritual authority to make some sense out of their lives.

These answers were all interesting enough, but by the end of the semester I felt that something was lacking. I could understand the words people were saying to us, but somehow the key dimension seemed missing. Little by little, as the notebooks piled up, I began to wonder what it would feel like to be on the *inside* of one of the movements. Is such a feeling ever available to outsiders? No one can hope to know another person's God as she does, nor experience his faith as he does. As a Christian and a professional theologian, I realized I was neither a genuine Oriental pilgrim nor an authentic seeker. I was intrigued, curious, fascinated; but I was not a devotee. Still, I began to see that I would have to pursue some kind of "inside" knowing and feeling if I were going to understand the disciples I was studying. So I tried another method.

In this, Phase Two of my work, I tried to become as much of a participant as I could. I was still an investigator, but I no longer simply hovered on the edge of things. I did not merely observe the Sufi dancers, I whirled too. I did not just read about Zen, or visit centers; I "sat." I chanted with the Hare Krishnas. I stood on my head, stretched my torso and breathed deeply with the Yoga practitioners, and spent hours softly intoning a mantra to myself in a favorite form of Hindu devotional practice. I became a participant, not because I thought there was actually something in it for me, but because I wanted to nourish my capacity for empathy. I wanted to find out what I could about the lure of the East on the visceral level. This participant-observer phase of my inquiry, I should add, took me far away from Benares-on-the-Charles. It led me to spiritual centers in California, Texas and Vermont, and into long conversations with Zen abbots, Sufi drummers and Divine Light devotees. Eventually this second phase of my search brought me to Boulder, Colorado, where my investigation took a completely unexpected turn: Phase Two ended and Phase Three began.

I find it hard to characterize Phase Three. In the previous stages of participant-observation research, I had always continued to be more an observer than a participant. True, I had long since gone beyond simply reading descriptions and asking questions, but even in the dancing, the chanting and the breathing I retained a certain inner distance. It was all designed to make me a better observer and commentator. I was still asking what it all meant for other people, for the church, or for Western society. I was not asking what it meant for me, and I could not imagine myself as an East Turner.

Then something I had not anticipated happened. I discovered that when someone is studying beehives up close, regardless of how much inner distance is retained there is still a distinct possibility that the investigator can be stung. While trying to find out what it would feel like to be an East Turner, I found myself—contrary to all my expectations and prejudices—"turning East." While wondering what kind of personal void an Orientally derived spiritual discipline might fill in someone's life, I discovered something that filled a previously unnoticed void in my own. Almost without noticing what was happening, I slipped across the border between "them" and "us." Consequently, a book which had started out as sympathetic description became, at least in part, critical autobiography.

I did not become a convert. I have not shaved my head, adopted an exclusively brown-rice diet or taken up public chanting and drumming. In the course of my investigation, however, I became aware that many of the hopes and hungers that motivate people to turn toward the East were not just observable in others: they were also present in me. I believe, in fact, that nearly everyone in our society feels them in some measure. But I went a little further. I also discovered that at least one of the spiritual disciplines taught by one of the neo-Oriental movements—in my case it was the meditational practice taught by the Tibetan Buddhists in Colorado—met a deep, if previously unrecognized, need in my own life. Although I rejected nearly all the theological trappings the Buddhists have attached to meditation, the "shamatha" practice itself became an integral part of my life.

Now I had to cope with a difficult decision. Since the Turn East had become a personal rather than a merely professional consideration for me, I had to face the same problem I had struggled with earlier, this time from the other side. I considered the idea of discarding the book altogether. Since my study had unexpectedly come to mean so much to me personally, once again I had to ask how I could possibly be "objective." Even worse, would writing a book somehow undercut the subjective importance my quest had taken on? Troubled by both of these questions, I went back and reread all my notes. I was greatly relieved. I discovered as I went through the material again that, although I could now grasp the meaning of things that had eluded me before and could understand the whole Turn East much better, I was not more sympathetic. In fact, at certain points I was more suspicious. Contrary to what many social science theories insist, my being more or less "inside" the Turn East did not make me any less capable of sensing its dangers or noticing its foibles. To my great surprise, my own Turn East made me even more critical, and in rereading my earlier notes, I could now see why.

Before the change in my own perspective occurred, I had been going out of my way to see the best side of it all. Knowing my original anti-pietistic bias, I had been giving the benefit of every possible doubt to the Turn East, even to the point of repressing my hunches about impostors and humbug if the evidence was not unambiguously clear. I had been leaning over backward to be fair. After all, who wants to be accused of performing a hatchet job on someone else's religion? I had been a model of academic restraint and objectivity. Consequently, my conclusions had been tepid, commendably moderate, and above all, dull. After my involvement became personal, however, most of the scholarly restraint disappeared. I could give voice to my most troubling suspicions about many, indeed most, aspects of the Turn East, and I could express my anxieties about how badly Oriental teachings are misunderstood and misused in the West.

Furthermore, my other fear—that writing the book would endanger the personal reality of what I had found—also faded. Despite the popular belief that writing or talking about something invariably spoils it, I found that the attempt to describe my experience with the Turn East made it more real and more vivid. Without doubt there are mystical ascents and ecstatic visions that defy mere words, but my experience with the Tibetan practice of meditation had been nothing like that. In fact, it had been nearly the opposite—sane, clarifying, grounding, "ordinary." Furthermore, even though the inner essence of wordless meditation obviously cannot be described in words, one can say a lot about what the experience means for the rest of life. I have never liked the idea of *sacrificium intellectus*—that certain experiences, usually religious ones, require us to immolate our minds. Admittedly, language is an imperfect tool, but however imperfect it is, we must still use it to relate some parts of our lives to other parts and to share our experiences with our fellow human beings. I have found that writing about the spiritual discipline I learned has not eviscerated it, but has integrated it more fully into my life.

Not only did my experience with Buddhist meditation give me a clearer insight into both the perils and the possibilities of the new Orientalism; it also provided me with a central clue to the inner meaning of the whole phenomenon—something I had just not been able to find before. Now, as I look back, I can easily see why the clue had been so elusive. Indeed, how can anyone make sense out of the jumble of movements and the confusion of religious ideas and sentiments which I have lumped together under the phrase "the Turn East"? At first glance the problem of finding a focus seems nearly impossible. There are hundreds of neo-Oriental movements flourishing in America today, ranging in size from ambitious national networks down to tiny handfuls of disciples of this or that teacher. Here a quiet cabal gathers to listen to a tape of Ram Dass. There a study circle pores over the Lotus Sutra. Groups seem to appear and disappear overnight. Gurus come and go. Teachings and practices blend and overlap. Serious masters, parvenus and outright charlatans fly in and out. How can an inquirer sort through the confusion in an orderly way?

I began to study the Turn East as a confused, nearly bewildered, observer. I needed a map, and I tried two or three without hitting on one that satisfied me. Ordinarily I might have chalked up the failure of the first couple of maps to the initial difficulties one always encounters in trying to see patterns in what appears to be a hopelessly scrambled scene. But in this instance, I think, in retrospect, that my initial frustrations were helpful, because they eventually taught me something about the neo-Oriental movements themselves. The fact that they could not be adequately studied with the normal methods of religious research reveals a critical facet of their reality. New wine bursts old wineskins. Something is going on that the standard methods and categories cannot explain.

For example, it first seemed sensible to me to divide the movements into groups corresponding to the original religious traditions to which they claimed to be related. I called this the "great traditions" approach. But after I had sorted out dozens of groups and movements into the three categories of Hindu, Buddhist and Muslim, plus a special category for Sikhs, it was obvious that I did not understand the neo-Oriental phenomenon any better than I had before. The trouble was that what I had learned about Oriental religions in my previous years of reading their sacred texts and investigating their history seemed to have little connection with what was happening in Benares-on-the-Charles. People who claimed to be immersed in Hindu practices often seemed amazingly unfamiliar with the Hindu scriptures. Enthusiastic Zen disciples sometimes seemed to know very little about Buddhist philosophy. I talked with Sufi dancers who, though they could chant phrases from the Koran for hours, while twirling to staccato drums, had no inkling of what the words actually meant. One perspiring young dervish dancer, who told me she had been born Jewish, seemed a little nonplussed when I pointed out to her that the Arabic words she had been chanting all evening meant "There is no God but Allah, and Mohammed is his prophet."

The problem presented by trying to map neo-Oriental movements in relation to the classical traditions is that of radical adaptation. Adaptation takes place whenever a religious tradition travels to a new setting, but it seems to have reached new limits of elasticity in America. The fact is that most of the movements I looked into have altered the Oriental original so profoundly that little can be gained by viewing them in the light of classical ancestry. They are far more "neo-" than "Oriental." Their leaders have stirred in such generous portions of the occult, of Christian images and vocabulary, and of Western organizational patterns, that trying to understand them in relation to an older "mother tradition" can ultimately be quite misleading. By now most of them are Western movements and are best understood as such.

It took a real Asian to show me just how far this Americanizing of

Oriental religions can go. The lesson came when a student from India, who is a Sikh, asked me for permission to write a research paper on a group of American young people who have organized the Boston branch of something called the 3 HO (Happy, Holy, Healthy Organization), which was started in America by a Sikh teacher named Yogi Bhajan. Sikhism is an independent Indian religious movement which was founded by Guru Nanak (A.D. 1469–1539), who was a vigorous opponent of ritualism and the caste system. It differs considerably from any form of Hinduism. Sikhs are easily recognizable because of their practice of not cutting their hair and of wearing large turbans and tiny wrist daggers. My turbaned Indian student spent several weeks getting to know these young American "Sikhs" well. He visited their commune, attended their services and talked with them at some length individually. Afterwards he wrote an informative and sympathetic paper on the group. He had learned to like them all very much. But he also concluded that their religious practice and ideas bore only the faintest resemblance to the Sikh teachings he had been reared on his whole life. Although the outward forms appeared similar—these young people also let their hair grow and wore turbans and wrist daggers—the meaning they attached to these practices turned out to be a mixture of astral metaphysics and esoteric lore completely unfamiliar to the young Indian, who wrote with good humor that his fellow Sikhs in India would be very surprised to learn that in the 3 HO movement the long hair is gathered on the forehead and covered by a turban to protect a particularly sensitive area of the brain from malignant cosmic rays. Obviously, studying this group in terms of classical Sikhism would cause more confusion than clarification.

So I junked the "great traditions" map of neo-Oriental religious movements. For a time my thinking seemed to lack any focus, and the task appeared impossible. Then I considered comparing the various movements in terms of *how much* they had adapted themselves to American culture. On one end of such a scale would stand those movements which almost seem to have been invented and distributed to appeal to the Western mind. Surely the Transcendental Meditation movement and the Divine Light Mission of the Maharaj Ji, which has its own Telex system and public-relations firm, would be located near this "high adaptation" border. These groups seem much more Western than Indian.

At the other edge one could place those movements which retain such a dense Oriental ethos that only a very small number of Westerners can find access to them. The Hare Krishna people, who not only wear distinctive costumes and try to learn Sanskrit, but also create a miniature Indian religious subculture, would belong at this nonadaptation end. Most groups range somewhere in the middle.

I soon discovered, however, that this degrees-of-adaptation scheme had its pitfalls, too. The problem is that there are various *kinds* of adaptation. Some movements conscientiously try to relate themselves to specifically Western modes of thought. Others seem to have been redesigned merely to increase their sales appeal. Some of the movements, the Zen Buddhist, for example, appear able to adapt very well in the realm of outside forms while retaining an impressive "inner" authenticity. Most of the movements are a hodgepodge of "authentic" and "adaptive" elements. So much for map number two.

It was not until after my own Turn East that I finally hit on an approach which seemed both faithful to the movements and helpful in interpreting them to other people. I had made my own Turn East for personal reasons. I had also made it with a host of internal reservations and for purposes that were quite different from the ones advanced by the teachers themselves. I was quite sure that mine was a most unusual case. I soon discovered, however, that it was not. Once I got to know them, it turned out that many of the people I met in these movements were there for personal reasons that often had little to do with the official teachings of their leaders. This was an astonishing and humbling discovery, but it did provide me with the clue I needed. I decided to avoid long descriptions of the movements or of the leaders or even of the ideas taught by the neo-Oriental groups. These are covered in other books anyway. I decided instead to focus on the people themselves. I decided to concentrate not on what the movements and their leaders claim to offer but on what the individuals who turn to them actually find. The two are often quite different. This approach finally seemed to make sense of my own experience. I had found something in one of the movements which was both relevant to my own life history and different from anything the literature had prepared me to find. I suspected the same was true for other people as well, and soon found that it was.

This book then is the record of a journey which began as a tour and turned into a pilgrimage. It describes what happened to an investigation that became a discovery. It recounts what took place as I moved from onlooker to actor, from describer to partaker. It concludes with a section on what it all taught me about the meaning of the Turn East for American society and for the American Christian churches in particular. Throughout the book I use the term "neo-Oriental" to indicate that I am not talking in these pages about the great Eastern traditions themselves, about Hinduism or Buddhism as they exist in their Asian settings. That would be another book. I am talking about the American versions of these traditions, which have begun, literally, to knock on our front doors, and about what they mean to the people who find something in them.

I have not seen Harry, Denise or Michael since the day they knocked at my door. I do not know if they still belong to the Hare Krishna group. They may not. In any case, I am grateful to them and I hope that wherever they now are in their pilgrimages, things are going well for them. They helped start me along a path which took a totally unexpected course. The journey I made, while helping me to appreciate more deeply what the East has to teach us today, also made me in some ways more Christian than I had been at the beginning. My guess is that the same thing, or something very similar, will happen to a lot of us before many more years go by.

* * *

TOWARD A SPIRITUALITY OF THE SECULAR

We need an authentic contemporary form of spirituality. We must find it, I believe, in our own tradition, not somewhere else. But where do we begin to look for it? In the Buddhist spiritual path the whole lineage of masters through whom the dharma has been conveyed is honored, but the most important masters are the founders of the line at one end and one's own master at the other—the classical source and the living teacher through whom the dharma comes to me. In the meditation hall of the Boston Dharmadatu, for example, where I sometimes go to meditate, there are four prominently displayed pictures. One is of the Buddha. One is of Avilokitsvara, the founder of the lineage. Another is the master of the current teacher; and the last is of the current master himself. I believe this same principle of genealogical selectivity also applies in Christianity. Next to Jesus and the first Christians, it is our direct mentors in the faith who play the most significant role. We should honor these godfathers and godmothers more than we usually do. Not only honor them but, in a sense, become their disciples. They constitute the critical link between ourselves and our past. Thus I believe that as late twentieth-century Christians trying to work out a viable spirituality, there are two principal historical sources to which we should look. They are the earliest period of our history and the most recent, the first Christian generations and the generation just before us.

I believe we should look principally to the primal sources and to the Christians nearest us, because the ransacking of other periods for help in working out a contemporary spirituality soon becomes either antiquarian or downright misleading. The Catholic nostalgia for medieval culture—shorn of pogroms and plagues, of course—seems to be fading now. So does the Protestant idealization of an allegedly more godly small-town Currier and Ives America. It is just as well. We cannot recycle either of these highly mythicized eons for our own spirituality today. When we try, we soon recognize that the saints of those and other in-between eras were different from us in ways that make it virtually impossible to turn to them as models. They were saints, in fact, because they successfully shaped a mode of religious existence that reverberated with *their* cultures as ours must with ours.

When we study the first few generations of Christians, however, we feel a strange shock of recognition. They are different from us too, but to our surprise we find we have more in common with them than we expected. The first practitioners of the Christ dharma, for example, lived in a pre-Christian culture. We live in a post-Christian culture. They had little to go on except the Law and the Prophets and their own experience of Jesus and the Spirit. They did not even have the New Testament, since they were, in fact, creating it. We are also feeling our way with few available guidelines. Since no one else has ever had to live out the Christian vision in a culture that was once allegedly "Christian" and no longer is, we must rely mainly on the same sources they did. They constituted the first generations after Christ. We are the first generations after Christendom. They were a tiny minority in a none-too-hospitable world. We are swiftly attaining the same status. They had to hammer out what they believed in the face of a cascade of varying religious world views that swirled not just around their congregations but through them. So must we. They worked on the task of defining the Christ dharma with what appears in retrospect to have been amazing skill and subtlety. They boldly absorbed religious practices and ideas—eucharist, baptism, logos philosophy—from their environment with what many theologians today would reject as blatant syncretism. We are free to be equally bold. They also drew lines and made distinctions that others recoil from today as arrogant, but they did so because they wanted their bewildered contemporaries to hear the Christ dharma with unmistakable clarity. They were convinced it was "good news," the best news, in fact, that anyone could possibly hear. We have the same responsibility—to make sure that what people hear is the gospel and not a culturally disfigured caricature. At no time in the nineteen centuries since Jesus has the Christian movement had more to learn than we do from the early formative years. Those wavering backsliders and ecstatic dreamers of Corinth, Rome, and Philippi are our brothers and sisters in a more important sense than are all the popes and preachers in between. Any authentic postmodern spirituality must begin by going back to the sources.

This does not mean we can neglect the long and variegated history of Christianity that stretches from the age of the Apostles and their followers to the beginning of our time. We need to know this period. But I think we should read it more as a cautionary tale than as a treasure house of available inspiration. We Christians today need to understand our history much as a compulsive neurotic needs to understand his—in order to see where we veered off, lost genuine options, glimpsed something we were afraid to pursue, or denied who we really are. Indeed, the most therapeutic accounts of our history for us today may not be the official ones, which sound defensive and self-serving, and often read like the religious equivalents of campaign biographies. What we need more are the neglected and repressed histories of what happened to the Montanists and the Cathari, to the Hussites and the Waldensians, to those who were branded as witches, heretics and schismatics. We need to reabsorb these people into our history today much as a neurotic person needs to reclaim parts of the self that have been denied or projected onto others. The outcasts of our history were burned or banished—at the time the social equivalent of repressing and projecting—but they have more to teach us now than their orthodox judges do. Their vision may have been too early for their time, but it is not too early for ours.

A trite adage avers that we must learn from history or suffer the pain of repeating it. The fact is that religious people often seem to read their history fired by a blind determination to repeat it at all costs. But it need not be so. We should study our Christian history not to suffuse it with sanctity but to discover how much of it has been excrescence and grotesquerie, to realize that we—like those earliest People of the Way—have got to start all over, or almost. If we are going to have a spirituality for our time, then we cannot borrow it from the East or resuscitate it from the past. We will have to forge it ourselves with the materials at hand, just as they did.

To some, the challenge to shape a spirituality that is at once biblical and contemporary will sound impossible of attainment, a herculean

task in an age without heroes. But the nub of what I have just said about
starting over is not so much that we must as that we can. Imagine a contemporary Christian spirituality rooted in the Hebrew prophets, the
Christ dharma and the creativity of the early Christians. How much
spurious encumbrance and religious nostalgia it could cut through.
If we need not stagger into the twenty-first century dragging the full
impedimenta of nineteen previous centuries, all things become possible. Then we can look to St. Thomas Aquinas (whose books, after
all, were publicly burned by his contemporaries), St. Francis (who was
nearly excommunicated), Martin Luther (who was) more as explorers who went ahead by first returning to the sources. We honor them
today not by mimicking Franciscan piety or perpetuating Thomist or
Lutheran theology, but by returning to the same sources and risking
the same willingness to innovate. We should be careful, above all, not
to sanctify this or that allegedly golden period of the Christian past
into another storied realm of Prester John, removed from us not by
space but by time. For Christians, just as the Kingdom of God never
was situated somewhere else in space, it also never lies in some bygone
era in time. It is coming, and in the midst of us, or it is nowhere at all.

I have said that in order to work out a spirituality for our postmodern
times we need to come to grips with two generations of Christians, the
first one and our own. Both are crucial. From the first Christians we
can learn how to be born again, how to flourish as a fringe group, how
to use whatever is at hand to celebrate the Spirit, feed the widows, and
make known the Christ. But beyond that, the early Christians cannot
teach us very much else. As we avoid mythicizing other periods of history, we should also spare the first Christians this fate. We have little
to learn from them, for example, about dislodging ensconced power,
taming the atom, preventing the poisoning of the sea, or how to talk
with life on other galaxies. They have less than nothing to teach us, it
would seem, about the proper role of women, the place of slaves, and
some other matters. Like us, they were fallible and finite. They made
mistakes we need not repeat. But, unlike anyone else, they were there
when it started; so it is to them we must go in order to start again.
They teach us not by *what* they did but by *how* they did it—with serenity and the zestful conviction that they could risk untried stratagems
because God would survive their mistakes. The Christians of the New
Testament period remind us that we have the freedom to create an
authentic contemporary form of spirituality. For the concrete shape
of that spirituality, however, we must turn to each other and to our

immediate predecessors in this first post-Christian century, the earliest post-Christendom Christians. Who are they?

For each of us, the list of near-contemporaries who have nourished our spirituality will be different. But I believe there is a growing consensus about a few figures to whom all, or nearly all, of us are drawn as our own gurus, as the first generation of postmodern Christians, whose exemplary lives and teachings help us eke out our own way of being. When I returned from Naropa for the last time, grateful for what I had learned but certain that my journey would now wend westward, I found myself turning to some of these gurus, or at least to their books, since some of them are already dead.

The first contemporary I turned to in my own attempt to construct a workable spirituality was Dietrich Bonhoeffer. This may come as no surprise, since Bonhoeffer, like myself, was a pastor and a theological writer. But there are others who fill this description. Why Bonhoeffer in particular? Maybe because he was a twentieth-century man par excellence, and yet a man of deep faith. The elegant, brilliant—perhaps even somewhat conceited—scion of a notable aristocratic family in Berlin, Bonhoeffer was a world traveler, a lover of the arts, a connoisseur of vintage wines and string quartets. An admirer of Gandhi, he nevertheless was able to sacrifice his philosophical pacifism in order to join the plot to assassinate Hitler, an act for which he was hanged in Flossenbürg concentration camp in April 1945, hours before the camp was liberated by the advancing American army.

Bonhoeffer speaks to my search for a contemporary spirituality because he too returned to the sources, the New Testament itself, and came to read it as an invitation to begin again. His *Letters and Papers from Prison* sketch in barest outline the dream of a Gospel freed at last from the remnants of obsolete metaphysics and constrictive pietism. Bonhoeffer tried until his dying day, although never successfully, to find a spirituality that would enable him to live in a world in which, as he put it, God had allowed himself to be edged out, but Christ could be met "at the center" where earthy life is thickest and most worldly. Bonhoeffer is an indispensable guru for those of us who, as he said, need to "live before God as though God did not exist"—which is what it must mean in part to be a Christian in the late twentieth century. His ideas of "anonymous Christianity" and "secret discipline," his reliance on a cadre of compatriots and his adamant refusal to let God be used to make up for human weakness or ignorance—all provide us with the building blocks we need to assemble the spirituality he never lived to develop himself.

Along with Bonhoeffer, the second guru I have turned to most often is that stubbornly indigestible Frenchwoman, Simone Weil. Roughly the contemporary of Bonhoeffer, Weil grew up in an educated if not a privileged family. Like him she was also raised on the classics but came later to yearn for nothing more than to serve God among the godless. As it happened, Weil's entry into the "godless world" was different from Bonhoeffer's and took her to a different kind of prison—the Renault automobile factory. But while working there she learned, as he did in the cellblock at Tegel, about affliction, courage and cowardice, and the tiny but infinitely valuable joys fellow prisoners and co-workers can share with one another. Like Bonhoeffer, Simone Weil hated the boundary the church had erected between believers and nonbelievers. Bonhoeffer dismantled the wall by insisting that the "true church" is nothing else than the world, claimed by God and inhabited by Christ. But Simone was born Jewish, raised a pagan and became a quasi-Marxist. She did not really have to go anywhere to be in the godless world; she was already there. Consequently, for Simone Weil, it was her refusal to be baptized into the church she believed in which signified her conviction that the Christ she loved dwelt also among scoffers and sinners.

It seems that all our postmodern gurus hold in common a firm conviction that to encounter the holy today one must move deeper *into* the "godless" world, not away from it. For all of them the narrow road to the Kingdom of God leads through the terrestrial city. No one has thought out this dimension of modern spirituality better than Amos Wilder in his essay on the "lay mystery" in which he says:

> Is it not true that Christianity has a need of recurrent baptism in the secular, in the human, to renew itself . . . to be saved over and over again from a spurious and phantom Christ? . . . Theology and witness today will be impoverished unless they take account of the secular man in all his dynamics; of the lay mystery that gives evidence of itself precisely in a desacralized world. (Wilder, *The New Voice*, 1969)

Dietrich Bonhoeffer and Simone Weil died within a year of each other. Neither ever read Wilder's words. But both dramatize how right he is. Both represent the rebaptism of the holy in the secular, a dawning awareness of the mystery that evidences itself in the desacralized world. Their paths into that mystery were different. Bonhoeffer's took him into the dark demiworld of conspiracy and espionage, and eventually to the gallows. Weil's took her into the often petty and acrimonious world of French intellectualism, and then to an early death in England caused in part by her refusal, though she was ill, to eat more than was permitted to her countrymen in occupied France. Both, however, died determined to share fully in whatever it means to embrace life in a century that believes it has left God behind, yet feels a hunger for a holiness that no churchly provision seems to feed. Both, from different sides, refused to allow the church wall to cut them off from a world where they believed Christ is present among the least likely.

There are other immediate forerunners of our own generation. My own hagiography includes one doughty octogenarian, Dorothy Day, the founder of the Catholic Worker movement, herself a pacifist and anarchist. Dorothy started her adult life by purposely getting arrested in New York City on Saturday nights so that she could share the tank with the prostitutes. She got herself in jail again about twenty years ago by calmly refusing to crawl into an air-raid shelter during a test alert. Her most recent brush with the authorities came when she sat serenely on a picket line with Mexican-American farmworkers in California and sweetly refused to move when ordered. On the other side of the violence/nonviolence spectrum, my calendar of saints includes Father Camilo Torres-Restrepo. Torres is the Colombian priest-sociologist who tried to organize a united people's political movement in his country in the 1960s, failed, and finally abandoned the effort to join a band of armed guerrillas in the hills. He was killed a few weeks afterward in a skirmish with the army. His body was never recovered. The authorities no doubt wanted to prevent a cult from growing up around his remains. Their caution was probably justified, for already a popular Latin American song declares that "where Camilo Torres fell, there sprung up a cross, not of wood but of light."

It might seem strange at first to include both Dorothy Day the pacifist and Camilo Torres the guerrilla in a single list of exemplars of present-day spirituality. But it should not be. What Dorothy and Camilo share, in addition to a certain personal quality of intensity modulated by irony, is the recognition that the world has taken the place of the wilderness as the classical place for testing and purification. Though they might not have approved of each other's methods, and though they came from different social strata (Torres-Restrepo remains one of Colombia's most aristocratic families), still I suspect Dorothy and Camilo would have sensed a strong cord between them. Both had a commitment to the struggle for bread, spiced by a winning tolerance for the weaknesses of the flesh, even in themselves. Dorothy Day bore a child out of wedlock. Camilo is said to have enjoyed the companion-

ship of women in a manner that did not seem commensurate with his
vows of celibacy, at least to some of his acquaintances. In other words,
both Dorothy Day and Camilo Torres broke from the cloying custom of
identifying piety with moralism. They both felt that personal holiness
is a wrestling match with the powers of evil in high places, and that this
duel must be fought today eye to eye with monstrous corporate forces.
Here is the indispensable insight any genuine contemporary spirituality must incorporate. It is the lay mystery.

I could add more names to my list of contemporary gurus. Martin Luther King has been idolized too soon by many (his birthday
is already a legal holiday in some states) and discredited too quickly
by others. But those who were stirred by his preaching and followed
him willingly through the streets and into the jails know that he had
begun to represent an engaging example of being fully Christian and
fully immersed in both the joy and the pain of the urban world. Other
politically committed Christians come to mind, such as Chief Albert
Luthuli and Bishop Helder Câmara. But for most Americans—black or
white—King still seems closer and more credible. And his assassination
at the age of thirty-nine reminds everyone that modern discipleship
still exacts its price.

Sometimes as I immerse myself in the lives and writings of these
recent Christian voyagers. I think about those writers on "spirituality"
who are constantly exhorting us to cultivate the habit of reading devotional literature. They may be right, but the problem is that material
published for such purposes today is almost universally admitted to
be indescribably bad. Maybe these men and women I have just been
discussing are in fact the ones whose lives and words should become
our "devotional reading" today. There is an essential link between a
style of spirituality and the kind of literature that feeds that style. The
trouble is that most allegedly "devotional" literature today is actually a
kind of religious pornography. This is true in a very literal sense. The
pornography of sex and violence qualifies as pornography because it
presents sex and violence unrelated to the concrete lives and circumstances of recognizable human beings. It is faceless. But so is much
of the ostensibly pious literature of our day. Here, as elsewhere, we
would do well to avoid the pornography (which like all porn eventually becomes tiresome) and steep ourselves instead in the "Lives of the
Saints"—our own saints.

The Kings and Weils and Bonhoeffers and Days feed us today for
more than one reason. First of all they are not simple shepherds, fish-
erfolk or unlettered peasants. They are urban, postmodern people like

us. They know about Darwin, Freud, Marx, contraception, imperialism and ennui. Their lives span not some idealized past, but our own fractured times. They carry all the alleged handicaps to belief that we do, yet they still manage to be Christians. Not only does the Christ dharma come to us through them, but the temporal proximity of their lives to ours makes the gospel more credible. Watching them, we realize that we must now find a way to live faithfully in a world that is already in some measure different from theirs, in which another generation will look to us for credible models of Christian existence.

It is important to realize that to learn from our forerunners we need not always agree with them. I cannot accept whole sections in some of their writings. Bonhoeffer, for example, often seems to me never to have shed his aristocratic hauteur, even in prison. Simone Weil occasionally let her spirited criticisms of the history of Israel cross the border into something close to antisemitism. I have other difficulties with Dorothy Day and Martin Luther King. But our disagreements with our godparents need not prevent us from learning from them. Also, we ought to remember that each of these twentieth-century disciples had a singular style. We learn from each of them individually, not as mere representatives of a vague construct such as "contemporary spirituality." Still, when one examines their lives and writings with care, some common threads do emerge, and these also help us in our quest. For example, of the exemplary figures I have mentioned probably only Simone Weil would have been conversant with the Buddhist belief that the essential pillars of any spiritual path must include dharma (teaching), *sangha* (community), and Buddha or guru (the teacher or model). But the more I learn about the people I have named above, the more the presence of these three pillars becomes evident. It is here that my own search for a viable spirituality intersects with theirs. I know that I, like them, need a clear teaching I can believe with both head and heart, a dharma. Also I, like them, need a company of trusted comrades who will chasten, criticize and support me, be there when I need them, go away when I don't want them, and expect the same from me. This is what the Buddhists call the *sangha*. And, as is evident from this chapter, I need *provisional* gurus, partial exemplars, models not so much to emulate as to argue with, learn from and—eventually—discard.

Does everyone need all three components? Some people may be able to get along today without one or more of the three. There are some, for example, who seem to thrive on dharma alone. They read Auden or Eliot, or Tillich or C. S. Lewis, depending on their tastes, and seem to need *sanghas* or gurus only in very minor ways. Their worship is often confined to Christmas Eve and Easter Sunday plus periodic feast days and *rites de passage*. These Christian intellectuals are an imposing breed, but their spirituality seems a little airy to me. Personally, I cannot survive as a Christian on pure dharma alone.

Another species of contemporary Christian relies mainly on the liturgy or congregation but seems generally untroubled by the question of what message this medium is conveying. Like the Sufi dancers I mentioned earlier, who did not know—or care much about—the meanings of the Arabic words they were chanting, there are *sangha* Christians who seem genuinely uninterested in the content of the dharma except in the most conventional terms. These are the people who can lose themselves in the mass, soar with real fervor into Bach anthems or traditional prayers, or give of themselves unsparingly in social-action projects, but whose eyes assume a glazed quality when asked to tell anyone why. Again, I am not denigrating this communal-liturgical mode of spirituality. There are times in the history of any religion—and this may be such a time—when the dharma may seem confused and opaque but the community of concern goes on, sharing the uncertainty but sharing nonetheless. *Sangha* spirituality should not be viewed with contempt by the more content-oriented. In our lonely era especially, when so many people are so starved for friendship, *sangha* without dharma must be expected. But for me, as indispensable as a liturgical community is, it is not enough.

Finally, there is a form of spirituality that survives without either *sangha* or dharma but relies entirely on the one-to-one dyad. Let us call it "guru spirituality." It is less familiar than the other two because it has, by its very nature, become ever less institutionalized and therefore less visible. It consists in the spiritual direction given by one person to another in relationships ranging from single counseling sessions to extended psychoanalysis. For some people it is all they ever get by way of spiritual direction and nurture. We often hear today about the similarity between what a good guru and a skilled therapist can do for a person. There is much truth in the comparison. But there is much that is misleading in it too. In our culture the therapist operates, at least ostensibly, without either a dharma or a *sangha*. Even if his clients constitute a group, as they do in some forms of counseling, the group usually has few other characteristics of a *sangha*; and if there is a teaching it is some mixture of psychological theory and popular humanism that the best practitioners concede will just not do as real dharma.

Once more, it is important for dharma and *sangha* Christians not to be too severe with those who rely on some Westernized kind of guru in the person of a counselor or analyst. Since our own religious tradition, apart from a few scattered novice masters, is so deficient in providing spiritual directors, it is not surprising that hundreds of thousands of people have turned, often at great personal expense and sacrifice, to their secular equivalents.

But again, it is just not enough—at least for me, and I suspect for most people. All the most effective counselors or analysts can do is to help their clients to be able to make decisions on their own. They help bring about a condition in which the unconscious underbrush is hacked away and the person is ready to start making choices unimpeded by invisible encumbrances. But this is just the moment when both the Word and the Sacramental Community have their greatest importance. A spirituality reduced to the master-disciple or therapist-client scale is surely better than nothing at all. But because it lacks both dharma and *sangha*, it cannot suffice, not in the long run.

What, then, can our near contemporary spiritual masters teach us about *sangha*, dharma, and guru, the three pillars of any spirituality? To answer this question we have to probe their lives as well as their writings, for none of them dealt with this question in just these terms. But even a cursory examination of how they lived will quickly reveal the pillars.

Sangha: No one who reads Dorothy Day's column "On Pilgrimage" can possibly miss noticing that it reads almost like a travel diary and address book:

> It is a beautiful, sunny day, midwinter in Tivoli. No wind to chill the bones, and the children, those who are not napping, are out playing on the lawn. Only Tanya goes to school and she will be home soon.
>
> The men are hauling wood down from the hillside, clearing out dead trees, and Chuck Matthei and Charles Goodding have brought loads of driftwood from the Hudson. . . . There is no ice yet, but I just saw a wagon load of driftwood, tree trunks and logs go by the window towed by John Filliger's tractor. . . . The repairs of the ceiling were accomplished by two students from Iowa, who spent their strength and the three hundred dollars donated by their friends and by Jean's parents, Al and Monica Hagan. . . . (Day, *The Catholic Worker*, December 1976)

The rest of this column is studded, as are all her books and columns, with the names of people, living and dead, and places, near and far. For Dorothy Day the mystical body of Christ is not very mystical at all.

It is not even "The Catholic Worker" as an organization. It is the Joes and Marcias and Gordons she visits, eats with, travels with, and prays for. Dorothy Day's spirituality is utterly dependent on a *sangha*. Without it, her life and witness would be unimaginable.

The same centrality of the *sangha* principle holds for Bonhoeffer. During the early Hitler years, Bonhoeffer was deprived by the Nazis of any opportunity to teach or preach legally; so he organized an underground seminary. But, unlike a university theological school, Bonhoeffer's seminary-in-exile in Finkenwalde was a closely knit household where students and professors lived together and shared everything, including the constant danger of a Gestapo raid (which eventually came, causing the closing of the school). After the dispersal of the Finkenwalde brotherhood, Bonhoeffer expended long hours composing letters by the dozens to the students and colleagues who had been drafted into the army. But he did not find such companionship again until his brother-in-law, Hans von Dohnanyi, initiated him into the secret cabal that was planning to kill Adolf Hitler. Bonhoeffer's arrest on another charge in April 1943 deprived him of these friends too. It was then that, much to his own surprise, he began to discover a *sangha* among both the political prisoners and the common offenders with whom he shared the gray routine of incarceration. In his *Life Together*, based on the Finkenwalde years, Bonhoeffer writes explicitly about the indispensability of a disciplined supportive circle. Though he is sometimes seen as a lonely and isolated man—which he often was—I still believe Bonhoeffer's spirituality could have emerged only from his *sangha*.

In the individualistic religious climate of our time we have something to learn from the fact that all the godparents I have mentioned attached a great importance to *sangha*. Martin Luther King's Southern Christian Leadership Conference multiplied local branches during the 1960s and provided a web of confidantes and phone numbers for hundreds of civil-rights activists at a time when official church bodies often looked askance at pickets and demonstrators. And it supplied a *sangha* for King himself. Only Simone Weil, among our godparents, seems to be the exception. Although attracted by the Catholic Church, she never joined it. In fact she resisted joining anything. My own conviction is, however, that this resistance to organizations is not an expression of Weil's rejection of the idea of *sangha* but rather a mark of the earnestness with which she sought it. In her little book *The Mysticism of Simone Weil*, Marie-Magdeleine Davy attributes the striking lack of any corporate quality in Weil's spirituality to her sometimes overly zealous pursuit of self-denial and solitude. Weil often consciously deprived herself of just what she wanted most, not to gain some other goal but in order to share in the historic suffering of humankind. Her rejection of organizations was both a self-discipline and a criticism of the artificiality of the solidarity proffered. "She rejected [the collective]," Davy writes, "with a violence which is only explicable through the purity and intransigence of her search for the holy. . . ." She was such a perfectionist that she never found the friendship she so obviously longed for.

Dharma: The most striking thing to me about our godparents' understanding of the Teaching is that no one of them is a "liberal." They all have more or less orthodox theologies, so much so, in fact, that this makes them appear radical in light of the dominant interest of modern theology in modernizing and accommodating.

Bonhoeffer, for example, was often considered a maverick by his scholarly colleagues. Like Karl Barth, the leading "neo-orthodox" theologian of his time, whom Bonhoeffer admired—though with reservations—he rejected most of the liberal German theologians' efforts to accommodate Christianity to modern culture. Thus, in one of his better-known letters, Bonhoeffer sharply criticized Rudolf Bultmann, a fellow theologian, for the "typical liberal reduction process," he used in interpreting the New Testament. Bonhoeffer asserted that he was of the view that ". . . the full content, including the mythological concepts, must be maintained." The New Testament "is not a mythological garbing of the universal truth; this mythology (resurrection and so on) is the thing itself—but the concepts must be interpreted in such a way as not to make religion a precondition of faith. . . . Not until that is achieved," Bonhoeffer concludes, "will, in my opinion, liberal theology be overcome."

Although Bonhoeffer often seems to be criticizing his colleagues for being too timid, what he really was striving for was a devastating rejection of all conventional Christianity, a rejection based on a bold reappropriation of the most thoroughgoing reading of the Incarnation. His point was that since God had already joined the human race irrevocably in Christ, no further accommodation was needed. The ultimate accommodation, so to speak, had already taken place. Bonhoeffer's ultra-orthodoxy made him a radical among the liberals.

Exactly the same can be said, in their own ways, for both Dorothy Day and Simone Weil. Dorothy Day's discomfort with some aspects of the Vatican Two "*aggiornamento*" is well known. She has never advocated women priests, a vernacular Mass, or even a rethinking of infallibility. It is said that she once scolded Father Daniel Berrigan for not treating the host with sufficient deference during a war-protest Mass. She describes herself as an angry but loyal daughter of the church, and she has been able to coax so many people toward a more radical social stance in part because she has remained so conservative in other respects. Like Bonhoeffer and Simone Weil, who was also no modernist, Dorothy Day demonstrates how a genuinely orthodox dharma can provide a more cutting, critical perspective on the world than a grossly accommodated one. Our other godparents have discovered the same thing. Even Martin Luther King, who came closer to being a liberal theologian in some of his writings than the others do, was at his best when his preaching and protest were grounded in the Hebrew prophets and the spiritual tradition of the Black Baptist church.

Guru: Finally, all our immediate forerunners had a strong sense of the role of the spiritual friend, the Christian *kalyanamitra*. Dorothy Day hardly writes a paragraph without mentioning the name of Peter Maurin, her own teacher and example. She not only looked to him for guidance and inspiration while he was alive, but returns to his *Easy Essays* and his memory now that he is dead. Simone Weil carried on a lifelong correspondence with the people she met whom she considered her spiritual guides. Bonhoeffer's most memorable book is not a book at all but a posthumous collection of the letters he sent from prison, many of them to his lifelong friend and colleague Eberhard Bethge.

Throughout the *Letters and Papers from Prison* Bonhoeffer reveals the trust and confidence he feels for Bethge. "They keep on telling me," he writes from his cell on April 30, 1944, "that I am 'radiating so much peace around me,' and that I am 'ever so cheerful.' Very flattering, no doubt, but I'm afraid I don't always feel like that myself. You would be surprised and perhaps disturbed if you knew how my ideas on theology are taking shape. This is where I miss you most of all, for there is no one else who could help me so much to clarify my own mind." On June 5 he writes, "I don't see any point in my not telling you I have occasionally felt the urge to write poetry. You are the first person I have mentioned it to. So I'm sending you a sample, because I think it's silly to have any secrets from you. . . ." Other similar passages appear in letter after letter. Bethge was Bonhoeffer's *kalyanamitra*, though neither man knew the word.

Simone seems to have placed the same kind of confidence, at least for a while, in her adviser and correspondent Father Perrin. "I owe you an immense debt of gratitude. Sometimes, through my friendship, I have given some human beings an easy opportunity of wounding me. Some have taken advantage of it, either frequently or infrequently, some consciously, some unconsciously, but all have done it at one time or another. But you never."

Martin Luther King, Jr., was more fortunate than most. He grew up in a tradition in which the role of spiritual master still obtains, at least for preachers. It continues in the apprenticeship practice of the black churches, the custom by which aspiring young pastors work closely with an older pastor, not just learning how to preach but also being schooled in a religious way of life. All of our predecessors in the faith had their gurus or, more importantly, they knew how to discover the *kalyanamitra* in friends and co-workers, how to seek personal guidance and criticism not only from books, but also from loving persons. We need to do the same.

Where does this leave me in my personal quest for a spiritual path and discipline today? My goal is summed up in a quotation from one of my oldest teachers, Professor Emeritus Amos Wilder. "If we are to have any transcendence today," writes Wilder, in the essay on the lay mystery to which I alluded earlier, ". . . it must be in and through the secular. . . . If we are to find any grace it is to be found in the world and not overhead. . . ." I think Wilder is right and that to uncover this "lay mystery" I need a "worldly" form of spirituality—one that includes a group of actual flesh-and-blood human beings who will nourish me without extricating me from society. I need a gospel that makes sense not of some special religious realm but of the actual day-to-day world I live in. And I need guides, *kalyanamitras*—both living and dead—to whom I can apprentice myself. In my case the *sangha* is a struggling little church in my neighborhood, a place where I must contend with younger and older people some of whose views I appreciate and others of whose ideas I find intolerable. The music is often stirring, sometimes off key. The preaching is uneven. There is never enough money for the oil, despite numerous potluck suppers. How often I have been tempted to jettison this all-too-human little freckle on the Body of Christ and stay home on Sunday with better music (on the hi-fi) and better theology (from the bookshelf). But I do not. A voice within me keeps reminding me that I need these fallible human confreres, whose petty complaints never quite overshadow the love and concern underneath. This precarious little local church may not be the ideal Christian *sangha* for our time, though it has done more to become one than many other parishes have. Still, it exists. It is where Word becomes flesh, and it offers something of what a *sangha* should. I do not believe any modern Christian, whether a returnee from the East or not, can survive without some such grounding in a local congregation. Although this may require vast patience and tenacity, I see no other way it can be done. "One Christian," as Péguy said, "is no Christian."

As for the Christian dharma today, I have already indicated my decision to focus on the biblical roots. This is just what I do. When I was invited to teach the one course on Christianity at the Naropa Institute, I consciously decided to make it a course on Jesus and the beginnings of Christianity. I chose this topic as much for myself as for my students. I still believe there is no "spiritual reading" that can compare with Isaiah, Amos, Mark, and John, especially when they are read in tandem with the diaries of our contemporary saints. Admittedly, in concentrating on the biblical dharma as normative, there are serious problems today. One is residual American fundamentalism, which distorts the Bible into a magical oracle. The other is a kind of arid scholarship that details every critical theory about a text but never asks what it would mean to live by it. My struggle with the dharma will continue to concentrate on the sources themselves and on their most recent appropriations. I strongly suspect that people who are looking elsewhere will eventually come to this view too.

Admittedly, the resources I have catalogued here for constructing a postmodern spiritual discipline sound unpromising—the shards and clinkers of a disintegrating culture, the remnants of previously taken paths, the often preoccupied and theologically unsophisticated people around me. But it is all I have. And it is all anyone has today. If we look for something else, or somewhere else, we will look, I fear, in vain. But I hope that does not discourage us. As a first-century *kalyanamitra* once wrote to a confused little urban *sangha* that was trying to understand a dharma that had recently come from the East, ". . . the divine weakness is stronger than man's strength. To shame the wise, God has chosen what the world counts weakness. He has chosen things low and contemptible, mere nothings, to overthrow the existing order" (1 Corinthians 1:26-28).

8

Religion in the Secular City (1984)

These selections are taken from Religion in the Secular City: Toward a Postmodern Theology *(New York: Simon & Schuster, 1984), 11-24, 175-80, 205-15, 262-68.*

RELIGION RETURNS TO THE SECULAR CITY

Not many years ago the world was full of dire prophecies about the future of religion. The great "sea of faith" which Matthew Arnold had once watched receding with a roar at Dover Beach seemed to have reached such a low ebb that it would never return again. We were entering, it was said, into a post-Christian era. The influence of religious institutions and traditional forms of piety were in irreversible decline. The distinguished Italian sociologist Sabino Acquaviva wrote in his book *The Decline of the Sacred in Industrial Society*, "From the religious point of view, humanity has entered a long night that will become darker and darker with the passing of the generations; and of which no end can yet be seen."[1]

Not everyone viewed the prospect of a religionless future with the same feelings. Preachers bewailed it, especially the erosion of spiritual influence on public morals. The latter-day children of the Enlightenment on the other hand greeted it as a liberation from ignorance and credulity. Theologians began to ponder the meaning of the "death of God."

Even the United States, which because of the strong religious influences on its early history had stood out as an exception to the global sweep of secularization, no longer appeared to be exempt. Religion was persisting here, the scholars declared, but only because it had settled for a much reduced place in the sun.

---

1. Sabino Samele Acquaviva, *The Decline of the Sacred in Industrial Society* (New York: Harper and Row, 1979), p. 201.

Students of religion were of the nearly unanimous opinion that whatever religion remained would have no connection with the public political realm. It would be restricted completely to the sphere of personal and family values. In a widely heralded article published in 1972, the American sociologist Richard Fenn said that here, as in all modern industrial societies, ". . . a normative order based on religious beliefs and values is no longer possible." The fact that political systems in such societies as ours had achieved "considerable independence from political control," he added, might well "reduce to near zero the level of interdependence between social factors and religious change." Consumption and political participation were what people wanted now, Fenn said; therefore, "Cultural integration on the level of religious beliefs and values is . . . under these conditions no longer possible or even necessary for the maintenance of motivation and order."[2]

What Fenn and his colleagues were arguing was that secularization does not actually drive religion from modern society completely. Rather, it fosters a type of private religion that has no real function for the society as a whole. In other words, despite the upsurge of gurus and charismatic revivals, the link between religion and the public domain—politics—was gone forever.

When theologians heard these forecasts about the decline of religion they naturally began to speculate about the theological and ethical implications. It did not seem premature or irreverent to think about how God and faith and morality could be envisioned in a world in which at least traditional forms of religion were disappearing. The once puzzling ideas of the German theologian Dietrich Bonhoeffer about a "world come of age" and a "nonreligious interpretation of the Gospel" now appeared more plausible.[3] By the late 1970s and early 1980s, however, the ebb tide appeared to be turning. Religion seemed to be staging a comeback.

One particularly powerful symbol of the sea change occurred on January 26, 1979. On that day a green-and-white Alitalia DC-10 landed in Mexico City and the newly elected Pope John Paul II climbed down the stairs and knelt to kiss the runway. I was teaching in Mexico City at the time, and I watched the pontiff's arrival on a tiny color TV screen with some friends in the San Angel section of the city. None of them found it all that significant. But I saw something click into place, the

---

2. Richard F. Fenn, "A New Sociology of Religion," *Journal for the Scientific Study of Religion* II, 1 (March 1972), 17.

3. See Dietrich Bonhoeffer, *Letters and Papers from Prison* (rev. ed.; New York: Macmillan, 1967).

kind of sharp image that suddenly appears when a kaleidoscope is turned one more notch. Why I thought I discerned an epiphany when my companions saw only a middle-aged prelate kissing some asphalt will take a little explaining.

Mexico City—at least legally and constitutionally—is one of the most secular cities in the world. It is the capital of Mexico, and since the constitution of 1861 Mexico has been an officially secular state. Its laws controlling religion are severe. Parochial schools are technically illegal. It is against the law to wear a Roman collar or any other clerical costume on the streets. All religious properties, including church buildings, are the legal property of the state. Holding religious ceremonies including masses, in public, is prohibited. Diego Rivera's vivid murals depicting bloated priests and armored conquistadores maiming Indians and plundering their gold embellish the walls of official government buildings. On the surface, Mexico City is the embodiment of a sprawling, modern secular megalopolis, one of the largest in the world.

But underneath it all does Mexico City, like New York or maybe even Moscow or Beijing, conceal some artesian religious quality, barely covered by its veneer of official secularity? Does some subcutaneous spirituality still animate not only its people but millions of others all over the modern world despite the enormous impact made by public education, scientific technology, urbanization, and other allegedly secularizing forces? Furthermore, is there something in the air that has brought this dormant piety to the surface? Has the sleeping giant of traditional religion awakened? For me, the coming of Pope John Paul II, the head of the oldest and largest Christian church in the world, to what may be the world's largest "secular city" posed all these questions in a single flash.

In their own way, Mexican politicians were impressed by the Pope's arrival, too. Whatever its religious significance, for them the papal journey was also a *political* event. It made them jittery. Admittedly there seemed to be some reason for the apprehensiveness. Just a few weeks earlier another religious leader, the Ayatollah Khomeini, had returned to an allegedly secular country and displaced the whole government. No one thought John Paul II had that in mind, but officials knew that the Catholic bishops in Brazil had become the main opposition to the military regime there. They were aware that nuns and priests were cooperating with insurgent movements in Central America, just across the border. The new Bishop of Rome was an unknown quantity. The night before his arrival a queasy minor official told me he had dreamed that the Pope stood up in his open limousine, pointed to the president's palace, and said, "Seize it!" and the crowd had drawn machetes and obeyed.

The Pope of course gave no such command. But from any politician's perspective, his visit was an enviable success. Millions of people lined the Avenida de la Reforma, named, ironically, for the secular Reform of 1861 which had resulted in the expropriation of the church's property, to cheer and wave. With blithe disregard for the anticlerical laws, John Paul II appeared everywhere in resplendent white papal garb, and celebrated mass in public. Watching the huge crowds, members of the ruling party could not help but reflect on the efforts needed to cajole even small and unenthusiastic groups into attending their appearances. As the departing Pope's plane circled the city on its way back to Rome and thousands of Mexicans flashed *adiós* with tiny hand mirrors (the idea of an enterprising local glassware dealer), one could almost hear the collective sigh of relief that went up from the Palacio Nacional.

The surprising weight attached by the local politicians to the visit of a priest from Cracow who commands no divisions highlighted another issue. Not only are we witnessing a resurgence of traditional religion in the world, this resurgence has an undeniable—if still indeterminate— *political* significance.

The ambiguous character of this political dimension of the new revival of religion was underlined for me by two visits I made in the summer of 1982. While making a return trip to Mexico in July, I stopped in Lynchburg, Virginia, to acquaint myself with the work of the Reverend Mr. Jerry Falwell, minister of the Thomas Road Baptist Church there and the founder and president of Moral Majority, Inc. During my brief stay I attended the Bible Study Hour and the regular Sunday morning service at Thomas Road Baptist Church. I visited Liberty Baptist College and Seminary, also founded and headed by Mr. Falwell. I inspected the imposing headquarters of the Old Time Gospel Hour, Mr. Falwell's widely viewed national network TV program. I talked at some length to the staff members of Moral Majority, Inc., about their efforts to enlist hundreds of thousands of Americans into bringing a conservative influence to bear on public policy in America. Mr. Falwell himself served as my affable host for a luncheon at the local Hilton Hotel restaurant. I left Lynchburg with the impression that I had met a man who personifies the most conservative side of the return of religion—both religiously and politically—one was likely to find anywhere in the world today.

A few weeks after my visit to Lynchburg I attended Sunday mass at the venerable old cathedral in the city of Cuernavaca, Mexico. The Bishop of Cuernavaca, then in his final weeks of service before his retirement, was Don Sergio Mendez Arceo, one of the most prominent voices of the "Catholic left" in Latin America. The guest preacher for the day was Father Ernesto Cardenal, the controversial priest, poet, and symbol of Christian participation in revolution. A few months later Pope John Paul II, during a visit to Nicaragua, would publicly scold Cardenal for remaining at his post as his country's Minister of Cultural Affairs. Standing next to the high altar that day in August, however, Cardenal did not appear to be a man who would be much affected by scolding. He spoke with great feeling about how Christians were becoming active in the struggle for justice all over the continent, especially in El Salvador and Guatemala. Within the span of a couple weeks I had touched down on the two most antipodal outposts of Christianity to be found today: Jerry Falwell and Ernesto Cardenal represent the polar antitheses of the Christian world.

Falwell and Cardenal are not merely mirror images of each other. They are enormously different men temperamentally, and they occupy different places in the two wings of the religious movements they represent. Nonetheless, there are some intriguing similarities. Both underwent life-changing religious conversions as young men. Both moved from a deep suspicion of the world of politics toward finding themselves immersed in it. Both are charismatic figures whose persuasiveness springs more from personal conviction than from polished eloquence. Both take positions that sometimes embarrass their more cautious colleagues. Still, Falwell and Cardenal embody both the return of religion and its powerful but contradictory political significance as well as anyone could. Taken together, the question they pose is this: What is the meaning of the present dramatic reappearance of religion as a potent political force all over the world just when the experts had thought it was all over?

Subsequent events in the world have made this question increasingly more pressing. Shortly after the Pope's visit to Mexico a band of Shiite Muslims seized the American Embassy in Tehran and held a number of its staff as hostages. Back home the average American was not only angry but confused. Having heard for years that our nation's enemies were godless atheists, they found it hard to understand bearded mullahs who called the United States "Satan" and were depicted in the news as religious fanatics. Then, in December 1980, four American Roman Catholic women missionaries were shot to death in El Salvador, not, it appeared, either by godless Communists or by fanatic Muslims but by soldiers carrying rifles supplied to them through the ruling junta by the United States government. Religion and politics were not only being mixed but in highly unfamiliar ways.

Every week new evidence suggested something was astir. The Roman Catholic bishops of Canada issued a sharp criticism of their government's economic policies, claiming discrimination against the poor. The *New York Times Magazine* carried a cover article about the Protestant and Catholic churches of South Korea and their strong public opposition to the regime there.[4] The Catholic Bishop of Manila called on the businessmen of his nation to join him in opposing the Marcos government. Even in Communist countries religion appeared to be assuming a more prominent public role. In Poland, members of the Solidarity trade union movement, which was repressed by a martial law decree in December 1981, sang hymns at their rallies and carried pictures of the Blessed Virgin on marches. The leaders, including Lech Walesa, appeared to be motivated by Roman Catholic values. Visitors to the USSR reported a growing interest in traditional Russian Orthodoxy among young people and intellectuals. And in February 1982 nearly four thousand youthful East Germans gathered in a Protestant Church in Dresden to listen to talks by two Lutheran pastors in support of European nuclear disarmament. They met under a banner stretched across the baroque organ pipes that bore the motto "Frieden schaffen ohne Waffen" (build peace without weapons), a phrase which directly contradicts the official East German government's position expressed by the slogan "Peace Must Be Armed."[5]

In Western Europe also, once thought of as the epicenter of secularism, churches reappeared in the public realm. A popular movement against nuclear weapons suddenly came into world visibility in 1981, and the churches—of Holland and West Germany especially—were at its core. Laurens J. Hogebrink, a Protestant pastor, often spoke for the Dutch Interchurch Peace Council. The British campaign for nuclear

4. Henry Scott Stokes, "Korea's Church Militant," *New York Times Magazine*, November 28, 1982, p. 67.

5. For descriptions of the role of the Church in Poland and in East Germany see Syzmon Chodak, "People and the Church Versus the State: The Case of the Roman Catholic Church in Poland," in *Occasional Papers on Religion in Eastern Europe* II, 7 (November 1982), 26; James Will, "Reflections on the Role of the Catholic Church in Mediating the Present Crisis in Poland," in *Occasional Papers on Religion in Eastern Europe* II, 6 (September 1982), 20; Mary Lukens, "The Churches in the German Democratic Republic: Notes of an Interested Observer," in *Occasional Papers on Religion in Eastern Europe* II, 1.

disarmament was led by a Roman Catholic priest, Monsignor Bruce Kent. Even in Sicily, Protestants and Catholics were working together to oppose the stationing of nuclear missiles in the small city of Comiso.

In the United States the new vitality of religion in the public sphere assumed a more ambiguous form. Falwell had organized Moral Majority, Inc., in 1979, and in the fall of 1980 he and other TV evangelists—strongly hinting that they had helped elect Ronald Reagan President—began to push vigorously for government action on restoring prayer to the schools, banning pornography, outlawing abortion, and controlling what they considered immoral themes in the mass media. By the fall of 1982, however, none of these goals had been attained, and nearly all candidates running on these issues lost their electoral contests. The question of how much influence political fundamentalism would have on American society remained unanswered.

Church members also began to notice a renewed series of attacks on the National Council of Churches and the World Council of Churches. They were often orchestrated by a politically conservative group called the Institute for Religion and Democracy, and their polemics focused on certain activities of these ecumenical bodies that their critics asserted did not reflect the ideas of the average person in the pew.[6] But there no longer seemed to be a one-to-one correlation between conservative theology and conservative politics. In 1978 an organization appeared called Evangelicals for Social Action, which presented itself as offering "education, support, and analysis toward biblical social change." Its statement of purpose declares:

> We are unique in that our agenda for social change is not derived from liberal or conservative social agendas, but from the Scriptures.[7]

Today ESA describes itself as adhering to a "pro-life" stance on "such issues as peace and nuclear disarmament; the rights of the unborn; wealth and poverty; the sacredness of the family; the elimination of racial and sex discrimination; human rights at home and abroad; and the protection of the environment." The Sojourners Fellowship

6. See *Christianity and Democracy*, issued by the Institute on Religion and Democracy, 1835 K St. N. W., Washington, D.C. 20006. For a critical discussion of this group see the March 21, 1983, *Christianity and Crisis* XLIII, 4, articles by Leon Howell, Wayne Cowan, and the editors. See also Cynthia Brown, "The Right's Religious Red Alert," *The Nation*, March 12, 1983, 301.

7. "Evangelicals for Social Action" (pamphlet), 25 Commerce St. S.W., Washington, D.C. 20005.

in Washington, D.C., an influential group of theologically conservative but politically radical Christians, resembles ESA but puts more emphasis on direct action, pacifism, and the development of new forms of spiritual community.[8]

Evangelicals in fact were emerging as a "third force" between the vociferous fundamentalist and the establishment-liberal wings of American Protestantism. As they did, they were leaving behind the posture which at least since the 1930s had made theological and political conservatism synonymous. Dr. Billy Graham, once viewed by most Americans as a streamlined version of sawdust-trail revivalism and a stalwart defender of conservative causes, had assumed a new role in his mature years. He was becoming a kind of church statesman, mediating between the various theological currents, and a vigorous critic of nuclear armament. Against the advice of the State Department he made a highly publicized visit to Moscow in June 1982, both to preach and to attend a peace conference. He had become "ecumenical," with only the far-fundamentalist right and the ultraliberal left continuing to regard him with suspicion.[9]

In 1982 the role of the American Roman Catholic bishops in the formation of public policy also took a dramatic turn. Issuing a draft of a pastoral letter on war and peace that was highly critical of American nuclear weapons policy, the bishops served notice that Catholics were not interested merely in abortion or the institutional problems of parochial schools. Monsignor Vincent Yzermans, who once served as information director for the U.S. Catholic hierarchy, wrote in November 1981:

> Something is stirring in the Roman Catholic Church in the United States that portends an explosion between church and state that will make the abortion issue, the school-aid controversy and the tax-exempt status of churches look like a child's sparkler on the Fourth of July. Stated simply, the church in the United States is becoming a "peace" church. . . . This revolution is being waged painfully in the hearts and minds of Catholic thinkers and leaders. . . . The American bishops are shouldering their responsibility of leading this revolution, at times to the chagrin and vocal opposition of their flocks.[10]

8. See *Sojourners Magazine*.

9. The principal voice of the most representative evangelical body is *Christianity Today* (465 Gunderson Drive, Carol Stream, Ill. 60187).

10. Vincent Yzermans, "The Catholic Revolution," *Christianity and Crisis*

Monsignor Yzermans emphasizes the Catholic bishops' collective support for nuclear disarmament. Some individual bishops have gone further. Archbishop Raymond Hunthausen of Seattle announced that he would withhold the portion of his income tax going for military purposes, and Bishop Leroy Matthiesen of Amarillo, Texas, has asked Catholics who work in any phase of nuclear weapons development to consider seeking employment elsewhere. In addition the bishops have sharply criticized the U.S. policy of supplying arms to repressive Central American regimes. Although the "explosion" Yzermans predicts has not occurred, both the Vice President and the Secretary of State have publicly questioned the bishops' policies.

By the early 1980s it had begun to look as though a revival of religion, one with important implications for political life, was underway everywhere. The old secular city just wasn't what it used to be. The evidence pointed to a resurrection of religion, and of traditional and theologically orthodox religion at that, worldwide. It appeared to be a revival, furthermore, which was not restricting itself to the sanctuary but was reaching into the barricades and the corridors of power. But there are still gnawing questions. Is it simply that the dirge was played prematurely? Is the death of God, or at least of religion, simply taking longer than expected? Are we witnessing a genuine revival of traditional religion, or is the new religious wave a creature of the mass media, or the fevered bloom on the cheek of a dying consumptive? Is it no more than a cynical misuse of religion for extraneous purposes? If there is a genuine spiritual upsurge, why has it assumed such a political stance, and why are the political postures so disparate—revolutionary in Latin America; democratic in Poland; mixed in the United States?

In 1965, much under the influence of Bonhoeffer's theology and greatly concerned about what the expected decline of traditional religion might do to the relevance of Christianity, I wrote a book called *The Secular City*.[11] In it I drew upon the anticultic preaching of the Hebrew prophets and Jesus' opposition to the priestly establishment of his own day to argue that religion is not always and everywhere a good thing, and that secularization might not be the unmitigated scourge it was often seen to be. I suggested that instead of bemoaning the waning

---

XLII, 3 (March 1, 1982), 39. For an interesting attempt to reclaim traditionally conservative symbols for a more progressive political purpose see Joe Holland, *Flag, Faith and Family: Rooting the American Left in Everyday Symbols* (Center for Concern, c. 1979, 3700 Thirteenth Street N. E., Washington, D.C. 20017).

11. Harvey Cox, *The Secular City: Urbanization and Secularization in Theological Perspective* (New York: Macmillan, 1965).

of ecclesial power or the disappearance of the sacral, Christians should concentrate instead on the positive role they could play in the modern secular world. I still believe in that thesis. The problem is that the world of declining religion to which my earlier book was addressed has begun to change in ways that few people anticipated. A new age that some call the "postmodern" has begun to appear. No one is quite sure just what the postmodern era will be like, but one thing seems clear. Rather than an age of rampant secularization and religious decline, it appears to be more of an era of religious revival and the return of the sacral. No one talks much today about the long night of religion or the zero level of its influence on politics.

The current reappearance of religion does not, however, make the message of *The Secular City* obsolete. It remains true that biblical faith is often critical of human religiousness. The Hebrew prophets inveighed against solemn assemblies. The religious authorities of his day saw Jesus as a dangerous threat. If secularization was not always bad, religion is not always good. If the challenge modern theology took on was to define and defend the faith in an era of religious decline, the task of a postmodern theology is to interpret the Christian message at a time when the rebirth of religion, rather than its disappearance, poses the most serious questions.

This is a book about the unexpected return of religion as a potent social force in a world many thought was leaving it behind. It is about the place religion has come to occupy in the modern age and about the role it should play in the postmodern world presently coming to birth. I write as a theologian. In doing so I accept that theology is an old-fashioned discipline that deals not just with what is but with what ought to be. Clearly, theologians possess no monopoly on the study of religion. Historians, sociologists, psychologists, psychiatrists roam freely through its sacred precincts as well. Still, there is a difference. When anthropologists and sociologists move as they often do from description to prescription, from telling us what religion is to advising us what it ought to be, then we must ask: What normative vision of religion and what plumbline of its proper relation to the secular world inform their prescription? Where do they get their oughts and shoulds? As soon as they begin to answer such questions we will have left social science and crossed over into theology.

Theology is unapologetically prescriptive. It does not claim to be value-free or neutral. Theologians draw upon the beliefs of a particular tradition to suggest a course of action, an appropriate response, a way of life commensurate with what the faith teaches. Theology can be wrong; it cannot be noncommittal.

In this sense, then, this book is not just about religion in the post-modern world. It makes a theological case which is in three parts.

The *first* is that with the passing of the modern age, the epoch of "modern theology" which tried to interpret Christianity in the face of secularization is also over. A fundamentally new theological approach is needed.

The *second* is that the essential rudiments of that new theology need not be invented out of whole cloth but are already appearing, borne by vigorous antimodernist religious movements. They need only to be discerned, clarified, and articulated.

The *third*, however, is that these indispensable components of the coming theology can be assembled only if we appreciate and use the accomplishments of modern theology, including "liberal" theology, rather than rescind them. I am writing not to bury modern theology but—at least in some measure—to praise it, or at least to learn from the courageous way it tackled the modern world how we might now begin to tackle its postmodern successor.

Where will the resources for a postmodern theology come from? My thesis in this book is that they will come not from the center but from the bottom and from the edge. They will come from those sectors of the modern social edifice that for various reasons—usually to do with class or color or gender—have been consigned to its lower stories and excluded from the chance to help formulate its religious vision. They will come from those parts of the world geopoliticians classify as the "periphery," regions also largely left out of participation in the centers of modern theological discourse which are located in the Western political and cultural milieu.

Before the bottom and the edge can be heard from, the present weakened "center" will have to be dismantled. Not destroyed, for there are parts of it which will be not only useful but essential to theology's next phase. Pope John Paul's arrival symbolized the return of religion to the secular city and the mixed political consequences of that return. It also brought together the two main agents of modern theology's end: the traditional and the radical. If the new theology will come from the edge and the bottom, I believe traditional religion will provide its content in some still unforeseen combination with radical Christianity. Here in the Pope's arrival were signaled all the elements—bottom and edge tradition and radicality. Here the most archaic and the most avant-garde wings of Christianity seemed, for a moment at least, to squeeze out the middle completely. Here Poland was meeting Latin America, and Rome was kissing the Third World.

The Polish Pope is an exemplary conservative religious leader. His opposition to birth control and his insistence on clerical celibacy and an exclusively male priesthood make this painfully clear to American and European liberal Catholics. He is also a traditionalist who has made highly publicized pilgrimages to the Black Madonna of Częstochowa in Poland, Fatima in Portugal, and the basilica of Our Lady of Guadalupe in Mexico. He is a staunchly *Roman* Catholic who will not permit his interest in Christian unity to erode what he believes are the unshakable pillars of the True Faith. But in climbing out of his jet onto Latin American soil, John Paul II—the custodian of traditional religion—arrived in the habitat of Christianity's most revolutionary wing. He was stepping onto the continent where young Catholics sing a song called "The Cross of Light," honoring the memory of the Colombian guerrilla priest Camilo Torres, and others light candles before photographs of the martyred Salvadoran Archbishop Oscar Romero; where Brazilian Bishop Paulo Evaristo Arns opened the churches of his diocese in São Paulo to illegally striking workers whom the military government had forbidden to meet; where the highly controversial "basic Christian communities," lay-led grassroots congregations involved in Bible study and political action, are blossoming by the thousands, and the much disputed "theology of liberation" originated.

The Pope's visit to Mexico brought the juxtaposition between traditional and radical Christianity into sharp profile. But it also revealed some elements of convergence between the two, not the least of which is their common aversion to "modern theology," the attempt to adapt Christianity to the modern world. The Pope's social pronouncements do not please conservative American advocates of supply-side and *laissez faire* economics. For their part, the revolutionary Christians of Latin America are quite traditional in some ways. They puzzle moral majoritarians who prefer to believe that all revolutionaries are devoted to the destruction of monogamy and the abolition of religion. An acquaintance of mine, a priest who identifies himself with the Catholic left in Brazil, once told me that the problem with North American theologians is that they will "never understand that we Latin Americans *like* tradition and ritual and hierarchy." Liberation theologians are cautious about the way liberal theologians apply modern historical methods to the study of the Bible, not because they oppose such methods but because they tend to confuse and mystify the ordinary people for whom the message is intended. As for public morals, when

Ernesto Cardenal became Minister of Cultural Affairs in Nicaragua after the victory of the Sandinista revolution, he immediately banned the importation of pornographic films. The meeting of the two wings of antimodernist Christianity involves consensus as well as collision.

These then are the two columns now engaged in ambushing the remnants of secular society and modern theology. But both wings are themselves improbable conglomerates. The conservative battalion, symbolized by the Pope, encompasses both arcadian poets who loathe television and Protestant preachers who own whole networks. It includes fashionable "neoconservatives," many of them Jewish, who write for *Commentary* magazine and whose grandmothers would light an extra Sabbath candle if they knew their progeny were keeping company with Texan revivalists and Polish prelates. Still, their shock could not exceed that of the shirt-sleeved fundamentalist predecessors of Mr. Falwell if they had seen the picture of a Romish Pope that was in a spring 1982 issue of *Moral Majority Report*. Whatever happened to "Rum, Romanism and Rebellion"?

Politics always makes strange bedfellows, especially when mixed with religion. If the conservative wing of the uprising against modern theology is a potpourri, the radical party is also a choir of mixed voices. It brings together not only Latin American Catholics but an increasing number of Asian and African Christians; a growing group of feminist religious thinkers; black American theologians; a scattering of white American inner-city Catholics and Appalachian Protestants, and—more recently—voices from the Asian American and Mexican American subcultures. Like the pope's division, this list includes people who until recently might have crossed the street to avoid meeting each other.

At first the convergence of the traditionalists and radicals seems odd. The conservatives dismiss the radicals and their liberation theology either as a collapsing of the faith into a political ideology or as just the latest sellout to modernity. The Latin Americans and their allies in the radical camp lump the sophisticated conservatives along with the fundamentalists as variations of the same religiously tinctured bourgeois ideology. But when it comes to evaluating modern theology, the two warring schools agree: they both find it a failure. Can a postmodern theology arise out of such cacophony?

I think it will, but one should not try to answer this question at the theological level alone. Theologies, unlike philosophical schools of scientific paradigms, do not make much headway in the world unless they are borne along by vigorous religious movements. They need a social base. The emergence of a postmodern theology from the bottom and the edges of the modern world will happen only as religious movements incorporating powerful critiques of modern theology and the religious sensibility on which it is based come more and more into prominence.

* * *

THE GREAT INVERSION

> There will be grinding of teeth when you see Abraham, Isaac and Jacob, and all the prophets in the Kingdom of God, and yourselves thrown out. From east and west people will come, from north and south, for the feast in the Kingdom of God. Yes, and some who are now last will be first, and some who are first will be last.
>
> —Luke 13:28-30

Dietrich Bonhoeffer was an amazingly prescient man. Sitting in his Gestapo cell and aware that his days were numbered, he also knew that the kind of theology he had grown up with would no longer do. "I have discovered," he wrote, just a few weeks before his execution, "that only by living fully in the world can we learn to have faith." But not even Bonhoeffer could foresee the massive changes in the world—and in theology—that were on the way.

Religion and theology in the dawning postmodern world are undergoing two jarring inversions. From all directions of the compass new peoples are arriving at the feast of the Kingdom, and many who were last are last no longer. Whereas once theology was manufactured at the center for distribution in the provinces, the direction of the flow is now being reversed. It is the periphery which is now threatening, questioning, and energizing the center. And, whereas the model once asserted that religious truth must be promulgated at the top and then "trickle down" through layers of hierarchy to the local level, now that vertical path has also been upended.

This capsizing of the movement of theological currents will require some important changes in the scope and method of theology. Listening to the edges will require a much more imaginative way of dealing with religious pluralism, for it is from the margins of Christendom that the most forceful challenge of other faiths comes. It will also require that theology deal more creatively with what has been known variously as folk religion, grassroots piety, and *religión popular*.

So far, the liberation theologies have dealt effectively with the poor as outsider and as "other." They are only beginning, however, to cope with the otherness of other faiths and with the significance of folk piety for any theology which is interested in the liberation of real folk. In confronting these two challenges—of popular piety and of other religions—theology comes up against the two most powerful vehicles bearing the traditional conservative complaints against modernity.

In previous chapters I have already defined "theology" as that activity by which human beings relate their faith in God (*theos*) to the patterns of meaning that prevail in any historical period or culture (*logos*). If Christian theology is to address itself to the modern-becoming-postmodern world, then it cannot fail to be explicit about both the God pole and the world pole. It must present a persuasive picture of the postmodern *logos*, showing its characteristic sensibility or ethos and how it differs from the modern one in which most of us have grown up. It must be equally clear about *theos*, the essential gist of the Christian message, the divine truth that must be conveyed to the temporal world.

Modern theology was Christianity's answer to the modern age. It assumed a variety of expressions, from Friedrich Schleiermacher to Karl Barth, from Jacques Maritain to the Roman Catholic modernists, from Nicolai Berdyaev to Paul Tillich. In fact, some theologians would argue that the differences among these thinkers are so great, it is misleading to call them all "modern." However, these disparate modern theologians were all preoccupied with one common underlying question—how to make the Christian message credible to what they understood as the modern mind.

In this sense, Friedrich Schleiermacher is recognized as the "father of modern theology." When he wrote his *Speeches on Religion to Her Cultured Despisers* in 1799, he set the agenda for an entire era. Writing the introduction to a reissue of that historic book more than a century later, the German religious scholar Rudolf Otto observed that what Schleiermacher was trying to do was "lead an age weary with and alien to religion back to its very mainsprings; and to reweave religion, threatened with oblivion, into the incomparably rich fabric of the burgeoning intellectual life of modern times." *Speeches*, adds the historian Wilhelm Pauck, was a "turning point" in the history of theology, since it marked "the first creative effort . . . to interpret the Christian faith in relation to the 'modern' world view."

Theologians have differed with Schleiermacher about what the modern world view is and how the "reweaving" should be done. Some, like Karl Barth, rejected his method completely. Barth had no patience with "liberal theology" and would probably have been deeply vexed even to be thought of as "modern," a term he found empty and useless. But the fact is that nearly all theologians since Schleiermacher have in common an imaginary interlocutor: the thoughtful troubled "modern person," wracked with doubts and misgivings about God, "weary with and alien to religion." Even those like Rudolf Bultmann who appealed to decision rather than intellect still employed critical-historical methods and fashionable philosophical movements, such as existentialism, to get their point across. Despite the variety of their approaches, their target audience was always "the burgeoning intellectual life of modern times," the cultured despisers of the faith.

Modern theology was a remarkable intellectual achievement. It created a wide variety of plausible answers to the question it set for itself: how to "interpret the Christian faith in relation to the 'modern' world view." The problem now is not that the responses created by modern theology are no longer credible. Rather, the question has changed. Every modern theology had a *theos* pole and a *logos* pole, a view of the nature of God and a theory of what the modern world essentially was. However, though neoorthodoxy and neoscholasticism and process theology differed from one another in defining these poles, the differences do not look as profound, in light of the postmodern situation, as they did to those who originally argued over them. What all these discordant schools had in common was a fervent desire to appeal to the thoughtful, educated, skeptical "modern mind." Neither Barth, Maritain, nor Tillich wrote for the masses, certainly not for the masses of ordinary believers. One might even argue that they were writing for that part of themselves which knew—from the inside—what it meant to be a skeptical "modern man."

With the coming of postmodern culture, all three ingredients of modern theology—its God pole, its world pole, and, most critically, its implied interlocutor—are thrown into question. By the time the impact of World War II had been fully absorbed, the picture of the modern world that informed modern theology began to lose its credibility. Doubts about the plausibility of that world picture multiplied as the unfolding history of modernity revealed sinister sides that had not figured in the modern theological equation. When the disclosure of what happened at Auschwitz did not lessen the modern world's capacity for mass slaughter, and the realization of what took place at Hiroshima did not evoke a shrinking back from the making of more nuclear weapons, something began to change. Growing numbers of people began to regard the modern logos not as something one tried to weave religion back into but as a world view which was itself fatally flawed. The modern mind became not the audience but the problem. The so-called crisis of modernity was upon us, and one secular philosopher [Joel Whitebrook] declared that it could never be solved until the world came to see that the "root of the crisis is the modern project itself."

This is the change that augured the end of modern theology. With its primary goal—the need to adapt religion to the modern world—now thrown into doubt, modern theology also found itself to be more a part of the problem than of the solution. Its world pole lay in shambles.

Modern theology's God pole also began to teeter. Previously theologians disagreed mainly about the details of this second component. There were many different "doctrines of God." But they all agreed that God was universal, equally approachable by all and available to all. There was little room in modern theology either for a partisan God who takes sides in historical struggles or for a God who has to be sought in radically dissimilar ways by different peoples. Now, however, this assumption of universality was questioned too.

From the periphery of the modern world and from the ghettos and *barrios* there came a strident challenge to this God pole in the form of a *theos* who takes the side of the disinherited against the powerful, and who can be known only in highly particularistic ways. All modern theologies had claimed to be, in principle, universal, commending themselves to all men and women of faith and reason. Now, however, that claim to universality was questioned. Blacks and women, poor people and non-Westerners all insisted that these allegedly all-inclusive theologies were narrow and provincial—white, male, Western, "bourgeois"—and inadequate because they seemed blithely unaware of their own nearsightedness. The God pole of modern theology swayed and finally fell in the face of what seemed to many of its practitioners to be a nearly polytheistic upsurge of partial and even idiosyncratic perspectives. Was God black or poor or red or female? Each image seemed to issue from a highly particular experiential base.

The most telling challenge to modern theology did not come from the questioning of its two poles. It came rather as a rejection of modern theology's implicit understanding of its "audience." The new generation of postmodern theologians, many of them Latin American, African, and Asian, refused to agree that their labors should be addressed primarily to the "cultured despisers" of religion. Instead, they began to forge a theology in conversation with the disinherited and the culturally dominated sectors of the society. Their interlocutors were now the "*non*cultured despisers," but these were not people who despised religion. They were the despisers of the modern world itself. This is what made the real difference.

Trained to concentrate on the content of theology rather than on the process of theologizing, modern theologians hardly noticed this change. Still, the transformation of interlocutors was by far the most significant dislocation. One could safely debate various ideas of God and world within the parameters modern theology was used to. But when one changes the social and institutional setting within which the whole theological enterprise proceeds, and when one alters the definition of *for whom* one constructs theology and *why*, when theologians turn from the despisers to the despised, then something fundamental has been altered. It is the game itself, not just the plays that are possible within it, that has been changed. Modern theology, with its astonishing capacity for inventiveness and creativity, might have survived a radical shift in its paradigms of God and world. It could not survive a fundamental redefinition of its purpose and agenda, with whom it was to be discussed, and by whom it was to be held accountable. But this is just the kind of challenge postmodern theologies were bringing.

We must be careful not to paint a monochrome picture of modern theology. Thinkers as wildly disparate as Dostoyevsky, Kierkegaard, Blake, and Pius IX questioned the modern theological program. Yet when we read these men today they often sound modern despite themselves, preoccupied as they were with the new age and the mistakes they believed their contemporaries were making in dealing with it. It is unclear how much help any one of them can offer in the task theology now faces, that of moving beyond the challenge of "modern times" to the construction of a theology that speaks to a world neither the modern theologians nor their critics could have foreseen.

In this final section of the book I will draw on the ideas of certain, contemporary social philosophers who have thought carefully about the postmodern world into which we are now moving. After that I will go on to suggest why the type of religiousness that became characteristic of the modern world is no longer adequate. I will conclude by suggesting that two massive realities, both virtually ignored by modern theology—global religious pluralism and popular piety—must replace the "cultured despisers" of religion as the principal conversation partners of a truly postmodern theology.

* * *

THE RESURRECTION OF LIFE

In the sixth century, Saint Benedict abandoned the worldly city and took refuge in the mountains so as to be able to find a favorable environment in which to seek God and live the Gospel. This led him to create a community of men who lived the same life as "the poor of the earth." Today, perhaps, St. Benedict would abandon the countryside and the mountains, now covered with gracious and comfortable villas. Perhaps he would abandon all those places where the rich and powerful have chosen to live and would go live among the dependent and exploited masses of the city in search of the "right place" to reread the Gospel.

—Giovanni Battista Franzoni
(St. Paul Christian Community, Rome)[12]

Our emerging postmodern period will be a religious one. This is not necessarily good news at all. Religion is always a mixed blessing, a source of good and of evil. It produces the sublime and the perverse: Torquemada and St. Francis, hospitals and inquisitions, *The Cloud of Unknowing* and *The Protocols of the Elders of Zion*. But since we are going to have religion in the postmodern era, Bonhoeffer's pursuit of "non-religious Christianity" cannot be theology's purpose today. Still, this definitely does not mean that theology should restrict itself, as modern liberal theology sometimes did, to dealing with "religious experience" or the inner content of the faith or the primitive *kerygma*, while ignoring the all-important question of the roles religion actually plays in society. Before we move on to consider what resources we will need to undertake this postmodern theological task, we have one more important lesson to learn from our predecessors. It has to do with which religion or religions we will encounter in the postmodern world.

Auguste Comte is known as the founder of positivism. This word has now come to mean many things. For him it meant simply that the exclusive way to truth lay through scientific experiment. He hoped passionately that science could establish ethics but his careful investigation of the history of ethics led him to the unwelcome conclusion that

---

12. Giovanni Franzoni, "The Earth Is God's," *NTC Summer Special* 1978, V, 13 (July 1978) (Italian Ecumenical News Agency, 00184 Rome, via Firenze 38, Italy).

people are not moved to morality by cold empirical data. They need something warmer. Comte called it "affection," and through further historical studies he came to believe that religion was the only source powerful enough both to inspire and to discipline the affections.

But here Comte hit a snag. As a scientist he felt he could not believe in the miracles and the absurdities of religion. Further, he was afraid that as scientific knowledge spread, no one else would be able to either. Thus the dilemma: morality had to be supported by religion, but it could not be the only religion Comte knew, Christianity.

Comte refused to retreat from the unnerving logic of his own reasoning; the only thing left to do was to invent a new religion, one that everybody—including the most scientifically trained—could believe in. For Comte it would have to be a religion in which humanity would be the object of devotion, not God.

Today no one except a few specialists has ever heard of Comte's "new" religion—complete with mass, saints' days, and all the rest. But the old religion, the one he thought would disappear, is still very much alive and includes among its adherents many people even Comte would have accepted as scientifically sophisticated. The lesson of the heroic and also tragicomic story of Auguste Comte is that he was right to recognize that morality and religion are intertwined inextricably. He correctly sensed that the "affections" play a decisive part in the ethical life of the race. He knew as Taine did that "the human mind itself," and not just women and savages, thinks with pictures. He was mistaken, though courageous, to try to invent a new religion.[13]

Like any other world, the postmodern world will need religion. Will it need a new one? Since religions, as Comte and many others have demonstrated, cannot be invented, the question must assume a somewhat different form. Is it possible that a new religious vision will appear, one that will help move us out of the dying and death-obsessed modern age and into the next?

One cannot merely pass over the possibility. New religions have appeared in the past, and Christianity is one of them. In fact, as religions go, it is one of the more recent ones. Some seers once looked to communism or socialism as the faiths of the future. Few do today. Some have tried to invent a comprehensive world faith like Bahai by assembling various elements of existing ones, a kind of spiritual Esperanto. Both Bahai and Esperanto are alive and well, but they can hardly be said to have swept the world before them. Some feminists have tried

---

13. Auguste Comte, *Positive Philosophy* (New York: AMS Press, reprint of 1855 edition); *The Catechism of Positive Religion* (New York: Kelley, 1973).

to revive or create a contemporary cult of the goddess, but so far their efforts have appealed to only a small number of women.

Given the lack of evidence that any new religion is waiting in the wings to enliven the postmodern era, the next logical question is what spiritual resources, if any, are appearing which might provide the basis for the new world we need and want? We are back to the dinosaurs and the field mice.

I do not mean to imply that Christianity will provide all the religious resources for the postmodern world. I do believe, however, that Christianity can and will make a decisive contribution to this new global civilization, and will do it in a manner completely different from the way it contributed during the modern age. Only a radically transformed and "demodernized" Christianity, can possibly make such a contribution. Is a postmodern or "demodernized" Christianity possible?

At first glance, the prospect does not appear promising. Most of the institutions of Christianity and most of its doctrinal and ethical formulations are so encased in the dying modern world that it is hard to see how they could possibly either move us or serve us in a postmodern future. But there are some theologians who, although they have given up on modern religion including its Christian variant, have not given up on a Christianity released from its current captivity. Pablo Richard suggests that the only way to recuperate what he calls the "liberating core" of Christianity from its alliance with the modern world is to look at it from the perspective of those who are Christian but in some sense not "modern." We must rethink the Gospel from the viewpoint of those who have been excluded from or trampled by the modern world. They constitute the "absolute other" of this world, he says, and since they have not fully internalized the modern world/liberal theology synthesis, they stand in the only possible position to transform or subvert it.[14]

For Richard the modern world's "absolute other" is the poor. I would add some of the "others" on Taine's and Mill's lists—women, "barbarians," the "simple working people." All these have internalized modern Christianity in some measure. It is the dominant current religious ideology, and no one who lives in the world can avoid it entirely. But these "others" have not absorbed it completely and have frequently even relied on their own interpretations of parts of it as alternative sources of meaning and identity. Some have even drawn on Christianity as a point of leverage for subversion and rebellion. These "other faces of Christ," embodied both in religious communities and in theological

---

14. Pablo Richard, "El Evangelio entre la Modernidad y la Liberación," *Servir* XIV, 76 (1978), 471.

162   **A Harvey Cox Reader**

reflection, because they have resisted being utilized to make modernity credible, supply the only secure launching pads for moving beyond it. It is these interpretations alone that can provide the Christian contribution to the religious core of a truly postmodern world.

The main stimulus for the renewal of Christianity will come from the bottom and from the edge, from those sectors of the Christian world that are on the margins of the modern/liberal consensus. It is coming from those places where Christians are poor, especially Latin America; from areas where they live as small minorities surrounded by non-Christian cultures as they do in Asia; from the churches that live under political despotisms as they do in the Communist world and in parts of South and Central America; from the American churches of blacks and poor whites; from those women who are agonizing together over what it means to be faithful and female in a church that has perpetuated patriarchy for two millennia. These are disparate peoples; but what they have in common is that they were all dealt in and dealt out, included and excluded from modernity and its religious aura. Their forced removal to its sidelines (or better, its basements, kitchens, slums, and colonies) is what now enables them to offer a version of Christianity that is liberating because it has not been squeezed through the concordat or distorted by the straitened function the modern world has assigned religion and theology.

Pablo Richard's formula for evolving a postmodern theology provides just the structural basis that is needed. A viable postmodern theology will be created neither by those who have completely withdrawn from the modern world nor by those who have affirmed it unconditionally. It will come from those who have lived within it but have never been fully part of it, like the women in Adrienne Rich's poem who, though they dived into the wreck, have not found their names inscribed within it. It will be created by those who, like black American Christians, have refused to accept the slavemaster's gospel but have also refused to jettison the Gospel altogether. As Marshall Berman points out in his *All That Is Solid Melts into Air*,[15] the nineteenth-century modernist always saw both the peril and the promise of the modern spirit. Only in the twentieth century has the all-or-nothing attitude that either canonizes or anathematizes it appeared. What is needed, however, is not some measured middle ground, some mellowed balance of what has been good and what bad in modern liberal theology, but a theology forged

---

15. Marshall Berman, *All That Is Solid Melts into Air: The Experience of Modernity* (New York: Simon and Schuster, 1982).

by those who have been both inspired and abused, both touched and trampled on by the religion of the modern age.

Modern theology was fascinated with the mind. It concentrated on ideas and was especially interested in the question of good and evil. Postmodern theology will concentrate on the body, on the nature of human community, and on the question of life and death.

This is not just a prediction. When one examines the emerging theologies of the various excluded Christian communities, the Resurrection or something clearly akin to it is central to each. The Latin Americans have been emphasizing an "antifetishistic theology of life" against what they view as a culture of lifeless commodities and gray death. Asians talk of the presence of a life-giving spirit of God in their Hindu and Buddhist neighbors. Blacks decry the lack of "soul" in a blanched world. Women speak frequently of the need to restore the human body with all its senses fully alive to a Christianity that has become arid and cerebral. Poor white church people do not theorize about it much; but what always strikes middle-class visitors about lower-class Pentecostalism, for example, is its embodied energy, its dancing and shouting and ecstatic utterances.

The religious foundation for a new world civilization does not have to be invented. It is already present. The mice are scampering among the mammoths. The puny congregations in Corinth and Rome and Ephesus thrived in the niches and interstices of an empire that was cracking apart. One tiny cluster of the saints apparently even met "in the household of Caesar." Later the monasteries and still later the conventicles of the Radical Reformation became the spawning grounds of the next phase of history. Today the rudiments of a postmodern civilization are sprouting on the edges and in the crevices.

The three ingredients needed before any civilizational era can reach its take-off point, a *style of personal existence*, a *theological vision*, and a *corporate form*, are all coming from the militant outcasts of modernity.

1. At the level of *personal life style*, we can see the appearance of a form of "worldly spirituality," of "engaged mysticism" that is replacing the monastic and pietistic modes inherited from the medieval and modern periods. The title of a recent book on spiritual direction, *Inviting the Mystic, Supporting the Prophet*,[16] reveals the focus of the new postmodern spirituality. Unlike that of St. Anthony, this new spirituality

---

16. Katherine Maria Dyckman and L. Patrick Carroll, *Inviting the Mystic, Supporting the Prophet: An Introduction to Spiritual Direction* (Ramsey, N.J.: Paulist Press, 1981).

is nurtured not by a single-minded withdrawal from the world but by a
rhythm of advance and retreat, of wading into the pain and conflict of
the secular realm, and repairing regularly into the sustenance of solitude and of a supporting community. A biography of St. Anthony says
of him, "Nearly twenty years he spent . . . pursuing the ascetic life by
himself, not venturing out and only occasionally being seen by anyone."
Eventually his friends became concerned about him and tore down
the stout door he had closed between himself and the outside. Then,
the biographer continues, "Anthony came forth as though from some
shrine, having been led into divine mysteries and inspired by God."[17]

Postmodern spirituality begins with the premise that periods of solitude are essential but that one need not meditate in a cell for twenty
years to find God. God is present in the confusion and dislocation
of the world. One encounters God not by turning one's back on that
world but by plunging into it with the faith that the divine–human
encounter occurs in the midst of the encounter of human with human,
especially in the struggle to create signs of the coming of God's reign
of peace and justice. Jon Sobrino, writing from the tortured land of El
Salvador, says:

> The novelty of the new lifestyle is spelled out programmatically
> in the Sermon on the Mount. . . . The kernel is the assertion
> that love, service and truth constitute the only kind of power
> capable of anticipating the kingdom. Seen in this light, the
> command to love one's enemies expresses the complete radi-
> calness of Jesus' demand . . . love of one's enemy is what verifies
> one's conversion, for the enemy is the most extreme and acute
> embodiment of other people.[18]

It must be emphasized that we are not talking here about a novel
theoretical spirituality being elaborated by a new breed of theologians,
but a form of discipline that is emerging in daily human living. Theologians like Sobrino would be the first to admit that what they are doing
is not commending or creating a style of spirituality but clarifying and
commenting on one that is appearing in their midst.

It is appearing among those communities, congregations, cultures, and peoples who have been willing to hold fast to the Christian
message while refusing the dominant modern interpretation of what

---

17. Quoted in Ernest Boyer, "Edges and Rhythms: The Spiritualities of Solitude and Community," *Sojourners* (June 1982), 14.

18. Jon Sobrino, *Christology at the Crossroads: A Latin American Approach* (Maryknoll, N.Y.: Orbis Books, 1978), 56.

that Gospel says. Should it be any surprise therefore that the exemplary "saints" of the postmodern world include a black preacher (Martin Luther King, Jr.), a woman (Dorothy Day), and a Latin American (Oscar Arnulfo Romero)? These were all persons of profound faith who instead of looking for a cave, or accepting the institutional insulation that separates most of us from the agony of the world, immersed themselves in that world. They did so, however, not just as "activists" or "change agents" but as followers of Jesus who were willing to run the risks of discipleship.

2. At the *theological* level, the new religious vision can be found in the spirited conversations going on within and among the communities of Christians we have called "the others." Using the term loosely, the theologies percolating from these communities are what we mean by "liberation theology." But there is no unified "school of thought." There is no single theology. What all these theologies do have in common is a determination to break loose from the dominant schools of theology hatched in the universities of Europe and the United States, encoded almost entirely by white males, and designed to respond to what are viewed as the religious needs of educated, "thinking" (read: doubting, questioning) readers.

What the liberation theologies have in common is their desire to reappraise Christianity and other religious traditions as well from the perspective of those who have been banished historically both from theological reflection and from the formulation of religious symbols. Despite differences, all the liberation theologies wish to effect what the Latin Americans call a *ruptura*, a radical disjunction from the methods, imagery, and agenda of the currently dominant theologies. This is not an effort to get away from Christian theology as such, but from those parts of it that have hurt them. Consequently, women, blacks, and Asians differ on exactly which features of this theological heritage they want to be liberated from; this is what produces the creative conflict among them.

There are those who believe these various theological tendencies not only have little relationship to each other but are moving in sharply different directions and are, ultimately, irreconcilable. Take for example the Asian liberation theology one now finds in the Christian churches of countries with predominantly Hindu or Buddhist religious traditions.[19] Some of the theologians who involve themselves in this work

---

19. See C. S. Song, "Many Peoples and Many Languages" (mimeograph), 1982; Tissa Balasuriya, *The Eucharist and Human Liberation* (Maryknoll, N.Y.: Orbis Books, 1979); Gerald H. Anderson, *Asian Voices in Christian Theology* (Maryknoll,

claim that Western liberation theologies, notably the black American and Latin American types, are too narrowly and uncritically Christian, too "Western," maybe even imperialistic. They fault the Latins especially for showing no interest in the challenge of religious pluralism. The Latins on the other hand complain that worrying about religious pluralism can lead to a kind of mindless tolerance and provide a respectable excuse for failing to confront the religious undergirding of unjust societies.

Women have accused blacks and Latin Americans of being blind to sexism, not only in the dominant theologies they criticize but also within their own. Blacks have criticized feminist theologians, most of whom are white and from middle-class educated backgrounds, of overlooking racism.

Despite all these frictions, I do not believe these various liberation theologies are necessarily antagonistic. Rather, they are particularistic. They do not pretend to be universally applicable but to articulate very specific settings. This suggests that the theology of the postmodern world will not be as coherent and systematically unified as modern theologies sought to be. They will be able to tolerate a higher level of jaggedness and lack of cohesion. There is a good reason for this. People who have lived within oppressed and dominated sectors of any society know that systems and symbols that emphasize universality and inclusiveness very often end up shortchanging diversity and particularity. Whatever their pretensions to evenhandedness and being all-encompassing, in the gritty dust of the real world unitive systems of thought usually become ideologies of domination. The effort of modern theology to be all things to all people everywhere may itself be one of the qualities of its modernity that should not survive into a postmodern world in which particularity will flourish. Likewise, narrative may now replace modern theology's near-obsession with systematizing and internal coherence, both of which tend to drain the color from religious expressions. Postmodern theology will thrive on stories.

3. At the level of *corporate form*, the resources for a postmodern Christianity also need not be invented but are pushing up through the cracking pavement of modernity. These new structures of Christian social existence take on as many shapes as liberation theology; but they all share the characteristics we have seen in the so-called base communities. Like liberation theology, the base community movement has come into being in the past two decades, starting among the impoverished

N.Y.: Orbis Books, 1980); John C. England (ed.), *Living Theology in Asia* (Maryknoll, N.Y.: Orbis Books, 1982).

and uprooted Christians of Latin America's rural villages and urban *favelas*. The movement has grown spectacularly, and has now reached Europe, Asia, and North America. It is made up of hundreds of thousands of local groups focused on Bible study and political action, and often critical of ideas, organizational patterns and liturgical practices of the more established sectors of the church.[20]

No religious movement in history has ever gone very far on ideas alone. Religions, unlike philosophies, are always embedded in rituals and symbolic practices, in songs and stories. Only when its ideas are coupled with such corporate realities—arising from them and influencing them—does a religious movement become significant. The Christian base communities of the Third World and their analogs in other places are providing that vehicle today. We have already visited La Chispa and examined the base communities movement. Here I want only to recall two features that underline the importance of these communities as the future form of corporate Christian reality.

The first is that like the various liberation theologies, the social shapes of postmodern Christianity also differ among themselves because they challenge different distortions in modern liberal Christianity. Women naturally tend to press for changes in polity that will permit them to exercise equal responsibility and leadership in the churches. They often support the ordination of women and the rewriting of hymns and prayers in a more inclusive language that does not use masculine words for everyone and does not always refer to the deity as "He." Black churches preserve and nurture the characteristic Afro-American qualities of worship and preaching that are often derogated in predominantly white congregations. South American base communities attack the traditional political alliance between the hierarchy and the oligarchy. European grassroots groups work for lay participation in a setting where churches have been extremely clergy-dominated. Thus all are pressing for the practical equivalent of the theological *ruptura* sought by liberation theology on the intellectual level.

Second, just as the Resurrection of Christ and of the human body is coming to supply a focal motif in the theology of postmodern Christianity, so the resurrection of the "mystical body," the rebirth of corporate community, is becoming the principal organizational quality of the new cells. In the modern period, Christian churches became a conglomerate of individuals. Congregations turned into collections of discrete persons (or at best households) who created a church through

20. Michael Bavarei, *New Communities, New Ministries: The Church Resurgent in Africa, Asia and Latin America* (Maryknoll, N.Y.: Orbis Books, 1983).

a kind of social contract—an idea with a distinctly modern pedigree. In the emergent base communities, however, the bonds are at once more particular and more holistic. Women discover sisterhood. Blacks affirm a kinship with others whose skin color has made their history what it is. The poor discover a closeness to others who share their disinheritance. The word "solidarity," with roots in the labor movement, has been used at times to describe this discovery of a deep bonding that the early Christians talked of as being "members one of another." In classical Christian theology this extraordinary tie was understood not as the result of mere natural consanguinity but as something made possible by the gifts of the Spirit and the presence in the assembly of the One who had risen from the grave. The theologies of the postmodern Christian movements celebrate life against death. Their organizational styles stress community against individualism, organic instead of mechanistic modes of living together. Their spiritual disciplines emphasize coming forth from cell and cloister into the surging stream of life. Wherever one looks it is the message of Easter, the one that enlivened the early church, which seems to be the central proclamation of the postmodern churches.

* * *

A NEW REFORMATION?

In reflecting on the various theologies of liberation and the different kinds of base communities from which they are issuing, I have frequently used the analogy of the Reformation of the sixteenth century. Once again in our time the currents that are promising to renew and reform Christianity are cropping up on the "margin," coming from what is often viewed as the periphery of cultural and intellectual life.

The Catholic theologians of his time eventually recognized Luther as a formidable opponent. But in the early years of his preaching they brushed him aside as a provincial upstart. They not only dismissed his theology as a squabble among the monks but looked upon him and his colleagues as "marginals," living in a hinterland comparable today to the boondocks of Latin America, Asia, and the ghettos and *favelas*. Yet religious renewal hardly ever begins in the capital. The Hebrew prophets trooped in from the sycamore forests to challenge the temple and the palace. Jesus grew up in a remote and suspect region of Palestine. Once again the question is being asked, "Can any good thing come from Nazareth?" and the answer is the same. It seems that genuine change must always begin on the edge.

Also, like the Reformation of the sixteenth century, the current reformation is not just an idea whose time has come. It is a theology intertwined with a series of social upheavals and political changes. Recalling
the nasty debates over the sale of indulgences and the popish milking
of the credulous, this one also involves money and power. Also like its
predecessor, which had its share of mad hatters and kooks, the current reformation is subject to misuse and cooptation. It will inevitably
attract its quota of charlatans, fanatics, opportunists, and easy riders.
Yet just as our study of the secular dimensions of the sixteenth-century
Reformation does not make it any less a religious movement, neither
do suggestions that the current reformation is "only political" or is too
wrapped up in earthly concerns sound convincing.

Finally, the sixteenth-century Reformation was sparked religiously
by the rediscovery and proclamation of a biblical truth that had for
years been neglected or underplayed. This came with Luther's seizing
on St. Paul's *sola fide*, the joyous declaration that grace is God's own
gift, something that could not and need not be earned. To a population strangled by religious duties and ecclesiastical obligations this
came as a welcome message. Retrieved by Luther from the back shelf,
the old news that "the just shall live by faith" became new news and
swept through much of Europe like a cleansing wind.

Today's reformation is sparked by an equally powerful biblical idea,
also lost for years but recently rediscovered. The idea is that of Resurrection: God alive in the world, life defeating death. But in liberation theology, especially in its Latin American version, the idea carries
a more specific edge. It is that the special locus of God's presence is
the poor and that therefore the poor have a singular and privileged
role to play in the divine intention for human history. The poor are
those through whom God chooses to mediate the coming of the divine
reign. If anything this idea of the *dios pobre* is even more central to the
Bible and is repeated more frequently than the idea of justification by
faith. Yet, for the reasons we have discussed, it was lost sight of and
denied during much of modern history and in nearly all modern theology. But, like the *sola fide* of the sixteenth century, the idea of *dios pobre*
has always been there. Smoldering, it has now been fanned into flames
and become the central religious idea of the new reformation.[21]

---

21. For a new approach to the interaction of religious and political strands
see Otto Maduro, "Extraction de la Plus-Value, Repression de la Sexualité et
Catholicisme en Amerique Latine," *Liaisons Internationales* 32 (September 1982)
(OELI Brussels, Belgium).

Still, comparisons with the earlier Reformation can be misleading. The main difference between the two is that since the current reformation is by its nature a grassroots movement it will not produce such larger-than-life heroes as Luther or Calvin. For all its eventual popular support and the local discontent that helped energize it, the sixteenth-century Reformation was led from above by determined and strong-willed men. When ordinary people did begin to assume some leadership, as they did among some of the Anabaptists and other sectors of the Reformation's radical wing, the elite leaders quickly tried to bring them to heel, and they usually succeeded. This is especially evident in those instances where lay people threatened the clerical control of the movement; or where miners and peasants applied the preaching about the equality of believers under God to the economic and political as well as to the spiritual spheres, and appeared at the manor house brandishing shovels and pitchforks. Whenever this happened, as it did in parts of Germany and in the Tessin sections of what are now southern Switzerland and northern Italy, the Protestant reformers persecuted the "left wing" as severely as the Catholics tried to repress them. Most of these radical groups were uprooted and scattered. Others withdrew or became socially quiescent. But the impulse never died completely. Indeed, it could be argued that many of the ideas now appearing in the base communities and in the liberation theologies were anticipated by these religious pioneers nearly five centuries ago.

There is one final comparison that suggests itself between the Reformation of the sixteenth century and the present one. One of the most telling results of the sixteenth-century Reformation was the change it wrought in the Roman Catholic Church, on the established religion and the reigning theology.[22] Scholars have filled shelves with arguments about whether the impact was, on balance, more beneficial or more detrimental. Did the Reformation frighten the Catholic Church into the rigidity and paranoia of the Council of Trent? Did it put a club in the hands of the church's reactionaries, one they gleefully used to clobber incipient internal reform sentiments before they could get on their feet? Or did it, if only indirectly, stimulate a form of renewal inside the Catholic Church, such as the mysticism of the Carmelites and the missions of the Jesuits, that might not have happened otherwise?

Questions of "what might have happened otherwise" are always dubious candidates for historical reflection. What we do know is that the Catholic Church that emerged from the era of the sixteenth-century

---

22. James Obelkevich, *Religion of the People 800–1700* (Chapel Hill: University of North Carolina Press, 1979).

Reformation did not act like a routed remnant. Changed it surely was, but it was also a robust and inventive religious community. If its theological development was retarded by the post-Tridentine (after the Council of Trent) atmosphere, still these were also centuries of astonishing growth in the number and variety of religious orders with their richly distinctive styles of spirituality and common life. Recent history always forces us to read past history through different lenses. Since the pontificate of John XXIII it has become more helpful to read the history of the sixteenth-century Reformation not as an event which split the church in two but as a painful period of renewal within the one Christian family.

Is a parallel with today possible? I think it is. The new reformation sweeping across the backlands and out of the pantries and alleys of Christendom carries a validity of its own. It must not be judged exclusively on how well it does in challenging or influencing the established churchly patterns and the dominant theological ideas of the day. Like its predecessor, this reformation needs a *ruptura*, part of which it creates by its own momentum, part of which is inflicted on it by the modern equivalent of bulls of excommunication and raw papal power.

Western "mainline" Christianity, both Catholic and Protestant, organized into roughly two hundred denominations, is the current equivalent of the Catholic Church at the beginning of the sixteenth century. If one objects that the Renaissance popes of that period, busy collecting Titians and dallying with their mistresses, bear little resemblance to today's church executives and curial administrators, it need only be pointed out that both groups faithfully reflect their respective Zeitgeists. The popes and their entourages were churchy editions of the vintage wines and baroque refinements of the Renaissance *uomo universale.* Today's ecclesiastical bureaucrats look and sound very much like the corporate board men with whom they peruse their newspapers on commuter trains. If a bit more Renaissance worldliness lingers in Rome, and a semblance of country-and-western flamboyance colors the Nashville headquarters of the Southern Baptist Convention, one can be relatively sure it is mostly on the surface. Structures of dominant ecclesiastical organization, like the personal life styles they elicit, are rarely innovative. In an imperial period they are imperial; in a feudal age they are feudal; and in our time they are bureaucratic. Only at the frayed edges and in unsupervised quarters do new modes of organization and new individual life patterns appear.

If denominational Christianity is the "Catholic" church of our modern Christendom, then what I have called "modern theology" provides the core of its system of religious ideas. Again my use of the term "modern" to categorize such a spectrum of theologies will be questioned by those who are accustomed to using the term to designate only some of the many schools of religious thought that have appeared in the modern centuries. I use "modern" to call attention to the otherwise overlooked common qualities of the various liberal, neoorthodox, neoscholastic, and evangelical theologies that students of this period study. Differ as they may, all of them either seek some *modus vivendi* with the dominant thought forms of modernity or else attack the manner in which other schools have undertaken this task. What is different about liberation theology is not, in the first instance at least, the content of its ideas but its view of the role and purpose theology should play in the world. I call those theologies "modern" which, regardless of the content of the concepts they use, largely agree on what theology should be doing: addressing itself to the modern world of ideas, and thus to those persons whose business it is to deal with such ideas. Liberation theology, on the other hand (and again, in a baffling variety of voices), is more concerned with the social sources and political uses of ideas. Its purpose is not to convince as much as to unmask, its intent somewhat more polemical than apologetic, its goal more social than individual.

My point here, in drawing this comparison with the sixteenth century, is that since it is unlikely that either denominational Christianity or modern theology will disappear completely, any more than the Roman church and Catholic theology did after 1550, the question of what impact the new reformation and its theology will have on the currently established church and theology cannot be avoided. It is not an easy question. Indeed, the two theologies seem now as irreconcilable as Catholic and Reform theology did to their most zealous advocates four hundred years ago. To the liberationist, the modern "liberal" insistence on analyzing and evaluating religious ideas with little reference to their social origins or political significances reveals a blind faith in a kind of disembodied reason, the hangover of an innocent Enlightenment prejudice. To modern establishment theologians, the liberationists' insistence on interrogating the social sources and weighing the political valence of religious ideas and practices smacks of reductionism and anti-intellectualism. Theologians from the two camps have a hard time talking with each other since they seem to be speaking at cross-purposes.

Things will change. The new reformation is young, noisy, and assertive. The established theologians, like the curial loyalists of the sixteenth century, continue to hope the whole thing will soon die out. But nothing stays the same. Already liberation theologians are modulating their voices and modern theologians are resigning themselves to the recognition that this is not just another flash in the pan.

Whatever happens, however they develop, I believe liberation theology and the base communities are here to stay. They are the germ cells of the next era of our culture, Toynbee's internal minority, bearing our common future. Unlike Auguste Comte, we need not break our heads to construct them. Rather, gratefully recalling the *sola fide* of a previous age, we can accept them and welcome them as the gifts of grace they are.

In the two decades since *The Secular City* was published I have gained the reputation in some circles of being a "liberal" theologian. I have never been satisfied with the label. Born and reared in a conservative Baptist milieu, I have never really abandoned that tradition. In recent years I have found myself increasingly drawn to Latin American liberation theology and have lived and taught in South America on numerous occasions. These two disparate streams of Christian faith do not seem contradictory to me, but in fact seem to confirm each other in ways I had not expected. I can feel at home in both.

As I have examined North American fundamentalism and Latin American liberation theology I have come to believe that the former has little to offer to a postmodern theology while the latter is enormously promising. Still, the liberation theologies are not export items. Eventually we North American Christians will have to develop our own liberation theology and our own base communities. When we do, however, I believe they will emerge more readily from the evangelical-conservative than from the liberal wing of American Christianity. We need a liberation theology that will draw on the folk piety of Baptists, Methodists, and the rest. We need it both to save our own valued religious tradition from being engulfed and deformed by the fundamentalists and also to absorb the liberation currents into a form of popular religion that is characteristically North American.

Perhaps I have come to appreciate my own Baptist tradition as well as the liberation theologies more in recent years because I too have been "detoxified." As this has happened I have come to believe that the great era of modern theology, of which what is loosely called "liberal" theology (in which I got my academic training) was the most characteristic expression, is drawing to a close, just as the modern era itself is ending. However, there is something different about my attitude toward this passing, and those who will still find me something of a "liberal" may not be entirely wrong. Unlike some of its conservative and radical critics, I do not believe modern theology was either a mistake or a betrayal. For me it arouses neither nostalgia nor disdain. It does elicit appreciation and admiration. It was a splendid and often inspired enterprise, a brilliant chapter in Christian history. I believe the postmodern world will require a different theology, and I have tried to suggest where that theology must come from and what it will be. But I believe that such a theology cannot be successfully formulated unless the modern liberal legacy is appropriated and incorporated. Only a theology that has taken the modern age seriously will be able to take seriously what is coming next. No one can move beyond the secular city who has not first passed through it.

9

Many Mansions (1988)

These selections are taken from Many Mansions: A Christian's Encounters with Other Faiths *(Boston: Beacon Press, 1988), 1-19, 195-212.*

JESUS AND DIALOGUE

Has the great dialogue among the world religions stalled, the dialogue that so many of us welcomed so warmly and so recently? Why has the "wider ecumenism," which had offered hope of crossing not only denominational but faith lines as well, begun to sputter and stammer and, in many instances, simply to stop? Why have relations among the ancient spiritual traditions of the human family, which many of us believed were improving a few years back, turned rancorous and even violent as new outbreaks of separatism, xenophobia, and hostility erupt?

To make matters worse, these same faith communities are increasingly divided within themselves, and the rifts are often exacerbated by political tensions. Sunni and Shiite Muslims declare each other to be worse than infidels. Jews, both pious and secular, who want to find some way to live at peace with Palestinians, despair over the zealotry of the Gush Enumin, who believe God has given their people land on which Palestinians have dwelt for generations. Christians who work for interfaith understanding have been shocked and perplexed by the attacks of fundamentalists who condemn them as traitors to the Gospel but who themselves seem willing to cooperate with those heathen if their politics are acceptable. Indeed, people in any religious tradition who are committed to dialogue often find themselves upbraided as turncoats by their own brothers and sisters.

Admittedly, the picture is not unrelievedly gloomy. Here and there, small circles of Muslims and Jews, Hindus and Sikhs, Buddhists and Christians, continue to meet and talk and even to work together, but they do so despite the currents that seem to be flowing against them. What has gone wrong?

I believe that the most nettlesome dilemma hindering interreligious dialogue is the very ancient one of how to balance the universal and the particular. Every world faith has both. Each nourishes in rite and saga its own unique and highly particular vision. Maybe it is the message of the one true God delivered without blemish to the Prophet. Or it is the fathomless Brahman from which all that is and all that is not come and return. Or the faithful Son of God dying on the cross. Or the supreme moment when enlightenment comes to the patient figure seated under the Bo tree. Or the bestowal of the life-giving gift of Torah on a chosen people. Whatever it is, the particular hub defines the center around which each world faith rotates, endowing it season after season and century after century with its characteristic ethos.

At the same time every world faith, if it is truly a world faith and not a local cultus, also generates a universal vision. Brahman embraces all ages, each drop of water, and every savior. The Koran names a God who created all people equal and who decrees that a unified human family should mirror his sublime unity. The dying Christ is raised to life by a God who favors the outcasts and the heartbroken and who summons all tribes and tongues into an inclusive community of service and praise. The bodhisattva compassionately refuses to enter nirvana until every sentient being can enter with him.

Thus each world faith has both its axis and its spokes, its sharply etched focus and its ambient circumference. Further, it is the mark of a truly world faith that these two dimensions are not only held together: they strengthen and reinforce each other. Somewhere, somehow, all that now seems fragmented and contradictory, all that appears tragic or inexplicable, is gathered into a single mystery of meaning and value.

The crisis in the current state of interfaith dialogue can be stated simply: the universal and the particular poles have come unhinged. Faced with a world in which some form of encounter with other faiths can no longer be avoided, the ancient religious traditions are breaking into increasingly bitter wings. Those who glimpse the universal dimension advocate dialogue and mutuality. They search out what is common and that which unites. Those who emphasize the particular often shun dialogue and excoriate their fellow believers who engage in it more fiercely than they condemn outsiders. This ugly chasm, running through all religions, gives rise to a "worst-possible" scenario one might envision if the current trend persists. Imagine a time when tiny cadres of "dialoguers" would perch on the fringe of each faith community, endlessly refining the language and concepts in which they converse with those on the universalist wings of the other faiths. Meanwhile, on the opposite side in each religion, zealous cohorts of radical particularists would congregate, anathematizing their backsliding coreligionists for compromising the truth by fraternizing with the reprobate. It is not an attractive prospect.

But we need both poles. I count myself as one of the universalists. Yet sometimes as I have sat in genteel—or even mildly acrimonious—gatherings of urbane representatives of different faith traditions, under the auspices of the World Council of Churches or the Center for the Study of World Religions at Harvard, my mind has strayed from the conference room out to those jagged corners of the world where other confessors of these same faiths are killing or proselytizing—or just frigidly ignoring—each other. I have wondered at such moments whether the "dialogue" has not become a tedious exercise in preaching to the converted and I have secretly wished to bring some of those enthusiasts in. Deprived of the energy such particularists embody, a dialogue-among-the-urbane can, and sometimes does, deteriorate into a repetitive exchange of vacuities. It could end with a whimper.

At the same time I fully believe that without the large-hearted vision of the universal that the interfaith conversation incarnates, particularism can deteriorate into fanaticism. And in our present overarmed world, zealotry can easily hasten the moment when everything ends with a bang. So we are left with a paradox. Without the universal pole, there would be no dialogue at all. But without the particular, the dialogue dissipates its source of primal energy. Without the Cross or the Koran or the Bo tree, the religions that were called into being by these sacred realities would atrophy and along with them the inclusive visions they spawned would fade away too. The paradox of the great world faiths is that they both create a dream of a single human family and threaten that dream at the same time. What can be done?

It seems too formulaic simply to say that the universalists and the particularists need each other, especially since they seldom think they do. Still, I believe they do, and as one who has participated in the dialogue for decades, I propose—in this book—to draw on my own experience to show how the indispensable element of particularity can be brought back in. To do so, however, will require me to point out, as I begin, the two most salient ways in which Christians who engage in the dialogue have—often quite inadvertently—neglected the hub in their commendable effort to enlarge the rim.

The first way the particular is diminished in interfaith dialogue is through the loss of the personal voice. Dialogue often climbs quickly to airy exchanges about "Christianity" and "Buddhism" or one of the other faiths. The dialoguers, who are frequently trained to think in abstract, conceptual terms, are sometimes reluctant to say much about "my" faith in Jesus Christ, or "my" devotion to Krishna, or "my" path toward enlightenment. Even the language of "our" faith or "our" path is often left behind as the talk soars into that realm of discourse (invaluable for its own purposes) one finds in an academic seminar on comparative religion. Soon people are yawning and glancing at their watches.

I believe a certain careful and modest restoration of personal narrative—call it "testimony" if you will—can help restore some of the life-giving particularity to the dialogue among religions. After all, it is never the religions themselves that converse but individual people who embody those religions. I have seen more than one interfaith colloquium that was drifting toward death by tedium restored to life when someone had the courage to speak personally rather than in general terms. For this reason, the essays in this book grow almost entirely from my own encounters with actual people of other faiths—enriched and broadened of course by reading and reflection. They are unified by the lived experience of one person. *Many Mansions* is not about "the" Christian dialogue with other religions but about one Christian's encounters with particular people of other faiths.

The second way Christian participation in the dialogue has sometimes lost sight of the particularity pole has been by soft-pedaling the figure of Jesus himself. There are many exceptions to this sotto voce treatment of Christ. Still, I have noticed—as will become evident later on—that when reference to Jesus is postponed or downplayed, conversations between Christians and people of other traditions tend to become arid, but when the figure of Jesus is brought to the fore, either by the Christians or—as sometimes happens—by the others, the dialogue comes alive.

One can of course understand why Christians who believe in the dialogue do not want to push Jesus down other people's throats as soon as the opening gavel has been rapped. After all, Jesus is in some ways the *most* particularistic element of Christianity, and in an interreligious dialogue one is presumably trying—at least at first—to present the less divisive aspects of one's own tradition. The trouble is that not only has this understandable reticence deprived the dialogue of the vigor it needs to survive, but it has also produced another unfortunate consequence. This secondary result is that Christians who think of Jesus as a model in other areas of their lives do not look to his example or teaching for direction in the dialogue itself. I think this twofold neglect of the figure of Jesus—both as a theme and as a source of guidance—has exacted a heavy toll.

I do not mean to suggest that those Christians who even now are working with great dedication in talks with Buddhists or Muslims or Jews never mention Christology (that branch of Christian theology that deals with the meaning of Jesus Christ). They do. Often they seek to find some bridge to the other faiths through a "cosmic Christ" such as the one portrayed in the Epistle to the Ephesians, a Christ who is said to be present throughout the universe and therefore presumably can be also found in the lived worlds of Hindus and Muslims. More frequently, however, the Christian participants have tried to base the dialogue on completely different facets of religious tradition. Sometimes, for example, they turn to the idea of God the Creator, the Mystery out of whom all that is emerges. At other times, they focus on the Divine Spirit, present in every person or even in every sentient being. In recent decades, they have preferred to explore the experience of faith itself as a universal human experience that exhibits common stages of development through the succeeding phases of human life. Most recently, they have sought to wrestle—together with people of other faiths—with the awful issues everyone must confront today—nuclear war, hunger, disease, the despoiling of the ecosphere—and to reach into the various traditions as possible sources of values and visions for facing such horrors. These paths to interfaith encounter differ markedly, but they all have one thing in common: they keep the historical Jesus of the Gospels distinctly in the background.

Each of these approaches to the crafting of an adequate Christian grasp of the multiplicity of faiths has its value. Each has advanced the dialogue in some measure. We need to continue to try to work with all of them. Still, I confess that I find these approaches, all of which hold the Jesus-fact in abeyance, not wholly satisfactory. The problem with them is twofold. First, for the vast majority of Christians, including those most energetically engaged in dialogue, Jesus is not merely a background figure. He is central to Christian faith. Not only do the Christian dialoguers recognize this, but so do their Muslim, Buddhist, Shinto, Hindu, and Jewish conversation partners. Wherever one starts, whether with creation (which, incidentally, is not a particularly good place to begin a dialogue with Buddhists, who reject the whole notion), with the omnipresent enlivening Spirit, with the faith experience as such, or with something else, any honest dialogue between Christians and others will sooner or later—and in my experience it is usually sooner—have to deal with the figure of Jesus.

Yes, some might say, but is it not better to delay so potentially divisive a topic until some more inclusive groundwork has been laid? This may be the case in some instances, but I have never been persuaded that an interfaith dialogue is enhanced by designing it like one of those elementary collections for teaching the piano that begins with "Frère Jacques" and works up to Chopin preludes at the end. Everyone always knows that the question of who Jesus was and is, and what he means today, will inevitably appear. Until it does, it sometimes feels as though one is—at least to some degree—engaging in the necessary pleasantries that often precede a genuine conversation but are really not integral to it. When will the other shoe drop?

The second part of my problem with dialogue tactics that play down the Jesus factor is that—surprisingly—it is just this factor that the non-Christian participants often seem most interested in and most eager to get to. This is not something one is led to expect will happen in inter-faith dialogue. But it does. Indeed, it happens so often that it raises serious questions about the other approaches, at least insofar as they try to proceed—ever so carefully and judiciously, they suppose—with-out this central point up front.

It took me a lot of time and many false starts to learn this. I too wanted to minimize the possibility of giving needless offense to the people of other faiths who had taken the venturesome step of entering into dialogue with me: to steer clear of unnecessary roadblocks or any suggestion of proselytizing. But I kept discovering that my tactics for nurturing the tender shoot of interfaith exchange did not connect with those of my partners across the table. I too tried to avoid talking about Jesus too quickly, but I soon discovered my interlocutors wanted me to, and their bearing sometimes suggested that they did not believe they were really engaged in a brass-tacks conversation with a Christian until that happened. Of course in this respect they were right.

The "others" want to hear what Christians think about Jesus. When Chogyam Trungpa, a Tibetan lama, invited me to teach summer school at the Naropa Institute in Boulder, Colorado, the first Buddhist higher educational institution in the United States, I accepted. I then suggested several alternative topics for my lectures and semi-nars, all leaning toward a comparative approach to religion. Trungpa and his fellow Buddhists were not interested. Instead, the course they encouraged me to offer was "The Life and Teachings of Jesus." A few years later, when I had my first serious conversation with a Muslim, he immediately wanted to compare Jesus with the prophet Muham-mad. Shortly afterward, when I was asked to address a gathering of Vaishnava Hindu scholars during a trip to India, I carefully chose a safe "universal" topic—I think it was something like "the role of reli-gion in the modern world." The Indian teachers sat patiently through my presentation and the long translation that followed. But, when the discussion period came, the first question they asked me was what I believed about Jesus and the form of love he exhibited (*agapē*). Soon we were all talking about Jesus, and then about the love Krishna shows to a devotee and the devotee to Krishna. My efforts at theological prudence, going slow, avoiding possibly thorny issues—although I certainly meant well—had merely succeeded in delaying the real exchange for two hours. I came away convinced that, whatever might be said for the other modes of dialogue, in my own future opportunities I would not assume that my partners wanted me to hold the Jesus factor in abeyance. More recently, other Christians who have engaged in difficult but real dialogue have come to the same conclusion. The only person I know who has ever met the Ayatollah Khomeini told me that the first thing Khomeini wanted to talk about was Jesus.

Of course, merely suggesting that Jesus be made more central to the dialogue does not solve anything at all. The questions of *what* role Jesus plays and *how* he is introduced still persist. This is why I have always been so intrigued by the "many mansions" Jesus speaks of in John 14:2, which I quoted at the beginning of this book, as well as by John 14:6: "I am the way, the truth, and the life: no man cometh unto the Father, but by me." These verses stand only a few lines away from each other in the same chapter of the same Gospel. But they have traditionally supplied both the dialogic universalists and the antidialogic particularists with their favorite proof texts. Those who look with appreciation on other faiths frequently cite John 14:2 and suggest that the "many mansions" may refer to the heavenly palaces in which Hindus and Buddhists will dwell—alongside Christians—in the hereafter. Those who insist that all others must accept Christ or be damned, however, prefer to cite John 14:6 and declare that Jesus alone is the one true way to salvation. What can we say about this curious juxtaposition of seemingly contradictory texts? Could it be telling us about the need to hold the universal and the particular together and about the central place Jesus must have for Christians even in the most expansive interfaith dialogue? The thoughts and experiences recounted in this book document my continuing struggle with these questions. I present them, not as a formula for all future dialogue, but as an addition and a complement to approaches I have found only partially satisfying. Thus my first point has been that, to place the figure of Jesus on the agenda of interfaith dialogue, far from killing it, actually enlivens it. My second point is related but different. It is that Jesus does have something vital to teach us about how to participate in interfaith dialogue. At first this may sound quite improbable. So far as we know, the rabbi from Nazareth never met a Buddhist or a Hindu. Islam did not appear until 600 years after his crucifixion. Despite speculations that regularly appear about his "hidden years," probably Jesus' interreligious experience was confined to the different sects and movements within the Judaism of his day and to the people, mainly Romans, even he called "heathens." At first glance, it hardly seems we can learn much from him on this subject.

Jesus also had no direct experience with many of the other vast questions we deal with today: runaway technology, genocidal weapons, AIDS, and the ethical issues involved in corporate takeovers, disinvestment, advertising, and insider trading. He never had to cope with the temptations that arise in filling out an expense account or an IRS form. But this misses the point. To be a disciple of Jesus does not mean to emulate or mimic him. It means to follow his "way," to live in our era the same way he lived in his—as a sign and servant of the reign of God. To "follow" Jesus does not require us to choose twelve disciples or to turn water into wine but to take his life project—making the coming of God's reign of Shalom real and immediate—our own. I believe that friendship among the peoples of the world faiths and the nurturing of a sense of "species consciousness" is an indispensable facet of the coming of God's Shalom. I also believe there are at least four ways in which the Jesus of the Gospels, he who "came preaching the Reign of God," provides useful guidelines for building such an interfaith consciousness.

The first is that a focus on Jesus moves the encounter from the theoretical level to the practical one. The reign of God is not an abstract ideal. It is a reality actualizing itself in history. Consequently, as soon as this Kingdom becomes the focus, we see that religions do not exist apart from their local manifestations. Further, these concrete expressions of a tradition vary markedly from place to place. Except in the minds of textbook writers, there is no such thing as Buddhism or Hinduism, or Christianity for that matter. There are only *persons* who think of themselves as Buddhists, Hindus, or Christians. Comparing classical religious texts can be misleading unless one understands what these texts mean to the actual people who chant them, study them, and try to live by them. And these meanings change from time to time and from place to place. Genuine interreligious dialogue occurs only when we recognize how a tradition actually shapes people's lives. Those who ignore this insight soon find themselves touring a never-never-land of "religions" that do not exist except in comparative religion monographs. To follow Jesus means to deal with specifics, not generalities.

Such a down-to-earth approach to interreligious conversation is anything but easy. It makes what was already an arduous undertaking even more difficult. Christians committed to dialogue with the people who live according to other faiths can no longer be content with the "library" versions of those traditions. Nor will it help to complain that the actual Buddhist or Islamic movements we meet today are not the real thing but decadent or "politicized" corruptions (as though "pure" editions existed once upon a time). The example of Jesus' own life demonstrates that any dialogue must take place with actual people. A so-called interreligious dialogue with the Platonic ideals of what this or that religious tradition ought to be in its pure essence leads nowhere.

The second way the Jesus of the Gospels facilitates interfaith dialogue is by reminding us that religion is always a mixed blessing. Jesus, after all, was fiercely opposed by many (not all) of the religious people of his day. His attacks on the misuse of religion remind us that, wherever religion exists, we can be sure that someone is trying to use the gods to dominate, frighten, or oppress someone else. Indeed, any honest attempt at interfaith dialogue must deal with the fact that our century has not only spawned hundreds of new religious movements but that some of those movements are destructive and some of the most demonic claim to be expressions of Christianity.

What are the limits of tolerance? Were the Christians of Japan being intolerant when they opposed the state Shinto that the military used during World War II to lead their nation to ruin? Was Bonhoeffer being narrow-minded when he refused to be cozily ecumenical with the *Deutsche Christen* who supported the Nazi effort to synthesize Christianity with the spirit of the German *Volk*? Should no one raise questions about human sacrifice, or consigning widows to their husbands' funeral pyre, or collecting Rolls Royces in the name of Christ? The more we think about it, the more obvious it becomes that a benign tolerance, which sees anything religious as good, will simply not do.

Intimidated by this need to "grade" religious practices, some gentle souls suggest that maybe we should simply declare a kind of moratorium both on proselytizing and on interreligious discussion. Why not just live and let live? The idea is not without its attractions.

But it is impossible. People travel today at the speed of sound, and ideas travel at the speed of light. It is idle to hope that various cultures and religions could simply leave each other alone. There will always be interaction. Some kind of encounter, even dialogue, is unavoidable. The hard question is how to enter into a genuinely open encounter without losing sight of the need to make judgments and, at times, even to take sides.

This is where the example of Jesus is most pertinent. Jesus was not a model of vacuous tolerance. He did make judgments about the faith of the people he met. In fact, he did so all the time. He argued with the Pharisees and excoriated the rulers of the temple. But the key to Jesus' approach to any religious perspective was, "By their fruits shall ye know them." He seemed singularly uninterested in the doctrinal content or ritual correctness of the different religions he encountered. He was, however, terribly concerned about the practical outcome of people's spiritual commitments. He once told a pagan Roman he had not found such a faith as his anywhere in Israel.

Third, Jesus' example also reminds us that the search for human oneness-in-diversity in interreligious dialogue is not *only* a matter of making judgments. It also sometimes requires refraining from judgment. This has its rewarding and even its lighter side. When I was living among Tibetan Buddhists, for example, it took me some time to appreciate the frolicsome way they approach even the deepest tenets of their faith. They sometimes called it the "crazy wisdom." I found that, as a Christian, I eventually had to lay aside the notion that dialogue must always be serious. The same is true with the so-called primal religions. At a conference in Japan, a pioneer of Christian dialogue with tribal peoples once observed that Western Christians tend to be at ease only with those adherents of other faiths who are as precise and sober as they are. Perhaps we need to place the "theology of play" at the service of interfaith encounter, especially with Buddhists and those who used to be called "primitive" peoples. Jesus often responded to people's serious questions by rattling off a story, and some of his stories—like the one about the speck in the neighbor's eye and the two-by-four in my own—are downright hyperbolic. I am sure people laughed when he told them. To insist that dialogue must always be about clear and distinct ideas is to impose a narrowly Western verbal-doctrinal style. What occurs, then, is nothing but a more subtle form of religious imperialism. Exchanging jokes and anecdotes is also a form of dialogue.

Can Christians allow themselves to enter into this friskier and more "ludic" expression of interfaith exchange? There's reason to believe that the tragic schism between the Byzantine and Latin churches deprived Western Christians of a tradition that preserved this roguish element. There was for many years in the Orthodox world the tradition of the holy fool. Harking back to Saint Paul's words in the Epistle to the Corinthians about being "fools for Christ," the holy fools were not only accepted but venerated. Alexander Syrkin describes, for example, one Symen, a contemporary of the Emperor Justinian I (527–565). Symen is said to have dragged a dead dog through the streets and then gone to the church and thrown nuts at the worshipers. Sometimes he would creep through the village on all fours, get himself beaten by a town ruffian, trip people as they walked, and stroll through the market with no clothes on. Apparently, the theological tactic behind all this tom-foolery was to awaken his surprised audiences from their lethargy, lampoon conventional values, and bring people to religious insight without accruing any praise or credit to himself.

When we look for an analogous tradition in Western Christianity, the closest we come is to Saint Francis and his earliest friars. Clearly, the behavior of the saint himself was viewed as mad by many of his contemporaries, beginning with his parents. Legend says that Francis, like Symen, stripped himself of the finery his well-to-do family had provided and stood naked in the town square, and that the citizens inveighed against him until the local bishop protected him. Francis said he wanted to "become naked" so he could "follow the naked Christ." But Francis also had a comic streak. As a boy, he had admired traveling troubadours. Later he called himself and his followers *joculatores Domini* (jesters of the Lord). Many of the stories about them handed down in *The Little Flowers* are strongly reminiscent of the capers attributed to the Russian holy fools. Once, for example, Francis is said to have sent Rufinus through the streets to the church to preach clad only in his underwear. On another occasion, the inimitable Brother Juniper cut the adornments and decorations from a church and gave them to poor people so they could get money to buy food. The famous pilgrimage Francis himself took through the battle lines of the crusading armies to visit the caliph was a classical fool's errand. The reason the Muslims did not kill him is that they also had a certain respect for holy madness.

In an interreligious dialogue, this crazy wisdom has an important theological meaning. It implies that the participants realize—as mystics also do—that even their best words fall far short of the divine reality, so far short as to be somewhat ridiculous. This insight undercuts distinctions that are very precious to the West: correct/incorrect, secular/sacred, wisdom/folly, purity/dirtiness. It thus points toward what mystical theology calls the *coincidentia oppositorum*, the ultimate union of what appear to be opposites.

The fourth way the Jesus of the Gospels helps facilitate interreligious encounter is that he teaches us to expect to find God already present in the "other," including the one with whom we are in dialogue, no matter how strange or unfamiliar that other's ideas or religious practices may seem. Christ meets us in and through the stranger. I have always known that this is true "in principle," but by participating in the dialogue I have learned it is also true in reality. To step into real dialogue, as Martin Buber knew, is to step onto holy ground. It invites both blessedness and pain. No one who enters—really enters—remains unaffected. If they do, there is room for doubt whether they have entered at all. Dialogue changes those who risk it. It upsets more than stereotypes and preconceptions about the "other"; it works an even more subtle transformation of the way I understand and live my own faith. To enter honestly into dialogue is to embark on a perilous personal voyage with no clear destination in view. Unforeseen things can happen. One of the risks is running the possibility of being viewed by one's coreligionists with suspicion or distrust. "Why do you want to bother with *them?*" Another is to find oneself asking questions, perhaps only inwardly, about what one's own faith really means, questions that would never have come up without the provocation of the other. The fearful gatekeepers who have insisted throughout the ages that "pure religion" can be maintained only in a ghetto or compound have not been entirely wrong. To expose one's tradition to dialogue is willy-nilly to open it to change, ferment, and internal debate. I believe God can and does speak to us through people of other faiths. And as people of faith have always known, when God speaks, mountains melt and the seas roar.

Christians have entered into serious dialogue with people of other faiths only very recently. As we have seen, one of the questions this conversation has sparked *within* Christianity itself concerns what Jesus means for the dialogue. But the question of what Christ means for our encounter with the other inevitably raises the even more basic one of what Christ means for us as Christians. It never fails. I invariably return from a conversation with a genuine believer in one of the other faiths with Christ's famous question to Peter ringing in my mind: "Who do you say that I am?" But, as I listen, I find I am not putting the question to the other. I am putting it to myself.

Perhaps the most unexpected thing I have learned in the dialogue with people of other religions is how important it is for me to keep in touch with those of my own faith community who remain suspicious and fearful of that dialogue. This has sometimes proven difficult, and I have often found it easier to converse with universally minded Buddhists or Hindus than with fellow Christians who not only dismiss such people as pagans but also want to dismiss me for not recognizing it. Still, I believe the critically important conversation among people of diverse faiths could founder and fail if we—the dialoguers—lose touch with our fellow believers who cluster on the particularistic side. We may not admit it, but we do need each other. They remind us that without the radical particularity of the original revelation, we would have no faith to share. We remind them that without the universal dream they falsify the message and diminish the scope of the original vision.

Multiple specters stalk the human enterprise today. We have reached a point where strife between nations and religions could lead to the final apocalypse. We need more than ever to doxologize the fragile oneness of the whole earth and all her inhabitants. Yet for men and women of faith, the sacred stories by which we hymn the unity of our species and its animal and cosmic neighbors need not be invented. Paradoxically, those stories and symbols are already embedded in the same traditions that sometimes threaten to tear us asunder. Our task is to claim these reminders of our common destiny from within the desperate sources that first gave them voice.

I invite my readers to journey with me through some of the discoveries and disappointments that have marked my attempts to cultivate the conversation with people of other faiths while trying to nurture the vital sources of the faith that motivates the conversation. From Jesus I have learned both that he is the Way and that in God's house there are many mansions. I do not believe these two sayings are contradictory. In fact I have come to see that only by understanding one can we come to understand the other.

* * *

THE FUTURE OF RELIGION

When all is said and done, is there anything we can confidently predict about the future of religion? Why not hazard a few guesses? After all, past predictions about other forms of human endeavor have often been borne out. Observe: we do have space ships, death rays, annihilation weapons, and happy pills, just as Jules Verne and Aldous Huxley once imagined. But religion is notoriously harder to predict. What Nostradamus could have foreseen the resurgence of militant Islam, a tongue-speaking charismatic revival among middle-class Americans, a Korean evangelist resurrecting the old American civil religion with himself as the presumptive messiah? Or a twentieth-century pope who poses for photographs with a sombrero on, like an American presidential candidate? Or the reemergence of witchcraft? In taking on this most perilous of all fields of forecast, it might be useful to recall three of the more notable past predictions, all of which seem to have come to nought.

The *Philosophes*

Let us begin with a distinguished company: the eighteenth-century French philosophes. Since they believed the Age of Reason was dawning, the philosophes confidently predicted that religion and superstition were fated for extinction, presumably quite soon. Their *Encyclopedia* was to be a compendium of all knowledge, shining the bright light of human intelligence into the darkest abyss, expelling the noisome remains of priestcraft and sorcery. Religion, they believed, was the product of ignorance compounded by clerical greed and political reaction. It was a poison whose only antidote was clear and courageous thought. "Not until the last priest is hanged with the entrails of the last king," Voltaire once declared, "will mankind finally be free." So they enthroned the goddess Reason, carried her in solemn procession through Paris, accompanied by young girls strewing flowers, bore her into Notre Dame Cathedral, hymned her virtues, and dedicated the dawning new age to her.

How were they to know that with procession, enthroning, and hymning they were perpetuating religion, not abolishing it? Human beings have made the same mistake before and since. Auguste Comte, the founder of positivism, was in some ways the last of the philosophes. He thought he saw humankind leaving behind mythical and metaphysical explanations of reality and entering the "positive" age. In fact, he became so enchanted with his vision that he went on to compose a whole Mass for the era of positivism. It is a curious and wonderful artifice, this Mass, containing all the traditional pillars of the Roman original but reworked for a positivist *Weltanschauung*. Religion seems to reassert itself even among those who most avidly desire its demise. The predictions of the philosophes seem not to have come true, even for them.

Lenin and Marx

Lenin is another case in point. With a mind somewhat more programmatic and less flexible than Marx's, he took quite woodenly his master's ideas about religion and enlarged them into a metaphysical worldview he believed would soon replace religion. Lenin utilized some of the evolutionist and physical materialist ideas then prevalent to produce his own theory of materialism, one which was, however, ontological, not dialectical like Marx's. Lenin's concoction, although popular with Russian Communists for many years, is rarely defended nowadays. Most Marxists prefer to follow Marx instead of Lenin and to make their judgments about religion on a political, rather than an ontological, basis. Ironically, a half century after the October revolution, not only has religion not died out in Lenin's Soviet Union, but the most widely appreciated Russian writers, Aleksandr Solzhenitsyn and Andrei Sinyavsky, are Orthodox believers, as was the late Boris

Pasternak. Whatever else his accomplishments, as a religious fore-
caster Lenin, like the philosophes, seems to have failed.

Lenin's predictions were confounded by his own fate. When this
enemy of all pilgrimages and icons and superstitious devotions died,
his body was embalmed and placed in a mausoleum in Red Square in
the shadow of Saint Basil's. There, to this day, thousands of pilgrims
wend their way, lining up in every kind of weather to file past the sacred
bier. The lights are dim in the tomb of Lenin. An atmosphere of sanctity and hushed awe pervades the stone temple. Some older pilgrims
from the far provinces are seen to cross themselves as they shuffle by
the glass-encased remains of the saint. And behold, as young Alexis
Karamazov had vainly hoped for *his* idol, Father Zossima, the body
remains uncorrupted—the result this time not of a miracle but of the
embalming techniques of modern science. The enemy of icons has
been made into an icon himself.

Freud and Jung

Let us look at one more prediction before—duly humbled by these
discouraging precedents—we venture a few of our own. No catalog
of "past futures" of religion would be complete without that of Sig-
mund Freud, whose *Future of an Illusion* represents his most concisely
worded entry into this precarious enterprise. Freud believed that
religion consisted of the projection of inner fears and anxieties—and
hopes and fantasies—onto the external world. He interpreted it as a
kind of infantile delusion writ large. As the inventor of psychoanalysis,
he had strong confidence in the efficacy of his method. He saw it as
the ultimate application of the scientific method—which had formerly
scanned the skies—to the inner, secret workings of the human mind.
He hoped that eventually the utilization of this method would enable
people to set aside religious delusions and face reality without blinders
and crutches.

But Freud did not seem to believe this psychoanalytic remedy would
take effect very quickly or even in the foreseeable future. The illusion
was too widespread and too well grounded in the culture itself. In fact,
there are passages in which Freud appears to have resigned himself to
a kind of pessimism, in which he seems to be saying that, since his solution will never be generalizable to the whole populace, the "illusion"
may have a promising future indeed.

Freud's body was never enshrined in a holy sepulcher, as Lenin's
was. But before his death, as though to prove once again the futility
of making predictions about the fate of the gods, Freud's criticism of

religion was turned inside out by one of his own disciples, Carl Gustav Jung. His thought may be for Freud what the Red Square tomb became for Lenin.

The son of a Swiss Reformed pastor, as a child Jung once had a dream in which an immense divinity squatted in the sky over the local cathedral and defecated on its soaring tower. Although this does not appear to be the dream of a man who would later start from Freud's thinking and then move toward a whole new rationale for the religious understanding of life, that is in fact exactly what Jung did. His theories, and the form of therapy associated with his name, have conspired to produce an attitude toward religion for numerous twentieth-century people who can no longer be religious in conventional ways. Like Freud, the Jungians see the whole pantheon of the gods as an internal universe, not something "out there." But in contrast to Freud, they believe these gods are not to be abolished, outgrown, unmasked, or eviscerated. Rather, one should learn to know them and serve them, for in so doing one is serving one's own deepest and most authentic self.

At this point, any sensible student of the history and philosophy of religion would stop. Having demonstrated the precariousness of extrapolations in the realm of the spirit, the best expression of wisdom would be a Buddha-like smile—and silence. It was Jesus himself who said, "The spirit bloweth where it listeth, and no man knows from whence it comes or whither it blows." (He also held in singularly low regard those who thought they could predict "the day or the hour of the coming of the Son of Man," a secret that, he said, was known only to the Father in heaven.) In short, all evidence, both historical and theological, seems to point to a strategy of restraint, abjuring all predictions. But who—despite the cautionary tales of past failures—can resist making at least some attempt to predict something about the future of religion? I will ignore the evidence and plunge ahead.

After this dismal recitation of failed fathers, I still contend that all three of the predictions I have just cataloged about the future of religion—those of the philosophes, of Marx, and of Freud—though flawed in detail, have turned out to be *essentially* accurate. In one sense, they all seem to have missed, but I believe they each teach us something valid, or at least useful.

Let us look at them once again, in order. First, the philosophes. They were correct, in my view, to foresee the disappearance of religion as an extension of that way of knowing the external world we now call magic or superstition. Religion is not the descendant of magic. The magical impulse is the desire to control and direct nature, to use it for human ends, to tame its sometimes malevolent side. This impulse developed through the centuries not into religion but into empirical science. The true successors of the sorcerers and the alchemists are not the priests and theologians but the physicists and the computer engineers. They merely use another method to accomplish the same end. Religion has nothing to do with supplying answers to questions that can be answered by empirical investigation and observation. Religion concerns questions of human meaning and purpose that are in principle unanswerable in an empirical way. (This holds unless one believes that ethical imperatives and human meaning can simply be deduced from how things are, a questionable theory that cannot itself be proven by observing how things are.)

In other words, the notorious nineteenth-century "Warfare between Science and Religion" arose from mistaken notions of what religion and science are. Although there are still occasional border skirmishes, most theologians and scientists now recognize that religion overstepped its boundaries when—at least in the West—it tried to make geological and biological history into matters of revelation. On the other side, although some scientists once believed they had discovered the universal method for solving all conceivable questions—rather than one very useful way of dealing with some—it is very hard to get an argument going between scientists and theologians over issues of this kind any more. At the international conference on "Science, Faith and the Future" sponsored by the World Council of Churches at the Massachusetts Institute of Technology in July 1979, there was virtually no debate along the old science-versus-religion lines at all. Rather, the scientists implored the theologians and religious leaders present to take more of an interest in the pressing ethical issues emerging from the newest advances of science. Theologians, especially from the poorer parts of the world, did not criticize the scientists for being too self-important. Rather, they took them to task for making big hardware for the multinational corporations instead of supplying appropriate technologies to the poorer countries. The issues, in other words, were political and ethical, and it was clear that the deepest divisions pitted North against South, rich against poor, East against West, radical against liberal.

As it turns out, the philosophes' attack on religion had a kind of purgative effect. More and more, religion is now concerning itself with questions of human meaning and ethical policy, not with dogmatic formulations about what time of day it was when God created the world (a question that had vexed the nineteenth-century British Anglican Bishop Ussher).

Even in Iran, where a form of Muslim zealotry has reemerged, it is significant to notice that the ayatollahs and imams have not attacked the domain of science as such but have concentrated on what they see as issues of public order. The direction the philosophes set out is still, when its exaggerations are combed out, what we too can expect in the future: realizing its limitations, we will turn to science for help in answering the how and why questions. At the same time the perennial riddles of human meaning and personal obligation will continue to be debated in categories derived from the great religious traditions.

How else could it be? The most important questions we will face in the future must be answered on the basis of premises about the nature and destiny of humankind for which no empirical proof can be mustered. What is human life, and when does it begin or end? Is every human life really worth respecting? If so, why? Has the present generation any responsibility for those who will inherit the planet millennia from now? Does the human species have any special responsibility at all in the cosmos? Is there a meaning that transcends my meaning or even the collective total of all our human meanings? Is there anything worth dying for? All these questions press the questioner ultimately into those strata of human reality where our primal terrors and hopes—expressed in myth and rite and symbol—remain the only sources of wisdom.

But what about Marxism? Surely Lenin's idea that religious life can be reduced to emanations from material particles that are then used to justify class oppression in no way depicts the future of religion. Again, let us step back from the precise manner in which Lenin (and Marx, in a much more subtle way) actually enunciated their theories and look instead at the overall intention of their program. Although Lenin's metaphysical views are dated ones and now appear positively quaint, there are three aspects of his and of Marx's ideas about religion that I consider basically sound.

First, they insisted that religion must be understood not in isolation but in relation to all other dimensions of life, including the way human beings use the natural world to feed and clothe themselves. Religion, they believed—and quite rightly—does not fall like fire from the heavens. It is part and parcel with all other human activities and cannot be fathomed without reference to them. Lenin called his way of analyzing this totality "materialistic" because of his neo-Democritean (from Democritus, the Greek atomic materialist) ontology. Marx preferred the term "dialectical." What they both wanted to say is that the study of "religion" *as such* can teach us nothing. We must study it as an integral element of the world of work and power and social arrangements. In this, they were right. More and more I am suspicious of that method of studying religion represented by Joseph Campbell and Mircea Eliade. The typical approach of these highly influential scholars is to assemble the myths and legends of several cultures into a collection in a skillful way but with few descriptions of the social settings within which actual people told, sang, chanted, or danced the myths. They are set down in print, often thematically organized. Tribes and continents are juxtaposed with very little indication of who tells them and who listens, how the tribe feeds itself or is governed, to say nothing of what happens to the people—if there are any—who don't like the story. In short, the error of this widespread method is that it lifts out something called "religion" from the intricate human corpus in which it lives. The result is a kind of collage of disparate elements that disfigures the religious dimensions. For all their understandable nineteenth-century philosophical narrowness, Marx and Lenin did not want this kind of excising to happen, and in this they were right.

Second, Marx and his followers saw that, in an unjust society, religion is a powerful tool of oppression. It is an opiate, a mystification, a way of trying to solve through fantasy what can be solved only in history. Again, although they were undoubtedly heavy-handed in the way they laid out this criticism, no one can doubt that they were largely correct, at least for the societies in which they lived. During the nineteenth century, religious institutions played an almost exclusively reactionary role nearly everywhere. Marx and his followers took deadly aim; they pointed out that, since religion is part of a sociocultural whole and culture is almost always controlled by the dominant group, religion can be a tool of manipulation. This leaves us to wonder what religion might look like in a nonexploitative society, where there would be no need for opiates to keep people subdued and mystified. I will return to this point later.

Third, Marx and his school believed that religion would eventually disappear. Again, though this may come as a surprise to the reader, I believe they were right. Marx's notion about the "disappearance" of religion can be understood best by comparing it with his theory about the "withering away of the state." This idea has also been roundly ridiculed, largely because it is so badly misunderstood. What he meant was that there is nothing eternally fixed about any human institution, the state included. It is a perfectly reasonable idea when one thinks about it for a moment. For millennia, human societies existed and governed themselves before the institution of the state appeared. National states emerged at a certain point in recent history, served and will serve a certain purpose, but will not endure forever. As awareness expands and new forms of consciousness and culture evolve, new patterns of governance, which are not as distant and hard to control as the state, will also appear, Marx thought.

The comparison with religion is quite exact. Just as some thing called the "state" differentiated itself from that great complex organism we now call "society" at one stage in its history, so we also began to speak of certain acts and persons and institutions as "religious." But this is a very recent category of human thought and I believe also a "reified" one. The Balinese, it is said, claim they have no art: they just do everything beautifully. There was a time, not too long ago in the full scale of cultural evolution, when one would have been hard put to discover anything separate and distinct in human societies that could be called "religion." People just "did everything" with awe or joy or with a sense of mystery or with a recognition of the incandescent power within persons, places, and things. Prayer was as much a part of planting as invocation was of hunting. It is possible that, in our efforts to understand the cultures of the Orient and of nonliterate peoples, much mischief and confusion has already resulted from our imposing on them the—Western and recent—term "religion." What Marx meant, perhaps, is that we now live in an unnatural epoch, one in which we have separated and elevated (and mystified) something we call "religion." Eventually, when conditions allow for the transition, this artificially segregated element will be reabsorbed into the whole.

Finally, what about Freud, Jung, and the psychological predictions about religion? Although religious scholars often prefer Jung since he is notoriously "soft" on myth, magic, and astrology, I prefer Freud. The old master of the Bergstrasse was right that much of religion consists of the projection of inner fantasies onto an imaginary external screen. Unlike Jung, Freud did not want to come to terms with this projecting, but he could not see how we could get beyond it either. He chose to live with the tension, and his choice has given rise to two remarkably differing interpretations of what the next step after his own work should have been. Some sought to help people do the best they can in a world in which some degree of neurotic projection will inevitably continue even after it is minimized in individual patients. Most practicing therapists settle for this interpretation of the master. The other side will not accept this compromise. The "radical Freudians" claim that there is implicit in Freud the idea that we should alter the conditions that produce this "surplus repression" with its resultant neurosis. If we did, alienated human thinking and living would be transcended, not by treating two billion people one by one for four years each at seventy-five dollars an hour, but by a quantum leap in human awareness, growing out of a qualitative change in the basic organization of human life. If this great leap could happen, then the present, unconscious inclination to segregate religious impulses from the rest of life would slip into the past, and we would deal with the universe, our neighbors, and ourselves without the mediation of mystified phantoms.

This vision of the radical Freudians, represented most eloquently in the thought of the late Herbert Marcuse, admittedly sounds terribly utopian, maybe even "millenarian." It is at least—to use a very theological term—"eschatological." It suggests a Messianic Era or a Kingdom of God. Freud remained stalwartly antireligious to his dying day. But the logic of his thought, at least as it is interpreted by his radical disciples, conjures up images similar to that of the prophet Jeremiah, who spoke of a coming time when no one would have to speak the name of God or teach the law since God would be within us and the law would be inscribed on our hearts. The New Testament book of Revelation tells of a heavenly city where there is no need for a temple because God suffuses everything. Ironically, the radical Freudians are closer to the Bible than the pious Jungians.

True, one could argue that all the predictions I have mentioned were wrong. Despite the *Encyclopedia,* religion has not disappeared. Despite Marx and Lenin, there is a religious revival going on in Eastern Europe and the USSR, and in Latin America the Catholics are more revolutionary than the Communists. Fifty years after Freud's death, psychoanalysis is dying. Still, each of these prophets had a point. The philosophes' forecasts remind us that religion should not be mistaken for a method of examining and managing empirical reality. Marx and Lenin are right that religion is part and parcel with the whole of the human world, and its use for exalted and debased purposes cannot be understood if it is studied in isolation. They also teach us that religion is not simply a part of "nature," given once and for all, but a part of "history" and therefore subject to conscious criticism and reconstruction. Finally, the Freudians remind us that even if religion springs from deep and possibly distorted needs in the human psyche, its inner logic points to the possibility of a fundamentally different kind of world order.

Where does all this leave us? It seems appropriate to conclude our reflections on the future of religion with a parable, this one the true story of one American congregation. During the War for Independence, there were many patriots in the new nation who thought that a new day had come in religion also. They were sure they were the midwives for this new religion, which they intended to deliver, not just to America, but to the world. The case of King's Chapel in Boston serves as a particularly good example. It had been, in the period before independence, an Anglican chapel serving the needs of the small community that still adhered to the Church of England in that Puritan theocratic outpost. When the war began, the position of theological and political loyalists became a bit less secure than the rock of ages. Eventually, when the British troops themselves evacuated Boston, King's Chapel suffered the hasty departure of its rector and many of its more Tory-minded parishioners.

The remnant was left in an unusually precarious but promising position. In fact, their canonical situation was virtually unique. Since the king of England, who had headed the Anglican church since Henry VIII, no longer ruled this realm, their ties with the Anglican hierarchy were severed with one hurried sailing. Also, since they had never been subject to the Standing Order—the established Puritan-Calvinist church of the Massachusetts Bay Colony—they now found themselves, in effect, the freest church in Boston. But what should that freedom mean?

A long discussion ensued about what a truly "republican religion" should be. Would it be deist, evangelical, unitarian? In one sense, the congregation of King's Chapel undertook the same task the French philosophes had accomplished by creating the goddess Reason. But unlike them, or Marx and Lenin, who saw no need for any religion, they wanted to formulate a religious doctrine that would be patriotic, enlightened, and in keeping with that special destiny many Americans believed "nature's God" intended for the new republic. The argument raged on, and the mixture of religious theories and political posturing that appeared was heady stuff indeed. The result, as might have been expected, was a fascinating compromise that any visitor to Boston can still sample by stopping in at King's Chapel. The "republican religion" for the new nation turned out to be an admixture of unitarian theology and Anglican liturgical forms. The church now belongs to the Unitarian-Universalist denomination, but the shape of its liturgy is "higher" than even that of many American Episcopal churches. In few other places can parishioners actually chant liberal theological paeans in something close to Gregorian plainsong.

To the question of whether the congregants of King's Chapel actually anticipated the religion of the future or even the religion of the new republic, one can offer only an inconclusive answer at best. True, their deliberations produced what harsher critics might call a potpourri of ingredients whose proportions did not catch on with the rest of the population of the new nation. Still, the important thing is that they made the attempt. Some political historians argue that it was not until the English revolution of the seventeenth century that people began to realize that the forms of governance they had simply taken for granted as being "natural"—the monarchy, for example—were not "natural" at all but were products of human construction in history and could therefore be altered or abolished. The people of King's Chapel were merely applying this same principle to religious life. They were taking what had once been viewed as a "given" into their own hands and consciously shaping it for human ends. They were "defatalizing" their religious lives just as they were also applying the human tendency to reshape, remold, and reform in other realms. They teach us something important about the future of religion not by what they did but by the courage and initiative they showed in daring to do it. We now have the chance to do the same thing—not to wait and see what religious forms will emerge in the next century, but to use our imaginations to shape them.

So what then about the future of religion? Personally, I believe those kinds of questions we currently segregate and call "religion" will not disappear so long as there are people around to ask them. Human beings come into life without having asked for it. They inherit a skin and sex and culture they never chose. They are buffeted with pain, lifted with joys, strangled by deprivation, awed by the inevitability of death. They are enraged by injustice and dream of a better way. Human beings always spawn more questions than they can answer. If they could only be *either* goats or gods instead of this curious combination, there would be no "religion." Still, as long as there is something recognizably human to hope for and ponder and question, there will be the "religious dimension." But will it always have the strangely segregated and fenced-off place it now seems so "naturally" to occupy in our epoch?

I doubt it. Students of Chinese history have often remarked on the way the sacred seems to be imbedded in the everyday. One writer calls Taoism "the sacrality of the secular." But does this mean the Chinese are "less religious"? Or more so? Perhaps future historians will look back on our modern Western age as an aberration, one in which the spiritual ingredient of life was distilled, drawn off, encapsulated—with disastrous results.

I do not believe my future vision of a religion reintegrated into the secular conflicts with Christianity. Dietrich Bonhoeffer, the German pastor who wrote his *Letters and Papers from Prison* while awaiting his execution by the Nazis, once said he never really wanted to become a saint; he just wanted "to be a man." To be a Christian, he said, was, in the final analysis, to be fully human. He rejected any "magic helper" notion of God and insisted that God had become a partner in the earthly reality, sharing our weakness, eliciting our strength. He even talked about the need for a "non-religious interpretation of the Gospel," but he was hanged by the Gestapo before he could begin to work out his ideas.

Bonhoeffer died in the spring of 1945, just hours before the advancing American forces reached the concentration camp where he was incarcerated. A few months later a plane named the Enola Gay flew over the city of Hiroshima and dropped the first atomic bomb. These two events, taken together, symbolize something unprecedented about the questions human beings ask about themselves and their futures, including the future of religion. In the last weeks of his life, Bonhoeffer glimpsed a new world emerging in which Christianity would assume a shape so radically different that he predicted it would be virtually unrecognizable to his contemporaries. The dropping of the atomic bomb, however, wrote a mushroom-shaped question mark after any and all speculations about the human future. It has also radically altered the question of the future of religion.

In his essay "The Mysticism of Science," Pierre Teilhard de Chardin, one of the most influential Catholic thinkers of our time, remarked that the two essential ingredients of any religion are "hope and the vista of a limitless future." In this short phrase he has put his finger exactly on the only authentically "religious" question of the post-Hiroshima era. Stated in its simplest form, our religious concern about the future must not be about the "future of religion" but about the future per se. Any "religious hope" today must begin with the hope that there will in fact be a human future. Such a hope must be "religious" because the empirical basis for it is ambiguous at best. Since Hiroshima and the stacking up of nuclear armed rockets, the answer to the question is in no way self-evident. For the first time in human memory there is room to doubt whether our species has any future at all. Teilhard envisioned humankind as just now entering on that exciting and critical new phase of evolution—its next "nodal point," as he called it—in which, at last, the future would be in human hands. But he did not foresee The Button, which is also in human hands.

Reviewing past forecasts about the future of religion can be helpful, but only up to a point. Making predictions can be valuable, but
also misleading. The great new fact of the possibility of species sui-
cide transforms not just the context in which our question about the
future of religion is voiced but the nature of the question itself. As
creatures embedded in history, we cannot ask these questions from
some Copernican vantage point situated outside the threats and uncertainties of terrestrial existence. To think in such an abstract way can
only be an ominous symptom of our refusal to take responsibility for
the real world in which we must live. "Predicting" the future subtly perpetuates the idea that someone or something else controls it, when the
truth is, as both Bonhoeffer and Teilhard knew, it is now in our hands.
And, as religious people would say, it is in our hands because God has
placed it there. Thus, the possibility of self-annihilation requires us to
put all our questions not in the form, What will happen? but rather in
the form, What must we do? We cannot merely speculate on whether
rites and myths will someday cease to divide and stupefy people; we
must so shape and reconceive them that they unite and enlarge us.
We cannot afford to wait and see whether the "religious dimension"
ceases to be a segregated precinct; we must set about making it an integral dimension of all we do. We cannot allow denominations, hierarchies, and confessional strife to continue to run their course as though
what happened in the "sacred realm" lay outside our human capacity
to mold and steer. But we cannot, like the God of scholastic theology,
create the future ex nihilo. As time-bound creatures, we must work
with the stubborn stuff of past and present. Among the "givens" are
our existing religious traditions, which, far from dying out, appear to
be leaping into a period of resurgence. But neither can we wait for kis-
met to deliver us into a new era in which we no longer need to project
our inmost terrors onto the heavens or onto other peoples and nations.
We must now take the initiative, not just to predict the future—including the future of religion—but to shape it.

10

The Silencing of Leonardo Boff (1988)

In March 1985 Cardinal Joseph Ratzinger, Prefect for the Vatican's Congregation for the Doctrine of the Faith (and later Pope Benedict XVI) issued a Notification regarding theological errors in a book by Leonardo Boff, a Franciscan theologian from Brazil, and one of the prominent pioneers of the theology of liberation. In May of the following year, the Congregation imposed a period of silence on Boff. This episode inspired the book from which the following brief excerpts are selected: The Silencing of Leonardo Boff: The Vatican and the Future of World Christianity *(Oak Park, IL: Meyer Stone Books, 1988), 141, 145-47, 149-53, 158-62, 166-67, 170-73, 175-78, 184-88. Harvey Cox saw this conflict as a tension between two competing visions for Christianity, one represented by "the Prefect," which presupposes a traditional, Eurocentric model, and the other, represented by "the Friar," which reflects the emerging features of a "world church," especially attuned to the perspective of the poor. Toward the end of the book, Cox illuminates this tension by reference to the traditional "marks" of the church (that the church is "one, catholic, holy, and apostolic," as described in the Nicene Creed), and concludes with brief reflections on the meaning and the inherent dangers of "silencing."*

THE MARKS OF THE CHURCH

The argument between the friar and the prefect is not about whether theology should be "ecclesial" or about the necessity of the church's learning to live and work in different "worlds." Both agree that the principal task of theology should be to help the church do its work in these worlds. The dispute, however, goes deeper. It is about the very *nature* of that church, and *what* its work in the different worlds should be. . . .

As acrimonious as all this sounds, it is hardly a new debate. It has raged within the Catholic Church and in other churches for many centuries. The "friars" of the world, broadly speaking, have always longed for a more fraternal church that expects of all its members a serious commitment to following the way of Jesus, a church that identifies itself closely with the underdogs, that plunges deep into divergent cultures, and that envisions itself as a band of pilgrims celebrating a Mystery that already suffuses the world. The "prefects" prefer a more hierarchically ordered church, that mediates Grace from heaven to earth, that relies on alliances with those who already bear the discipline and responsibility of power, and that bases itself primarily in the culture the church has already nourished for centuries.

This argument about what the church is and what it should be doing today echoes the very old controversy over what have traditionally been known as the four "marks of the church," the so-called *notae ecclesiae*. The "true" church, according to the historic creeds, must be *one, holy, catholic,* and *apostolic.* The rule of thumb is that where these marks can be discerned, there the true church of Jesus Christ exists, but that where one or more of the marks is missing the church is not truly present. Something essential to the church is missing. Neither side in the present debate disputes this ancient rule; but the argument between Ratzinger and Boff opens the old discussion about the marks of the church again.

The clamor over the silencing itself receded quickly after the Vatican ended it in March 1986. But ensuing events demonstrated that the divisive issues brought up by the Boff case remained. The disputes he had stirred up about the relationship of the hierarchy to grassroots religious communities, the place of the poor in the church, and the challenge of religious and cultural diversity had not been resolved. Furthermore it had also become clear that each of these issues leads back to an even more fundamental one about the historic marks of the church:

1. The assertion by liberation theology that fidelity to the message of Jesus requires a partisan option for the poor constitutes a claim about *apostolicity,* the nature of the connection between today's church and its origins.

2. The vexed problem of how the institutional churches' leadership should deal with *religión popular,* internal dissent, and the volatile new religious movements springing up from the grassroots—such as the Christian base communities—raises the question of the church's *holiness,* its ability to exemplify in its own life what it is teaching the world.

3. The emergence in recent decades of a culturally pluralistic world church with a non-Western majority poses the mystery of the church's *catholicity,* its universal inclusiveness, in a particularly sharp way.

4. Finally, the problem of how the church can remain in some real sense a single church despite all this tension, conflict, and diversity is clearly a matter of its mark of *oneness.*

Thus, we find ourselves in the midst of a new debate about an old subject: the marks of the church. Will it ever be possible for the two major parties in today's controversy to agree on what the historic marks of the church should be in this radically altered environment of the late twentieth century? This question is an urgent one because it concerns something both the friars and the prefects believe is essential: norms. It has to do with making the difficult but necessary judgments about what the church should be doing and what it ought to be teaching, about what is authentically Christian and what is not. . . . Both the liberation theologians and the supporters of Cardinal Ratzinger agree that the church has strayed from the narrow path Christ marked out and that it needs discipline, a term derived from the same root the word "disciple" comes from. But they differ on what this discipline should be. For Ratzinger, as we have seen, the church's present flaccidness is traceable to its excessive accommodations to the modern world and its mistaken interpretations of an alleged "spirit of the Council." The tightening up he wants will require, therefore, a "recentrage," a reassertion of firm papal authority, a slowing down of ecumenical momentum, a renewed emphasis on what is Roman about the Catholic Church.

Even some liberation theologians trace at least part of the flabbiness back to Vatican II, but in a different way. Jon Sobrino writes that he once warmly welcomed the Council's shift in imagery about the church from "body of Christ" to "people of God." He saw it as an appropriate expression of the Council's distrust of elitism (a church centered on the hierarchy and the priesthood). But he has come to believe, he says, that it turned out to be a mistake for the Council and its interpreters to underscore so much the "all" who constitute the people of God. Though this "all" had a certain positive democratizing value, at the time, he says, it soon misled people into thinking of the church as "universal in a vague sort of way." Sobrino fears this vague universalism allows too much slippage and can even be read to imply that the church need not demand much from its members. Like Ratzinger, both Boff and Sobrino want the church to be more disciplined, not less. What is at issue between the two parties is not *whether* there should be norms and discipline but *what* they should be.

The "friaral" view of the church and the "prefectural" one move in different ways to answer this question. Are their differences unresolvable? I believe the divergences between these two approaches are deep and serious. I also believe, however, that by examining how each side looks at the four historic marks as they re-emerge in the central questions raised by the Boff case (the role of the poor, *religión popular,* cultural pluralism, and church unity), it becomes possible to sort out the differences between the parties. Having done this we can then go on to distinguish between those issues on which some consensus might appear, and those on which, since there seems little likelihood of an agreement very soon, the primordial litigation between the friars and the prefects will probably continue for a long time to come.

Apostolicity and the Poor

Apostolicity is the mark of the church that refers to its continuity with Christ and the apostles. Both sides in the Boff dispute agree that apostolicity is an essential quality of the Christian church. But what does it mean for the church to be apostolic today, and what does apostolicity have to do with the "preferential option for the poor" or with becoming what John XXIII called for: a "church *of* the poor"? Here is where the disagreement sets in.

For most conventional Catholic theologians, the litmus test of apostolicity is to ascertain whether any claimant to Christian identity today can demonstrate *visible institutional continuity* with the apostles of Christ and their present-day successors, the pope and the bishops. For Boff and the friars on the other hand, apostolicity means faithfully *continuing the work* and *ministry* Christ and his apostles actually did, and this obviously entails, as it did for them, a preference for the outcasts. To be truly apostolic for Boff requires taking the side of the poor—whether one calls this "love" or "option." It is the gospel itself that requires the preference. And where this mark is missing, where the church remains neutral or allies itself with the powerful, one is justified in harboring at least some doubts about its genuine apostolicity.

Can the dispute over this norm ever be settled? *The Modern Catholic Dictionary* states that the word "apostles" refers to the "followers of Jesus who spread his message." During Jesus' own lifetime, the entry continues, these men are referred to as "disciples," but "following his ascension they are always called apostles." "Apostolicity," then, refers to two aspects of the church. The first is its origin in the life and ministry of Jesus and his followers. The second has to do with its "mission," its *being sent* by God to do something in the world. The Greek word *apostolos* actually means someone who is sent to do some task. In order to grasp the import of the difference between Boff and Ratzinger and their respective supporters on this point we must first ask how they envision the church's link to Jesus; and we must then find out how they believe this link should be expressed in its apostolate, its "sent-ness" today.

The difference between the friars and the prefects on these issues can be evoked in one question: how much continuity is there between a "disciple," one who seeks to follow Jesus, and an "apostle," one who carries the gospel to the world? Another way to put the question is this: how much should the earthly life of the Jesus of the Gospels shape the current life of the church nineteen centuries later? In other words, how much does "representing" Jesus today (apolostolicity) entail "following" him (discipleship)?

The answer to this question is that for the liberation theologians there is a great deal of continuity between the historical Jesus of the Gospels and the task of the church today, and therefore between discipleship and apostolicity, between following and representing. For the other side in the debate, there is not only much less continuity between Jesus and the early church, there is in fact a great gulf. The mission of the church begins not with the disciples but with those who met the Risen Christ, the apostles. Easter changed everything. Therefore, the church should *not* be traced back to the historical Jesus. Properly speaking it begins only after the Resurrection of Christ, and its mission is not so much to "follow Jesus" but to represent Christ, not to be disciples but to be apostles. . . .

For Jon Sobrino (and most of the other liberation theologians) one simply cannot represent Christ today without also following him. Apostolicity entails discipleship. Ratzinger and his school of interpreters generally deny that there is or should be a strong element of continuity between the actions of the historical Jesus and his followers on the one side, and the nature and task of the church today on the other. They criticize the liberation theologians for underlining the continuity too much. . . .

Both sides insist that "Jesus" and "Christ" must always be held together. But for Boff and Sobrino, Jesus gives the *content* to Christ, while for Ratzinger his being *the* Christ is what ultimately is essential about Jesus. The liberation theologians contend that the life and teachings of the Nazarene give substance to the Christ of faith. It was not just anyone who was raised on Easter, it was a particular man, along with what he said and did. Their critics think this emphasis loses the essential combination by putting too much weight on "Jesus." . . .

Holiness and Praxis

The debate about the mark of the church's holiness comes up with the issues the Boff case raises about *religión popular,* religious populism, dissent, and grassroots movements. At first the connection is not so evident. Perhaps because of our secular atmosphere today, the word "holiness" sometimes evokes overtones of the spectral or the uncanny. Or it suggests some unattainable degree of moral perfection. But the word "holy," as it is used in the Bible, has another force. It means "whole" and is derived from the same root as "heal" and "health." We have a helpful hint to its derivation in the English phrase "hale and hearty." This suggests that God promises the church a certain kind of health that is necessary for its task of healing the hurts of the nations and helping the world itself become whole. Thus at least in some measure the church should *be* what it talks about: whole. But its holiness should *not* call undue attention to itself. Its wholeness or holiness is strictly instrumental. It is intended ultimately not for the church's own benefit but for the world's.

Both the liberationists and their opponents accept the mark of holiness as essential, and both agree that it means God both gives holiness and wholeness to the church and expects them from the church. But from there on disagreements set in. Traditional Catholic theology has often viewed the church as a kind of repository holding God's gift of holiness "like a treasure in an earthen vessel." God bestows this holiness on the world *through* the church, by means of its teaching and its sacraments. Furthermore there are always individuals within the church, the saints, who became particularly luminous mediums of God's holiness. Not only are these holy people held up as moral exemplars, they are often believed to have the power to heal. The custom the Catholic Church retains of requiring proofs of healing before a deceased person can be officially canonized as a saint may seem quaint, but it preserves the ancient connection between health, holiness, and exemplary goodness.

For their part, liberation theologians emphasize that "holiness" refers to the *whole* church and not just to extraordinary persons. The New Testament (1 Peter 2:9) speaks of the entire people of God as a "holy nation." This suggests that the whole church, and not just a few individuals within it or certain of its acts, must in some way be an *example* of what it is teaching. The problem is that clearly this is not always the case. It seems easier in practice for Mother Church to condemn the injustice and corruption of the sinful world than to admit she often shares this lack of wholeness in her own life, a failure that makes her message sound like a pot calling a kettle black. It was for pointing out this embarrassing contradiction so unsparingly and in such grim detail in his book *Church: Charism and Power* that Leonardo Boff got his Alitalia ticket to Rome. For the liberation theologians, God is helping the church—as a people—to bring wholeness to the world. It is holy but it is not exempt from human failures, or from the equally human need to repent and be forgiven. Therefore, in order to be the humble exemplar it is intended to be, the church must not be afraid to admit its own flaws and ask God's help in correcting them. In fact, this willingness to concede one's own imperfections is one expression of exemplary holiness. A "wounded healer" is often in a better position to heal others, but only when the healer recognizes her own woundedness.

The special contribution of liberation theology to the discussion about what constitutes the holy or exemplary quality of the church appears most clearly in its idea of "orthopraxis." Sometimes this word is mistakenly counterposed to "orthodoxy" and is then said to mean little more than "actions speak louder than words," or that the church's actual conduct in the world says more than its preaching. But the idea of orthopraxis is more nuanced than that. It goes well beyond the familiar idea that faith entails both belief and action. It suggests that the two are no more than different moments in the same total response, that they constantly interact with each other. The idea of "praxis," from which orthopraxis comes, challenges both Descartes and Dewey, both the old idealistic notion that all actions are derived from previous ideas, as well as the reductive modern theory that holds that thinking is little more than a reflection of the organism's acting.

Once again Franciscan spirituality provides a good example of orthopraxis. The early Franciscans did not disdain preaching. They proclaimed the message of the gospel in meadows and markets wherever they roamed. But they believed this gospel required them to demonstrate as best they could, in their own lives, what following Jesus meant. St. Bonaventure taught that the same uncreated "inner light" illuminated both thought and action. St. Francis himself believed not only that Christians should *love* the poor but that they came to know Christ *in* the poor. Consequently, these early friars also had a preferential option for the poor. However, they dealt with poverty through a form of compassion in which they sought to know the "poverty of Christ" in the actual poor people of their time. The present-day friars, on the other hand, want to fuse compassionate knowing and doing in a way that might help change the world and contribute to justice rather than merely to charity. They speak therefore of "accompanying" the poor in their struggle against oppression. Still, in their own way, both the early friars and the liberationists, their latter-day successors, exemplify the idea of orthopraxis.

Liberation theology thus combines the old and the new. It does not differ from conventional theology principally in the ideas it advances, but in its understanding of what theology is: namely, the effort to help the church become "holy" so that it can be a credible bearer of its message in its own life. But can the actual church exemplify reconciliation in a world so cruelly split up between races and sexes; between Overeaters Anonymous and malnourished children; those with enormous power, who are wary and uneasy, and those with no power, who are restive and resentful? In such a world, the church itself, because it lives within history and not in some transcendent realm, is also inevitably torn and dismembered. Those who share the body of Christ are supposed to be examples. Still Christians rob, kill, cheat, and maim each other with disconcerting regularity. But if God's will for the world is love, reconciliation, and justice, then one of the church's primary tasks is to exemplify these qualities in its own life. This is what holiness means. How, given its own obvious brokenness, can the church nurture and advocate the wholeness of the nations?

Many conventional theologians deal with this dilemma by advocating a transcendental definition of the church's exemplarity. The world may indeed be riven with conflict, they say, but in principle Christ has already reconciled these divisions on the cross. Slumlords and tenants, muggers and victims, revolutionaries and reactionaries may be at each other's throats outside the doors of the sanctuary, but—it is argued—around the altar these differences should be temporarily set aside, while, in the sacrament of Christ, everyone savors the ultimate peace and unity they possess in God. In this view, to involve the church on one side of any of these divisions is terribly dangerous because it could exclude certain people from the single place or occasion that might afford them a taste of wholeness. This is one reason why the critics of liberation theology look with such deep suspicion on what they regard as its advocacy of a partisan church. Individual Christians, they say, can and should engage in such activities. But not the church.

The liberation theologians . . . will not settle for a church that merely talks about God's justice, or worse, one that declares that in the light of eternity all earthly injustices are insignificant. They want church people to play a role in working for real community in the actual world, even though the community achieved will always remain partial and fragile. . . .

For liberation theology holiness has little to do with spookiness or claims of moral superiority. The holiness of the church means the embeddedness of the entire people of God in a suffering world, in which hope must be concretely exemplified and religious language must point to genuine possibilities of deliverance from the real sins of impoverishment, exclusion, and cynicism. . . .

* * *

CATHOLICITY AND CULTURAL PLURALISM

Catholicity, another traditional mark of the church, means universality or all-inclusiveness. But how can any church claim to include all when in most areas of the world Christians constitute small minorities and when the world itself is culturally piebald and religiously pluralistic? The answer often given to this question is that catholicity should mean "culturally inclusive." It should signify the church's hospitality to all tongues and nations, its willingness to sink roots in any soil, and its freedom from captivity to any one tribe. What especially annoyed the Brazilian bishops about the Boff silencing was that it seemed to them an expression of European cultural imperialism. It did not allow the church in Brazil to "be Brazilian." It appeared to be a violation of the principle of catholicity. Asian and African Christians often join the Latin Americans in rejecting Rome's insistence that every theology and every liturgy, no matter what its cultural matrix, must eventually be judged by what they view as European or Roman standards, even if these standards are touted as those of the universal church. Cardinal Ratzinger, like most modern churchmen, is in favor of a culturally inclusive church. But, he is deeply worried that regional or ethnic particularities could overshadow what he describes as "essentially catholic about Christianity."

How can catholicity and cultural diversity be reconciled? Enrique Dussel, the Argentine theologian, likes to quote the famous dictum of the Indian Cardinal Paracattil, "The Catholic Church is neither Latin nor Greek nor Slav, but universal. Unless the church can show herself Indian in India, and Chinese in China, and Japanese in Japan, she will never reveal her authentically Catholic character."[1] If Dussel is right,

---

1. Enriqui Dussel, "Theologies of the 'Periphery' and the 'Centre': Encounter or Confrontation," in Claude Geffré, Gustavo Gutiérrez, and Virgil Elizondo,

and to be universal means to be present within every culture, then a truly "catholic" church would not only allow but encourage a thousand flowers to blossom. It would recognize that different climates nurture different flowers.

But this only states the issue. It does not resolve it. All that blossoms does not necessarily bear fruit. As Ratzinger might put it, eventually one must distinguish flowers from poison ivy, healthy diversity from proliferating malignancy, the genuine from the spurious. The Latin Americans recognize this too. But the question is how?

The principal difference between the prefects and the friars on the question of catholicity is that the former claim it is a quality that *already exists* in the Catholic Church. It is indeed the name by which that church is most commonly known. Therefore it is cherished as an invaluable asset, as a gift from God that the church can share with other religious bodies (which can now be called "churches") and eventually with the whole world. To become "catholic," according to this interpretation is to become a part of the Catholic Church and of its beliefs, values, stories, and meaning patterns. Consequently, it means becoming, at least in some way, a participant in "catholic culture," whatever that may mean.

For the liberation theologians, on the other hand, catholicity is indeed a gift, but it is also a task. In our new age of global pluralism it can be realized only when the church is "de-Europeanized," when it is released from its captivity to one culture so that it can enter fully and deeply into others. They believe catholicity is present in the Roman Catholic Church today more as a promise than a reality, more as a goal than an accomplished fact. Consequently, it must not only be shared, it must also be sought. At the level of theology this quest for catholicity requires what Eduardo Hoornaert calls "de-northification," the leaving behind of bondage to "northern" (European and American) forms of thought, not so either church or theology can be culture-free, which is both impossible from an anthropological perspective and entirely non-Catholic, but so they can enter in fruitful fusions within other cultures as well. . . .

For the prefects, a more universal and united world is also a goal of the Catholic Church. This helps explain their opposition to the rampant nationalism of the last two centuries and the support recent popes have given the UN. But when it comes to religious and cultural disunity, the Catholic Church's official formula for universal accord

---

eds., *Different Theologies, Common Responsibility,* Concilium 171 (Edinburgh: T&T Clark, 1984), pp. 87ff.

has not changed: the various parties must come to recognize that the Roman church is the authentic custodian of catholicity. Catholicity is not just spiritual or invisible. It takes historical shape. Consequently, though the Vatican never spells out exactly what form it must take, the achievement of catholicity requires incorporation into the visible institution that now nurtures it, and this in turn requires some form of submission to the papal authority, which guarantees and symbolizes visible unity. There are no shortcuts.

The liberationists agree and disagree. They also insist that catholicity must be real, not just ideal. But they emphasize that if the quest for catholicity in church and world is to be guided by the spirit of the poor Christ, then there can be no question of a universality achieved through submission. Submission by someone also implies domination by someone else. Domination is always a false form of universality, and, when it is done in the name of a man who washed his followers' feet, it is a grotesque anomaly. This is why the friars have always argued that the symbols of monarchy, such as the papal tiara and episcopal thrones, that Catholics have traditionally utilized—often with the best intentions—to symbolize an inclusive spiritual dominion, can be dangerously misleading. John Paul I, the thirty-three-day pope, may have sensed this. He refused to accept the tiara during his papal inauguration.

For the friars, Christ himself is the exemplar of the mystery of catholicity. He consistently fought against the barriers and taboos that excluded people from the religious and civil communities of his day, but he did so by becoming a servant, not a monarch. There is no doubt that, in the *Pax Romana*, the Roman Empire of Jesus' time had created the most inclusive, i.e., "catholic," political entity the world had ever seen. But Jesus rejected Caesar's solution. His quarrel with the empire, however, was not about the goal of bringing all the world's diverse communities into one imperium. His argument was about what *sort* of imperium it would be, and *how* it would be instituted. He called it the Reign of God, and said that the power to build it did not come "from this world." The finale of Jesus' life, his face-down with Pontius Pilate, provides the denouement of the clash between polar visions of the meaning of "universal," and of how to bring it about: Christ's way or Caesar's.

Cardinal Ratzinger and his supporters recognize the failure of previous definitions of catholicity as well as the liberationists do. They know that the chances of literally initiating all peoples and nations into the existing Catholic Church are very remote. Consequently, in recent years, they too have begun to envision a different form of catholicity, one which teaches that the church, even if only as a tiny minority, should be *present* in all cultures. They have also begun to advocate what they call "inculturation." The word suggests the effort to enter other cultures, not by imposing Christianity, but by allowing it to become thoroughly suffused with the culture itself. If, as Cardinal Paracattil says, the church must be Indian in India and Japanese in Japan, then—so the argument goes—it must immerse itself fully in the symbols and stories, the history and perhaps even the traditional religious systems of these lands. It must in-culture-ate itself.

Just as liberation theologians tend to be suspicious of imperial notions of catholicity, they are also skeptical about most attempts at inculturation, because they are aware of the oppressive ways the church has sometimes sought to insert itself into various cultures. Their apprehensiveness arises from the experience of the underclass people they work with and from whom they have learned that culture itself can be despotic. It can be used to exclude and dominate, for example, when a dominant culture imposes its language or legal codes on subordinate minority ones. Some liberation theologians have personally suffered, and seen their people hurt, by repressive measures taken by authoritarian governments in the name of such potent cultural symbols as "homeland" or "Western Christian civilization" or "patriotic duty." They know first hand how powerful elites can skillfully manipulate cultural patterns, folk beliefs, and pious practices of poor people to keep them in poverty and ignorance. They have learned to be suspicious of advocates of inculturation who do not recognize that culture is never neutral. But they also know that no faith, Christianity included, can exist without some cultural vehicle. The key question then becomes: how can Christianity become an integral part of a culture without perpetuating that culture's injustices?

For liberation theology, the history of Jesus' interaction with his culture hints at the answer to this question. Jesus was fully steeped in the traditional religion of his own people. He was not counter-cultural. Nevertheless he did not hesitate to point out how the elites of his day were misusing this heritage. Jesus invoked old cultural and religious traditions such as the Jubilee Year (which decreed a redistribution of land and the cancelling of debts) in the face of economic inequality. He regularly cited the Law and Prophets against his religious critics. He neither embraced nor rejected culture uncritically. Rather he loved it, reshaped it, and then *used* it against its procrustean distortion. He drew on the psalms and the ritual law of his people to expose those who were exploiting religious tradition for their own gain: "It is written, that my house shall be a house of prayer for all people, but you have made it a den of robbers."

For liberation theologians, the concept of "inculturation" is too uncritical and too formal a term. It lacks content. In line with their emphasis on the model Jesus set for the churches, they prefer "incarnation" as the description of how the church should become present within a culture. Incarnation has more contour because it calls to mind the selective way Jesus himself dealt with culture. It was to highlight the church's need to incarnate itself that Boff chose the title *And the Church Became People* for the book that caused the new storm of protest after the silence.

Cultures exist in a constant state of internal conflict between those who control the symbols of power and those who do not. Inevitably some cultural forms and religious patterns become the tools of tyranny while others provide hope and vision to those who fight against it. The Duvalier family clung to power in Haiti for several decades in part by cruelly exploiting such popular spiritual practices as voodoo. Men still subject women to an undercaste in most parts of the world by appealing to traditional definitions of womanhood, many of them sanctioned by religion. Racism is an integral component of many cultures today. But on the other hand the songs and legends and heroes of tyrannized peoples, often borne by their religious beliefs, have inspired dignity among the despised and fired opposition to despots.

Incarnation differs from inculturation because it recognizes this unavoidably conflictual character of culture. If the church models its approach to cultures on the incarnation of Christ it will not seek to diffuse itself equally throughout all strata. Even less will it work principally with the most powerful and privileged sectors. Rather, if the church practices discipleship and *follows* Christ into a culture, it will position itself, as he did, principally (though not exclusively) among the alienated and the rejected. It will incarnate itself among the people, not as their tribune, but as their servant and companion in struggles and defeats. It will partake in the mystery of the presence of Christ among the poor. . . .

Ironically, as Christianity gropes its way toward becoming—at last—a world faith, and not a Western religion with outposts and enclaves around the globe, Catholic theologians may have a certain advantage over Protestants. True, the Roman party erred in trying to wed Catholic theology eternally to St. Thomas Aquinas and thus to an idealized Western medieval culture. But Protestants, faced with the same dilemma, made an even more disastrous mistake. They tried, earlier in the present century, to create a theology that ostensibly needed no culture at all. Karl Barth grumbled that *Kulturprotestantismus* was Christian theology's greatest foe. He tried to fashion a theology founded on the naked

Word of God that allegedly needed no cultural vehicles. Now, however, it has become clear that *every* theology—including Barth's—must express itself in and through some set of cultural patterns. Consequently some Catholic theologians, having grown accustomed to the old inculturated manner of thinking, do not find it as hard as Protestants do to enter into other cultural systems. The problem is they can often become too uncritical of an environing culture. The Protestant suspicion of uncritical "inculturation," on the other hand, therefore preserves an invaluable balancing insight. The gospel must say both yes and no to a culture at the same time: yes to those parts of it that nurture life, and no to those that perpetuate domination and exclusion.

Perhaps the time has come for Christianity to stop trying to deal with world cultures as it tried to deal with Judaism, by—in the pope's ill-chosen words—"assuming" and "surmounting" them. The model of Jesus is one of serving, not one of surmounting or of merely assuming. Incarnation means not just that God became flesh but that God became human, and the human always includes culture. It is important to emphasize, however, that the incarnation took place not in an abstract or universal culture, but in a particular one, the culture of Israel. Further, God chose to come to the subculture of the poor, the landless, the religiously suspect, and Christ contested those elements of the dominant culture he found oppressive to the human spirit. . . .

The prefects are surely right that catholicity cannot be some airy spiritual feeling. It must take visible shape in the real world, and it must be clearly linked to the apostolic character of the church. But the friars are also correct that catholicity today will require a form of inculturation that takes the self-humbling of God in the incarnation and in Jesus' preference for the underclass as its model; this will require making painful choices and taking sides. It appears certain that the church's catholicity will never be perfected this side of the Reign of God. It also appears that unless Rome is prepared to silence many hundreds of Leonardo Boffs, not just in Brazil but in Taiwan and Ghana and Sri Lanka, the debate about what catholicity is and how it should be pursued can hardly be expected to subside for a long time to come.

* * *

ONENESS AND DIVERSITY

The riddle of the one and the many antedates the birth of Christianity by many centuries. But, since the church's earliest years, it has been a major preoccupation of theologians as well. The world is so obviously many. It is peopled by many tongues and nations, many classes and conditions, many philosophies and faiths. Yet Christians confess that God is one and that the church is, or should be, one. But this is exactly what troubles the conscientious critics of liberation theology most: they are genuinely fearful that it threatens the church's unity. They are afraid its partisan stance could tear the flesh of the body of Christ. . . .

What kind of "oneness" in the church might the approach liberationists represent eventually lead to? Probably never again to the attempt to devise a single, all-encompassing theological formula—however minimal—to which everyone everywhere must subscribe. Rather, it could lead to the culturally and theologically pluralistic church Karl Rahner once foresaw, united not from the past or from the top, but by its hope for that which is yet to be. The Latin Americans believe they have grounds for hope, since signs and portents of just such a church are already appearing on their own continent. It is a church, which though weak and vulnerable by worldly standards, is nonetheless moving toward apostolicity, catholicity, holiness, and unity. It finds the oneness in its stumbling attempt to follow the poor Christ into the depths of diverse cultures in order to demonstrate the beloved community only God makes possible.

It seems that Karl Rahner, too, toward the end of his life, imagined a church bound together more by this venturesome love than by dictums and dogmas. Maybe that is why one of his last acts was to send a warm letter of support for Gustavo Gutiérrez, who was then under attack by Rome. In any case, writing in his *Theological Investigations,* Rahner said in 1974 that he hoped one day there will "no longer be any one single and universal basic formula of the Christian faith applicable to the whole church." If that day comes, and welcomed by both the prefects and the friars, by the pope and the Congregation for the Doctrine of the Faith, then the Catholic Church will have taken a decisive step toward an authenticity that now seems so elusive. And if it does, all the nations of the world—and all the other churches—will be greatly blessed.

The trial of Leonardo Boff is not yet over, nor is the trial of liberation theology. When will we learn that within the church we have had quite enough trials? What is beginning now is the trial of the church itself. That trial will test whether the church can in fact "become the people," and whether Christianity, for so many centuries a largely Western and "northern" faith, can live in and speak to the tribes and nations of the whole world. This will require a good deal of venturesome theology. Obviously, some of that theology will be true and faithful and some will not. What we will need, therefore, is not indictments and censures but patience, humility, and a genuinely open debate. But a debate does not have accusers and defendants. It has partners and protagonists who respect and listen to each other. In a debate no one tries to silence anyone else. Both sides expect to learn from the clash and resolution of ideas. Boff and his fellow liberation theologians know as well as anyone that they are not always right, nor their opponents always wrong. What they ask is not for agreement, but for the opportunity to contribute to the conversation, to speak and to listen.

* * *

SILENCING AND COMMUNITY

Indeed, as the conversation continues, it will no doubt become clear that liberation theology, like every other theology, has no final answers. Human life and history being what they are, the time will come when new voices with concerns we cannot now foresee and perspectives we can scarcely imagine will arise in the household of faith and seek to be heard. But whether the church as a whole will hear and respond to such voices tomorrow depends in considerable measure on whether it learns to heed the cries of the voiceless today. This is why someone's right to be heard within the Christian community is not just a procedural question or a matter of fair play. It has to do with the very nature of the religious community itself.

Leonardo Boff is not the only Christian to be silenced. There have been many before him. And it may be well to remember that the first silencing to occur in the church, and in some ways the primal one, was that of women. The "original silencing" made an impact in some ways analogous to that of original sin: it has stained everything since. Why and how did it happen? It is incontestable that women played critical leadership roles in the early Christian church. Priscilla, for example, seems to have been at least the equal of her husband Aquila in the work they did together as teachers (Acts 18:2, 18, 26; 1 Cor. 16:9; Rom. 16:3). The Apostle Paul taught that women could lead worship and that the sexes were equal before God. In some ways the early Christian movement appears to have been a bold experiment in egalitarian inclusiveness. But as the church began to adjust itself to its environing culture, something changed. In the generation that followed Paul, the male leaders surrendered to the pressure they felt to deprive women of the role they had once played (1 Tim. 2:11-12). Most scholars now explain the notorious passage in Paul's 1 Corinthians (14:33-35) in which women are admonished to remain silent in the churches—a blatant contradiction of what he says elsewhere—as an insertion that was placed there during the less venturesome generation that followed him.

Whether this was the case or not, the result of this "original silencing," which antedated Leonardo Boff's by nineteen hundred years, was not just to deprive half of the church's members of their full humanity, a wounding that would be serious enough in its own right. It also set an ugly precedent, and it fundamentally distorted the entire structure of Christian worship and teaching. Insofar as it was actually enforced it deprived the community's prayer and hymnody of the symbols that could be brought to it only from the lives of women. It impoverished its ethical life and its diaconal service by assigning less weight to those particular forms of pain that women, as the bearers of children and the objects of patriarchal power, bring to expression. It thinned out the celebration, not just for women, but for everyone, by preventing the unique joys and ecstasies women feel from being shared by all.

The deformation that resulted from the silencing of women is that the whole body was crippled and its capacity to hear anything or anybody seriously attenuated. One cannot tune out some without at the same time tuning out others. By muting the sisters, the early church inflicted on itself a form of deafness that has persisted ever since. Women were the first to be silenced, and in many respects that archetypal silencing continues today. But women were not alone. Once silencing found its way into the company of the faithful, there were others whose songs and stories were also stifled. Women share this disallowance of speech, of saying one's word, with many, many others. Their enforced quiet is also the lot of millions of the world's poor, and of those who are rejected or excluded for a variety of other reasons from full participation in the human family. This is probably why women everywhere have responded with enthusiasm to those theologies that take as their starting point the perspective of the voiceless, a preferential option for the silenced.

In the biblical tradition, God is known as the Holy One who speaks to human beings and who expects them to answer. Therefore, to silence someone, it could be said, is a type of blasphemy. It denies that person the opportunity to respond to God's call, and it therefore denies God. To silence is to fashion a kind of idol, a false God who calls everyone but who does not expect everyone to answer, or who expects some to answer for others. The Christian church, however, understands itself to be a community that is constituted by the Word which God spoke to it in the life of Jesus and to which a response *must* be given. This is why the practice of silencing and excluding stands in opposition to the spirit that is needed if the church is to become an inclusive world church.

Bishop Casaldáliga said it with elegance when, in the poem he wrote at the time of the silencing, he reminded Leonardo that by becoming silent for awhile, he would partake of the condition in which those who have no voice—either in the church or in the world—live all the time. But the hope to which the church gives voice—or should—is that this unnatural silence will not last forever, that by God's grace the mouths of the mute will be unstopped and one day all will sing the Lord's song together.

11

Seven Samurai and How They Looked Again

Theology, Social Analysis, and Religión Popular *in Latin America (1989)*

This essay was first published in Marc H. Ellis and Otto Maduro, eds., The Future of Liberation Theology: Essays in Honor of Gustavo Gutiérrez *(Maryknoll, N.Y.: Orbis Books, 1989), 229-39.*

Twenty years ago an unlikely combination of actors surveyed Latin America and saw a specter haunting the land. The specter was *religión popular* and the odd coalition that descried its threatening visage was made up of seven fierce warriors who normally viewed each other with considerable suspicion. It included (1) pre-Vatican II Roman Catholic integralists intent on holding the line; (2) post-Vatican II liturgical and theological reformers intent on changing it; (3) Protestant missionaries from North America and the local clergy they had trained; (4) Pentecostal preachers, nearly all of them Latin Americans; (5) liberal developmentalists from agencies such as IMF, AID, and the World Bank; (6) Marxist activists; and (7) liberation theologians. These seven samurai agreed on virtually nothing else. But they could—and did—join hands in common opposition to popular religion. They could—and did—form a united front against unauthorized cults of the Virgin, "patronales," and raucous fiestas, against the use of holy water to cast spells, against pre-Christian healing rites and scapulars designed to ward off evil. The specter, it appears, bore many faces, but its presence was so menacing and so manifold that this heterogeneous cohort of ghost busters set aside other differences to track it down.

Of course the different members of the alliance opposed popular religion for their own quite different reasons:

(1) *Integralists* saw in the local cults remnants of pagan piety and the subversive syntheses of official saints with pre-Columbian deities. Undiscouraged by four hundred years of spotty successes, they were still pursuing the "cut and burn" policy initiated by the Franciscans at the time of the Conquista.

(2) *Post-Vatican II reformers* longed to gather congregations around the altar (newly moved out from the wall), which now became the table of the family of God. They did not look kindly on worshipers saying beads during Mass or siphoning off energies in individual devotions at side chapels. Christians were to become (in Vatican II terms) a "people of God," and popular religion—the reformers thought—worked against this goal.

(3) *Protestant missionaries and local evangelical leaders* saw popular religion as yet another example of the debased Roman Catholicism that had been disparaged since the Black Legend first appeared in the sixteenth century: superstition and magic blended with popery and ignorance. For them, to embrace Protestant faith obviously required eschewing all that.

(4) *Pentecostal preachers*—mostly Latin Americans themselves—railed against devil worship, and the drunkenness and lusty excess that often accompany fiestas and patronales. In their opposition to popular religion they seem—if anything—more zealous than their other Protestant colleagues.

(5) *Liberal developmentalists* saw popular religion as an unfortunate obstacle to the introduction of modern agriculture, education, and especially health care, for *curanderos* were often key leaders in popular religion.

(6) *Marxists*—rarely masters of nuance in making judgments about religion—dismissed popular religion along with all religion as one more opiate of the masses. Like other rural idiocies it would evaporate once capitalism was abolished.

(7) *Liberation theologians*—most of them at least—tended to see popular religion as a fundamentally alienated expression of religiosity, a form of false consciousness that prevented Christians from responding to a gospel that called them to become aware of their role as subjects and agents of the historical project of building the kingdom of god.

Thus the seven samurai harbored their own peculiar *causae belli,* but for each the struggle against the perversions of popular piety was one they took up with enthusiasm.

This grim catalog of reasons why so many different actors showed so little sympathetic interest in what has accurately been called "the

religion of the poor" seems remarkable given the "preferential option
for the poor" some of the same parties trumpeted so widely at the same
time. Yet, in retrospect, what now seems equally remarkable is that
during the same period the "high" forms of scholarly and academic
theology displayed equally minimal interest in the religion of ordinary
persons. Protestant theologians were busy refining historico-critical
methods and reappropriating the theologies of the Reformation, most
of which were not sympathetic to popular piety. Catholics were absorbing the impact of Vatican II and reveling in their newfound freedom
to engage in critical biblical studies. With the possible exception of a
few French Catholics who were still interested in "spirituality," and of
an even smaller handful of "liberal" Protestants who continued to be
intrigued by "religious experience," most of theology simply ignored
religion, popular or otherwise.

This benign neglect of the phenomenon of religion by most theologies was even more evident with reference to the non-Christian religious traditions. One can hardly locate a memorable paragraph in
Gilson or Maritain about the other religions of the world. The same
lapse is true of Barth, Bultmann, and Bonhoeffer. Hendrik Kramer,
the only neoorthodox theologian who addressed himself to the issue,
argued, in effect, when it comes to world religions, the less said the
better.

But by the late 1960s this picture was changing. The Vatican had
established secretariats for dialogue with Jews, Protestants, and non-
Christian religions. In his last book published just before he died, Paul
Tillich declared that the vexing question of the relationship between
Christianity and the non-Christian faiths of the world now loomed as
the most important theological issue, one he had scarcely addressed at
all in his fifty years of scholarly theological production. By the early
1970s other Protestant theologians followed suit, and "theology of the
religions" became a central preoccupation. Even so, it has taken years
for theologians to recognize that in order to deal with this issue they
must move beyond old comparativist methods (which had focused
largely on the scriptures of other faiths) and learn something from
more recently developed approaches to religious studies, including the
need to study both "high and low," both official and popular versions,
of world religions.

This brings us to the threshold of the 1990s where, due in no small
measure to the vast influence of the theology of Gustavo Gutiérrez and
his co-workers, the entire situation vis-à-vis attitudes both of activist
parties and of academic theologians toward *religión popular* has shifted

dramatically. What I wish to do now is to chart briefly how parallel changes occurred in each of the seven samurai, focusing especially on liberation theologians. In doing so I want to suggest why this change signals a possible quickening of the sometimes limping conversation between theologians and those who study religion from the perspective of psychology, anthropology, and sociology. After that I wish to hazard some tentative hunches about what all this might mean for the more general question of the "theological problem of religion."

Changes: The First Six Samurai

How did the seven samurai come to look at the ever-present reality of popular religion in Latin America in a new way? In each one the change came about both because of internal developments within the party itself and also because of changes in the functioning of popular religion itself.

1. *Pre-Vatican II integralists* continue to play some role in the Catholic Church, but their influence is waning. Admittedly, Pope John Paul II has appointed conservative bishops nearly every time a vacancy has occurred in Latin America. But the men he appoints cannot usefully be described with the old-fashioned term "integralist." Rather, they represent the school of thought within Catholic ecclesiology that holds that the reforms of Vatican II have gone too far, and that the time has come for retrenchment and consolidation. The most articulate spokesman of this line is of course Cardinal Joseph Ratzinger, prefect of the Sacred Congregation for the Doctrine of the Faith, who declares repeatedly that the most pressing need in the Catholic Church today is for what he calls *recentrage*. He uses this French term to refer to a tendency he welcomes, in particular within the French church, to look more to Rome and to deal sternly with the various forms of democratization and decentralization that have crept in since the 1960s.

When it comes to popular religion Cardinal Ratzinger is hardly an exclusivist or integralist. During a visit to Canada a few years back, he responded to a question about the prospects of Christianity with characteristic comprehensiveness by dividing the battlefield—as a previous dweller by the Tiber once did—into three parts. In the First World, he declared, consumerism and moral decay are the main challenges to the church. In the Second World—countries with communist governments—he found a growing disillusionment with Leninist ideology and a hunger for faith. He was most enthusiastic, however, about the Third World, including Latin America, where he suggested that "the natural piety and deep religiousness of the people present a genuine opening for christianization." This telling remark of the prefect parallels the position taken by Cardinal López Trujillo, the president of CELAM (the Latin American Bishops' Conference), who frequently declares that in time of rapid social change and jarring cultural dislocation the simple piety of ordinary persons should not be disturbed since it is what enables them to survive the traumas of history. This idea represents a conservative, in fact "functionalist," view of the role of religion, which differs from integralism in that virtually any faith that performs this role can be viewed with sympathy.

2. *Post-Vatican II reformers* who once swept through the churches of Latin America removing statues of saints, relics, and the accumulated detritus of previous waves of popular devotion, have now begun to take a second look at *religión popular*. The conviction is emerging among them that much of the enthusiasm for liturgical renewal that sprang from Vatican II had a certain elitist cast and that for liturgy to become the "work of the people" it has to incorporate elements of the local folk heritage. A good example of this rethought strategy can be seen in the history of the cathedral in Cuernevaca, Mexico. There, Bishop Don Sergio Mendez Arceo (now retired) first zealously removed all the saints' images and the traditional trappings from the church. But then, sensitive to popular tastes, he initiated the famous Mariachi Mass, using the instruments not so much of folk culture but of the regional music tradition of his people. A form of popular devotion was thus readmitted.

3. *Protestantism* of the "mainline" variety has not officially altered its abiding suspicion of popular religion. But this form of Protestantism appears to be one of decreasing vitality in Europe. On one wing its youngest leaders are drawn toward liberation theology and therefore toward a form of cooperation with Catholics, which their grandfathers—most of whom were converted from folk Catholicism—would have rejected. A decade ago the North American sponsors of the Baptist Seminary in Mexico reacted with deep dismay when the local leaders of the school began including Roman Catholics not only in the student body but on the faculty as well. On the other level, mainline Protestantism is beginning to merge with Pentecostalism. Indeed, it is often difficult for a visitor to a Protestant congregation in Latin America to detect its denominational affiliation. All these developments suggest that the Protestantism introduced by missionaries in the nineteenth century will probably not continue to nurture its animus against popular religion as ardently in the future.

4. *Pentecostal* changes in attitudes have also taken place but more as a result of the actual structure of Pentecostal worship than as the fruit of theological analysis. With the exception of Afro-Brazilian spiritism, Pentecostalism represents the most thoroughly indigenized expression of non-Roman Catholic religion in Latin America. Nearly all its preachers and leaders are themselves Latin Americans (this in contrast to Catholicism, which still relies on a high proportion of foreign-born priests and religious). This, along with the highly decentralized organization of Pentecostalism, means that hierarchical forms of social control are less workable, so the censoring out of the folk elements that persons bring with them to worship is more difficult. Also Pentecostalists encourage the use of indigenous musical instruments and melodies, and this inevitably allows elements of popular religion to sift in. Finally, the explicitly emotional tone of Pentecostal worship and the "speaking in tongues" phenomenon permits images from what might be called the "cultural unconscious" to come to expression. Pentecostal leaders still vigorously discourage their members from taking part in most popular rituals and fiestas, but there is considerable evidence that at another level Pentecostal spirituality may be preserving elements of folk piety that might otherwise have been eradicated by urbanization and other types of social change.

5. Among *developmentalists* who are interested in stimulating changes in societies, especially in matters such as food production, health care, and education, again the attitudes toward religion have begun to change. Though they once saw popular religion as the primary obstacle to any form of change, developmentalists now tend to be much less sweeping and judgmental in their assessment of religious practices and institutions. The general shift in attention among developmental theorists away from more technological fixes and toward questions of culture has brought this concern into an even sharper focus, and developmentalists now try to cooperate with religious movements in the areas in which they are working. Some even look at them not as obstacles to innovation but as the main source of values and hopes by which persons may be motivated to make any changes at all.

6. One of the most dramatic changes has come in the *Marxist evaluation* of the significance of religion. Confronted with a continent where the only promising revolutionary activity seemed to be coming from Christian sectors, Latin American Marxists and their colleagues elsewhere were eventually forced to reassess some of the standard Marxist analyses of the role of religion in society. The most visible example of

their new attitude toward religion is the one demonstrated by none other than Fidel Castro himself in his widely read book *Fidel and Religion* (Simon & Schuster, 1987) in which the *comandante* not only does not condemn religion out of hand, but in fact insists that for large numbers of persons faith may provide the principal motivation for their participation in revolution. When the leader of the communist country, who has the longest claim to longevity in office, thus speaks, many listen:

> Basing themselves on their faith, believers can take a revolutionary stand and . . . there need not be any contradiction between their being believers and revolutionaries. As I see it, that phrase [that religion is the opiate of the people] cannot be, nor is it, a dogma or an absolute truth; it is a truth in specific historical conditions. Moreover, I believe that this conclusion is perfectly in keeping with dialectics and Marxism.
>
> I believe that, from the political point of view, religion is not, in itself, an opiate or a miraculous remedy. It may become an opiate or a wonderful cure if it is used or applied to defend oppressors and exploiters or the oppressed and the exploited, depending on the approach adopted toward the political, social, or material problems of the human beings who, aside from theology or religious belief, are born and must live in this world.
>
> From a strictly political point of view—and I think I know something about politics—I believe that it is possible for Christians . . . to work together with Marxist Communists to transform the world . . . even though, in the case of the Christians, their starting point is a religious concept.

At the more theoretical level, Latin American Marxists, who were once dazzled by Lenin's rather idiosyncratic views about metaphysical materialism, have now begun to study religion more from the perspective of the Italian theoretician, Antonio Gramsci. As they do, they make their judgments more on a political rather than on a metaphysical basis. Consequently their attitude toward all forms of religion tends to be much more nuanced.

Liberation Theology

In the case of the seventh samurai, liberation theology, the story is both more complex and more immediately significant for the larger issue of "the theology of religion." The fact is that even at its inception there was an active discussion in the liberation theology movement about the significance of *religión popular*. Liberation theologians after all did not appear out of nowhere. Many had been trained in some form of pre-Vatican II integralism. Most were understandably intoxicated by the reformist currents of the council. Some were touched by various expressions of Protestant theology. All, as Latin American intellectuals, had had to come to terms with one or another type of Marxism. They were men of their time and of their region, and as one follows their early debate about *religión popular* and notes the course it has taken more recently, two things become evident. First, the positions various of the theologians took were deeply influenced by their theological and even confessional commitments, and secondly, the present, more positive, appreciation of popular religions emerged as a result of ideas that were there from the beginning. Both these observations can be confirmed by a brief examination of some texts from an earlier stage of the discussion.

In 1976 José Míguez Bonino published a widely discussed article entitled "La Piedad Popular in América Latina" in the journal *Cristianismo y Sociedad* (no. 47, Buenos Aires, 1976, pp. 31-38). Relying on the earlier work of Aldo Büntig and on the declarations of the Medellín Conference of Latin American Bishops (CELAM) Míguez Bonino drew a very grim picture of popular religion. Referring to a report by the director of the CELAM Instituto Pastoral, Míguez Bonino quoted as follows: "The religiosity of poverty does not work to change life. It is well known that such Catholicism strengthens a dualistic vision of reality and, therefore, a religious attitude alien to the tasks of this world." In Latin America, he insisted, such popular Catholicism reinforces the social system with all its injustices, contradictions, and forms of oppression.

But Míguez Bonino was hardly alone. A paragraph from the international catechesis weekly published in Medellín in 1968 makes—if anything—a more severe judgment:

> The manifestations of popular religiosity—even if they sometimes show positive aspects—are, in the rapid evolution of society, the expression of alienated groups—that is, of groups that live in a depersonalized, conformist, and noncritical manner and do not make efforts to change society.

This document, reflecting as it did the enthusiasm of the post-Vatican II era, did not withhold its indictment of the church for allowing such popular piety to continue. "This kind of religiosity is maintained and encouraged," the report said, "by the prevailing structures of which the church is a part. . . . The expansion of this type of religiosity slows down changes in the structures of society."

Five major elements appear in the harsh post-Vatican II liberationist critique of popular religion. The first pointed to its alleged *fatalism:* it encourages persons to accept the situation in which they find themselves as the will of God or as according to the order of creation. The second criticism, directed especially at Pentecostal forms of popular piety, focused on *individualism,* on the attempt to "save my own individual soul" at the expense of corporate or cooperative action in society. The third had to do with what might be called *substitute satisfaction,* finding spurious solutions to genuine human dilemmas: lighting a candle before a saint's picture when a child is sick instead of summoning whatever health care is available. A fourth critique had to do with the *blessing of intergroup and interclass harmony* through an emphasis on love and reconciliation—a "false universalism." It was often noted that this universalism is gladly seized upon by those in power to maintain the status quo. Fifth, there was the critique (mainly of developmentalists) that immersion in the popular religious mindscape *prevented persons from "integrating,"* from participating in the development of the wider society.

Reading these critiques in historical perspective, it becomes evident, however, that both Bonino's widely read article and the Medellín catechetical material were written to attack other positions. Thus Bonino sounded an alarm about romanticism, and warned those who look for liberative potential in popular religion that it can never be found in a pure state. Folk religious expressions exist *within history,* he argued, and therefore in a context of class conflict and oppression. The Medellín paper echoed the same caution, adding that such movements are always to some extent misshaped by the distortions introduced by ruling elites in order to make use of religion to perpetuate the prevailing system of privilege. But both Bonino and the authors of the Medellín document realized that popular religion could not simply be ignored. It was present everywhere and had a special appeal for precisely the persons whom liberation theology was supposed to liberate. What was the answer?

Replies to the challenge of popular religion often followed theological positions in a remarkably predictable way. A Methodist, Bonino suggested that the only solution was that of conversion—*metanoia.* In order to encourage such a conversion, he said, popular religious movements needed to be brought to a point of crisis. The poor and marginated who participate in them had to be made to see the contradiction between the picture of the world religious movements project and the actual world in which they had to live. Out of the resulting breakdown would come a transformation not just of the person, Bonino hoped, but of the *tradition itself.* Its rudiments could be then redirected toward the proper historical task of human beings.

Míguez Bonino does not delineate more specifically what these rudiments might be, but his prescription drawn from the lexicon of Wesleyan theology is an understandable one: like individuals, religious traditions must also be brought to the mourner's bench, to a point of crisis, in order for a genuine conversion to occur. The resurrection comes only after the cross.

Similar prescriptions were advanced by many Catholic writers at the time, especially Juan Luis Segundo. Perhaps some of them were more influenced by protestantizing theological currents than they themselves were aware.

Still, neither Bonino's voice nor the Medellín instruction were the only sentiments being articulated. At about the same time Míguez Bonino's article was published, Juan Carlos Scannone, who like Míguez Bonino wrote from Buenos Aires, took a quite different position about what the appropriate attitude of liberation theologians toward popular religion should be. Scannone believed the Second Vatican Council had brought to Latin America two different forms of postconciliar theology. One was shaped by the European liberal enlightenment and its more rational way of thinking. Scannone criticized this stream for viewing popular religion with a thoroughgoing "hermeneutic of suspicion." It signaled a deep distrust of what he called the "sapiential wisdom" of ordinary persons, a wisdom embedded in their religious beliefs and ritual practices.

The other stream of postconciliar theology that Scannone noted was the one he himself represented. It is a theology that allows popular culture to provide what used to be called *locus theologicus* or *Sitz im Leben,* what Scannone calls the "hermeneutical locale." He argued that only this second theological approach could in the long run make a genuine contribution to the authentic liberation of Latin American peoples. "Without denying its ambiguities," Scannone wrote, "it [popular religion] is an expression of authentic Christian faith inherited from the past and received from the preaching of the first missionaries. It should continue to be evangelized but in terms of its own proper cultural values."

The heart of Scannone's argument lay in what Alisdair MacIntyre has since called the "tradition specificity" of any mode of reasoning. Scannone rejected outright the notion that universalistic and scientific modes of discourse were the only valid ones and argued forcibly that there are *different* traditions of reason. He further argued that incarnate in the religious practices of the Latin American peoples, there is a deeply symbolic mode of reasoning, which not only needs to be preserved in Latin America but has an invaluable contribution to make to other parts of the world. Scannone's point coheres well with the ideas advanced more recently by C. S. Song (*Theology from the Womb of Asia*, Orbis Books, 1986) about theologizing in the context of local symbolic codes.

Scannone's main argument with Bonino and the other liberation theologians who looked with suspicion on popular religion is posed by his most basic question: Who is the real subject of liberation theology? Granted that theologians make such theology explicit and critical, and that they reflect on it, who is the *original subject* of this discourse? Furthermore, who is the genuine addressee? Is the addressee of theology all persons of faith or is it mainly elites—religious or nonreligious—who have been conscientized into the process of social change and historical responsibility?

Scannone views the "hermeneutic of suspicion" with suspicion. He suspects that it is informed by a scientistic bias that prevents it from fathoming the full potential of popular religion. He calls for a radical incarnation of the theological enterprise into the "culture-specific" religion of a particular people. He asked for a hermeneutic of appreciation, one that would be open to the significance of symbolic modes of thinking and would recognize that mythic thought is not merely a stage to be outgrown but a permanent component in any thinking that is essentially human. Scannone's approach to popular religion, it seems, is just as "Catholic" as Bonino's is "Methodist."

In the past twenty years it can be said with a considerable degree of accuracy that the old argument between Bonino and Scannone has moved more in Scannone's than in Bonino's direction. Such influential figures as Gustavo Gutiérrez have published significant works on the necessity for drawing on the spiritual resources and traditions of the people for the project of liberation. Gutiérrez's book *We Drink from Our Own Wells* is a particularly good example of this thesis. Nevertheless the argument is not over. Other theologians, such as Jon Sobrino, when they adumbrate a spirituality of liberation, rely heavily on a reinterpreted version of the classic European Catholic tradition itself.

Sobrino for example refers hardly at all to popular religious devotions and movements in his work, *The Spirituality of Liberation*. Leonardo Boff, for all his difficulty with the Vatican and his radical criticisms of Catholic ecclesial forms, makes few references to popular religious movements in his writing. Still, a consensus seems to be appearing that those who do not take the religions of the poor with utter seriousness have fallen somewhat short of a genuine preferential option for the poor.

The "Theology of Religions"

What does all of this mean for the "theology of religion"? In the work that lies ahead on this vital subject, it seems clear that a deepened conversation between theologians and social scientists is required. In order to do their work theologians need to become students of religions not just in their classical scriptural expressions but in their *actual local* manifestations. Theologians, Marxists, and others have been forced to take another look at *religión popular* in part because, empirically, it has not conformed to the mental images they held of it. The revolutionary Christians of Central America and the Christian advocates of democracy in Brazil often came from the sector of *religión popular*. This suggests that the discussion, among theologians and others, about religion must move outside the abstract level on which it has often been lodged. It must also focus on highly particular expressions of popular religion. Only then can informed theological judgments and evaluations be legitimately made.

There can be no doubt that the religions of marginated and oppressed peoples frequently serve an absolutely indispensable positive function. Such religious expressions preserve a *mythic past*, which then can become a source of what Metz calls the *subversive memory* that can bring a critical perspective to the present world around them. Popular religion also nurtures the *values* and *moral practices* that hold together a culture under siege and without which a people collapses into anomie. As has been pointed out frequently, popular religions also to some extent *protect cultural minorities* from the intrusive domination of cultural and religious majorities, and in some measure inoculate them against the narcotizing effect that hegemonic religions (of elites) exert on those on whom they are imposed. Finally it has been pointed out that popular religions nourish a *Prinzip Hoffnung* (Ernst Bloch); they project the *hope for a better time*, a future redemption, a utopian realm. Without such hope any people becomes cynical and defeated. These are all persuasive reasons that are advanced to suggest why harsh judgments about popular religions are often inappropriate. In short, it is held, popular religion serves a genuine function and should not be tampered with until that function is clearly understood.

Theology, however, is an *evaluative* discipline and must eventually make judgments. It asks questions not only about the *functionality* of religious beliefs but about their truth and their value for life as God intends it. Theology has various ways of asking these questions but at least these ways—albeit "traditional specific"—are *explicit*. Theologians have much to learn from the empirical specificity of students of religious phenomena. But perhaps theology's value-explicitness should evoke from social scientists on the other hand a more candid clarification of the values and commitments that underlie their work. We can no longer accept the premise that social science is merely descriptive, while theology is normative. Both are both normative and descriptive, and their specializations must be seen to lie elsewhere.

A Christian theology of popular religion will be informed by an explicit and value-conscious anthropology. Therefore Christian theologians will probe specific expressions of popular religion with some of the following questions:

What is the *nature* of the mythic past preserved in ritual and legend? Does it sacralize oppressive patterns of rank and gender discrimination? Does it stigmatize certain groups within the society in a degrading way? Is it, to use a theological category, "idolatry"?

What about the values it perpetuates? *Which values* are they? How does one judge *among* values especially at a time when the word "values" itself has become a cliché? The mere "preservation" of values is surely not an ethically positive function. Which values should be nurtured? Which subverted?

In protecting minority groups against cultural domination, do popular religions sometimes erect an obstacle to that minimal degree of recognition and coping with the dominant culture needed to ward off extinction or lethal marginalization? What is the optimal form of human community and how can it be attained?

Finally what about transcendent hope? *How* transcendent is it? Is it so otherworldly as to undercut constructive action within the society? Is it individualistic rather than corporate? How does the kingdom of God impinge on the kingdoms of this world?

There are many questions to be asked from a theological perspective of any popular religious movement. This is how a positive and appreciative engagement must take place. After all, Christian theology itself projects a mythic past, a set of prescribed values, a circumference that delineates who is in and who is out, and a hope for the coming of a reign of peace and justice. Christianity is not completely asymmetrical to other religious movements in these regards. But in its prophetic mode Christianity is also highly critical of the dehumanizing and oppressive components of religious practices and institutions. Both Judaism and Christianity emerged initially as religious protest movements against a dominant sacral system. Both began as "liberation theologies." Still if this theological engagement is to be specific rather than merely general, if it is to be concrete rather than abstract, some of the tools of observation and modes of analysis that have heretofore been the monopoly of social scientists will need to become part of the tool box of theologians as well.

We may be entering a new and fruitful place of the sometimes troubled relationship between theology and the social scientific study of religion, one in which the latter can help the former to be more concrete, while theology can challenge social science to be more explicit about its value commitments.

If there is anything to be learned from the story of the seven samurai it is that history is open and that no theological or ideological judgments are final. Things change and persons change, even religiously. So in the matter of what "popular religion" is and what it might contribute to the liberation of women and men in the future, it is always useful to take another look.

12

Fire from Heaven (1995)

These selections are taken from Fire from Heaven: The Rise of Pentecostal Spirituality and the Reshaping of Religion in the Twenty-First Century *(Reading, MA: Addison-Wesley, 1995), xv-xvi, 3-17, 299-301, 302-4, 306, 308, 309-21.*

PREFACE

A few years ago the editor of a national magazine called to ask if I wanted to make a comment for an article they were preparing on the anniversary of *Time* magazine's famous "Is God Dead?" cover story. He told me that he and his colleagues were puzzled. Why did Presbyterians, Methodists, and Episcopalians seem be to losing members—down 20 to 40 percent in the twenty-five years since that cover hit the stands—while certain other churches, mainly pentecostal ones, had doubled or tripled their memberships in the same period. He had also seen reports that pentecostalism was growing very quickly in Latin America, Africa, and parts of Asia. Was there something ominous, he wanted to know, about all this? And furthermore what did I think of the rumor that President Bill Clinton used to play his saxophone at pentecostal revival services in Redfield, Arkansas? He sounded a little worried.

I thought I knew why he was calling me. Nearly three decades ago I wrote a book, *The Secular City,* in which I tried to work out a theology for the "postreligious" age that many sociologists had confidently assured us was coming. Since then, however, religion—or at least some religions—seems to have gained a new lease on life. Today it is secularity, not spirituality, that may be headed for extinction. I thought, perhaps the editor wanted me to eat a little crow in public. Instead I thanked him for the call and told him I was probably not the right person to ask. But his questions were thought-provoking. I had read some of the same amazing statistics, including the estimate that pentecostal churches are growing at the rate of 20 million new members a year and that their worldwide membership had now reached some 410 million. I had wondered myself why they have such an appeal, but the phone call pushed me into a more active inquiry. I decided to find out what I could about pentecostals, not just by reading about them but by visiting their churches wherever I could and by talking with both their ministers and with ordinary members. My project eventually took me to four different continents, to a score of conferences and conventions of pentecostal leaders, and to more congregations than I can enumerate.

Even before I started my journey through the world of pentecostalism it had become obvious that instead of the "death of God" some theologians pronounced not many years ago, or the waning of religion that sociologists had extrapolated, something quite different has taken place. Perhaps I was too young and impressionable when the scholars made those sobering projections. In any case I had swallowed them all too easily and had tried to think about what their theological consequences might be. But it had now become clear that the predictions themselves had been wrong. The prognosticators had written that the technological pace and urban bustle of the twentieth century would increasingly shove religion to the margin where, deprived of roots, it would shrivel. They allowed that faith might well survive as a valued heirloom, perhaps in ethnic enclaves or family customs, but insisted that religion's days as a shaper of culture and history were over.

This did not happen. Instead, before the academic forecasters could even begin to draw their pensions, a religious renaissance of sorts is under way all over the globe. Religions that some theologians thought had been stunted by Western materialism or suffocated by totalitarian repression have regained a whole new vigor. Buddhism and Hinduism, Christianity and Judaism, Islam and Shinto, and many smaller sects are once again alive and well. For many people, however, it is not always good news that religions that were once thought to be safely moribund or at most peripheral have again become controversial players on the world stage. We may or may not be entering a new "age of the Spirit" as some more sanguine observers hope. But we are definitely in a period of renewed religious vitality, another "great awakening" if you will, with all the promise and peril religious revivals always bring with them, but this time on a world scale. But why were the predictors so wrong? Why has this unanticipated resurgence of religion occurred?

As I began work on this book I was aware that pentecostalism is only one particularly dramatic example of this wider religious revival, of what the French writer Gilles Kepel calls "the revenge of God." Still, I gradually became convinced that if I could somehow decipher pentecostalism's inner meaning and discern the source of its enormous appeal, this would provide an essential clue to understanding the larger religious upsurge of which it is a part. So, it became important for me to try to fathom exactly what pentecostalism is and what about it is so attractive to such a wide variety of people around the world. . . .

* * *

THE LITTLE CHURCH AND THE BIG CITY

When the day of Pentecost had come, they were all together in one place. And suddenly a sound came from heaven like the rush of a mighty wind, and it filled all the house where they were sitting. And there appeared to them tongues as of fire, distributed and resting on each one of them.

Acts of the Apostles 2:1-3

The people who call themselves "pentecostals" today take their name from a story recounted in chapter two of the Acts of the Apostles. The plot describes how the confused followers of the recently crucified rabbi they believed was the messiah gathered in Jerusalem to mark the Jewish holiday called Pentecost that occurs fifty days after Passover. Suddenly there came a sound from on high "like the rush of a mighty wind." The Holy Spirit filled them, tongues "as of fire" crowned their heads, and to their amazement each began to understand what the other was saying even though they came from "every nation under heaven" and spoke many different languages. It seemed that the ancient curse of Babel—the confounding of languages—had been reversed and that God was creating a new inclusive human community in which "Parthians and Medes and Elamites and residents of Mesopotamia" could all live together.

The story then takes an unexpectedly comic twist. Passersby, the text says, were annoyed by the ruckus and thought a drinking spree was under way. It would not be the last time that people filled with the pentecostal spirit would be dismissed as inebriated. But the Apostle Peter, rising to his feet, assured the neighbors that his companions were not soused. What was happening, he said, was no less than the fulfillment of ancient prophecy. The Spirit was being poured out in anticipation of the Last Days. Soon this present world age would come to an end, the wicked would be punished, the just rewarded, and the visible Kingdom of Christ would be established on earth.

As months, then years, then centuries passed, however, the final consummation never seemed to come. Christianity, which began as an apocalyptic sect, gradually had to adjust to the long haul. Theologians gallantly tried to redefine what the Kingdom was and when it would materialize. Some decided that the church was the Kingdom, and since it was obviously already here, there was no need to look forward to any big changes. Others taught that the Kingdom is the eternity that begins when life on this plane is over. Most Christians seemed to adjust to the new situation. But throughout the centuries there were always some who read those early prophecies, noted certain portents and omens in their own eras, and declared that this time the End was indeed near at hand. Christianity has never completely shed the millennial hopes with which it came to birth, and the conviction that the climax of history is imminent has reappeared time and time again, especially during wrenching social dislocation and cultural collapse. It also seems to come back regularly during the final years of centuries and millennia. We are once again at such a juncture, and when I started to write this book the most popular play on Broadway was one called "Millennium Coming."

The story of the first Pentecost has always served as an inspiration for people who are discontented with the way religion or the world in general is going. They turn to it because it is packed with promise. It seems to presage a big change; and when people believe that the future will be different it transforms the way they feel about the present. Some like the story of Pentecost for other reasons. It is about the experience of God, not about abstract religious ideas, and it depicts a God who does not remain aloof but reaches down through the power of the Spirit to touch human hearts in the midst of life's turmoil. It should come as no surprise, therefore, that in our present time of social and cultural disarray, and with another century—indeed a new millennium—about to begin, pentecostalism is burgeoning nearly everywhere in the world.

Because pentecostalism is so widespread, I did not have to travel very far to begin my odyssey. I started by visiting three churches located within a twenty-minute drive of my home in Cambridge, Massachusetts. On a clear night in November, I attended the midweek gathering at a black church affiliated with the Church of God in Christ in the Dorchester section of Boston. The congregation was meeting in a former synagogue which still bore a Hebrew inscription over the doors. On the following Sunday morning I found my way to a small, mainly white and Asian, Assemblies of God congregation meeting in a rented hall in a changing neighborhood in downtown Boston. Then, on Sunday evening, I dropped in on about 400 Puerto Ricans and Central American immigrants at a rousing service in an independent Spanish-speaking pentecostal church that had taken over an abandoned Lutheran edifice in the South End.

What first struck me about all three of these lively congregations was how young the worshippers were. At the black church, for instance, though women made up the majority, young black men in baggy pants, hair clipped in the latest style, sang and clapped. The youth choir was twice as big as the young adult choir, and there was a Gospel choir and children's choir as well. At the downtown church a young white woman with honey-colored hair down to her waist, wearing a floor-length peasant-style skirt, played a guitar and led the songs while an Asian woman in a white jumpsuit sang along with her and two young men with shoulder-length manes manned the drums and the keyboard. At the Latino church four young women in tasteful multi-colored frocks stood at four microphones, snapped their fingers, and moved their shoulders as they led the singing, accompanied by triple fortissimo chords from an amplified guitar and an electric keyboard.

In each of the churches the worship followed the pattern I have now learned to expect in pentecostal churches: high-amperage music, voluble praise, bodily movement including clapping and swaying, personal testimonies, sometimes prayers "in the Spirit," a sermon full of stories and anecdotes, announcements, lots of humorous banter, a period of intense prayers for healing, and a parting song. At the coffee, punch, and cookie hours after the services I met medical secretaries, computer programmers, insurance salesmen, graduate students in microbiology, and actors and police officers, as well as people who were out of work and down on their luck. It was clear that the worshippers were not simply curios, survivors of a vanishing religious age, but modern city-dwellers, who were obviously relishing one of the rare occasions in which they could engage in some personal give-and-take in a setting not stifled by some specialized technical idiom. I was beginning to see already why pentecostalism is growing with particular rapidity in cities, and since I like cities, I was beginning to feel at home very quickly. It was then that I recognized the combination of ancestral and personal history that without my knowing it had prepared me for my errand.

My ancestors fled England for the new settlement in Pennsylvania in the early years of the eighteenth century. They left because they belonged to an unpopular religion whose members were derided both for their lack of respect for established civil and ecclesiastical authorities and for the unseemly intensity of their worship. They refused to bow or take off their hats for bishops or even for kings, and they sometimes shook with fervor when they prayed. Derisively, people dubbed them "Quakers." They seem to have borne up patiently in the face of insults, but when ridicule hardened into persecution and imprisonment they set off for another continent rather than yield to further humiliation. The original epithet stuck. Though they would never have chosen the name "Quaker" themselves, they learned to carry it with pride.

The early Quakers were an ecstatic sect if there ever was one. A contemporary observer described them as "froathing at the mouth, and scrieching with a horrible noise" as they awaited the descent of the Spirit. They were so persuaded of the urgency of their message that they sometimes interrupted other people's church services. There is no doubt that they were quite fervent, intense, and more than a little intrusive. They were undoubtedly more like today's pentecostals than today's Quakers like to think.

The man who led this band of eighteenth-century holy rollers to the new world, William Penn, was also a social visionary. Like many such prophets before and after him, he longed to build a colony that would, as far as possible, replicate the heavenly Jerusalem here below. When he founded Philadelphia, "the city of brotherly love"—a name he chose from the biblical book of Revelation—he made it clear that he wanted it to serve as a haven of the religious freedom and friendly persuasion the Quakers taught. It was to be an earthly version of the City of God.

By the time I was growing up in a small town in Pennsylvania some thirty miles from where Penn and his fellow refugees had landed more than 200 years earlier, the Quakers had lost most of their ardor and impertinence. They were no longer disrespectful of authority, and their worship was anything but emotionally fervent. There was no more "froathing" or "scrieching." They, or at least the Quakers who lived in our town, had become paragons of propriety. At their services they sat quietly, eyes lowered and hands folded, waiting for the Spirit to prompt someone to speak. The Spirit usually tapped the same distinguished elders, the ones who always sat on the facing bench, and the message did not vary much from week to week.

The Quakers did not seem very interested in building the New Jerusalem either. They had become the pedigreed aristocrats of the little town we lived in, Malvern, and had generally done rather well financially. They believed, as the town gossips put it, "in God and 6 percent interest." The "city of brotherly love" was a place to do their Christmas shopping but otherwise it was best to stay away. With a growing black and European immigrant population, and dirty streets, Philadelphia, in their minds at least, was no longer the shining example of God's will for the world, but a sinkhole of vice and corruption. What they were building was not an ideal city but prudent investment portfolios.

My parents had no portfolios, but they shared the prevailing local opinion of the city William Penn had hoped would be a beacon of virtue: they thought it was a good place to avoid. If we had to drive down Chestnut Street to cross the Delaware River bridge on our way to Cape May, New Jersey, they hurried through the city, even running yellow lights. If we went in to shop at Gimbels or Wanamakers, they would buy what they wanted quickly, in order to get out before nightfall. But already as a small boy I could detect that it was not just our safety that worried them. There was something about the city they did not want me to know about. I can still remember my fascination as I stared through the streaked windows of our 1936 Chevrolet at the forbidden sights we raced past. And I recall tugging at my father's hand as he pulled me along Market Street on the way to the train station while I gaped at the unusual looking people and flamboyant window displays we were passing. With a child's unerring instinct, I sensed that if it was prohibited, then it must be interesting. I quickly learned to associate the city with exciting disorder and taboo pleasure, not exactly, I fear, what William Penn had in mind.

I was only an occasional visitor to Quaker meetings in our little town. My paternal grandfather had been lured away from the Quakers as a young man when he married a Baptist, and since my own parents preferred to sleep in on Sundays, my grandparents assumed responsibility for my spiritual upbringing. It took place, for the most part, in the First Baptist Church, where there was a junior choir and lots of hearty congregational singing. But no one quaked or screeched. A certain amount of emotion was fine, but there were, after all, sensible limits. Mostly I enjoyed it. But sometimes it got terribly dull, and I remember counting the diamond-shaped figures on the brown wallpaper over and over again during what seemed like interminable sermons.

There was one church in Malvern, however, where things were never dull. It was a tiny stucco and cinder-block edifice located on Rutland Avenue, the street that marked the edge of town. Right behind it stood the rusting red tanks of the local heating oil company and the scrubby pine trees surrounding the water pumping station. It was known to the townspeople simply as the "little church." I don't think I ever knew its denominational affiliation or whether it even had one. It probably belonged to that family of churches designated with the term "Holiness" in which fervency in prayer, a strict moral code, and the presence of Christ within every believer were emphasized. It was certainly the closest thing in our town to what I later learned was pentecostal worship. People would say, "Well, I drove by the little church the other night and they sure was hollerin'," and someone else would reply, "Yeah, Doris said last Sunday you could hear 'em singin' as far as Woodland Avenue." Once in a while people referred to those who attended the little church as "holy rollers" and said they sometimes got down and rolled in the aisles. No wonder my curiosity was aroused. But it took some time before I found out for myself what they were like.

As a teenager, I began attending the little church occasionally when Lois, a girl with creamy skin and beautiful straight black hair, who was in my high school class, invited me to go with her. Frankly, I went at first since it seemed to be the only way I could spend any time with Lois. Because of her religion she could not attend dances, movies, or parties. So accompanying her to prayer meeting or the evening service was my only opportunity to be with her. My parents were not overjoyed by this. I think they harbored a few doubts, both about Lois *and* about what went on in the "little church." At first, I had some reservations too, at least about the little church, but I very quickly came to look forward to my visits.

I always had a wonderful time when we went, and not just because I was with Lois. People sang with gusto. They murmured and nodded when they prayed. Sometimes they sobbed and wept. The pianist threw in chords and runs I never heard at the Baptist church. Lois's wide brown eyes lit up as we sang "Love Divine, All Love Excelling," while she pressed my hand. Some of the members moved and clapped or did a little two-step to the music. Sometimes people went forward and kneeled at the altar while the pastor and the deacons placed their hands on their heads and prayed. I never saw anyone roll in the aisles.

But I remember having this one problem at the little church: the preacher. He was riveting, I have to admit; his sermons were masterpieces of suspense and melodrama, replete with vivid images from Revelation and Daniel of beasts and dragons and vials of fire—high-octane material our more reserved Baptist minister usually steered away from. He also hopped and bounced around a lot, and he sometimes acted out two sides of a conversation between, for example, God and the devil, or David and Saul, mimicking their different voices. Frequently he slid out from behind the pulpit and sauntered along the aisle as he spoke. It was dramaturgy at its best: I almost always liked the *way* he said things, but I often had serious questions about *what* he was saying, and I wanted to discuss it. Even at that age I was already fascinated by the similarities and contrasts among the various churches and denominations. But no one at the little church seemed very interested in the fine points of theology.

My romance with Lois did not survive our high school graduation, but I am grateful to her for several insights I picked up by going to church with her, ideas that have influenced me in ways I could not have foreseen then. One is that eros and agape, the erotic and the spiritual energies of life, may not be as distinct as some theologians would have us believe. Whenever I think of that little church I think of Lois, and how, even though she never wore a trace of rouge or lipstick, when she prayed, eyes closed, her head tilted back and her hands raised, the way all the people in her church prayed, I thought she was the most beautiful girl I had ever seen. But there was also something frankly physical about the congregation itself. People hugged each other, and on summer nights when they lifted their arms in praise, long streaks of perspiration reached down toward their waists. They wore their clothes in a less trussed-up way, and the men's collars always seemed to turn up at the points. They were the kind of people who sometimes put their hands on your shoulders and thrust their faces up close to you when they talked.

I learned something else at the little church too, though at the time I am sure I understood it only in the most inchoate way. I learned that the imagery, mood, and tempo of a religious service are not just add-ons. They are not superfluous. Human beings are physical as well as mental creatures, and therefore these more tactile elements are part of the substance of worship. And since life itself is so full of conflict and craving, of wild hopes and dashed expectations, any religion that does not resonate with the full range of these feelings, and provide ways of wrestling with them is not worth much. Whatever else you might say about the little church, it imparted to its people not just an idiom replete with lakes of fire and a city without tears, but the jubilant gestures and heart-rending wails to go with it.

My occasional visits to both the little church and the big city remain in my memory as exhilarating episodes in a happy but uneventful boyhood. Over the years, however, these two distinct experiences have blended together in my mind. I think I know why. Both exuded the allure of the forbidden; both could scare you; both also gave off a slightly seductive, mildly wanton scent. Both conveyed an unmistakable impression of a just-barely-controlled chaos. I often had the feeling that at any given moment something could happen without advance warning. Consequently, I was strongly drawn to both, but never entirely at ease in either. I remembered this later when during my study of pentecostalism I learned it is mainly an *urban* religion, the faith of choice for tens of millions of city-dwellers on five continents.

By the time I left my hometown after high school, my lifelong fascination with cities and with experiential religion was already firmly in place. Luckily, the university I went to allowed me to gratify both. Since there was not enough money for tuition at any of the colleges I had hoped for, my parents sent me to the University of Pennsylvania where I had a state senatorial scholarship. At first I was disappointed, but that did not last long. The university was in Philadelphia. Now, at seventeen, I could gambol in the forbidden delights of Elysium with no one tugging at my hand. The movies, the stage shows, the jazz spots, the political rallies, even the "Troc"—the fly-specked old burlesque house at 10th and Arch—were now all mine for a small admission fee and a streetcar fare.

I also quickly found out that the city was full of churches. I attended a different one each week—Catholic, Methodist, Apostolic, Pentecostal, and even some Baptist churches, black and white. Some of the services were wearisome, but others made even the worship at the "little church" seem subdued by comparison. In short, as a city buff and a religion junkie I had a splendid time during my undergraduate years.

When, decades later, I read James Boswell's *London Journals*, jotted down while he was about the age I was then, recording his coffee house conversations, his incessant church going and his constant amorous affairs, I felt I had discovered a soul mate. It was only the amorous affairs that were missing in my case. My fascination with the religion of the heart continued throughout those years, but so did my problem with it. Pascal once said that the mind builds walls that the heart jumps over, but somehow that did not satisfy me. Why did the mind and the heart have to be such antagonists, the one trying to fence the other in?

Looking back at my boyhood in the small Baptist church my grandparents took me to I have to admit that, tedious as it was at times, it had done a pretty good job of holding belief and experience—and head and heart—together. One evening in particular stands out from all the rest, and thinking about it now helps me understand why the themes of this book are so essential to me. It happened when I was thirteen, and the time had come for me, along with the other boys in my Sunday School class, to "make my decision" to be baptized and join the church. To do so, however, we had to be examined by the board of deacons. It was an intimidating prospect, and I arrived at the deacons' meeting with considerable anxiety. But the kindly elders who questioned me, along with the other four equally nervous candidates, asked only a couple of questions about my beliefs. Mainly they wanted to know whether I had *experienced* the love of God and the grace of Christ in my own life. They asked nothing about the inerrancy of the Bible or the doctrine of the Trinity or when I expected the Second Coming. Rather, with simple directness and genuine concern, they wanted to know what God meant to me. Not to someone else, but to me.

I do not recall what I said to them. I do remember that one of the other boys got the giggles during the prayer the presiding deacon offered, but he was accepted for baptism anyway. But what stays with me with complete clarity is that these serious older men were genuinely interested in *me*. Naturally they wanted to find out what I knew about the Ten Commandments and the Sermon on the Mount. But mainly, they wanted to know what I, at the deepest level of my bumbling preadolescent being, felt about what—even then—I sensed were the deepest things anyone could think or feel about. They wanted to be sure that, however I stammered about it, that God was real for me. Whatever I said must have satisfied them, for a few weeks later, on a clear Easter Sunday morning, I waded into the baptismal pool behind the pulpit and was immersed.

In college, and later as a doctoral student in religion, I gradually discarded or put on hold some of my church's beliefs. But I never rebelled or resigned, never felt that I had been brainwashed or coerced. Somehow I recognized that whatever the empirical improbability of some of those stories and lessons might be, the real point was something different. For me they continued to constitute what theologians call the "master narrative" that gives my life coherence. They have stayed with me not just as ideas and values but as a cluster of deep and ineradicable affective traces: feelings of joy, terror, awe, mystery, and well-being.

As I got older, my fascination with what I had once found in the "little church" kept coming back. I am a professor of theology, and that is both my delight and my dilemma. When you teach religion in a university, or even in a seminary today, you mainly investigate other people's ideas and other people's experiences. You study the history of religions, comparative religion, the scriptures of the world, maybe the psychology of religion. This is perhaps as it should be. Few seminaries and hardly any universities are equipped to help students enter into a mystical quest or spiritual journey. Also, in order to avoid myopia and provincialism, one must be familiar with how God has been envisioned in past ages and by other peoples, both in one's own religious tradition and in others. But there is a genuine risk involved. As Ralph Waldo Emerson eloquently warned an audience at Harvard Divinity School in 1838, the danger of a steady diet of other people's religion is that it can dry up one's own resources. Studying *about* religion inevitably means studying ideas. But ideas can be very derivative, and they can take the place of experience, which must in some way be personal.

I have sensed this peril acutely during my years as a teacher and—perhaps as a consequence—have always felt drawn to those religions which major in what Jonathan Edwards once called the "religious affections" rather than in doctrines. I find myself constantly asking what experience, what encounter with the numinous, lies behind and beneath this or that theology? All in all, it was probably inevitable that one day I would—figuratively—retrace my steps across town to the "little church." After all, pentecostalism is the most experiential branch of Christianity, a movement that first arose at the turn of the century as a protest against "man-made creeds" and the "coldness" of traditional worship. This contrast may be why the telephone call from the puzzled editor rekindled my interest.

One of the first things I discovered as I began to study the history of the pentecostal movement was that I would have to do it mainly on my own. Universities do not generally offer courses on the subject, and their libraries do not condescend to stock pentecostals' often fiery tracts. At Harvard, for example, where I teach, a student can take courses in Sufism or Tibetan Buddhism. There is even a class on Hindu Goddesses. But, until I introduced a small research seminar two years ago, there were no offerings on pentecostalism.

As I delved into the history of pentecostalism and began visiting all the pentecostal churches I could, some discoveries surprised me. The first was how *many* pentecostals there are. David Barrett, a leading expert in religious statistics, estimates that pentecostalism in all its varied forms already encompasses over 400 million people. It is by far the largest non-Catholic grouping, accounting for one in every four Christians. It is also the fastest growing Christian movement on earth, increasing more rapidly than either militant Islam or the Christian fundamentalist sects with which it is sometimes confused. In Africa, pentecostal congregations, usually called "African independent churches," are quickly becoming the main expression of Christianity. Several Latin American countries are now approaching pentecostal majorities on a continent that had been dominated by Roman Catholicism for five centuries. The movement is also growing in Korea and China.

Second, I was interested to find that the pentecostal movement worldwide is principally an urban phenomenon, and not a rustic or "hillbilly religion," as some people still believe. It is proliferating most rapidly today in the gigantic megacities of the third world such as São

Paulo, Seoul, and Lusaka. Sometimes the only thriving human communities in the vast seas of tar-paper shanties and cardboard huts that surround many of these cities are the pentecostal congregations. In effect pentecostalism is a kind of communitarian counterforce within these bloated conurbations as they continue to swell and become progressively less livable.

I also learned that it is a serious mistake to equate pentecostals with fundamentalists. They are not the same. Fundamentalists attach such unique authority to the letter of the verbally inspired Scripture that they are suspicious of the pentecostals' stress on the immediate experience of the Spirit of God. This should not be surprising. Text-oriented believers in any religion tend to be wary of mystics. However, this does not mean that pentecostalism does not embody a complex of religious ideas and insights. It does. The difference is that while the beliefs of the fundamentalists, and of many other religious groups, are enshrined in formal theological systems, those of pentecostalism are imbedded in testimonies, ecstatic speech, and bodily movement. But it *is* a theology, a full-blown religious cosmos, an intricate system of symbols that respond to the perennial questions of human meaning and value. The difference is that, historically, pentecostals have felt more at home singing their theology, or putting it in pamphlets for distribution on street corners. Only recently have they begun writing books about it.

I was also in for another surprise. As I sang and prayed with pentecostals in various parts of the world I discovered that their worship constitutes a kind of compendium of patterns and practices from virtually every Christian tradition I had ever known. It would have been startling, and maybe upsetting, to the members of St. Patrick's Church, or the Quaker meeting, or the African Methodist Episcopal church in my home town, for example, to know that much of what went on in the "little church" was derived more or less directly from their traditions. Pentecostalism, while it looks to many like a narrow cult, is actually a kind of ecumenical movement, an original—and highly successful—synthesis of elements from a number of other sources, and not all of them Christian.

As I neared the end of my personal pilgrimage through the pentecostal world I found that my original ambivalence about it had not disappeared. I am still intrigued by its drama and fascinated by its ideas. I know a lot more now about why so many different kinds of people find it so appealing. But I also find myself distressed by certain features of the movement, especially the political alliances some of its members have recently entered. I still want to argue and to differ. Maybe I am still looking for the conversation I never got—despite those debates between God and the devil—at the little church. But I now harbor—paradoxically—both more hopes and more misgivings than I did so long ago in the stucco and cinder-block building on Ruthland Avenue. Maybe it is because I can see that the stakes are now higher.

When I first became acquainted with the pentecostal movement forty years ago, it was little more than a small sect. Today it is a major, worldwide religious movement. When I went to church with Lois, she was not allowed to go to the movies because they were "worldly." Today, at least in America, many pentecostals have become terribly comfortable with "this world." They started out in a faith that brought hope to society's losers and rejects. Today some of their most visible representatives have become ostentatiously rich, and some even preach a gospel of wealth. When I attended Lois's church no one asked me to sign any creeds. Indeed, pentecostalism began as a rebellion against creeds. But today many of their preachers cling tenaciously to such recently invented dogmas as the verbal inerrancy of the Bible. Pentecostals also started out teaching that the signs and wonders that took place in their congregations were not some kind of spectacle but harbingers of God's new day. But today, some pentecostal preachers seem so obsessed with the techniques of rapture that they have forgotten the original message.

There have been other changes. Pentecostals began as rebellious antagonists of the status quo, refusing to serve in the armies of this fallen age, but many have now become impassioned superpatriots, easy marks for the high rollers of the religious right. They started out as a radically inclusive spiritual fellowship in which race and gender discrimination virtually disappeared. That is hardly the case, at least in most white pentecostal churches, today. In short, as I came to know the pentecostal movement in its present incarnation I discovered that the pentecostals themselves are facing a dilemma they may not survive. At least they may not be able to survive it and still remain true to their origins.

* * *

THE LIBERATING SPIRIT

As the first days of the new millennium draw closer, the prospects for the human spirit seem both promising and chilling. For the past three centuries, two principal contenders—scientific modernity and traditional religion—have clashed over the privilege of being the ultimate source of meaning and value. Now, like tired boxers who have slugged away too long, the two have reached an exhausted stalemate. As British rock singer Sting laments in one of his most popular songs, many have now lost faith *both* in "science and progress" *and* in "the holy church." People are still willing to rely on science for the limited things it has proven it can do, but they no longer believe it will answer their deepest questions. They remain vaguely intrigued with the traditional religions, but not with conventional churches. They want to pick and choose and are less willing to accept religions either as systems of truth or as institutions. But the loss of direction Sting sings about also has a positive side. Increasing numbers of people appear ready to move on, and are on the lookout for a more promising map of the life-world.

There is no shortage of cartographers marketing their guidebooks. Rarely in history have so many models of reality and so many metaphors of what human life is intended to be made their cases with such vigor and in such jarring proximity to each other. To some observers the religious bazaar of our age resembles the riotous confusion and heady potential that enlivened the first axial age, some 2,500 years ago, when the archaic gods were already in retreat but the classical religions had not yet taken hold. To others it seems more like the Hellenistic period, when the first generations of Christians competed both with the decaying paganism of the Roman pantheon and with the exuberant cults of Cybele, Isis, and Mithra, streaming into the Mediterranean basin from the Middle East. To some it seems that today our shrunken world is heading for spiritual chaos, but others hope that out of the churning a new and unifying style of sanctity and a fresh planetary awareness may well appear.

As both scientific modernity and conventional religion progressively lose their ability to provide a source of spiritual meaning, two new contenders are stepping forward—"fundamentalism" and, for lack of a more precise word, "experientialism." Both present themselves as authentic links to the sacred past. Both embody efforts to reclaim what is valuable from previous ages in order to apply it to the present and future. Which of these two rivals eventually prevails will be decided in large measure by which one grasps the nature of the change we are living through. Philosophers, theologians, poets, and many others—both famous and not so famous—have tried their hand at comprehending that change. Forty years ago the Roman Catholic philosopher Romano Guardini became the first to refer to "the end of the modern age." Then the British historian Arnold Toynbee wrote that Western civilization had entered a period of decline and that only a spiritual renewal could save it from destruction. The Russian Orthodox philosopher Nicholas

Berdyaev thought that we might be on the threshold of a "new age of the Spirit," but T. S. Eliot foresaw only a desiccated wasteland peopled by hollow men. Others spoke of the decline of the West, or the death throes of patriarchy, or the twilight of either capitalism or socialism.

There is an underlying thread that connects many of these diverse portrayals of the emerging Zeitgeist. Most agree that we are entering a period in which we will see the world and ourselves less cerebrally and more intuitively, less analytically and more immediately, less literally and more analogically. Most depict the self and the world as moving beyond subject-over-against-object. The great Asian religious sages have always sensed this, but they have sometimes lost the self altogether in an undifferentiated whole, a drop of water merging with the boundless ocean. Perhaps it has taken the very recent and unprecedented meeting of East and West to produce this new stage of consciousness. In any case, these thinkers find evidence for a new phase of history in virtually every field of human endeavor—in atonal and improvisational music, in the environmental movement, in new styles of painting and sculpture, in experimental architecture, and especially in poetry. I think one can also find it in pentecostalism. . . .

Although there appear at first to be certain parallels between fundamentalism and experientialism, their differences are much more important. The fundamentalists are the most visible. Zealous, unswerving, and impassioned, the devotees of the new fundamentalist movements, although they confess a variety of convictions and creeds, and are frequently at each other's throats, seem curiously similar in many respects. The word "fundamentalist," which was originally used in the early twentieth century to characterize a particular tendency within American Protestantism, is now applied to the Hindus who tore down the Muslim mosque in Ayodya, India, the Buddhists who harass the Hindu minority in Sri Lanka, the Jewish members of Gush Enumin who insist that God has granted them the land of their Arab neighbors, and the Muslims who want to enforce Islamic law on everyone through state power, along with those Christians who believe in the verbal inerrancy of the Bible.

The use of the label "fundamentalist" to describe such a heterogenous miscellany of movements and sects may stretch the word. But there is no denying that these diverse legions of resolute believers all bear what Martin E. Marty and Scott Appleby, who have written about them at some length, call a "family resemblance" to each other. Each presents itself as a revival, drawing upon what its leaders insist are the "fundamentals," the non-negotiable bedrock beliefs of a religious tradition which have undergone cultural erosion or direct attack by secular forces in the modern age. Furthermore, each fundamentalist movement claims to be the sole authentic representative of the religion it speaks for, and fundamentalists often treat fellow believers who do not grant them this prerogative with more venom than they do outsiders. Inquisitors are always quicker to stoke the fires for heretics than for mere unbelievers.

There is one important feature to be pointed out immediately about fundamentalists. Though they insist they are "traditional" in one way or another, these movements are really what the British historian Eric Hobsbawn calls "invented traditions." In their own distinctive ways they are all modern by-products of the religious crisis of the twentieth century. As Marty and Appleby put it, "Fundamentalists do not simply reaffirm the old doctrines; they subtly lift them from their original context, embellish and institutionalize them, and employ them as ideological weapons against a hostile world." The great irony of Christian fundamentalism, for example, is that it shares the same disability that plagues and cripples the modern rational mind—literalism. In their frantic effort to oppose modernity, Christian fundamentalists have inadvertently embraced its fatal flaw. Their prosaic view of the Bible and their cognitive conception of faith—epitomized by a shrill defense of scriptural "inerrancy"—place fundamentalists squarely in the modern camp. Fundamentalism is not a retrieval of the religious tradition at all, but a distortion of it. The fundamentalist voice speaks to us not of the wisdom of the past but of a desperate attempt to fend off modernity by using modernity's weapons.

The various "fundamentalisms" abroad in the world today are recent reactions to different forms of modernity and, however much they claim to be the original article, they differ in essential respects from the classical historical expressions of their traditions. At first this might seem to undermine their plausibility. But their claim to have a firm grip on absolute truth attracts those who have become weary in their searches or who are afraid even to begin the quest. The problem with such hermetic certainty, however, is that while it might work in an isolated ghetto where one religion predominates, it is very difficult to maintain when one is surrounded by other people who are also making absolute claims. The increasing religious diversity of today's world pits different kinds of fundamentalists against each other in a no-holds-barred conflict. The dissension is especially volatile when some variety of religious fundamentalism combines, as often happens, with some form of nationalism. The emergence of an assortment of fundamentalists in recent decades, and the inevitable discord between them, raises the awful specter that instead of a new beginning for the spirit, we may be heading for an ugly replay of something like the Thirty Years' War between the Catholics and Protestants in Europe—only this time on a global scale.

The other contender for spiritual ascendancy in the next century is "experientialism." By its nature, however, it is more disparate and inchoate, harder to describe than fundamentalism. It also assumes different forms, but is unified by a common effort to restore "experience," albeit defined in different ways, as the key dimension of faith. In recent years liberation theologies and feminist theologies—among many others—have shared this penchant for experience. Like fundamentalism, this bent toward experientialism is also appearing within a variety of different religious traditions. Also, just as the various fundamentalisms in different religions bear a striking family resemblance to each other, the experientialist tendencies in different religions are more like each other than like the fundamentalist wings in their own households of faith. Thomas Merton once claimed he felt closer to Buddhist monks and Hindu mystics than to certain people in his own Catholic Church.

Like the fundamentalists, the experientialists also try to reach back past current distortions to the sources of the faith and to make these sources freshly available in the present. Unlike fundamentalists, however, they do not always claim to be the single authoritative voice of their tradition, and—like Merton—they often find much in common with people on other paths. In a troubled time, these two prevalent tendencies—fundamentalism and experientialism—stand like mirror opposites of each other, our benign and the malignant angels. . . .

This new environment puts religious authorities in an uncomfortable position. The traditional clergy plays a much less privileged role. Neither ecclesiastical ordination nor theological education guarantees that anyone will pay any attention to them. At worst, certified religious leaders are sometimes viewed as obstacles to a genuine personal appropriation of the faith. At best they are seen as useful, but not indispensable counselors and guides who help other people reach into the reservoirs of archetypal symbols and exemplary stories. Consequently it is not surprising that many religious functionaries staunchly oppose the experiential current. I often hear priests and ministers complain about what they call "cafeteria-style spirituality" or "religion à la carte." Professional theologians insist on maintaining the elegant intricacy of the whole doctrinal system and resist any effort to adopt part of it without accepting the entire bundle. Theologically trained and ordained religious leaders often feel that their authority derives from the fact that they represent *the* tradition in its fullness, and they resent the nonspecialists who are not impressed by their credentials. Hervieu-Léger compares this situation among religious institutions to "deregulation" in the economic sphere.

The other feature of "experiential" spirituality that religious professionals resent is that today's seeker is often looking for some very practical results. The postmodern pilgrims are more attuned to a faith that helps them find the way through life here and now. There is something quite pragmatic about their religious search. Truths are not accepted because someone says they are true, no matter what that leader's religious authority may be, but because people find that they connect, they "click" with their own quotidian existence. . . .

The contest between the fundamentalist and the experientialist impulses has barely begun. The question of which one will eventually supersede the spent and weary forces of scientific modernity and conventional religion as the principal source of coherence and value in tomorrow's world is still undecided. The stakes are very high, and the battle is raging on several fronts at once. . . .

Which way will it eventually go? As I returned to my writing desk after all my reading, conversation, and travel through the many worlds of pentecostalism, I found myself asking not only this question, but also another one: how will pentecostalism itself weigh into this struggle for the soul of humankind? The question is important because the people who are attracted to pentecostalism around the world, although many critics dismiss them as an anachronism, are actually more of an avant-garde. They are the very people who are already bearing the brunt of the same numbing social dislocation and cultural upheaval that is in store for us all. Despite themselves they are the pioneers of the vertiginous world the rest of us will also be trying to negotiate in the decades to come. So the question of how pentecostalism will influence them is a critical one. Will it stoke the fires of xenophobia and hostility? Will it channel the emotions it releases into perpetuating and deepening the ruptures that divide us? Or will it open people to new outpourings of the divine spirit and a fresh recognition of the motley oneness of the human family and its multitudinous fellow dwellers on our frail planet? . . .

Some pentecostals want to cooperate with ecumenical groups. Others do not. Some feel at home in the evangelical or even fundamentalist household. Others want to dissociate themselves from those groups. When I attended a service at the church associated with the international headquarters of the Assemblies of God in Springfield, Missouri, a couple of years ago during a meeting of the Society for Pentecostal Studies, some of the denomination's leaders seemed upset when the president of the society suggested that pentecostals had their own history and a particular message of their own for the world and should not be subsumed under an evangelical or fundamentalist umbrella. When a woman teacher from a pentecostal college excitedly told about representing their tradition at the National Council of Churches, some in the audience looked skeptical. Wasn't the National Council that "liberal superchurch" their evangelical friends had warned them about?

The divisions between third world pentecostals and their North American brethren are more political in nature. For instance, when I talked with some Mexican pentecostal leaders in Guadalajara, they complained that their North American brothers and sisters had gotten so carried away by the health-and-wealth gospel and were so much under the sway of the right-wing group known as the Christian Coalition that they had forgotten their original mission to the downtrodden. And even within North America there is little cooperation between white pentecostals and their black fellow pentecostals, some of whom contend that the Assemblies of God was founded at least in part to take the leadership out of the hands of blacks.

The divisions are not just trivial. While perhaps a majority of white pentecostals in the United States strongly supported American aid to the Contras in Nicaragua's civil war and the effort to eradicate the guerilla rebels in Guatemala, many pentecostals in both these Latin American countries were actually fighting on the other side. A missionary to Guatemala told me that in that country alone seventeen pentecostal pastors had been killed by the army in its effort to root out insurrectionaries. Few white American pentecostals welcomed the news that many of their brothers in Chiapas joined their Catholic neighbors in the Zapatista uprising that surprised both the Mexican government and the world in January 1994. Meanwhile the leaders of the Christian Coalition's strategists are making every effort to enlist the pentecostal churches in their efforts to take power in every institution in the land. The political split in pentecostalism is deep and—it seems—widening.

Because the organizational pattern of pentecostalism is so anarchic, or so lacking, it is not easy to discern the battlelines. Relations between the large black pentecostal denominations such as the Church of God in Christ and the predominantly white ones such as the Church of God and the Assemblies of God are often tense and edgy. Black and Latino pentecostals within all of these different denominations often find themselves closer to each other than to their fellow denominationalists. Almost everyone is embarrassed about Jimmy Swaggart and Jim Bakker, but no one knows whom to blame. The pastors of the small, struggling pentecostal churches that are still serving the lower-class people with whom the movement started out often feel overshadowed and ignored by the pastors of the new "megachurches" who have achieved splashy celebrity status. Tensions among the "classical" pentecostals who date back to Azusa Street, the "charismatics" who appeared in the established churches in the 1970s, and the Third Wavers who emerged in the 1980s and claimed the gifts of healing and prophecy but did not want to bear the onus of the "pentecostal" label, continue to simmer. Meanwhile, the growth of pentecostalism among white people has slowed considerably, while its expansion among minorities and in the third world continues to accelerate.

These internal struggles will go on for a long time and may never be fully resolved. But the answer to the larger question of whether pentecostalism will contribute more to fundamentalism or to experientialism will depend on two key features of pentecostal life and theology. The first is the problematical term "experience" itself, and the second is the idea of the "Spirit." Both of these concepts are utterly central to pentecostal self-understanding; consequently, to raise questions about them is to go to the core of what the movement is.

Pentecostals talk about *experience* a lot. The old tent-meeting adage that "a man with a doctrine doesn't stand a chance against a man with an experience" is still frequently quoted. But if pentecostalism is to become a strong ally in what I have called the "experientialist" side of the attempt to shape a spirituality for the next century, then pentecostals will have to be much clearer about what they mean by "experience." Otherwise a vacuous "cult of experience," too much in keeping with the contemporary celebration of "feelings" and the endless search for new sources of arousal and exhilaration, could undermine its authenticity. Pentecostalism could disappear into the vogue of New Age self-absorption. The popularity of health-and-wealth theology shows how quickly this could happen. Some pentecostal preachers I have heard and watched are so fascinated by sensational displays of rapture that they appear to have forgotten the original meaning of the "signs and wonders" which were seen as tokens that a new day was coming, that the reign of God was breaking into history. Speaking in tongues, especially, which became so important for the early pentecostals, was not just an "experience" that one sought for its own sake; it was the "initial evidence" of the Spirit's baptism, a sign that God was about to "do a new thing in the world."

Pentecostals often talk about experience without being very precise about what they mean. In fact, they sometimes claim, like the mystics from whom they have descended, that the experience they are referring to defies verbal expression: "When it happens to you, you'll know, and you won't have to ask." There is some truth in this. However, virtually anyone can claim anything in the name of experience. The results are often exciting but confusing. For instance, liberation theologians insist that the Bible must be read and Christian theology worked out anew in the light of the experience of poor and oppressed people. Feminist theologians base their work on the experience of women, and one feminist theologian, Paula Cooey, identifies pentecostals as among the forerunners of this experiential approach. It seems that pentecostals, though some of them might feel uncomfortable in the company of liberationists and feminists, are actually making a very similar claim, and were making it long before these others did. But each of these approaches has its own take on what "experience" means.

What they actually mean by "experience" is the keystone on which the pentecostal enterprise depends, and the answer is not all that clear. But it would be wrong to single out Pentecostals for their lack of precision. Some years ago the German philosopher Hans-Georg Gadamer wrote, "However paradoxical it may seem, the concept of experience seems to me one of the most obscure we have." The great American thinker Alfred North Whitehead was even more forthcoming. "The word 'experience,'" he remarked, "is one of the most deceitful in philosophy." Nonetheless, whether it is obscure or even deceitful, most Christian theologians have included experience—sometimes precisely defined, most often not—as one of the authoritative bases for religion and theology, along with scripture and reason (and tradition among Catholic). But just how much relative weight should be assigned to each of these has never been settled, and a kind of low-intensity skirmishing has gone on for a very long time. Periodically one or the other—sometimes reason, sometimes tradition, sometimes experience—emerges from the pack to insist that it has been wrongly denied its rightful place.

The argument seems to come in waves. During the Protestant Reformation, Luther and Calvin stressed scripture against tradition. During the Methodist revivals, Wesley and his followers accented experience over both. During my boyhood, the emphasis on religious experience in my own Baptist denomination was being sharply challenged by fundamentalists who were insisting on doctrinal purity. When I was in seminary, the "neo-orthodox" theologians such as Karl Barth and Emil Brunner were once again stressing the Bible against what they feared was a wave of hazy subjectivity. Later, when I went to Harvard to study for my doctorate, the spirits of Jonathan Edwards, William James, and Ralph Waldo Emerson, all of whom stressed religious experience, were still very influential. More recently . . . experience has made another comeback via liberation theologies. But no sooner had that happened than a new anti-experientialism once again became the rage among academic theologians. Highly influenced by current anthropology, these "post-liberals" such as Professor George Lindbeck at Yale argue that religious experience is not primary at all. They believe that religions are cultural and linguistic systems that shape and define the kinds of religious experiences the individuals within them have. Thus, "religion" comes first, and experience is secondary. So the argument goes on. It seems that once again, as Gadamer and Whitehead warned, "experience" is proving to be a slippery concept.

For pentecostals the crux of this renewed debate between the primacy of belief systems and that of personal experience may lie in precisely that feature of their life which has sometimes brought upon them the most reproach and caused them the most embarrassment: ecstatic worship—which I believe is a kind of populist mysticism. What pentecostals call "speaking in tongues," or praying in the Spirit, has appeared in history before, and it is always a sure signal that the available religious idiom has become inadequate. Glossolalia is a mystical-experiential protest against an existing religious language that has turned stagnant or been corrupted. But glossolalia does not occur in a vacuum. It almost always takes place among people who are themselves culturally displaced, and often politically or socially disinherited as well. It is a form of cultural subversion, a liberating energy that frees people to praise God in a language of the Spirit that is not controlled by dominant modes of religious discourse. Furthermore, glossolalia helps to create a new religious subculture, one that in turn amplifies and affirms personal experience.

There is one thing the crisis of experience-based theologies overlook when they claim that culture and language always precede and shape experience. They overlook pain. They forget that some human experiences are so intense that they defy words and compel us to create new words, sometimes whole new worlds. Of these world-creating experiences, perhaps the principal ones are spiritual and physical suffering. Pentecostals, unlike feminist and liberation theologians, usually like to stress the more joyful dimension of their meeting with the Spirit. But, as the pentecostal theologian Steve Land has pointed out, this encounter also involves anguish and yearning. I think this is the key. Anyone who has felt real pain knows that not all moans of distress are culturally patterned. Suffering is sometimes expressed in available cultural motifs, but sometimes it also forces us to reconstruct our worlds. Pain changes us. It compels us to break out of our normal modes of thinking and to see life in a different way.

The final word has not yet been said about what the oh-so-simple-sounding but "obscure" and "deceitful" concept of "experience" means. The debate is sure to go on, and if the past is any guide, professional theologians and ecclesiastical leaders will usually be skeptical of "experience," while lay people will tend to trust their experiences more than they trust theology. For me the question ultimately is not whether experience should be important. I agree with Paul Tillich—who was surely not a pentecostal—but who maintained that all religious belief *must* be subject to what he called "experiential verification." Experience, after all, is the experience *of something*. Even in the most "experientially" oriented spiritual movements, experience itself is not the Source, it is the means by which the Source is known. Experience does not create the spiritual reality. It makes something real *for me* which was not so real before. If the pentecostals can clarify this, they could become a major ally of the experientialist against the fundamentalist party in today's battle. But in order to grasp what the spiritual experience they talk about is an experience *of*, pentecostals will have to become more precise about the meaning of the second key term in their vocabulary, "Spirit."

A special encounter with the "Holy Spirit" (which they called the "Holy Ghost") was at the heart of the early pentecostal movement. But they were not talking about just any spirit. They said it was the same Spirit who hovered over the primal chaos when God created the world, who spoke through the prophets, who dwelt in Jesus Christ and—most important—who had begun to fulfill all the biblical promises by creating a new heaven and a new earth where justice and compassion would reign. The early pentecostals saw themselves positioned "between the already and the not-yet," witnesses to the "first fruits of the Kingdom" but not yet to its fullness, living in the light that precedes the dawn. In other words, the *experience* they testified to was an encounter with a Spirit who has a purpose not just for them but for the whole world. And for the unemployed janitors and domestic servants who gathered at Azusa Street, this purpose was no less than the coming of the Kingdom of God as it had been taught and demonstrated by Jesus.

Therefore they believed that when it came, the poor would be lifted up, the hungry fed, and the brokenhearted comforted; while the mighty would be brought low and the rich sent away empty. It is hard to imagine a more radical vision of the future than the one this life-changing experience of the Spirit awakened in them.

Not only did the early pentecostals believe that the Kingdom of God was coming soon, they also believed they themselves were the evidence of its arrival. The future was already breaking into present. What theologians call "eschatology" was not merely one conviction among others. It was their escutcheon, their trademark, their rallying point. It was utterly focal to the other features of the movement. Healings and tongues and prophecies were seen as certain signs of the imminent arrival of the reign of Christ the King. This vivid millennial expectation continued for decades. When Aimee Semple McPherson set out across the country in her "Gospel Car," the words emblazoned on the side read "Jesus Is Coming Soon: Get Ready."

But now things have changed. My impression, after visiting churches on four different continents, is that today pentecostals are even more uneasy about this radical vision of the future than they are about speaking in tongues. In most churches today the message centers on the immediate presence and compassionate availability of the Spirit of Jesus Christ as helper, healer, and companion. The expectation that the Lord will come again soon, though it is voiced now and then, seems muted. It surely does not hold anything like the pivotal place it once did.

I have a very ambivalent attitude about this change. As one who has imbibed at least some of the liberation theology's practice of rethinking theology from the vantage point of the poor, I regret in some measure that pentecostals seem to have dampened their early eschatological fire. The confident hope that God's judgment and blessing were on their way soon has both comforted and catalyzed oppressed peoples for centuries. But today many middle-class pentecostal congregations appear very much at ease with the status quo. Now they seem confident not that Jesus is coming soon, but that He probably isn't, and that therefore nothing will interrupt their pursuit of success and self-indulgence. The Kingdom Now movement and the "name-it-and-claim-it" preachers have elevated this complacency into a theology.

On the other hand, I frankly hope that pentecostals do not try to reclaim the *literal* End Time urgency that swept the world in the early years after the Azusa Street revival. But they *are* faced with a difficult dilemma. The disappearance of eschatology produces stagnation, comfort, and the consumer religion of the Kingdom Now preachers; a short-term apocalyptic vision, on the other hand, makes it impossible to address the long-term issues that Christians, along with all human beings, must confront, particularly the environmental crisis. When a former Secretary of the Interior said that he saw little purpose in trying to preserve rainforests since Jesus was coming soon anyway, he did not speak for all pentecostals. But clearly any theology that allows Christians to ignore the threats of water and air pollution, resource exhaustion, and the destruction of the atmosphere, all because they believe our delicate orb is only the "late great planet earth," is both morally irresponsible and patently unbiblical. If pentecostalists do not reformulate their eschatological vision of what the Spirit is doing in world history, they end up supporting the fundamentalist party, and telling us not to fret about the ruination of the environment since Daniel and Revelation teach that we are in the Last Days and there will be no future generations anyway.

I am heartened to find among the younger generation of pentecostal ministers a serious effort to rethink pentecostal eschatology. They teach their congregations that what the Bible envisions is not the fiery dissolution of this world, but its transformation into the promised Kingdom, and that the scripture strictly warns against setting dates and timetables. These same young pentecostal leaders also believe that the fact that their movement started among the disowned and dispossessed is not a mere historical memento, but a decisive indication of what the Spirit wants them to be doing today. Unlike the Kingdom Now preachers who court the well-to-do and advocate the takeover of worldly institutions, these leaders recognize that Jesus promised His kingdom to the poor and to those who suffer for righteousness' sake.

Much to the chagrin of the political right-wingers, a kind of pentecostal liberation theology is now emerging. The Puerto Rican theologian Eldin Villafañe, a pentecostal himself, believes that the genius of pentecostalism is an encounter with the power of the "liberating Spirit," and he believes that this Spirit has a "project" that is being worked out within human history. His sketch of a pentecostal liberation theology is an exciting prospect, and it is not a passing chimera. Sociologist Cecilia Maritz, who studies the small Catholic "base communities" in Brazil, the local study and action groups from which liberation theology arose, has noticed that in some places these groups function very much like pentecostal communities. Father Pablo Richard, a Costa Rican Catholic who spends most of his time teaching

Bible courses for the lay leaders of these base communities all over
Latin America, claims that the difference between them and pentecostal congregations is diminishing rapidly. If these two powerful movements, both of them on the "experientialist" side of the ledger, were
somehow to combine their strengths in the coming decades, the result
would be extraordinarily potent. If the pentecostals, following Villafañe's lead, absorb something of the social vision of liberation theology, and the Catholic base communities shed the residual elements of
vertical authority they still sometimes retain, the offspring could be
more powerful than either of its parents.

Whether pentecostals will come down on the side of the fundamentalists or on the side of the experientialists is an open question
since vigorous forces are pulling both ways. Whether such core ideas as
"experience" and "Spirit" are interpreted in ways that push the movement—against the grain of its history—in the fundamentalist direction
remains to be seen. But whatever happens, given the nature of the
pentecostal impulse, I doubt that it will be settled through theological
debate. Pentecostal theology is found in the viscera of pentecostal spirituality. It is emotional, communal, narrational, hopeful, and radically
embodied. Furthermore, whatever changes occur in pentecostalism
will begin in the lives of its hundreds of thousands of congregations.
Answers to the questions about what experience is and what the Spirit
is doing in the world will not appear first in journals but in the ways
that these little outposts of the Kingdom *live* in a world that is both
hostile and hungry. The reason I am hopeful that pentecostalism will
emerge from the current fray on the side of the angels comes not principally from what I have read, but from what some of these outposts,
especially a very small but very symbolic one, are actually doing.

The Grove Hall area in Dorchester is one of the most neglected and
crime-ridden sections of Boston. Many of the stores are boarded up,
and commuters who drive through lock their doors. The police call it
"Beirut West." In the middle of this desolation there is a tiny congregation of young black pentecostals, many of them graduates of the elite
universities of the Boston area, who have chosen to return to live in
the ghetto as an expression of their Christian faith. They do not own
a building, but meet to pray and sing and study in a rented hall. They
attend court, monitor the police station, train young people in work
skills, and encourage them to stay in school. Amid continuing setbacks
and great discouragement they try to include people who live in the
neighborhood in their fellowship and to build a basis for hope in an
atmosphere of anger and corrosive cynicism. They know about early

pentecostalism, and with a finely honed sense of history they call themselves the "Azusa Christian Community."

The day I visited the regular Sunday worship of the Azusa Christian Community in Dorchester the members sang with gusto, shook tambourines, and worshipped with infectious jubilation. But what impressed me most was the intensity of their prayers. A shooting had taken place just outside the apartment of one of the members, so they prayed for the victim and his family. They prayed that God would touch the hearts of the drug dealers who pandered their wares openly just down the street so they would see the error of their ways. They prayed for the sick, including, when I requested it, my sister-in-law who was suffering from leukemia. But they also prayed for help in getting through their exams, finishing their lab projects, and finding a job. I was touched. Here were people who had chosen to be actual witnesses to the kind of community their pentecostal ancestors foresaw. But they know they cannot do it without each other's support or without prayer. The Reverend Eugene Rivers, who leads the congregation, makes the rounds of the Massachusetts Institute of Technology, Harvard, and Boston University, challenging young graduates to forgo moving to the suburbs and to join the Azusa community on the urban frontier. "But if you don't pray," he warns them, "don't come."

The service at the Azusa Christian Community lasted longer than I anticipated, so I had to slip out a bit early. The streets were glum and the sky was gray. Orange peels, cigarette butts, and dented cans littered the gutter. Three children played on the hood of an abandoned car. As I climbed behind my steering wheel I heard a siren. A police van raced by, followed by a fire engine. I waited until they turned the corner onto Blue Hill Avenue and the sound of the siren grew dimmer as it moved south toward Mattapan. But then, just as I put my key in the ignition, I heard the congregation inside start to sing again, and when I looked back I saw that one of the young men had come to the door to smile and wave goodbye.

My visit to the Azusa Christian Community in Dorchester brought me full circle. The fire from heaven had first fallen on a tiny handful of people at a place called Azusa Street. It crackled and hissed, then caught on and leaped across continents and oceans. Eventually it reached around the world. I had seen the evidence of its effects in many, many places. But never had I felt closer to the original spirit of Azusa Street than when I visited its namesake, in a rented hall forty minutes from my doorstep.

13

The Papacy of the Future: A Protestant Perspective (1998)

This essay was originally published in Gary McEoin, ed., The Papacy and the People of God *(Maryknoll, N.Y.: Orbis Books, 1998), 144-57.*

In *Ut unum sint* Pope John Paul II reminds his readers that the supreme vocation of the bishop of Rome is that of striving for the unity of Christians. I welcome this historic encyclical and I am especially grateful that the pope seems to have invited all Christians into a conversation about how this quest for unity might be advanced. But how serious is this invitation? We have some reason to be hopeful. Immediately after the encyclical appeared the dean of the Waldensian (Protestant) Seminary in Rome, Paulo Ricca, telephoned the Sacred Congregation for the Doctrine of the Faith and asked if it really meant that non-Catholics were to take part in this exciting conversation. Not only was he assured that we were, but a short time later Cardinal Joseph Ratzinger himself came to the Waldensian Seminary and, before a packed house, discussed the encyclical with Dean Ricca and other members of the faculty. Since then, Vatican officials have participated in other high level discussions on the topic with Protestant and Orthodox church leaders and theologians. I do not believe non-Catholics should underestimate the importance either of the pope's invitation or of Cardinal Ratzinger's demonstration that it is genuine. I do feel, however, that what Protestants could contribute to the conversation might be quite different from what the pope or his prefect anticipate.

No doubt, of course, there will be Protestants, especially those in the more "catholic" and more ecclesially self-conscious denominations who will be only too happy to take up the old debates about the validity of orders, what infallibility means, the significance of Marian piety, maybe even the current status of the *filioque* clause. I will have some-

260

thing to say about these venerable polemical chestnuts later on, but I rather believe that everything that could possibly be said about them has already been said, most of it more than once, and that the chance of a breakthrough coming on such an agenda is fairly remote. What attracts me most about *Ut unum sint* is the pope's suggestion about "leaving behind useless controversies" and his intriguing allusion to a "new situation." Just what is this new situation that makes it possible to carry on a discussion among all Christians about how the pope's vocation for unity could best be carried out?

I will not try to summarize the wide array of Protestant points of view of this topic. They range from those who think that, with a few modifications in the more recent enlargements of the papal claims, the bishop of Rome might well be endowed with some symbolic primacy, to those who continue to feel the whole history of the papacy has been a calamitous mistake from the start. Then of course there are those—and there are many—Protestants who are so busy evangelizing Latin America or just trying to stay alive in China that they rarely if ever think of the papacy, except maybe when they see the pope on television emerging from an Alitalia jet or waving from his specially designed limousine. I also realize that the questions the other authors in this volume have dealt with so ably, about the pope's role in the governance of the Catholic Church, are crucial ones. But they have discussed them so thoroughly I prefer to take a different approach. I wish to enter the very personal observations of one particular Protestant and to concentrate on my hopes—perhaps even my fantasies—for the future ministry of the papacy to the whole world.

I

I remember well the first time I found out there was such a thing as a pope. It was in February 1939, and I was nine years old. Walking down our street in the small town of Malvern, Pennsylvania, where I grew up, I noticed that the doors and lintels of the imposing, greystone St. Patrick's Church, which stood almost next door to our two-family brick house and on the same block as the Baptist church we belonged to, were hung with yards of somber black ribbon. When my father came home from work that evening, I asked him what it meant. My father, the non-churchgoing offspring of two churchly Baptist parents, pursed his lips for a moment before answering. "Well," he finally said, "their pope died. He lived in Italy, but he died, and those are mourning decorations. It's the way they show their sadness."

He may have hoped I would be satisfied with the answer, but of course I wasn't. I wanted to know what a pope was—it was a term I had never heard before—and why anyone from Malvern would be that sad about the death of someone who had lived so far away. He paused and then tried to explain as best he could what the pope meant to Catholics. Sixty years later what impresses me about his reply is how free it was from bigotry or papist-baiting, something I only learned about much later, and never heard at all either in church or at home. My parents' attitude seemed to be that if Catholics, whose ways were a bit mysterious anyway, wanted to have an Italian who lived far across the ocean as the head of their church, that was their business. It had nothing much to do with us.

Like many Protestants, however, I have had a continuing fascination with the popes and the papacy. As I grew, I also came to see that the pope, even though we were not Catholics, did have something to do with us. The pope who had died on that cold February day in 1939 was, of course, Pius XI, the librarian-diplomat, whose memory tends to be overshadowed by his flashier protégé and eventual successor, Pius XII. It was that pope whose somewhat sour visage and rimless glasses I came to recognize during my teenage years as the Italian who headed the Catholic Church. I never saw him as a very warm or welcoming figure, but I have also discovered that many Catholics didn't either. Still, as I began to study—and become unendingly fascinated—with history, first in high school and then in college and ever since, I could not help noticing that whatever period or problem I was reading about, the popes were always there. Try to study the history of political institutions, philosophy, art, science, or literature without bumping into popes everywhere. They did, after all, have something to do with us for they were significant actors in a history we all share. Besides, whatever you might say or think of the claims made about the popes, it would be hard to find a more fascinating collection of men (I am leaving out "Pope Joan," whose credentials and historicity, it seems, are still in some dispute). The bishops of Rome have included saints, rakes, scholars, schemers, administrative geniuses, reformers, egomaniacs, tyrants, art collectors, warriors, builders, and even an occasional personage with an interest in theology. Somehow, as I plunged deeper into history, then theology and the history of religion, it was the sheer persistence and virtual omnipresence (for blessing or for bane) of the papacy, that impressed me. I began to see at least a glimmer of plausibility in the hoary Catholic argument that any institution which has survived that long, despite the fornicators and four-flushers who had actually occupied the office, must be taken with some degree of seriousness. If the

God of the Bible, as I believe, acts in and through human history, then it has to be conceded that the papacy, and not just in the West, occupies a not inconsiderable chunk of that history.

I was already a doctoral student in the history and philosophy of religion at Harvard in 1958 when Pius XII died and a roly-poly character named Roncalli was elected and took the name John XXIII. His choice of this name was a bit puzzling to those of us who knew a bit about papal history since the previous John, who had reigned seven hundred years earlier, had become a slight embarrassment to the church. John XXII had sat in Avignon and thus represented an episode in church history some Catholics would prefer to forget. He had worried theologians (is anything really new?) by talking about his mystical visions of what would happen after the final judgment. But there you had it again: persistence. The Catholic Church had waited seven hundred years, but now seemed an opportune time, at least to Roncalli, to retrieve and refurbish a perfectly good biblical name. It was touching to be reminded by John Wilkins' essay in this volume of something I had read, but nearly forgotten, in Peter Hebblethwaite's biography of Angelo Roncalli, that virtually the last words he uttered on his deathbed were, *ut omnes unum sint.* I think it is safe to say that, given Roncalli's short but spectacular papacy, the name John has now been fully restored and vindicated. The Catholic Church, it seems, is not in any particular hurry about these things.

John XXIII did far more than reclaim a papal name. He demonstrated, in a thrilling and imaginative way, the kind of freedom a pope has if he is willing to exercise it. John XXIII not only issued encyclicals like *Pacem in Terris* that still reverberate, and not only assembled a council that changed the church forever, he also redefined the religious, cultural, and moral meaning of the papacy itself. He did this, moreover, not through any sweeping juridical reforms but simply by the way he lived. I continue to be astonished when I remember how not only Protestants, Jews, and members of other religions, but also atheists, skeptics, and agnostics seemed to admire and even love him, and how genuinely sad hundreds of millions of people were when he died. I am also somewhat baffled by it. Why should so many people who, like my parents, think of this pope business as an odd but harmless thing Catholics indulge in, have any interest in whether a pope is generous, expansive, humble, or not? It almost suggests that there was, and is, something deep in even the most unpapal (as opposed to anti-papal) soul that hopes for a pope we can all feel fond of. It is the evolution of this cultural-spiritual and moral dimension of the papacy that is left out of most of the suggestions I see about the future of the papacy. Maybe the omission occurs because most of those who engage in the discussion are Catholics, and since they tend to be preoccupied with other aspects of the papal office, they might miss this one. Perhaps you almost have to be something of an outsider, and therefore not so wrapped up with issues of collegiality, infallibility, and curial power, to appreciate it.

II

The first pope I met personally was Paul VI. It was at a consultation in Rome sponsored by the Vatican's then newly established Secretariat for Nonbelievers, whose president was Cardinal König of Vienna. It was a meeting that altered forever my ideas about the papacy and about what its future course might be. I was not, however, invited to the conference as a nonbeliever. Vatican II had made it clear that Protestants were now to be viewed in a much more favorable light, and a Secretariat for Christian Unity had just been established. I was invited because it was shortly after the appearance of my book *The Secular City* and someone at the Vatican, possibly even prompted by the pope, thought I knew something about secularization and modern unbelief. When at the conclusion of our talks Pope Paul VI received the scholars who attended, he took my hand and, with gentle eyes looking over his hawk-like nose, told me that he had been reading my book and that although he disagreed with some of it, he had read it "with great interest." I was immensely pleased but also sorry the next day that I had not asked him to put it in writing. It would have made a marvelous blurb for future editions.

What was important about that consultation, however, was not meeting the pope. ("It's like visiting the Statue of Liberty when you go to New York," the monsignor who administered the Secretariat told us before the audience.) The important thing was that this was a meeting sponsored by an official organ of the Vatican curia to which not only Protestants and Jews but nonbelievers and even Marxists were invited. It suggested a vast new arena for papal leadership, a transformation of the Vatican itself into an open meeting ground where representatives of various contending world views could come together for uncoerced and honest conversation. This hope is voiced by Giancarlo Zizola in his essay in this volume when he suggests the possibility of the Vatican becoming "such a point of concentration of spiritual authority in the eyes of all Christians and of all peoples as to become a kind of agent of unification of all forces that tend toward the good, without losing at the same time continuity with what had previously been considered good." This represents a truly catholic vision of what Christ's prayer, *ut omnes unum sint,* could mean.

To my mind, that meeting was a truly remarkable gathering, but I regret to say that the Secretariat for Nonbelievers soon fell upon hard days. Perhaps it was just a little too daring, a bit in advance of its time. Still, I like to think of its courageous work almost as an eschatological sign, a token of future possibilities. After all, the authority of the bishop of Rome in the early years of Christian history arose when he was looked to as the one to hear out and settle otherwise intransigent disputes among contending parties within the church; so the kind of meeting I attended would represent a logical extension of that practice. Someone reported a few years ago that the reason the Secretariat for Nonbelievers has declined into insignificance is because neither Cardinal König nor the people who administered it in Rome were cagey enough to deal with the hardball of internal curial politics. This may well be the case, but again, maybe one has to be a non-Catholic, or at least blissfully uninvolved in the internecine power struggles of Rome, to appreciate just how powerful and promising that historic gathering was. I still believe, despite more recent reverses, that it presages a role the papacy—and quite possibly only the papacy—could play in the next century.

Theologians sometimes use the word "proleptic" to describe those hints and foretastes of the final consummation that are already appearing here and there in earthly human history. The sacraments are such proleptic signs, especially the Lord's Supper. But the church itself is also called to be a sacrament, a "provisional demonstration," as Karl Barth once wrote, "of God's intention for all humankind." A couple of years ago I witnessed just such a proleptic demonstration in Milan, where Cardinal Carlo Maria Martini has created an annual series of meetings in which believers and nonbelievers gather to share insights and opinions about some issue of vital common concern. It is an immensely popular event, drawing tens of thousands of Milanese away from their offices, style shows, and discotheques. Tickets are free but one must request them and they are always in short supply. The year I participated, priests and lay people, scholars and politicians—including the mayors of the four largest cities in Italy—came together to discuss "The City: Blessing or Curse?" Cardinal Martini himself, in full vestments, ably presided over the meetings and made his own comments. Despite film openings, theatrical productions, concerts, and numerous art exhibits going on in the city at the same time, it was clear that Martini's gathering was the one no one wanted to miss. It was "the open church" at its best, a demonstration not only of what the church should be but what, at times, it already is. Its only limitation was that it was a bit provincial. It was Italian, even Milanese. The setting and sponsorship lacked the historic resonance and universal sweep of Rome and the Vatican. John Paul II had taken a couple of initiatives in this direction, such as the memorable prayer meeting for members of the different world religions in Assisi and his historic invitation to the head rabbi of Rome to say Kaddish in the Vatican. What interested me most about these events was how eagerly people responded to his initiative and how grateful they were. The future papacy, it would seem, does not have to be invented out of whole cloth. Strands of it are already in hand. They need only be woven together and spread.

III

The ending of the cold war may be one of the most important features in the "new situation" the pope refers to. But the world is still tormented by divisions, the most painful and salient of which do not run along denominational or even religious fault lines. What separates us today is the way hunger and misery are distributed—or maldistributed—in the world Jesus Christ came to "make one." Thirty years go, when the Second Vatican Council adjourned, the countries of the North were roughly twenty times richer than those of the South. Today, after decades of development programs, loans, aid and marketization, they are fifty times richer. According to the UN Development Report for 1996, the world's 358 billionaires are wealthier than the combined annual income of countries with 45 percent of the world's population. The gap between the hungry and the satiated has never been wider and it deepens every year. Since nearly two billion of the world's population are Christians—and this includes hundreds of millions of the world's impoverished—it is self-evident that what dismembers and disfigures the Body of Christ today and makes "visible unity" such a painful challenge is not the divisions among churches. It is the chasm between the minority of the privileged and the majority of the poor, sick, and abandoned to whom Christ addressed most of his ministry.

This is not to say that some kind of ecclesial "visible unity" among Christians is not important. It is indeed important, but not as an end in itself. The unity of Christians is vital, but it is instrumental, not ultimate. When Christ prayed, in the words quoted in the encyclical, that "all might be one" (John 17:22), he himself recognized this instrumentality. He prayed for unity *so that the world might believe the Gospel.* I doubt that any Catholic or Protestant theologian would deny this. But the Gospel we hope the world will believe is about the coming of God's reign of justice which signifies the vindication of the poor and the ingathering of the excluded and forgotten. So the question we need to ask is this: how can the quest for Christian unity, which the pope acknowledges is the highest goal of his ministry, be understood as a means to healing the wounds of the nations and overcoming the cruel sunderings that are tearing the flesh of the human family?

IV

This takes me back to the old ecumenical agenda, what the pope refers to as the "useless controversies." I realize these endlessly debated questions cannot be set aside completely. But when we recognize that the unity of Christians, which the pope says he embraces as the main goal of the Petrine ministry, is a means toward achieving human unity, this casts the timeworn agenda in a new light. It enables us to approach seemingly obsolete questions from a new angle. The stubborn dilemma about valid and invalid orders, for example, might seem less intractable if we kept in mind that the whole church, in all its many twigs and branches and including the laity, is called by God to be a minister/servant to the world, and that the various orders of ministry are principally various forms of servanthood. Several writers in the present collection have already reminded us of this, and it seemed significant to me that John Paul II refers to himself in this encyclical as *servus servorum Dei*. Admittedly in the past popes have not always used this title to signal a readiness for humility and servanthood. Can we hope that this time he may be quite serious about it?

The issue of humility brings up another feature of the papacy which has sometimes been a sticking point in the past: pomp and pageantry. Catholics who have drunk deeply of the fountains of St. Francis sometimes suggest that the palaces and the regalia one encounters around St. Peter's create an unnecessary obstacle to unity. Consign them all to the bonfire of vanities, or better still sell them all and give the proceeds to the poor, they urge, and the separated brethren will flock into the newly trimmed-down bark of Peter.

Not so. I believe most non-Catholics enjoy the baroque and theatrical aspects of the papacy, albeit sometimes a little secretly and guiltily. But there is a reason for this. Ever since the pope was stripped of his earthly fiefdoms in 1870, it is obvious that he is not a king or emperor in the earthly sense. His guards, after all, carry halberds, not uzis (although I assume that since the assassination attempt there are some real bodyguards with real semi-automatic weapons just offstage). When the pope really ruled over worldly domains, the plumes and maces were a genuine offense. They are not today. But they are not just camp either. Their somewhat operatic staginess reminds us that, in a strange way, the pope does have his divisions, but they consist entirely in the moral and spiritual authority symbolized by the living tradition these colorful antiques recall. The outcome of what Pius IX considered a great catastrophe, the loss of the Papal States in the *Risorgimento,* has turned out instead to be a blessing. It resulted in a papacy that wields more genuine power than it ever did, none of it coming from the barrel of a gun. Maybe next the papacy will discover that its real spiritual power does not come from the barrel of an excommunication notice either.

Also, on the vexed issue of Marian piety, I think a fresh approach might eventually help diminish the rancor and tone down the rhetoric. The "new situation" that is pertinent here is the worldwide triumph of the culture of market capitalism and the individualistic consumerist mythology that supports it. Is a counter symbology available? Recent feminist scholars have sagely pointed out that the relationship of the mother (or the primary parent) to the child reminds us that the current economic model of human beings as calculating decision-makers who base their choices on rational self-interest leaves out a huge piece of reality. It leaves out most of the relationships we really have, and certainly the most important ones. No one makes the calculated choice to be a child. No child chooses its parents. Parents and children rarely enter into contractual relationships, and choosing to become a parent is rarely a profit-motivated decision. In addition, the child-parent relationship is one in which the power equation changes over the years. One partner begins weak and becomes strong, the other eventually grows weaker and needs the strength of the one who began in total dependency. We should not overlook, as Protestants often have, that Marian piety is often the major devotion precisely of those masses of people who tend to be left out—or pushed out—of the self-interest-centered market culture. Also, the symbol of the parent and child is an immensely powerful ecumenical one. It is a folk icon you can find in almost any home of any denomination. Rightly understood, the place of Mary in Christian spirituality (and not only Christian) could be an asset rather than a liability to Christian unity. At the same time it could serve as a desperately needed counterweight to the pervasive image of the calculating economic decision-maker which provides the basis for the religion of the market with its sacrament of endless consumption.

The other contributors to this volume have already presented convincing arguments about how one might re-think such questions as infallibility and collegiality. Regarding the former, it has always seemed odd to me that the papacy, which has been one of the most stalwart foes of the acids of modernity, has inadvertently allowed itself to be taken in by one of the most corrosive of these cauterants—literalism. The very concept of infallibility assumes a view of language and its relationship to God, to persons, and to the world which is highly reductive and distinctly modern. It implies a wooden, even lifeless notion of language, a view which has been challenged not only by the best poets of the century but also by the most insightful philosophers. It is especially surprising that a pope who before his elevation was a respected phenomenological philosopher (and gave a lecture on this subject at Harvard Divinity School) should be caught in such a contradiction.

Doctrines are of course an essential element in the life of the church, but a deeper and more nuanced understanding of the nature of doctrine—and its kinship to poetry, song, liturgy, and prayer—might eventually make the whole infallibility question moot. But on this question I am afraid that Catholics do not have much to learn from Protestants, who have sunk even deeper into the abyss of literalism. Not only the fundamentalists but also their mirror image, the historical critical zealots who vote with variously colored balls on which words are and which are not the *ipsissima verba* of Jesus, have fallen into the literalist mire. Both have forgotten the essentially mythic and symbolic quality of religious language. It were as though one of the most unattractive components of modernity had taken its revenge on religion by seeping like some invisible but lethal vapor into the inner sanctum of the churches themselves. Maybe at some level the Pentecostals and charismatics have sensed this. For them, language, including religious language in its present debased state, is suffocating faith. Therefore glossolalia seems to be one way to start breathing again. There is a crisis of language in the churches, but the concept of infallibility is a symptom of it, not a cure. It is not for nothing that thoughtful observers of worship have detected a surprising similarity among Quaker silent worship, speaking in tongues, and the Latin Mass.

Protestants may have a little more to contribute when it comes to questions of collegiality. Not that all non-Catholic forms of polity have always worked perfectly. They have not, but there are so many of them that they provide a sort of laboratory, a thousand flowers blooming. And there is no such thing as a failed experiment since we learn from our mistakes as well as our successes. The down side of the "new situation" however is that the modern world has taken its secret toll here as well. What literalism is to doctrine, bureaucracy is to polity. Whether it be a free church, connectional, presbyterial, or episcopal polity on paper, almost all Protestant churches—and Catholic churches as well—have been thoroughly bureaucratized. Does the pope really know or care about what is going on day by day in those anonymous labyrinthine offices that line the Via della Conciliazione? When the buses stop and the traffic lights change, the busy clerical pen pushers who file into those buildings carrying their briefcases look like Xerox copies of their counterparts at Dean Witter or the Prudential Life Insurance Company, except for the clerical collars.

If anything, Protestants seem to have learned a bit in advance of Catholics, that new, de-centralized, more loosely organized forms of polity are urgently required. If centralization, hierarchy, and top-down vertical authority came close to putting IBM and General Motors out of business, why should they work for us? This is hardly a heretical thought. "Subsidiarity" is, after all, a very old and established principle in Catholic social teaching. There is no reason why it should not apply within the church itself. In his thoughtful lecture on "The Exercise of Primacy" given at Campion Hall in 1996, Archbishop John Quinn quoted these words which Archbishop Giovanni Benelli uttered while he was serving in the Roman Curia as Substitute Secretary of State:

> The real, effective jurisdiction of the pope over the whole Church is one thing. But centralization of power is another. The first is of divine law. The second is the result of human circumstances. The first has produced many good things. The second is an anomaly.

Protestants would of course have their doubts about what "effective jurisdiction" means. But they would say a loud "amen" to the peril of centralization. We have lived through a period of massive defections from national and international church headquarters. Consequently, today Protestants the world over are experimenting with all kinds of polity changes. Some will no doubt be disastrous. Others could work. And, as long as we keep reminding ourselves that the purpose of all church polity is ministry and service to the world, then these experiments might be useful for everyone.

V

I began these highly personal reflections on the papacy of the future with my early memory of the passing of Pius XI. I conclude with a much more recent papal encounter that also taught me a lot about Christian unity. In the summer of 1995, just weeks after the appearance of *Ut unum sint*, I was teaching in Rome at the same Waldensian Seminary on the Piazza Cavour where Cardinal Ratzinger would soon come to discuss the encyclical before an eager audience with the dean, Paulo Ricca. During that summer the pope held a smaller-than-usual audience after his return from Slovakia where, to the astonishment of his hosts, he had knelt in prayer at the grave of some Protestant martyrs. He wanted this particular audience to take place in St. Peter's Basilica itself, not in the new Hall of Audiences next door. It was a moving occasion. The pope obviously still had his recent visit in mind and he spoke eloquently about the need to put old dissensions and suspicions behind us and affirm what we hold in common. He then made a special point of greeting and shaking hands with the Protestant delegation of which I was part. When he took my hand he smiled as an aide told him of my connection with Harvard Divinity School where he had once given a lecture on phenomenology (which I regretfully admit I did not attend). He seemed a bit puzzled, however, and his brow knit when he learned that I was there with a delegation from the Waldensian Seminary in Rome. "Here," he asked, raising his eyebrows slightly, "in Rome?" Yes, I assured him, the seminary was indeed right here in Rome. It is hard for me to believe he did not know of its existence. Maybe he had simply forgotten, or was confused about why I should be there. But to me the symbolism seemed wonderfully appropriate. We were his neighbors.

Founded by Peter Waldo as the "Poor Men of Lyon," the Waldensian movement began two hundred years before the Reformation, at about the same time as the Franciscans, and embraced many of the same principles. They did not seek papal approval, however, as Francis had done, and immediately became one of the targets of the Inquisition. Most fled to the northern mountains of Italy or to remote regions of Sicily. Then, when Rome was incorporated into the new united Italy, some returned to Rome where they published the first Bible in Italian to appear in that city. They have been there—as well as in other parts of Italy—ever since. They like to point out to guests that their seminary, which adjoins a Waldensian church and a bookstore, stands within five hundred meters of the Vatican. I like to think that the presence at the audience of Waldensians from just across the Tiber reminded the pope that ecumenism is not just a matter of ecclesial diplomacy and encyclicals. It is also an issue for Main Street. To paraphrase my favorite Catholic politician, the man who represented my home district in Congress for many years, namely Tip O'Neill, all ecumenism is local. It is local or it isn't anything. The real test of *Ut unum sint* will be what happens between St. Patrick's parish in Malvern, where I first saw those mourning drapes, and the Baptist church down the street, and the A.M.E church across town. My hope is that the somber ribbons may be replaced by the garlands of a festive new chapter in ecumenism, one that inspires even the most remote churches to move together into the "new situation" with the kind of hope that can only come from the realization that Christ himself—not we ourselves—is the author of our unity, a unity that is intended to include not just the churches but the world God loves.

14

The Rise and Fall
of "Secularization" (1999)

This essay was published in Gregory Baum, ed., The Twentieth Century: A Theological Overview *(Maryknoll, N.Y.: Orbis Books, 1999), 135-43.*

History may be servitude,
History may be freedom. See, now they vanish,
The faces and places, with the self which, as it could, loved
    them,
To become renewed, transfigured, in another pattern.
                        —T. S. Eliot, *Little Gidding*

One hundred years ago, as the nineteenth century ended, predictions of what the twentieth would hold were varied and often contradictory. Some prophesied the final disappearance of religion, ignorance, and superstition. Others confidently predicted a "Christian" century, and some American Protestants even christened a new magazine with that name. A hundred years later, both these forecasts appear to have been wrong. In this essay I wish to inquire into the career of one idea that became a touchstone for both the theology and the cultural criticism of the twentieth century. Indeed, it became for some the single most comprehensive explanatory myth of its era. I want to ask what became of that myth and of the reality it was supposed to illuminate. The myth, of course, is secularization.

Max Weber initiated the discussion by suggesting that although Calvinism had provided the original value foundation for modernity, the religious substance was being displaced by the very worldview it had spawned. This was a revolution that was devouring not its children but its parents. Then, throughout the twentieth century, students of large-scale social change saw religion and modernization within a kind of zero-sum equation: the more modernization, the less religion. The larger the role religion played, it was held, the less chance modernization—which was widely held to be a desirable process—had to bestow its benefits. Conversely, the more modernization—with its subversion of traditional patterns, urbanization, high mobility, and technical rationality—the more religion, including the religion that had laid the groundwork for modernity, would be undercut and marginalized. Modernization and secularization were both the offsprings and the murderers of religion. Max Weber was the clearest proponent of this view. Religion was seen to play the role of John the Baptist to modernization's Messiah: preparing the way, but then pointing its long bony finger and announcing, "I must decrease; he must increase."

Today this zero-sum construction seems entirely implausible. Religion has not only survived, it has even thrived in some of the most modernized areas of the world. There is every indication that in many places it has even continued to stimulate the modernization process. Japan, for example, is in some ways the most modern society in the world. (Few other countries can boast taxi doors that open by themselves!) By most criteria, however, modern Japan can hardly be thought of as a secular society. Both local and state Shinto are undergoing a certain revitalization, to the dismay of democrats, Buddhists, and Christians, who view this development with alarm. The so-called new religious movements continue to proliferate, in part—some observers say—precisely because they enable people to cope effectively with the dislocations of modernization. In Africa, Latin America, and Asia both Christianity, mainly in its Pentecostal form, and other new religious movements—which are often creative adaptations of traditional religions—are burgeoning. In the United States, religion, though changing in important ways, is hardly in decline. In the so-called Third World some traditional and many innovative religious movements appear to prosper. Only Europe, some claim, is an exception to this global process. But even that is not clear. Is religion, in a characteristically European way perhaps, also making a comeback there? Paradoxically, by some standards the world may be even less secular at the end of the twentieth century than it was at the beginning. How are we to explain the dramatic failure of the secularization thesis as an explanatory paradigm for religion, culture, and politics in the twentieth century? Where does that leave us as theologians of culture at the beginning of the twenty-first?

Religious revival, unlike some other large-scale cultural trends, often begins on the periphery and only subsequently works its way to the center. This has happened time and time again in the history of the several religions. The Israelites were never a major power in the ancient world. Jesus came from an outlying province. The Mecca in which Mahomet was born was not at that time a leading city. Spiritual energy, it seems, comes from "the bottom and the edges." The current Islamic resurgence began in the slums of Cairo and other Middle-Eastern cities. The base communities of South America generated the energy for liberation theology. The fastest-growing Christian groups in the world today are probably the Pentecostal/Charismatic ones, which began in the poorer sections of cities and still grow most quickly there. Some observers forecast that by A.D. 2010, Pentecostals will account for one of every three Christians in the world. Why such phenomenal growth?

The pattern of growth tells us something important about religion and secularization. Pentecostals, though they are theologically and cultically very different from Max Weber's worldly ascetic Puritan, generate a functional equivalent to the work ethic that makes them particularly well suited to certain features of modernization. This may help explain why Pentecostalism is growing most dramatically in regions and among classes that are not yet in the mainstream. For example, there are already nearly 400,000 Pentecostals in Sicily. But in that epitome of traditional Catholic, patriarchal, southern-European culture, the Pentecostal movement is often associated (in the traditionalist mind and quite unfavorably) with women. In particular, it is associated with the women who opt out of the existing religious culture, often against the express wishes of husbands and fathers, to become healers and prophetesses. Studies have shown that Pentecostal sermons and testimonies in Sicily markedly alter existing patriarchal images of God, emphasizing God as lover and companion. It will be important to note whether the growth of this movement in other parts of the world will have an effect not just on the roles traditionally assigned to women in more conservative areas, but on the hegemonic religious symbol system itself.

In France, on the other hand, the charismatic movement (a milder form of Pentecostalism) has appeared within the educated/technical classes, a sector not usually considered marginal. Why? Perhaps in part because these people must spend so much time immersed in the flat, homogeneous language of the computer world. For them, the charismatic practice of glossolalia (speaking in tongues) provides an alternative, emotionally rich but less denotative idiom for expressing human emotion. It could be a protest against the technological reduction of language.

The vigor and expansion of new religious movements often create both collisions and fusions with "modern" societies. For example, the rapid spread of Islam in Europe through immigration is forcing people to rethink long-cherished notions about church and state and the proper place of religion in culture. The debate assumes different forms in different places. The result of the famous conflict in France about whether Muslim girls were to be allowed to wear scarves to school indicated that French officials are reluctant to allow what they see as ethnic differences to assume a religious coloration. True to a secularist tradition dating back to the Revolution, religion is supposed to be a strictly *private* affair, but schools are *public*.

Islam, unlike Pentecostalism, provides a difficult test for prevailing definitions of religious liberty in liberal societies. Pentecostals separate faith from state power even more emphatically than most traditional Protestant denominations. It would be hard to imagine an established or specially favored Pentecostal church comparable to the Anglican or Lutheran churches of the UK or Scandinavia. In Islam, though there are clear ideas about religious tolerance in the Qur'an, discussions about a Muslim equivalent to the liberal conception of separation of church and state are just beginning. But such a development will need to recognize that in Islam the faith is expected to guide the polity and inform the culture. There are other religious and ethical considerations that make the integration of Muslims into Western societies more problematical than that of previous waves of immigrants. Among these are differences in marriage laws, in beliefs about the proper age for women to marry, and whether boys and girls should be educated together. The situation is different in the UK, where some people have begun to notice the logical inconsistency of providing tax support for Protestant, Catholic, and Jewish schools but not for the country's growing Muslim population. These conflicts will soon become a matter of public debate. The result could be ironical. It could force a recognition that we are moving neither into a secular nor a Christian century but into a pluriform one. For example, if in order to prevent public funding for Islamic schools, the UK should reverse tradition and give up all public support for confessional education, then the society would have taken a long step into a kind of secularization most Britons firmly reject. On the other hand, if Muslim and then eventually other religious schools are accepted and publicly supported, it would mark a step toward a de jure as well as a de facto religiously *pluralistic* (not secularized) culture.

In many places in eastern and western Europe today, churches established for centuries either in culture or in law are now facing a much more radically pluralistic and therefore competitive situation. There is every indication that various forms of Pentecostalism and evangelical Protestantism will burgeon in some areas of the former Soviet Union. Some years ago an American religious magazine featured on its cover a picture of well-groomed young Southern Baptist missionaries handing out Russian-language Bibles both to the crews of the tanks surrounding the Russian White House during the August coup and to the people picketing them. The smiles on the faces of both groups of recipients suggested that they were pleased. This response is a matter of grave concern to the Russian Orthodox hierarchy, which has pushed for laws to guarantee its hegemony if not its monopoly.

In many places in Europe today one gets the distinct impression that although the *institutional* forms of religions may be weaker than they once were, religion still plays a strong role in public culture. References and allusions appear in such widely disparate places as poetry and drama, film, political debates, and even popular music. Pope John Paul II's avowed hope for the restoration of a Christian Europe finds an echo in a vague popular nostalgia for religious roots. Indeed, hundreds of thousands of young people from France, the rest of Europe, and other parts of the world gathered two years ago for a papal visit in—of all places—Paris. This in the city of the Boulevard St. Michel and Pigalle, a metropolis closely identified with the radical secularism of the French Revolution, and more recently with atheistic existentialism and consumer hedonism. Also in allegedly post-Christian Europe journeys to the old pilgrimage sites such as Lourdes, Fatima, and Santiago de Compostella are increasing. Could Christianity in Europe be moving away from an institutionally positioned model and toward a culturally diffuse pattern, more like the religions of many Asian countries, and therefore more difficult to measure by such standard means as church attendance and baptism statistics? Again, though this would make a significant change in religion, it can hardly be thought of as secularization.

The key theological question is how we are to evaluate *both* the demise of the secularization myth as an explanatory paradigm *and* the subtle but important changes that are going on in the religious situation of the world today. Are existing techniques of cultural analysis suitable to address this question? There is a contradiction here. One of the reasons for the religious renaissance is said to be a restlessness and dissatisfaction with the values and meanings of modernity. But the very tools of modern social and cultural analysis often used to analyze this shift are themselves squarely based on modern assumptions about the nature of human life, the good society, and the meaning of freedom. All this seems to press us toward a more explicit declaration of what the underlying, often unspoken, "theologies" of secular modernity really are. How would the emergence of a genuinely postmodern culture in Europe, one presumably free of all culturally established master narratives (including secular ones), change all this? Might it alter the present anomalous situation in which a liberal/modernist critique of religion is generally presumed to be a legitimate part of public and scholarly discourse, but a religious critique of modernity is viewed as the inappropriate intrusion of a private or inaccessible argot into the public realm?

Beneath these rather large questions lurk even larger ones. Forms of discourse and modes of inquiry gain their legitimacy because they rest on worldviews that are encoded in subtle and frequently unexamined cultural patterns. The unanticipated renaissance of religion in many parts of the world today, which surprised so many cultural observers, *might* turn out to be ephemeral, a merely superficial adjustment. But it could also mark the beginning of a long and fundamental reordering of worldviews, one in which cultural patterns that have endured since the Enlightenment would be markedly altered or even replaced. But our mental equipment for understanding a sea change on such a scale seems woefully lacking. How then are we to talk about it intelligently?

This is an especially urgent question for those theologians—including myself—who once accepted the secularization view of modern history in whole or in part. My own work on this topic has led me to the tentative conclusion that what we are witnessing is *neither* secularization *nor* its opposite ("resacralization"). Rather, it is a fascinating *transformation of religion,* a creative series of self-adaptations by religions to the new conditions created by the modernity some of them helped to spawn. Viewed in this light, I can see more continuity than discontinuity between my earlier work on the theology of secularization, especially as it was voiced in *The Secular City* (first published in 1965), and my current work on the theological significance of new religious movements.

The thesis of that earlier book was that God, despite the fears of many religious people, is also present in the "secular," in those spheres of life that are not usually thought of as "religious." But current religious movements have vigorously reclaimed many of these "secular" spheres as places where the holy is present within the profane. My early book was also, at points, a severe criticism of the traditional churches for ignoring the poor and marginalized populations of the world. Now, many of the new religious movements appeal to millions of people the traditional religious institutions have consistently failed to reach. I also argued in *The Secular City* that there was a kernel of truth in the over-blown claims of the so-called (and now largely forgotten) death-of-God theologians. They saw, in a somewhat sensational way, that the abstract God of Western theologies and theistic philosophical systems had come to the end of his run. Their forecast of what would come next was dramatically mistaken, but the eruption of new movements that rely, as most of them do, on the direct experience of the Divine rather than on creeds and philosophies seems to corroborate the death-of-God theologians' diagnosis while it completely undercuts their prescription. The fact is that atheism and rationalism no longer constitute (if they ever really did) the major challenge to Christian theology today. That challenge comes not from the death of God but from the "re-birth of the gods" (and the goddesses!).

As the twenty-first century begins, a momentous change *is* under-way, and it is not just a "religious" one. No thoughtful person, believer or nonbeliever, can ignore it. In the last few years I have focused a good deal of my attention on the astonishing growth of Pentecostal Christianity in large part because it provides such a useful x-ray, a way to understand the much larger mutation of religion of which it is an expression. In turn, change in the nature of religiousness provides an essential key to understanding the other big change or changes.

Many people, of course, have tried to fathom the meaning of the current religious revival, and some have even focused on the Pentecos-tal movement as a prime example. Earnest sociologists, puzzled psy-chologists, and diligent anthropologists have all taken their turns. But the picture they paint is often confused and contradictory. They point out that Pentecostalism seems to spread most quickly in the slums and shantytowns of the world's cities. Is it then a revival among the poor? Well, they concede, not exclusively. Its message also appeals to other classes and stations. Pentecostals vary in color and gender and nation-ality. They may be teenagers or old folks, though young adults lead the way. They may be poverty stricken or perched somewhere in the lower ranges of the middle class; there are not many well-to-do. They are what one writer calls the "discontents of modernity," not fully at home with today's reigning values and lifestyles. Another scholar even describes the movement as a "symbolic rebellion" against the modern world. But that does not quite jibe either, for the people attracted to the Pentecostal message often seem even more dissatisfied with traditional religions than they are with the modern world that is subverting them. For this reason, another writer describes them as providing a "different way of being modern." Both may be right. They are refugees from the multiple tyrannies of both tradition and modernity. They are looking for what it takes to survive until a new day dawns. Is there anyone who does not find a little of this wistfulness within?

But how much does all this tell us? Are sociological or psychological analyses really enough to explain such a truly massive *religious* phenomenon? One historian has called the Pentecostal surge the most significant religious movement since the birth of Islam or the Protestant Reformation. But these previous historic upheavals have for centuries defied attempts to explain them in exclusively secular categories, however sophisticated. The present religious upheaval, of which Pentecostalism is such a vivid example, also seems to slip through such conceptual grids. What does it mean?

As I have tried to reflect theologically on the significance of the new religious movements, it has become clear to me that they represent a clear signal that a "Big Change" is underway. Indeed even the most skeptical observers are beginning to concede that—whether for weal or for woe—something quite basic is shifting. It is a change, furthermore, that is not confined to some special religious or spiritual sphere. Granted, there are many reasons to doubt whether such a metamorphosis is actually at hand. It is true that in philosophy and literary criticism something called postmodernism is the rage of the journals. But intellectuals like to imagine themselves on the cutting edge, and postmodernism could be one more pedantic self-delusion. Gurus and crystal gazers talk about a New Age, but they sound suspiciously like the aging hippies who thirty years ago were hailing the imminent dawning of the Age of Aquarius. The "new world order" that President Bush's Desert Storm was supposed to introduce has turned out to be something of a mirage, and elsewhere in the international political arena we seem to be reeling backward to an era of ethnic and tribal bloodletting, not moving into anything very new at all. There is every reason to heed the skepticism of Ecclesiastes about whether there is ever any "new thing under the sun." Still, the question stubbornly persists. Do the Pentecostal movement and the global religious stirring of which it is undoubtedly a part point to something larger and more significant?

I think so. As a lifelong student of religions—Christian and non-Christian, historical and contemporary, seraphic and demonic—I have come to believe two things about them. My first conviction, which is widely shared among my colleagues today, is that religious movements can never be understood apart from the cultural and political milieu in which they arise. I do not believe religious phenomena are "caused" by other factors, economic or political ones, for example. Still, they always come to life in close connection with a complex cluster of other cultural and social vectors. You have to look at the whole configuration.

I have also come to a second working premise, one that is not as widely shared among my colleagues. It is that although religion neither causes nor is caused by the other factors in a complex cultural whole, it is often the most accurate *barometer*. It can provide the clearest and most graphically etched portrait, in miniature, of what is happening in the big picture. Freud once said that dreams are the royal road to the unconscious. This may or may not be the case. But I am convinced that religion is the royal road to the heart of a civilization, the clearest indicator of its hopes and terrors, the surest index of how it is changing.

The reason I believe religion is such an invaluable window into the whole edifice is that human beings, so long as they are human, live according to patterns of value and meaning without which their life would not make sense. These patterns may be coherent or confused, elegant or slapdash, rooted in ancient traditions or pasted together in an ad hoc way. People may adhere to them tightly or loosely, consciously or unconsciously, studiously or unreflectively. But the patterns exist. They are encoded in gestures, idioms, recipes, rituals, seasonal festivals and family habits, doctrines, texts, liturgies, and folk wisdom. They are constantly shifting, mixing with each other, declining into empty usages, bursting into new life. But they are always there. Without them human existence would be unlivable. And they constitute what, in the most inclusive use of the term, we mean by *religion*–that which binds life together. Even that most famous of atheists, Karl Marx, after all once said that religion is "the heart of a heartless world."

Naturally, just as it takes practice and experience to "decode" dreams, it also requires the combined efforts of many people—insiders and outsiders, observers and participants—to understand what the densely coded symbols and practices of religion tell us about their culture. Religions always contain a mixture of emotional and cognitive elements, often fused into powerful yet compact bits of highly charged information. Understanding them requires a particular form of what the anthropologist Clifford Geertz calls "close reading," one that brings historical and comparative methods together with both intuitive and critical perspectives. But the result is worth the effort. Knowing the gods and demons of a people and listening to their prayers and curses tell us more about them than all the statistics and case histories we could ever compile.

The twentieth century began with wildly disparate predictions. It was to be the "Christian century" in which science, democracy, and Christian values would triumph. Or it would be the century that would witness the final demise of superstition, obscurantism, and indeed, religion itself. For both parties of forecasters, paradoxically, "secularization" became a central focus, sometimes almost an obsession. The religious party saw it as an awful threat. The modernizers welcomed it as a deliverance. It now turns out that both predictions were wildly wrong, and the myth has faded. As the next century begins we are left with another question: What is the inner meaning of the massive transformation we are living through, a change within which the current religious mutation is an integral dimension, a sure sign, and perhaps even the determinative impulse? So far only faint harbingers of the new era are discernible. If the qualities of most of the new religious movements presage anything, we may expect a world that prefers equality to hierarchy, participation to submission, experience over abstraction, multiple rather than single meanings, and plasticity rather than fixedness. There will, of course, be countercurrents and backlashes—some of which we also see foreshadowed in various examples of fundamentalism, religious terrorism, and reaction. But the overall profile has, however dimly, begun to emerge. And the myth of secularization is dead.

Ultimately, of course, only the future will disclose what the future will be. But in the meantime, exploring the present, unanticipated, worldwide explosion of new religious movements, decoding their hidden messages, and listening to their inner voices will give us some valuable hints.

15

The Market as God (1999)

This essay was originally published in The Atlantic Monthly *(March 1999).*

A few years ago a friend advised me that if I wanted to know what was going on in the real world, I should read the business pages. Although my lifelong interest has been in the study of religion, I am always willing to expand my horizons; so I took the advice, vaguely fearful that I would have to cope with a new and baffling vocabulary. Instead I was surprised to discover that most of the concepts I ran across were quite familiar.

Expecting a terra incognita, I found myself instead in the land of déjà vu. The lexicon of the *Wall Street Journal* and the business sections of *Time* and *Newsweek* turned out to bear a striking resemblance to Genesis, the Epistle to the Romans, and Saint Augustine's City of God. Behind descriptions of market reforms, monetary policy, and the convolutions of the Dow, I gradually made out the pieces of a grand narrative about the inner meaning of human history, why things had gone wrong, and how to put them right. Theologians call these myths of origin, legends of the fall, and doctrines of sin and redemption. But here they were again, and in only thin disguise: chronicles about the creation of wealth, the seductive temptations of statism, captivity to faceless economic cycles, and, ultimately, salvation through the advent of free markets, with a small dose of ascetic belt tightening along the way, especially for the East Asian economies.

The East Asians' troubles, votaries argue, derive from their heretical deviation from free-market orthodoxy—they were practitioners of "crony capitalism," of "ethnocapitalism," of "statist capitalism," not of the one true faith. The East Asian financial panics, the Russian debt repudiations, the Brazilian economic turmoil, and the U.S. stock market's $1.5 trillion "correction" momentarily shook belief in the new dispensation. But faith is strengthened by adversity, and the Market God

283

is emerging renewed from its trial by financial "contagion." Since the argument from design no longer proves its existence, it is fast becoming a postmodern deity—believed in despite the evidence. Alan Greenspan vindicated this tempered faith in testimony before Congress last October. A leading hedge fund had just lost billions of dollars, shaking market confidence and precipitating calls for new federal regulation. Greenspan, usually Delphic in his comments, was decisive. He believed that regulation would only impede these markets, and that they should continue to be self-regulated. True faith, Saint Paul tells us, is the evidence of things unseen.

Soon I began to marvel at just how comprehensive the business theology is. There were even sacraments to convey salvific power to the lost, a calendar of entrepreneurial saints, and what theologians call an "eschatology"—a teaching about the "end of history." My curiosity was piqued. I began cataloguing these strangely familiar doctrines, and I saw that in fact there lies embedded in the business pages an entire theology, which is comparable in scope if not in profundity to that of Thomas Aquinas or Karl Barth. It needed only to be systematized for a whole new *Summa* to take shape.

At the apex of any theological system, of course, is its doctrine of God. In the new theology this celestial pinnacle is occupied by The Market, which I capitalize to signify both the mystery that enshrouds it and the reverence it inspires in business folk. Different faiths have, of course, different views of the divine attributes. In Christianity, God has sometimes been defined as omnipotent (possessing all power), omniscient (having all knowledge), and omnipresent (existing everywhere). Most Christian theologies, it is true, hedge a bit. They teach that these qualities of the divinity are indeed there, but are hidden from human eyes both by human sin and by the transcendence of the divine itself. In "light inaccessible" they are, as the old hymn puts it, "hid from our eyes." Likewise, although The Market, we are assured, possesses these divine attributes, they are not always completely evident to mortals but must be trusted and affirmed by faith. "Further along," as another old gospel song says, "we'll understand why."

As I tried to follow the arguments and explanations of the economist-theologians who justify The Market's ways to men, I spotted the same dialectics I have grown fond of in the many years I have pondered the Thomists, the Calvinists, and the various schools of modern religious thought. In particular, the econologians' rhetoric resembles what is sometimes called "process theology," a relatively contemporary trend influenced by the philosophy of Alfred North Whitehead. In this school although God wills to possess the classic attributes, He does not yet possess them in full, but is definitely moving in that direction. This conjecture is of immense help to theologians for obvious reasons. It answers the bothersome puzzle of theodicy: why a lot of bad things happen that an omnipotent, omnipresent, and omniscient God—especially a benevolent one—would not countenance. Process theology also seems to offer considerable comfort to the theologians of The Market. It helps to explain the dislocation, pain, and disorientation that are the result of transitions from economic heterodoxy to free markets.

Since the earliest stages of human history, of course, there have been bazaars, rialtos, and trading posts—all markets. But The Market was never God, because there were other centers of value and meaning, other "gods." The Market operated within a plethora of other institutions that restrained it. As Karl Polanyi has demonstrated in his classic work *The Great Transformation*, only in the past two centuries has The Market risen above these demigods and chthonic spirits to become today's First Cause.

Initially The Market's rise to Olympic supremacy replicated the gradual ascent of Zeus above all the other divinities of the ancient Greek pantheon, an ascent that was never quite secure. Zeus, it will be recalled, had to keep storming down from Olympus to quell this or that threat to his sovereignty. Recently, however, The Market is becoming more like the Yahweh of the Old Testament—not just one superior deity contending with others but the Supreme Deity, the only true God, whose reign must now be universally accepted and who allows for no rivals.

Divine *omnipotence* means the capacity to define what is real. It is the power to make something out of nothing and nothing out of something. The willed-but-not-yet-achieved omnipotence of The Market means that there is no conceivable limit to its inexorable ability to convert creation into commodities. But again, this is hardly a new idea, though it has a new twist. In Catholic theology, through what is called "transubstantiation," ordinary bread and wine become vehicles of the holy. In the mass of The Market a reverse process occurs. Things that have been held sacred transmute into interchangeable items for sale. Land is a good example. For millennia it has held various meanings, many of them numinous. It has been Mother Earth, ancestral resting place, holy mountain, enchanted forest, tribal homeland, aesthetic inspiration, sacred turf, and much more. But when The Market's *Sanctus* bell rings and the elements are elevated, all these complex meanings of land melt into one: real estate. At the right price no land is not for sale, and this includes everything from burial grounds to the cove of the local fertility sprite. This radical desacralization dramatically alters the human relationship to land; the same happens with water, air, space, and soon (it is predicted) the heavenly bodies.

At the high moment of the mass the priest says, "This is my body," meaning the body of Christ and, by extension, the bodies of all the faithful people. Christianity and Judaism both teach that the human body is made "in the image of God." Now, however, in a dazzling display of reverse transubstantiation, the human body has become the latest sacred vessel to be converted into a commodity. The process began, fittingly enough, with blood. But now, or soon, all bodily organs—kidneys, skin, bone marrow, sperm, the heart itself—will be miraculously changed into purchasable items.

Still, the liturgy of The Market is not proceeding without some opposition from the pews. A considerable battle is shaping up in the United States, for example, over the attempt to merchandise human genes. A few years ago, banding together for the first time in memory, virtually all the religious institutions in the country, from the liberal National Council of Churches to the Catholic bishops to the Christian Coalition, opposed the gene mart, the newest theophany of The Market. But these critics are followers of what are now "old religions," which, like the goddess cults that were thriving when the worship of the vigorous young Apollo began sweeping ancient Greece, may not have the strength to slow the spread of the new devotion.

Occasionally backsliders try to bite the Invisible Hand that feeds them. On October 26, 1996, the German government ran an ad offering the entire village of Liebenberg, in what used to be East Germany, for sale—with no previous notice to its some 350 residents. Liebenberg's citizens, many of them elderly or unemployed, stared at the notice in disbelief. They had certainly loathed communism, but when they opted for the market economy that reunification promised, they hardly expected this. Liebenberg includes a thirteenth-century church, a Baroque castle, a lake, a hunting lodge, two restaurants, and 3,000 acres of meadow and forest. Once a favorite site for boar hunting by the old German nobility, it was obviously entirely too valuable a parcel of real estate to overlook. Besides, having been expropriated by the East German Communist government, it was now legally eligible for sale under the terms of German reunification. Overnight Liebenberg became a living parable, providing an invaluable glimpse of the Kingdom in which The Market's will is indeed done. But the outraged burghers of the town did not feel particularly blessed. They complained loudly, and the sale was finally postponed. Everyone in town realized, however, that it was not really a victory. The Market, like Yahweh, may lose a skirmish, but in a war of attrition it will always win in the end.

Of course, religion in the past has not been reluctant to charge for its services. Prayers, masses, blessings, healings, baptisms, funerals, and amulets have been hawked, and still are. Nor has religion always been sensitive to what the traffic would bear. When, in the early sixteenth century, Johann Tetzel jacked up the price of indulgences and even had one of the first singing commercials composed to push sales ("When the coin into the platter pings, the soul out of purgatory springs"), he failed to realize that he was overreaching. The customers balked, and a young Augustinian monk brought the traffic to a standstill with a placard tacked to a church door.

It would be a lot harder for a Luther to interrupt sales of The Market's amulets today. As the people of Liebenberg discovered, everything can now be bought. Lakes, meadows, church buildings—everything carries a sticker price. But this practice itself exacts a cost. As everything in what used to be called creation becomes a commodity, human beings begin to look at one another, and at themselves, in a funny way, and they see colored price tags. There was a time when people spoke, at least occasionally, of "inherent worth"—if not of things, then at least of persons. The Liebenberg principle changes all that. One wonders what would become of a modern Luther who tried to post his theses on the church door, only to find that the whole edifice had been bought by an American billionaire who reckoned it might look nicer on his estate.

It is comforting to note that the citizens of Liebenberg, at least, were not put on the block. But that raises a good question. What is the value of a human life in the theology of The Market? Here the new deity pauses, but not for long. The computation may be complex, but it is not impossible. We should not believe, for example, that if a child is born severely handicapped, unable to be "productive," The Market will decree its death. One must remember that the profits derived from medications, leg braces, and CAT-scan equipment should also be figured into the equation. Such a cost analysis might result in a close call—but the inherent worth of the child's life, since it cannot be quantified, would be hard to include in the calculation.

It is sometimes said that since everything is for sale under the rule of The Market, nothing is sacred. But this is not quite true. About three years ago a nasty controversy erupted in Great Britain when a railway pension fund that owned the small jeweled casket in which the remains of Saint Thomas à Becket are said to have rested decided to auction it off through Sotheby's. The casket dates from the twelfth century and is revered as both a sacred relic and a national treasure. The British Museum made an effort to buy it but lacked the funds, so the casket was sold to a Canadian. Only last-minute measures by the British government prevented removal of the casket from the United Kingdom. In principle, however, in the theology of The Market, there is no reason why any relic, coffin, body, or national monument—including the Statue of Liberty and Westminster Abbey—should not be listed. Does anyone doubt that if the True Cross were ever really discovered, it would eventually find its way to Sotheby's? The Market is not omnipotent—yet. But the process is under way and it is gaining momentum.

Omniscience is a little harder to gauge than omnipotence. Maybe The Market has already achieved it but is unable—temporarily—to apply its gnosis until its Kingdom and Power come in their fullness. Nonetheless, current thinking already assigns to The Market a comprehensive wisdom that in the past only the gods have known. The Market, we are taught, is able to determine what human needs are, what copper and capital should cost, how much barbers and CEOs should be paid, and how much jet planes, running shoes, and hysterectomies should sell for. But how do we know The Market's will?

In days of old, seers entered a trance state and then informed anxious seekers what kind of mood the gods were in, and whether this was an auspicious time to begin a journey, get married, or start a war. The prophets of Israel repaired to the desert and then returned to announce whether Yahweh was feeling benevolent or wrathful. Today The Market's fickle will is clarified by daily reports from Wall Street and other sensory organs of finance. Thus we can learn on a day-to-day basis that The Market is "apprehensive," "relieved," "nervous," or even at times "jubilant." On the basis of this revelation awed adepts make critical decisions about whether to buy or sell. Like one of the devouring gods of old, The Market—aptly embodied in a bull or a bear—must be fed and kept happy under all circumstances. True, at times its appetite may seem excessive—a $35 billion bailout here, a $50 billion one there—but the alternative to assuaging its hunger is too terrible to contemplate.

The diviners and seers of The Market's moods are the high priests of its mysteries. To act against their admonitions is to risk excommunication and possibly damnation. Today, for example, if any government's policy vexes The Market, those responsible for the irreverence will be made to suffer. That The Market is not at all displeased by downsizing or a growing income gap, or can be gleeful about the expansion of cigarette sales to Asian young people, should not cause anyone to question its ultimate omniscience. Like Calvin's inscrutable deity, The Market may work in mysterious ways, "hid from our eyes," but ultimately it knows best.

Omniscience can sometimes seem a bit intrusive. The traditional God of the Episcopal Book of Common Prayer is invoked as one "unto whom all hearts are open, all desires known, and from whom no secrets are hid." Like Him, The Market already knows the deepest secrets and darkest desires of our hearts—or at least would like to know them. But one suspects that divine motivation differs in these two cases. Clearly The Market wants this kind of x-ray omniscience because by probing our inmost fears and desires and then dispensing across-the-board solutions, it can further extend its reach. Like the gods of the past, whose priests offered up the fervent prayers and petitions of the people, The Market relies on its own intermediaries: motivational researchers. Trained in the advanced art of psychology, which has long since replaced theology as the true "science of the soul," the modern heirs of the medieval confessors delve into the hidden fantasies, insecurities, and hopes of the populace.

One sometimes wonders, in this era of Market religion, where the skeptics and freethinkers have gone. What has happened to the Voltaires who once exposed bogus miracles, and the H. L. Menckens who blew shrill whistles on pious humbuggery? Such is the grip of current orthodoxy that to question the omniscience of The Market is to question the inscrutable wisdom of Providence. The metaphysical principle is obvious: If you say it's the real thing, then it must be the real thing. As the early Christian theologian Tertullian once remarked, "Credo quia absurdum est" ("I believe because it is absurd").

Finally, there is the divinity's will to be omnipresent. Virtually every religion teaches this idea in one way or another, and the new religion is no exception. The latest trend in economic theory is the attempt to apply market calculations to areas that once appeared to be exempt, such as dating, family life, marital relations, and child-rearing. Henri Lepage, an enthusiastic advocate of globalization, now speaks about a "total market." Saint Paul reminded the Athenians that their own poets sang of a God "in whom we live and move and have our being"; so now The Market is not only around us but inside us, informing our senses and our feelings. There seems to be nowhere left to flee from its untiring quest. Like the Hound of Heaven, it pursues us home from the mall and into the nursery and the bedroom.

It used to be thought—mistakenly, as it turns out—that at least the innermost, or "spiritual," dimension of life was resistant to The Market. It seemed unlikely that the interior castle would ever be listed by Century 21. But as the markets for material goods become increasingly glutted, such previously unmarketable states of grace as serenity and tranquility are now appearing in the catalogues. Your personal vision quest can take place in unspoiled wildernesses that are pictured as virtually unreachable—except, presumably, by the other people who read the same catalogue. Furthermore, ecstasy and spirituality are now offered in a convenient generic form. Thus The Market makes available the religious benefits that once required prayer and fasting, without the awkwardness of denominational commitment or the tedious ascetic discipline that once limited their accessibility. All can now handily be bought without an unrealistic demand on one's time, in a weekend workshop at a Caribbean resort with a sensitive psychological consultant replacing the crotchety retreat master.

Discovering the theology of The Market made me begin to think in a different way about the conflict among religions. Violence between Catholics and Protestants in Ulster or Hindus and Muslims in India often dominates the headlines. But I have come to wonder whether the real clash of religions (or even of civilizations) may be going unnoticed. I am beginning to think that for all the religions of the world, however they may differ from one another, the religion of The Market has become the most formidable rival, the more so because it is rarely recognized as a religion. The traditional religions and the religion of the global market, as we have seen, hold radically different views of nature. In Christianity and Judaism, for example, "the earth is the Lord's and the fullness thereof, the world and all that dwell therein." The Creator appoints human beings as stewards and gardeners but, as it were, retains title to the earth. Other faiths have similar ideas. In the Market religion, however, human beings, more particularly those with money, own anything they buy and—within certain limits—can dispose of anything as they choose. Other contradictions can be seen in ideas about the human body, the nature of human community, and the purpose of life. The older religions encourage archaic attachments to particular places. But in The Market's eyes all places are interchangeable. The Market prefers a homogenized world culture with as few inconvenient particularities as possible.

Disagreements among the traditional religions become picayune in comparison with the fundamental differences they all have with the religion of The Market. Will this lead to a new jihad or crusade? I doubt it. It seems unlikely that traditional religions will rise to the occasion and challenge the doctrines of the new dispensation. Most of them seem content to become its acolytes or to be absorbed into its pantheon, much as the old Nordic deities, after putting up a game fight, eventually settled for a diminished but secure status as Christian saints. I am usually a keen supporter of ecumenism. But the contradictions between the world views of the traditional religions on the one hand and the world view of the Market religion on the other are so basic that no compromise seems possible, and I am secretly hoping for a rebirth of polemics.

No religion, new or old, is subject to empirical proof, so what we have is a contest between faiths. Much is at stake. The Market, for example, strongly prefers individualism and mobility. Since it needs to shift people to wherever production requires them, it becomes wrathful when people cling to local traditions. These belong to the older dispensations and—like the high places of the Baalim—should be plowed under. But maybe not. Like previous religions, the new one has ingenious ways of incorporating pre-existing ones. Hindu temples, Buddhist festivals, and Catholic saints' shrines can look forward to new incarnations. Along with native costumes and spicy food, they will be allowed to provide local color and authenticity in what could otherwise turn out to be an extremely bland Beulah Land.

There is, however, one contradiction between the religion of The Market and the traditional religions that seems to be insurmountable. All of the traditional religions teach that human beings are finite creatures and that there are limits to any earthly enterprise. A Japanese Zen master once said to his disciples as he was dying, "I have learned only one thing in life: how much is enough." He would find no niche in the chapel of The Market, for whom the First Commandment is "There is never enough." Like the proverbial shark that stops moving, The Market that stops expanding dies. That could happen. If it does, then Nietzsche will have been right after all. He will just have had the wrong God in mind.

16

In the Court of the Gentiles (2001)

This appears as the Afterword to Common Prayers: Faith, Family, and a Christian's Journey through the Jewish Year *(Boston: Houghton Mifflin Co., 2001), 271-76.*

A few years ago, I borrowed a video for a course I was teaching that showed a computer-generated full-color reconstruction of the ancient Temple of Herod in Jerusalem. Based on the latest archaeological evidence, it was a remarkable feat. With just a tad of suspension of belief, my students and I could approach the towering stone walls, just as thousands of pilgrims and visitors, including Jesus, might have in the first century c.e. We could walk past what is now called Robinson's Arch, pass through the Huldah Gate, then pause in awe as the intricate facade of the central edifice came into view. But just as we paused it occurred to me that at that moment I was standing, virtually if not quite literally, in the Court of the Gentiles. After that, much of the rest of the fascinating visual reconstruction was lost on me. I lingered in the Court of the Gentiles. I rather liked it there.

After two thousand years of history and my fifteen years of marriage to a Jewish wife, I am still in the Court of the Gentiles. I still like it here. I have no intention of trying to enter the inner courtyard, where only male Jews are permitted. But I also have no inclination, having trod on the holy ground, to leave and go somewhere else. I appreciate the fact that many of the psalms refer to the temple, not just as a place to worship or visit, but as a "dwelling place." That suits me. I prefer its in-between, fluid, somewhat elusive character. I would not like a dwelling place that is too definitively demarcated. True, high stone walls surrounded the old Court of the Gentiles. But its gates opened on all sides, and I suspect no one paid much attention to who strolled in and out. That is the kind of space I value.

I realize full well, however, that although I am still in the Court of the Gentiles, the court itself is not the same. Both in stone and in metaphor, it is a different place. It is different because as the landscape around a location changes, the location itself changes as well. And the world around the Court of the Gentiles has shifted. When the Romans razed the Temple in 70 C.E., they also, of course, destroyed the Court of the Gentiles. Then the Jewish people, deprived of their central symbol and driven into exile, responded with dazzling spiritual creativity. They created an intangible Temple positioned within the ongoing life and prayers of the people, a Temple that could never be destroyed as long as this people survived. But if a spiritual Temple still exists, then presumably the Court of the Gentiles, with the generous space it allotted to people like me, still exists as well. But just where, in this eternal Temple, is the Court of the Gentiles now?

During the twenty centuries that have passed since the stone court was demolished by the legions, Jews have answered this question in many different ways. A final and definitive response has never been given, and probably never will. Jews have always insisted that they are different. There is "us" and there is "them." That much is clear, but not much else. The Talmud is full of disputes about where the borders should run. Should Jews patronize a Roman bath that displays a statue of a goddess? If a pagan temple shares a wall with a synagogue and the wall falls down, should the Jews rebuild it, and thus presumably provide shelter and indirect support for the worship of idols? The debates go on and on. Nothing much changed, in this regard at least, when Israel was founded in 1948 or when the Israelis occupied the Temple Mount at the conclusion of the 1967 war.

That was an ambiguous victory. After 1967, the huge structure on which the Temple—and the Court of the Gentiles—had stood was back in Jewish hands. But the area was now surmounted by the glistening golden Dome of the Rock, a site sacred to Islam. In the interest of civil peace, the Israeli authorities turned the administration of this area over to the city's Muslims and enforced a prohibition against Jews praying there. Orthodox Jews, in any case, are forbidden to pray there because in order to do so, they might inadvertently step on the site of the Holy of Holies, where only the high priest could enter. I have visited the Dome of the Rock, one of the most dazzling religious buildings I have ever seen, and since no one has ever warned me not to pray in or near it, I once did (albeit silently and standing, not moving my lips).

But none of this answers the question: Where, for Jews, is the Court of the Gentiles today? Exactly where do we gentiles stand in the Jewish religious view of the world? I do not expect a single answer to this question. Jews have no pope to issue teachings applicable to all of Judaism. Consequently, I have looked at it from the other side. How do gentiles define their relationship to Jews? To this I regret to say there have also been many varied answers, and from the earliest decades of Christianity most of them have been negative. Depending on time and circumstance, various gentile nations have ignored, expelled, forcibly converted, married, taxed, segregated, murdered, caricatured, made friends with, and lived next door to Jews. There is no Court of the Jews in the various temples of the gentile faiths. Muslims come closest to having one. They define Jews, along with themselves and Christians, as "people of the Book." But Christianity has no such category. Of course neither does Buddhism nor Shinto nor many other traditions. But that is understandable; until quite recently Jews were not part of the experience of these religions as they were, from the beginning, for Christians.

The way different faiths define their relationship to others, including Judaism, is not fixed. It changes from time to time, and sometimes a particular event can change the whole focus. I think just such an event took place in March 2000 when a frail, bent old man, clothed in white vestments, shuffled painfully across the rough cobblestones of Jerusalem, prayed quietly at the Wall, and then placed a scrap of paper with his prayer into one of the cracks that have received so many thousands of prayers for so many years. The pope's simple, silent gesture said more than a thousand encyclicals or a million words. I am not sure what or how much it said to Jews. But to hundreds of millions of Christians—and I think many others around the world—it said something like this: whatever our attitude toward the Jews has been in times past, from now on it will be one of profound respect. The pope, in effect, created a symbolic place of esteem and affinity for Jews in the Christian worldview, a sort of Court of the Jews. And he did so in a display, not of pomp and power, but of weakness and vulnerability. I do not think the importance of his gesture should be underestimated.

But the pattern of the pope's movements on that day also demonstrated something else. Just before he prayed at the Wall, he had visited the Dome of the Rock. Whether he prayed there or not, no one knows for sure. But, mystic that he is at heart, I believe he did, maybe as I did, without moving his lips. Then, after he prayed at the Wall, he stopped at the Church of the Holy Sepulcher, where he led an ecumenical Christian prayer service. Thus, within one short hour, the bent old man in white indicated that there is an ineradicable triangularity involved. He demonstrated that Jewish-Christian relations will mean very little unless they include Muslims. I would only add that once that principle is established, we must go on to quadrangles, pentagons, and hexagons. The other faiths must also have a place at the table. The much-touted Jewish-Christian dialogue cannot continue as a duet. It must become a trio, a quartet, and eventually a whole choir. This is not to say that as Christians and as Jews we do not have our own special issues. We do. So do Jews and Muslims, and so do Hindus and Muslims; the list could go on. But as Jews and Christians, we can no longer engage in dialogue as though we were the only performers on the stage.

One of the most attractive features of the original Court of the Gentiles is that the Jews made no distinctions among "the nations." We were all "them." From one perspective this may seem narrow, but from another it makes the Court of the Gentiles a wonderfully open space. There were, of course, no Muslims when it still existed in stone, and not many Christians (and most of them were Jews). But there were Hindus and there were Buddhists even then. It is tempting to fantasize about a dusty camel caravan of traders arriving in Jerusalem in those days, perhaps from India or China. They would surely have been welcome in the Court of the Gentiles.

As I write these concluding lines, I have recently returned from taking part in a modern scenario in Jerusalem that was similar, but not quite the same, as this fantasy. This time I joined six other teachers at what used to be a monastery only a few hundred yards from the Old City and, therefore, not that far from where the Court of the Gentiles once stood. My colleagues included two rabbis, a Jesuit scholar, a Hindu, a Buddhist, and a Muslim. Our caravans gathered in stifling 100-degree-plus heat under the auspices of something called the Elijah School, where we spent three weeks teaching students from several countries who wanted to explore the frontiers of interfaith relations today. Like previous encounters of this sort, the experience was both rewarding and difficult. Such a multifaith meeting inevitably raises questions that rarely come up when representatives of only two or even three traditions meet. There is, of course, also value in one-on-one dialogues. For example, when I, as a Christian, speak with Muslims, I get a sense of what Jews must feel about the claim Christians have often made, that we have absorbed and gone beyond them, for this is just what Muslims often say about us. I also realize, in conversations with Muslims, that Christianity has not yet developed a way to appreciate what I call postcanonical prophets, those like Muhammad, who arrived after the Bible was written. But I have also noticed that when the three "Abrahamic" faiths—Judaism, Christianity, and Islam—meet, they often tend to underline their common "monotheism." This, however, opens a gulf between us and hundreds of millions of Buddhists and Hindus. Conversations with these Asian faiths, on the other hand, tend to evoke from Christians their conviction, awkwardly formulated in the idea of the Trinity, that the one God has many faces. This, in turn, sometimes convinces Jews and Muslims that, as they suspected all along, Christians are not really monotheists after all. And so it goes. Perhaps what we need now are not just duets or quartets but a full oratorio that includes all these plus a complete orchestra and a mighty chorus, joining not just as background, but as full-voiced participants.

Nevertheless, I am still drawn to the idea of the Court of the Gentiles. It symbolizes something I wish every religion had. It has three essential components. First, it stands near, but separate from, a central sanctuary that is highly particular in its rites and its vision, a place that can make real sense only to those who share in its history. But its second component, the court itself, is a wide-open space, still sacred but in a different way, in which all the children of God can enter, mix with one another, and benefit in whatever way they can from its atmosphere. Third, there is the whole outside world, acknowledged as outside, but the gates are wide open. This three-tiered model of how a specific religious tradition presents itself—a central sanctuary, a spacious surrounding court, and an openness to the world—is one we especially need in our new epoch of global religious heterogeneity.

I started this book by saying that my personal gateway into the Court of the Gentiles and into the abundant legacy of the Jewish tradition began when I married a Jewish woman. I know I will never be able to appreciate that legacy in all its fullness. As the psalm puts it, "My cup runneth over." Like the gentile woman Ruth's famous words, "Whither thou goest, I will go," I have faithfully journeyed with my Jewish partner, and I have become, insofar as I could, a part of her people. Such a marriage can be a demanding and rewarding crash course in interfaith relations for both parties. It has been for us. But such a marriage is not for everyone. (Indeed, marriage itself is not for everyone.) Still, you do not have to be married to a Jew to enjoy the full benefits of the Court of the Gentiles. Its many gates remain open, and the traffic is heavy. Also, as we all speed into a truly global world, and religions that used to be distant phantoms are now neighbors, the spiritual open space symbolized by the Court of the Gentiles has become an ever livelier place. I like dwelling in it. I am here to stay.

17

When Jesus Came to Harvard (2004)

These selections are taken from When Jesus Came to Harvard: Making Moral Choices Today *(Boston: Houghton Mifflin Co., 2004), 259-66, 267-85. The book describes the experience of teaching "Jesus and the Moral Life," a popular undergraduate course at Harvard over many years.*

A WORLD WITHOUT GOD?

Now from the sixth hour there was darkness over all the land unto the ninth hour. And about the ninth hour Jesus cried with a loud voice, saying, Eli, Eli, lama sabachthani? That is to say, My God, my God, why hast thou forsaken me?—Matthew 27:46

Among the hundreds of students who took Jesus and the Moral Life during the two decades I taught it, many came from serious, often quite pious, Christian families. They often questioned some of my interpretations of the Bible, but I encouraged them to stand up for their convictions. Some had been taught that Jesus had always felt close to God at every moment of his life, that his profound sense of God's presence never left him. But those students had a very hard time handling the verse quoted above. Jesus seems to be saying that, even in his hour of severest need, God had abandoned him.

Here is Jesus at his most human. If the painful experience of the absence of God is at times a part of a genuine spiritual life, which the great saints like John of the Cross have insisted that it is, then this is also Jesus at his most spiritual. It is also Jesus at both his most Christian and his most Jewish. Here he is quoting Psalm 22, often intoned by Jews, then and now, to help them through the most difficult trials.

This part of the story sounds very authentic. Jews have learned over the centuries how to cope with tragedies by turning to their scriptures, and this is just what Jesus was doing. He was at the nadir of his life, the point at which he shared the lot of humanity at its worst. He had suffered not just betrayal by a friend, public humiliation, appalling physical pain, the apparent failure of his mission, ridicule, and death, but also the awful sense that even God had deserted him at the time of his most searing need. Still, since most people, even devout believers, suspect at times that God has forgotten or ignored them, the realization that Jesus once felt the same way can strengthen and reassure them.

Although that thought may be helpful, it is hardly enough to go on for very long when things get tough. So it is important to realize that these words have a much wider resonance and that they sound a Jewish timbre far beyond one particular psalm. They focus on a point at which the Jewish story and the Christian story reverberate with each other in numerous ways. Maybe that is why the German theologian Dietrich Bonhoeffer, who was killed by the Nazis in the Flossenburg concentration camp, maintained that Jesus' cry of abandonment from the cross constitutes not just the core of the Christian message, but also the heart of the whole Bible. Again, it is how this text resonates with the Jewish larger story that makes his claim clearer. Bonhoeffer did not seem to be familiar with the Kabala, the great Jewish mystical text. But if he had been, he would undoubtedly have appreciated the kabalistic teaching about the *zimzum*, the "withdrawal" of God from the world in order to give the Creation breathing space and genuine freedom. The influential American Orthodox rabbi Irving Greenberg, though certainly not a kabalist, has said something very similar: "To the question, 'Where was God at Auschwitz?' the answer is: God was there—starving, broken, humiliated, gassed and burned alive, sharing the infinite pain as only an infinite capacity for pain can share it." Rabbi Greenberg's point is that if God did not swoop down to smash the ovens during that most monstrous of crimes, if instead he was among the victims, then we should not expect him to intervene to deliver us from our self-inflicted depredations in the future. This is at least one meaning of being "forsaken."

Bonhoeffer, who had opposed the Nazis from the start, was arrested in 1943 when the Gestapo began to suspect that he was secretly working against the regime (which he was). He was first incarcerated in Tegel, the military prison in Berlin. But later, when the attempt to assassinate Hitler failed on July 20, 1944, and the Gestapo suspected that he was involved in the plot (which he was), they moved him first to their own prison on Prinz-Albrecht Strasse in Berlin, then to Flossenburg, where he was hanged just a few hours before the American army liberated the camp.

I had been an admirer of Bonhoeffer's life and thought ever since, as a young theologian with a recently minted Ph.D. in hand, I lived for a year in Berlin and came to know a number of people who had worked with him. Later I also met Maria von Wedemeyer-Weller, the woman to whom he had become engaged but had never married. They had planned their wedding for after the war, which he did not live to see.

While he was locked in Tegel prison, Bonhoeffer spent much of his time reading and writing letters, some to his parents, some to his fiancée, and some to his best friend, Eberhard Bethge. A friendly guard helped smuggle them out. I am sure Bonhoeffer never expected the letters to be read by anyone else. But a few years after the war, Bethge decided the ones he had received included such daring and provocative insights that they should reach a wider audience. He assembled them and they were published first as *Prisoner for God,* then later as *Letters and Papers from Prison.* Within a few years this book became one of the spiritual classics of the twentieth century.

What makes Bonhoeffer's prison letters so powerful is that even though he knew he was facing certain death, and with it the loss of all he held most dear in life, including his forthcoming marriage, there is hardly a melancholy or lugubrious sentence in them. They stand along with St. Francis's canticles to Sister Moon and Brother Sun as among the most buoyant and life-affirming documents in all of Christian literature. Even his famous poem about his approaching death has an underlying joyful tone. Bonhoeffer adamantly opposed any kind of Christianity that appealed to human weakness or despair. In one of his letters he told Bethge he despised the idea of a God whom we experienced "only at the edges of human life, i.e., in death, sin and suffering." This seems a surprising assertion for a man bolted behind bars and facing virtually certain execution. Still, he went on, "I should like to speak of God not on the boundaries but at the center, not in weakness but in strength; and therefore not in death and guilt but in man's life and goodness."

But how could Bonhoeffer turn to the words Jesus spoke at the moment of anguish and death to make such a statement? Again, it is the resonance with the Jewish story that makes this clearer. Bonhoeffer believed that when God did not rush down like a Greek *deus ex machina* to save Jesus from the cross, he was signaling to human beings that we have indeed been "forsaken" in the sense of being left to work things out, or to fail, on our own. God will not compromise our freedom even to deliver us from the most tragic consequences of the worst of our hatred and greed. In another letter, Bonhoeffer told Bethge:

> [God] is weak and powerless in the world, and that is precisely the way, the only way, he is with us and helps us . . . the God who is with us is the God who forsakes us [Mark 15:34]. The God who lets us work in the world without the working hypothesis of God is the one before whom we stand continually [Letter of 16 July 1944].

So far this echoes the kabalistic teaching faithfully. Then Bonhoeffer adds a highly paradoxical Christian twist: "Before God and with God," he writes, "we live without God. God lets himself be pushed out of the world onto the cross."

This is pretty radical theology. But I had learned so much both from Bonhoeffer's writings and from the example of his courageous death that I decided to invite the students in my class to read some of his letters. They did. But then a problem I had not anticipated arose.

Bonhoeffer had insisted for many years in his previous teaching and writing that God was to be found in the secular world, not beyond it. But while he was in prison, Bonhoeffer discovered an unanticipated confirmation of his theology. He came to know and admire many brave men who were in no way "religious." Some were communists, others secular intellectuals, others simply ordinary people who had somehow aroused the ire of the Gestapo. Some were dismissive of religion, others simply indifferent. But what Bonhoeffer noticed was that, even in the midst of Allied bombing raids, and even faced with death sentences, they did not turn to "the consolation of religion."

Living month after month in close quarters with such fellow prisoners, Bonhoeffer began to notice some changes in himself. He began to believe that these men were harbingers of the future, non-religious or post-religious men, and that in fact history might itself be moving toward a time when religion would be left behind. How, he wondered, could the message of Jesus be communicated in such a time? Maybe, he conjectured to Bethge, religion has only been the "outer garment" of Christianity, one that it was now time to shed. But then, as he so pointedly asked, can we devise a "non-religious interpretation of Christianity" for a "world come of age"? Sadly, Bonhoeffer never had a chance to answer his own question.

When we tried to discuss Bonhoeffer I could see that the students were painfully conflicted. They admired his courage and his celebration of what he called *hilaritas*, the sheer joy of being alive in the world. They found his story gripping and many passages in his letters inspiring. But what in the world could he possibly have meant by a "non-religious interpretation of Christianity"? Wasn't Christianity itself a religion? Didn't many people claim it was the best or the highest or even *the only* true religion? Well, maybe it is or maybe it isn't. But surely it is *a* religion. What would be left of it if it were not a religion anymore?

During this conversation I came to the stark realization that my students, especially the younger ones, had moved beyond both Bonhoeffer's worldview and my own. They were not living in a postreligious era at all. They were living in an era in which religion seems to have made a surprising comeback in the latter decades of the twentieth century, a riposte that Bonhoeffer seems not to have anticipated. This "return of the sacred," as some scholars have called it, has not always been welcome. It has included religiously motivated terrorism as well as increasing church attendance in some parts of the world. It encompasses crystals and channeling and a variety of other fuzzy New Age pieties, as well as the Muslim renaissance, the spread of Buddhism to the West, and the rebirth of both Christian and Jewish theological scholarship. Students all over America now eagerly enroll in courses in religious studies and seem to relish perusing the great classics of the field. Religion may never actually have declined at all, but it is certainly "in" again.

Bonhoeffer, on the other hand, thought human history had passed through the "archaic age" of myth, had moved past the "metaphysical age" of religious systems, and was now entering what he called, drawing on a phrase from Kant, a "world come of age." He did not mean by this phrase that our era was any better or more virtuous, merely that we would no longer need the "God hypothesis" to explain the world. He warned that if God were called upon only to fill in the gaps in human knowledge, there would soon be no place left for him at all. There might be some people, he conceded, who would remain more or less religious, but they would constitute a smaller and smaller minority. Christianity would have to learn to address the "'Third Man,'" the one who had left both myth and metaphysics behind, who was no longer in any historical sense religious. What was needed was a "non-religious interpretation of the Gospel."

It did not help when I explained to the students that Bonhoeffer was not just looking for this new expression of the message of Jesus so that he could convince someone else of the truth of Christianity. For him, it was a personal quest. He had never undergone what might be called a crisis of faith. If anything, his faith had deepened and matured during his imprisonment. But at the same time he increasingly recognized himself to be a "post-religious" man. In his impassioned letters he was trying to hold together two dimensions of his own life. He came to believe that there was no such thing as a spiritual realm, apart from the everyday world. He believed that the God who had, in one sense, "forsaken" the world was still alive and present in it. In fact, it was the very forsakenness of Christ on the cross that revealed *how* God is present. He is present suffering and struggling along with the despised and rejected people of the world, those whose lot is to be ignored, overlooked, and humiliated. Therefore the calling of the "post-religious" Christian is not to strive for transcendental salvation, but to enter joyfully into the "suffering of God in the world," and to strive for the renewal of Creation that only God himself could ultimately complete. With these words, and without knowing it, Bonhoeffer became one of the sources of inspiration for the liberation theology movement, which arose twenty years later.

My discussion with the students about "My God, my God, why hast thou forsaken me?" ended inconclusively. I had to concede that in the cultural climate of the late twentieth and early twenty-first centuries—a time swarming with a variety of religious movements, some healthy, some venomous—it was understandable why they could not wrap their minds around a "non-religious interpretation of Christianity." Bonhoeffer's cultural prediction may have been mistaken, or perhaps premature. But his portrait of how God is present in the seemingly "godless" secular world is still a powerful one. So I would not concede that Bonhoeffer is no longer relevant. True, we may never arrive in a fully non- or post-religious era. But if the kind of superficial religiousness that is engulfing us today continues to spread, then both serious Christians and serious Jews may find themselves insisting in a new way on the absence of the real God from such a world. Both the Jewish kabalists and the Christian mystics have taught that atheism is superior to the feeble complacency of so many people today.

Also, the divide between believers and nonbelievers may not be as wide, or as real, as many think. Even, or perhaps especially, the most truly religious people today have their dark nights of the soul, and they cannot escape being secular or even nonreligious at some moments or in some respects. And there are increasing numbers of nonbelievers in today's world who harbor gnawing doubts about the validity of their skepticism. We are all to some extent hybrids.

All in all, I have come to share Bonhoeffer's suggestion that Jesus' agonized cry, "My God, my God, why have you forsaken me?" is the

most important verse in the Bible, and the most decisive moment in
Jesus' life. If Christian faith teaches that in this man from Galilee
God shared the most racking pain and the most overwhelming sorrow human beings can know, including death itself, then he must also
have felt abandoned by God. He must have felt, in his own way, that he
had lost his faith. Of course, this is a paradoxical statement. How can
God feel abandoned by himself? But the fact that we cannot fully grasp
such an idea does not make it any less powerful. It merely deepens the
mystery of just how God was present in Jesus, and how God continues
to suffer the grief and heartache of human existence. All the doctrines
and theories that have been invented for nearly two thousand years
have not even come close to explaining how such a thing is possible,
and none ever will.

Once one of Bonhoeffer's fellow prisoners told him that his goal in
life was to become a saint. But Bonhoeffer responded that, for him,
being a saint was not an attractive prospect, that he simply wanted "to
become a man," fully human. Of course, not all of Bonhoeffer's theological ideas were accurate. He was, like all of us, a creature of his time.
Still, for me he remains a model of what it means to be a Christian in
the twenty-first century. Maybe the prisoner in cell 19 of Tegel military
prison was not a saint, but he came as close to being a fully human
being as anyone I know of, and he still has something worthwhile to
say to all of us.

* * *

THE EASTER STORY

But very early on the first day of the week they came to the
tomb bringing spices they had prepared. They found that the
stone had been rolled away from the tomb, but when they went
inside, they did not find the body of the Lord Jesus. While they
stood utterly at a loss, suddenly two men in dazzling garments
were at their side. They were terrified, and stood with eyes cast
down, but the men said, "Why search among the dead for one
who is alive? Remember how he told you, while he was still in
Galilee, that the Son of Man must be given into the power of
sinful men and be crucified, and must rise again on the third
day." Then they recalled his words and, returning from the
tomb, they reported everything to the eleven and all the others.

The women were Mary of Magdala, Joanna, and Mary the
mother of James, and they, with the other women, told these

things to the apostles. But the story appeared to them to be nonsense, and they would not believe them.—Luke 24:1-11

When I was a youngster in a small town, Easter Sunday was always a memorable day. But not for the reasons the minister and the church elders obviously thought it should be. It was the only day when all the church congregations in town gathered in the dark before dawn for an ecumenical sunrise service. All the churches, I should add, except for the Roman Catholics. This was years before the Second Vatican Council in the early 1960s softened Catholic attitudes toward Protestants. I can still remember shivering as my bare feet hit the cold floor when I got up while it was totally dark, pulled on my clothes, crept quietly out of the house, and made my way to the park amid throngs of townspeople, some carrying flashlights. I was secretly a little pleased that at least on that one day we were out of bed even earlier than the Catholic playmates who got up every Sunday for the seven o'clock Mass and never tired of telling the rest of us how heroic they were and how easy we had it.

The gathering took place in a large open park also used for Fourth of July parades and the annual Volunteer Firemen's Fair. An obscure skirmish had been fought there during the Revolutionary War, and two rusting iron cannons were perched near a flagpole at one end. By the time I got there I could hear the combined choirs of the various churches singing, not just to set the tone but probably also to keep warm. There were already a few gray streaks on the eastern horizon, but it was still dark. The service was timed so that the sun would rise about halfway through it, which it usually did except when it was drizzling or the skies were overcast. No one seemed bothered by the quasi-pagan admixture of the rising of the sun with the Resurrection of the Son. I doubt that even the ministers realized something I did not learn until years later, that the word for the Christian holiday we now call Easter is derived from the name of a pagan goddess—Oester—who was associated with the east, where the sun comes up.

The Easter sunrise service could be strenuous. It always lasted longer than a regular service, in part because every minister in town had to be heard from, with an invocation, a prayer, or a word of welcome. Fortunately, they took turns giving the sermon, passing it around from year to year. Otherwise we might have been there until the sun set. Still, with a different preacher each year, I was able to detect some of the nuanced differences in the ways they interpreted the Easter story. That may have sown some of the seeds of what eventually became a lifelong fascination with theology and comparative religion. The service was also taxing because the only chairs were those elderly or infirm people had brought with them. The rest of us stood, so that by the time it was over, the benediction was pronounced, and the choir had sung its final "amen," I was quite ready for what I knew was coming next: the annual Easter Sunday all-church pancake breakfast.

This was always a sumptuous spread that took place in the basement of one of the larger churches. There were platters stacked with piles and piles of steaming brown and white pancakes, topped with ladles of maple syrup and chunks of butter, with crisp bacon on the side and orange juice in paper cups. The adults sipped at mugs of aromatic coffee drawn from shiny silver vats. The atmosphere was always cheery, but I am sure, at least for the young people, the festiveness had as much to do with the food and the ecumenical camaraderie as it did with the event we were celebrating. It was one of our few opportunities to mix at a church event with the boys and girls from other denominations from whom we were usually separated by niceties of theological distinction that did not seem all that vital. By the time I got back home, where my parents, who were not churchgoers, were just coming down to breakfast in their bathrobes, I felt buoyant, and a little self-righteous. I do not remember giving much thought one way or the other to whether the biblical text quoted at the start of this chapter, which I had just heard read, or the sermon that had just been preached were true. It just never entered my mind.

That began to change when I became a teenager and—as with all teenagers—people I knew began dying. Thoughts of my own mortality often upset me. My awareness of death was no doubt deepened when I began to work part-time for my Uncle Frank, who was the town's only undertaker, or "mortician," as he preferred to be called. I went out with his crew to pick up the bodies of people who had just died and bring them to his morgue. I watched him embalm some of them on a white table with a formaldehyde solution. I helped carry caskets to the cemetery. Some of the people he buried were old, some young, some were stout, some thin. But to me they all had one thing in common: They all looked *very* dead. Yet at the graveside, whatever minister was in charge always talked about the resurrection of the dead, and they were not just talking about Jesus. They were talking about everyone— what is known as the "general resurrection."

I began to wonder. It was not long before I began to ask myself the question I had not asked as a youngster. Was what the Bible said, and what the songs and the ministers proclaimed, really true? And if there was eventually going to be a general resurrection, what was happening to all those dead people in the meantime? Now and then when a person died, someone in the church would say they were already in heaven, or had "gone to be with God." But that did not seem consistent with a general resurrection sometime in the distant future. Then, when I began to meet people who said there was no such thing as a life after death, that when you were dead you were dead, and that's that, the mystery deepened. Once in a while I would ask someone about what seemed to me a nest of contradictions, but I never got a satisfying answer. Eventually I just stopped asking.

The dilemma stayed with me when I went to college. In a sophomore philosophy course I wrote a term paper on the idea of the immortality of the soul in Plato, and got an A minus from the professor. I enjoyed attending a variety of different churches, so I heard a wide range of interpretations of life and death and resurrection. In my junior year I began reading the novels of Fyodor Dostoyevsky and was gratified to discover that he had not only wrestled with these questions his whole life, but that he considered them the most important things anyone could think or write about. By the time I graduated from college and began seminary, I knew three things. One was that the Resurrection of Jesus Christ, whatever it was, is not peripheral to Christianity but is at its core. Another was that I did not know what it meant or what I believed about it. Finally, I realized that I would probably never answer the questions I had, that I would have to live with an element of uncertainty, but that there were many thoughtful people—many of them exemplary Christians—who were in exactly the same situation.

Is it any wonder, then, that for the first couple of years that I taught Jesus and the Moral Life, I dodged the Easter narrative? Of all the stories told about Jesus, this one is the most potent and the most baffling. Yet for centuries many Christians—perhaps even most—have insisted that without it all the other stories lose their weight. Still, this outlandish tale of angels, grave clothes in an empty tomb, apparitions, and mysterious encounters between the man the Romans executed and his despondent followers defies all our everyday sensibilities. What are we to make of it?

At first I took the easy way out. I stopped the lectures about Jesus' life with the Crucifixion, then devoted the remaining few sessions to discussing some of the innumerable different interpretations of the moral significance of his life that have arisen in the centuries after his death. I passed over the Resurrection in part because I thought that talking about it in a core curriculum course at Harvard would be awkward, and might even seem inappropriate, especially with students from many different religious traditions present. I also knew how hard it would be to talk about an event that, unlike many other events in Jesus' life, stood on the borderline between the historical and the mystical. But then I changed my mind.

After a year or two I began to have a bad conscience about leaving out such a central element of the Jesus story. Even the most critical modern biblical scholars concede that undoubtedly the scattered and dispirited followers of Jesus experienced *something* after his crucifixion that convinced them that death had not finished him for good. Otherwise it is hard to imagine why they should have reassembled and insisted on continuing his hazardous work while the same brutal cliques that had put him to death were still in charge. The British New Testament scholar N. T. Wright catalogs half a dozen movements that were in some ways similar to the Jesus movement, and existed in the same historical period, but simply melted away after their leader's death or they selected a new leader. None of them claimed their leader was still alive. Furthermore, Jesus' followers ran the terrible risks of arrest and a death like their leader's precisely *because*, as they said time and again, they had encountered him as, in some sense, alive and in their midst. Their accounts of these meetings with a no-longer-dead Jesus are described in those passages scholars call the "Resurrection appearances." But because these experiences do perch on the precarious borderline of empirical history, they were impossible to portray in an ordinary vocabulary. Like any truly mystical experience, they could not be described in everyday language because everyday language describes everyday events. Mystical experiences always "break the language barrier," which is why mystics so often turn to symbols or song or silence.

But my own "resort to silence" did not satisfy the students, and ultimately it did not satisfy me either. The students let me know quickly, and in no uncertain terms, that having followed the story of Jesus with me from the manger to the grave, they were not going to permit me to skip so easily over its peculiar and baffling climax. And to my surprise, the objection came not just from the Christian students, who understandably wanted to hear my interpretation of Easter, which—with the possible exception of Christmas—finds more people in churches than any other celebration of the year. It also came from the nonreligious students and those from other religious traditions. Many of them had been drawn to Jesus as a rebel against the status quo, as a daring moral exemplar, or as an inspiring teacher of spiritual wisdom; still, they were puzzled, not just by this climax as it is told in the Gospels, but also by why it seemed so central in Christianity. No one had ever claimed that the Buddha or Confucius or Socrates or the Prophet Mohamet had returned from the dead. Why Jesus? I knew that somehow I was going to have to break the silence.

I also knew, of course, that the Easter story is sometimes no less problematical to Christians than to others. Many regular churchgoers do not know what to think of the Bible readings they hear on Easter, which sound to some like extracts from a Stephen King novel or the script for a Hollywood thriller, like the *Terminator* series in which the hero stubbornly staggers back time and time again even after he has been shot, incinerated, or blown to bits. One student told me that he attended church regularly but whenever he heard the Resurrection account read he could not help thinking of the scene in the Dracula films in which the pale "undead" count pushes open the lid of his coffin and climbs out to go on the prowl for some fresh blood. He quickly added that he knew it was wrong to think of Easter in the same frame with the prince of the vampires, but somehow he just couldn't help it. I was glad he had told me, because it reminded me once again that although today's worldview is quite different from the one in which these biblical accounts first circulated, there are also many troubling similarities, or at least what appear at first to be similarities. Like our first-century forebears, we in the twenty-first century are still both fascinated and horrified by death, and equally disquieted and intrigued when the dead do not stay dead. The idea of the Resurrection has been a "scandal" since it was first disseminated, but the reasons why it is hard to interpret change from age to age.

The young people of today are different from their twentieth-century grandparents, at least from the more "secular" of those elders. They no longer share the unshakable confidence in science that characterized the pre–World War I mentality. This sunny certainty about science had prompted that previous generation to reject the very idea of resurrection out of hand as simply nonsensical. Today's young people are not as wedded to the idea of a closed universe in which science has all the answers. They are open, sometimes uncritically, to possible other dimensions of reality that might impinge on or even penetrate the familiar one. They watch movies teeming with human-machine hybrids, time warps, dematerializers, and the million-dollar man. But this does not make the task of interpreting the Resurrection of Jesus any easier. Sometimes I am afraid it makes the danger of misunderstanding it even more acute. Jesus was not a benevolent first-century Terminator.

I also knew that, formidable as these obstacles were, there was another reason why I had been trying to steer around the Easter story: Classrooms, at least the ones I teach in, are not viewed as the proper venue for testimonies. What is supposed to go on in classrooms is "explanation." But not only did I not know how to explain the Resurrection to the class, I was not even sure what "explaining" it might mean. It eventually became clear to me, however, that all my excuses were, in the final analysis, unsupportable. By leaving out this part of the story I was not just being unfair to my students (albeit under cover of being evenhanded), I was also being intellectually dishonest, a little lazy, and cowardly. I realized that, at a minimum, I would have to sketch out some of the current interpretations of the Resurrection and suggest that they would have to decide among them on their own. I had a feeling that this was not going to satisfy them, and it turned out that I was right. But I set out to move from silence into at least some kind of conversation.

In preparing for this step I went back and carefully scrutinized the Resurrection accounts in the four Gospels, together with some of the many commentaries that have appeared about them. I knew that the Christians had not invented the idea of resurrection, that it was already present in the Hebrew scriptures. So I also went back to the passages there that deal with God's vindication of innocent suffering and of God's gift of new life, at times even to the dead. And I read the Jewish commentaries on these. Once again, the Jewish sages and the rabbis came to my aid.

Since I had not been talking about the Resurrection in class, I had not made a careful study of the key passages for some time, and when I did I was in for a few surprises. First, it immediately became evident that stories of raising the dead in the Old Testament *did not have to do with immortality*. They are about *God's justice*. They are expressions of a human hope that is born of a *moral*, not a metaphysical, impulse. They did not spring up from a yearning for life after death, but from the conviction that ultimately a truly just God simply had to vindicate the victims of the callous and the powerful. The prophet Isaiah declares this hope with particular eloquence. He looks forward in lyrical anticipation to the day when "the inhabitants of the world learn what justice is" and "the wicked are destroyed" because "they have never learned justice" (Isaiah 26:9, 10). But he goes on to foresee that even though the righteous now suffer and die, "your dead will live, their bodies will rise again. Those who sleep in the earth will awake and shout for joy" (Isaiah 26:19). The same sentiment is voiced in the poetic passage in the

prophet Ezekiel about how God breathes across the valley filled with
the bleaching bones of the vanquished casualties of imperial conquest,
and they reconnect with each other and stand.

> The Lord's hand was upon me, and he carried me out by his
> spirit and set me down in a plain that was full of bones. He
> made me pass among them in every direction. Countless in
> numbers and very dry, they covered the plain. He said to me,
> "O man, can these bones live?" I answered, "Only you, Lord
> God, knows that." He said, "Prophesy over these bones; say: Dry
> bones, hear the word of the Lord. The Lord God says to these
> bones: I am going to put breath into you, and you will live. I
> shall fasten sinews on you, clothe you with flesh, cover you with
> skin, and give you breath, and you will live." (Ezekiel 37:1-6)

The Protestant theologian Jürgen Moltmann correctly notes that for
the Israelites, resurrection did not "refer to everlasting life or happi-
ness"; rather, it was "a theological symbol to express faith in God's
justice at the end of history. . . . It was not a longing for life everlasting
but a thirst for justice." Clearly the story of God's resurrection of the
righteous rabbi from Nazareth is meant to be a continuation of these
ancient stories of his people. As with so much else about Jesus, we mis-
understand him badly if we remove him from the ongoing saga of his
people.

Reading the Easter story in the context of this previous history
makes one thing quite clear: It is at least as much a story about God
as it is about Jesus. The Resurrection is not something Jesus does; it is
something God does. Strictly speaking, the accounts do not say that
Jesus awakened himself from the dead. Most of them say, "*God* raised
him." As with Isaiah and Ezekiel, God is the principal actor in the
drama. For obvious reasons this reminded me of the exodus story that
Jews retell at every Passover seder. I had noticed when I participated in
these celebrations that although Moses, along with his brother Aaron,
led the Israelites out of their Egyptian captivity, Moses is scarcely mentioned in the Passover liturgy. This reflects the wisdom of the rabbis.
They avoided casting Moses as the central figure because they wanted
to make sure people realized that God was the real liberator. This
rabbinical insight suggests yet again that we need to see Jesus not just
against the Israelite background that went *before* him, but in light of
the continuing Jewish history that came *after* him. As we will see in
a moment, the Jesus story continued the old story, but added a new
dimension.

The exodus from Egypt, kept alive by song and story for 3,500 years, is one of the most important events in human history. By liberating the Israelites from bondage, God not only humbled one despot, the Pharaoh, he also established a precedent that would pose a constant threat to any future tyrant as well. It has worked out just that way. The original exodus inscribed the conviction that people have a God-given right to be free within the Jewish psyche, and from there it eventually found its way into Christianity and into cultures all over the world. It started something irreversible in human history. When Benjamin Franklin was asked to design a great seal for the new American republic, he asked an artist to sketch the destruction of the Egyptian army at the Red Sea. (That design was eventually not the one chosen.) Black Americans identified completely with the exodus story. While still in slavery they sang "Let My People Go," and during the civil rights movement they sang "We Shall Overcome" because "God is on our side." The exodus is a key theme in liberation theology. It is completely understandable, therefore, why it provided the first Christians—all of them Jews—with the historical paradigm for the Easter story.

This is why for centuries Christians have spoken of Easter as a "second exodus." The idea is that in the original liberation of Jesus from the grip of death, God inflicted a mortal wound not just on human mortality but on the tyrannical forces that murder innocent people like him. The victory was not yet complete, just as the Israelites' escape from Egypt did not complete the destruction of despotism and servitude. But now both Jews and Christians could anticipate the final victory of God over all that deforms and destroys life, with confidence that the turning point had come and the decisive battle had been won.

At Passover, Jews eat the bitter herbs and the unleavened bread to make vivid the memory of their deliverance from captivity. Jesus told his followers to eat the bread and drink the wine "in remembrance of me." Memory is basic to both these observances because both commemorate massively subversive events; they become reminders of what one theologian has called the "subversive" memory that becomes the basis for hope, even in the worst circumstances. In short, the early Christians believed that the same God who had manifested himself in the exodus as the One who empowers human freedom had acted again at Easter, enlarging and deepening the scope of his liberating energy. This makes the Easter story, like the exodus, mainly a story about God.

Of course, the Easter story is also about Jesus. God, these puzzling old stories state, did not raise just anyone from the dead. He raised an innocent man who had placed himself alongside the misfits and the outcasts of his day, who taught people to love their enemies, who boldly confronted the rapacious elite, and who was tortured and killed—like so many others before and after him—by a depraved system of law and order. Furthermore, he was murdered *because of* who he was and what he did and said. He died because of the way he lived. It is also enormously significant that according to the Easter story, God vindicated a teacher of the Jewish law who had spent the night before his execution celebrating Passover. Christians often overlook this inconvenient fact, but this causes us to forget the corporate dimension of the exodus and reduce the Resurrection to an individual affair.

How Jesus died is very important. In the biblical texts he is not just described as "dead" but as "crucified." There is a difference. To restore a dead person to life might be seen to strike a blow at mortality. But to restore a crucified man to life means to strike an equally decisive blow at the system that caused his wrongful death, and the death systems that continue to cause the suffering and fatality of millions in what the Latin American theologian Jon Sobrino calls "a world of crosses." The Resurrection story points not just to the ultimate victory of life over death, but of God's shalom over cruelty, greed, and atrocities.

We need these three different searchlights to illuminate the Resurrection. Reading the Easter story against both its biblical background and its rabbinical foreground is a good start. But seeing the way both narratives have inspired freedom movements all through history brings the narratives up to date. Taken together, these three interpretive lenses help us glimpse what the New Testament writers were saying in the only language they had.

As I had anticipated, however, my students were still not content. We were left with the unanswered question both they and many church members raise. Yes, they say, it's a powerful story with an inspiring biblical pedigree; yes, it has empowered freedom struggles throughout history, but *did it really happen?* If it is true that "something" reinspired and regathered the shattered band of disciples and propelled them out into the world to carry on the work of the Nazarene, what was that "something"? Why did they notice it and no one else did? Was it some form of hallucination, a clever fiction, a wild rumor they started believing because they so much wanted to?

These are perfectly honest questions, and the only honest answer I could give my students was that I could take them only so far and no farther. The "Resurrection appearances" texts are inconsistent and discrepant. The original Gospel of Mark, the oldest of the Gospel accounts, ends by describing the arrival of the three women—Mary

Magdalene, Mary the mother of Jesus, and Salome—to the tomb where the remains of Jesus had been laid. They planned to anoint the body with oils, an established mourning custom. They were worried about how they would move the large stone that had been used to close the entrance to the tomb, but as they approach they see that it has already been rolled away. Puzzled, they go into the tomb and find a young man in a white robe sitting there. They do not know what to say. The young man (he is not called an angel, just "a young man") says to them:

> Do not be alarmed. You are looking for Jesus of Nazareth, who was crucified. He has been raised; he is not here. Look, there is the place where they laid him. But go and say to his disciples and to Peter: "He is going ahead of you into Galilee: There you will see him, as he told you." Then they went out and ran away from the tomb, trembling with amazement. They said nothing to anyone, for they were afraid. (Mark 16:6-8)

Astonishingly, this is where the account ends: "they were afraid." Period. The oldest and most authentic version of the Gospel of Mark simply stops here. In most editions of the New Testament today, other verses have been added, some of which are found in later manuscripts of the Gospel. However, the scholarly consensus is that they were tacked on because succeeding generations of Christians found it hard to live with this cryptic, unsatisfying—even disturbing—"nonending." Terrified women running away, too frightened even to tell anyone? What way is that to conclude the story of Jesus? Now what? What happens next?

The original Mark does not answer any of these questions. The women are simply told that to see him again they should return to Galilee, the impoverished land where Jesus had taught and healed and made himself controversial by talking about a new kingdom of God that would replace the divine Caesar's. There, where he had spent most of his life among the pariahs and the disinherited, is where they would find him.

This terse version of the Easter story has startling implications for the question of why some people could "see" the no-longer-dead Jesus and others could not. The story contains what philosophers call an epistemological point. It helps explain why some people find the idea that "Christ is risen" nothing but a far-fetched superstition, while for others it is the sustaining capstone of their lives (and there are many somewhere in between). As Jesus had frequently said in his teaching, the kingdom of God "does not come by observation." Likewise the Resurrection, as the continuation of God's vindication of the left out and the trampled upon, is something that by its nature is not observable or even remotely credible to impartial investigators. This is undoubtedly why the endless sifting through the scanty historical sources on Easter, which is obstinately carried on by amateur sleuths and scholarly analysts, convinces no one and is always so unsatisfying. These investigators will never prove or disprove something that is by definition not subject to the methods they employ. In order to "see" him, the women are told they have to go to where he will now—in some unspecified way—be carrying on with what he was doing before. One "meets" Jesus, the messenger of God who manifests God's reality, only by going where he is, to Galilee where he first initiated his audacious project. To "see God," Jon Sobrino has written, "one has to go to where God is."

In the other Gospels, the disciples encounter Jesus, but the accounts are not consistent. At times he appears, but the disciples do not recognize him, at least not at first. In the story of the road to Emmaus, two depressed followers meet a stranger who walks along with them but does not seem to know about the death of Jesus or the hopes they had attached to him. Only after they have sat down to eat with him do they recognize who he is. In another passage Jesus joins his disciples even though the doors and windows are barred. In another he sits on the beach and eats charcoal-broiled fish with them. St. Paul insists that he never met Jesus in the flesh, but that this Jesus spoke to him after he had been hurled to the ground while on the way to Damascus. Some of the disciples "see" Jesus. Some hear his voice but do not see him. Some, like Thomas, touch him. All the human senses are called on, stretched to and beyond their limits, to express something that by its nature transcends normal human senses.

Clearly these disparate reports, are *not* describing a revivified corpse. But they are not talking about a ghost either. Within the limitations of human language, they are describing something the disciples believed was both utterly real and unique. Obviously the passages do not encourage us to think that we can do much better, or can locate and describe in some unambiguous way the "something" they are desperately groping to express. On this score I simply had to disappoint the craving of my students to find out "what really happened." I had to leave them to puzzle over these elusive reports as generations before them had done.

Still, two elements do seem to tie all these stories together. The first is that the confidence that Jesus was still alive did not originate in people hearing *about* an empty tomb or *about* the Resurrection and then *assenting* to the reports. St. Paul, for example, whose letters date from immediately after the Crucifixion, appears never to have heard about an empty tomb. Also, the confidence that Jesus was somehow alive began with an experience that convinced a dejected gaggle of followers that Jesus was still with them. Experience came first and narrative second. Then, of course, the two became intertwined so that for succeeding generations they became inextricable. The story began to trigger the experience. The experience sustained the story.

Second, in each of these encounters Jesus has the same message: *He wants them to keep on doing what he was doing,* to continue to announce and demonstrate the reality—albeit hidden—of the dawning reign of God, the birthing pangs of the age of shalom. He assures them that he will be with them as they set out to tell his story and the stories he told. This fusion of experience and assignment, encounter and project, is what keeps them going in a world that had already proven what it could do to nobodies who circulated such ideas.

For some theologians, this continuation of the work of Jesus in the life and work of his followers *is* the elusive "something" to which the Resurrection stories point. "Jesus Christ is risen" means Jesus lives in the lives and actions of those who once followed him, and still do. "The cause of Jesus," as some of them put it, "moves forward," and this is what the disciples were straining to say in their contradictory descriptions of their encounters with their crucified friend.

This sounds plausible, and it appeals to many people today. But its logic merely pushes the question back one more step. Jesus not only announced his "cause," the coming of God's shalom, he also acted it out—by dining with sinners and embracing lepers, for example. At times he even seemed to identify himself with it, for example, by riding into Jerusalem on a donkey. He was not just its publicist, he was its initiator. The disciples of course remembered this, and they were convinced not only that "the cause of Jesus" was continuing, that his struggles and his project would still go on; they also personalized it. They refused to separate the person from the program. They were also convinced that he himself was somehow living in their midst—albeit in a manner quite different from the way he had been with them before his death—and that was *why* the project could and would go on. This integral connection between Jesus and his mission, between the personality and the program, has generated countless attempts at explanation. None of them is totally satisfactory. They revolve around issues like the connection between the "Jesus of history" and the "Christ of faith," or between Jesus as prototype or archetype and the "spirit of Christ" that inspired succeeding generations. The link between Jesus and his "cause" also reminds us that for many, if not most, of those who have seen themselves as advocates of God's shalom, some personal experience of Jesus, and not just his message, has been a large part of their motivation.

None of this makes it any easier to believe in the Resurrection. In fact, I think the words *believe in* are misleading in this context. Confidence, hope, and trust are more appropriate perspectives on the Resurrection. If what lies behind, and shines through, the Resurrection stories is true, as Christianity teaches, it requires a huge step. It involves not just a sharply modified view of God and of Jesus, but also of the whole of historical reality. If God's vindication of Jesus had been a once-only exception to the closed web of cause and effect, it could be dismissed as an anomaly. It might not be all that significant. Sometimes even the inexplicable happens. But to see beneath the culture-bound language of the Easter story and into its inner reality involves more than accepting an isolated aberration. It is to make a life choice, to live by the hope that this is what reality is really like. Therefore hope, not belief, is what the story seeks to evoke, a hope that is not based on weighing possibilities but on one's own perception of what is most real in life—what some people call "God"—especially at times when there seems to be no way out.

Such a perception is even more radical than achieving Zen enlightenment. The whole world takes on a different visage. What once seemed hopeless is no longer so. What appeared to be final and crushing defeats become temporary setbacks. One begins to see possibilities where there were once only immovable obstacles. As Martin Luther King, Jr., used to say, you can only keep going against what seem to be impossible odds if you have "cosmic allies." To nourish the Easter faith is to allow oneself to hope that despite eons of injustice, pain, and death, in some way that now eludes our most vivid imagination, God's shalom will triumph in the end. This is a hope, though based on different grounds, both Jews and Christians can share.

But surely others can share the hope, too. The exodus motif originated with the Jews. It was embraced by Christians and applied to the Resurrection of Jesus. Both are about the final victory of God's shalom. But there is no reason why the same hope for a world where violence and hatred are abolished cannot be embraced by people of other religions and by those who do not adhere to any religious tradition. The exodus story suggests that God—that ultimate reality—stands on the side of all peoples who cherish this hope, not just the ancient Israelites. The Easter story means that God eventually vindicates the victims of all forms of persecution, not just persecution at the hands of the Romans. If these stories cannot be parsed to include the hopes of all peoples, then we are left with a tribal god who will be rightly dismissed by those who hold no church or synagogue membership card.

After I broke my silence about the Easter story, I told my students I did not expect them either to accept it or reject it on my authority. I warned them that it would make no sense at all unless they were personally involved, whatever they called it, in what Christians call the coming of God's reign, that often discouraging effort to establish what Jews call God's shalom in a world that seems constantly to defeat and frustrate it. I told them they need not expect to have anything like the "Resurrection experiences" reported in the Gospels (though I would not exclude the possibility), but that they should be alert in their own lives for analogies. I once saw a vivid poster in El Salvador of a contemporary pietà, a young woman weeping over the body of a young man whose body is riddled with bullet holes. But from the wounds spring twigs and tiny leaves: life out of death. We need new and daring metaphors for what the earliest Christians coded in the language of resurrection. They used the most potent vocabulary they had available, and we must do the same.

I also conceded that a classroom in a comfortable university where detachment and critical observation are what everybody expects might be the least likely place to ponder the Easter story, or to decide whether to live as though life will eventually triumph over death, and shalom over injustice. I said that my own Resurrection hope is not based on understanding it, which I definitely do not, but on something much deeper in my marrow. I told them that I was surest about it when I was locked in a southern jail during the civil rights movement and heard the young black people with whom I had been arrested singing "We Shall Overcome" at the top of their lungs in the next cell. If you want to meet God, you have to go where God is.

This, of course, is only my own interpretation of what the Resurrection story means. I *do* recognize that there are many other possible interpretations, and I would not discount any of them. In fact, "interpretation" is a very secondary matter. The "something" eludes all our theories and interpretations. But we have the *story*, and when the experience it conveys and evokes makes a real difference in our lives, the various theories all begin to sound less important.

Telling the Easter story in a classroom, or anywhere, is a risky enterprise. Still, despite my initial reluctance to talk about them, the highly fragmented and enigmatic narratives of the Resurrection make up a story no one can skip over. The Passover narrative from which this story emerged, the impossible-to-define "something" to which it points; and the way the world looks from the angle it creates, all provide an indispensable lens. But the story fails unless it opens the listener to an underlying reality that no story can adequately tell.

I was glad I had finally made the slippery move from silence to speech. In making it I even felt I shared a bit of the early Christian bewilderment and exasperation about how to tell other people what had happened to their friend and to them. But, like them, I was left with a lot of loose ends, and my students would not let me forget them. And one loose end in particular they simply would not let go of: What *did* happen to that *body*?

18

The Future of Faith (2009)

This essay, "An Age of the Spirit," is taken from the first chapter of The Future of Faith *(New York: HarperCollins, 2009), 1-20.*

What does the future hold for religion and for Christianity in particular? At the beginning of the new millennium three qualities mark the world's spiritual profile, all tracing trajectories that will reach into the coming decades. The first is the unanticipated resurgence of religion in both public and private life around the globe. The second is that fundamentalism, the bane of the twentieth century, is dying. But the third and most important, though often unnoticed, is a profound change in the elemental nature of religiousness.

The resurgence of religion was not foreseen. On the contrary, not many decades ago thoughtful writers were confidently predicting its imminent demise. Science, literacy, and more education would soon dispel the miasma of superstition and obscurantism. Religion would either disappear completely or survive in family rituals, quaint folk festivals, and exotic references in literature, art, and music. Religion, we were assured, would certainly never again sway politics or shape culture: But the soothsayers were wrong. Instead of disappearing, religion—for good or ill—is now exhibiting new vitality all around the world and making its weight widely felt in the corridors of power.

Many observers mistakenly confuse this resurgence of religion with "fundamentalism," but the two are not the same. Fundamentalism is dying. Arguments still rage about whether the Christian Right in America is fatally divided or sullenly quiescent. Debates boil about whether the dwindling support for radical movements in Islam is temporary or permanent. But as the twenty-first century unfolds, the larger picture is clear. Fundamentalisms, with their insistence on obligatory belief systems, their nostalgia for a mythical uncorrupted past, their claims to an exclusive grasp on truth, and—sometimes—their propensity for violence, are turning out to be rearguard attempts to stem a more sweeping tidal change.

However, the third quality, the equally unforeseen mutation in the nature of religiousness, is the most important in the long run. Not only has religion reemerged as an influential dimension of twenty-first-century life; what it means to be "religious" is shifting significantly from what it meant as little as a half century ago. Since religions interact with each other in a global culture, this tremor is shaking virtually all of them, but it is especially evident in Christianity, which in the past fifty years has entered into its most momentous transformation since its transition in the fourth century CE from what had begun as a tiny Jewish sect into the religious ideology of the Roman Empire.

Scholars of religion refer to the current metamorphosis in religiousness with phrases like the "move to horizontal transcendence" or the "turn to the immanent." But it would be more accurate to think of it as the rediscovery of the sacred *in* the immanent, the spiritual *within* the secular. More people seem to recognize that it is our everyday world, not some other one, that, in the words of the poet Gerard Manley Hopkins, "is charged with the grandeur of God." The advance of science has increased the sense of awe we feel at the immense scale of the universe or the complexity of the human eye. People turn to religion more for support in their efforts to live in this world and make it better, and less to prepare for the next. The pragmatic and experiential elements of faith as a way of life are displacing the previous emphasis on institutions and beliefs.[1]

It is true that for many people "faith" and "belief" are just two words for the same thing. But they are not the same, and in order to grasp the magnitude of the religious upheaval now under way, it is important to clarify the difference. Faith is about deep-seated confidence. In everyday speech we usually apply it to people we trust or the values we treasure. It is what theologian Paul Tillich (1886–1965) called "ultimate concern," a matter of what the Hebrews spoke of as the "heart."

Belief, on the other hand, is more like opinion. We often use the term in everyday speech to express a degree of uncertainty. "I don't really know about that," we say, "but I believe it may be so." Beliefs can be held lightly or with emotional intensity, but they are more propositional than existential. We can *believe* something to be true without

1. Andre Corten and Marie-Christine Duran, "Immanence and Transcendence in the Religious and the Political," *Social Compass* 54, 4 (December 2007): 565. The phrase "horizontal transcendence" is used by the French philosopher Luce Irigary. See her *Key Writings* (London: Continuum, 2004), 172.

it making much difference to us, but we place our *faith* only in something that is vital for the way we live. Of course people sometimes confuse faith with beliefs, but it will be hard to comprehend the tectonic shift in Christianity today unless we understand the distinction between the two.

The Spanish writer Miguel Unamuno (1864–1936) dramatizes the radical dissimilarity of faith and belief in his short story "Saint Manuel Bueno, Martyr," in which a young man returns from the city to his native village in Spain because his mother is dying. In the presence of the local priest she clutches his hand and asks him to pray for her. The son does not answer, but as they leave the room, he tells the priest that, much as he would like to, he cannot pray for his mother because he does not believe in God. "That's nonsense," the priest replies. "You don't have to believe in God to pray."

The priest in Unamuno's story recognized the distinction between faith and belief. He knew that prayer, like faith, is more primordial than belief. He might have engaged the son who wanted to pray but did not believe in God in a theological squabble. He could have hauled out the frayed old "proofs" for the existence of God, whereupon the young man might have quoted the equally jaded arguments against the proofs. Both probably knew that such arguments go nowhere. The French writer Simone Weil (1909–1943) also knew. In her *Notebooks,* she once scribbled a gnomic sentence: "If we love God, even though we think he doesn't exist, he will make his existence manifest." Weil's words sound paradoxical, but in the course of her short and painful life—she died at thirty-four—she learned that love and faith are both more primal than beliefs.[2]

Debates about the existence of God or the gods were raging in Plato's time, twenty-five hundred years ago. Remarkably, they still rage on today, as a recent spate of books rehearsing the routine arguments for and against the existence of God demonstrates. By their nature these quarrels are about beliefs and can never be finally settled. But *faith,* which is more closely related to awe, love, and wonder, arose long before Plato, among our most primitive *Homo sapiens* forebears. Plato engaged in disputes about beliefs, not about faith.

Creeds are clusters of beliefs. But the history of Christianity is not a history of creeds: It is the story of a people of faith who sometimes cobbled together creeds out of beliefs. It is also the history of equally faithful people, who questioned, altered, and discarded those same

---

2. Simone Weil, *Notebooks,* 583, quoted in David McLennan, *Utopian Pessimist: The Life and Thought of Simone Weil* (New York: Poseidon, 1980), 191.

creeds. As with church buildings, from clapboard chapels to Gothic cathedrals, creeds are symbols by which Christians have at times sought to represent their faith. But both the doctrinal canons and the architectural constructions are means to an end. Making either the defining element warps the underlying reality of faith.

The nearly two thousand years of Christian history can be divided into three uneven periods. The *first* might be called the "Age of Faith." It began with Jesus and his immediate disciples when a buoyant faith propelled the movement he initiated. During this first period of both explosive growth and brutal persecution, their sharing in the living Spirit of Christ united Christians with each other, and "faith" meant hope and assurance in the dawning of a new era of freedom, healing, and compassion that Jesus had demonstrated. To be a Christian meant to live in his Spirit, embrace his hope, and to follow him in the work that he had begun.

The *second* period in Christian history can be called the "Age of Belief." Its seeds appeared within a few short decades of the birth of Christianity when church leaders began formulating orientation programs for new recruits who had not known Jesus or his disciples personally. Emphasis on belief began to grow when these primitive instruction kits thickened into catechisms, replacing faith *in* Jesus with tenets *about* him. Thus, even during that early Age of Faith the tension between faith and belief was already foreshadowed.

Then, during the closing years of the third century, something more ominous occurred. An elite class—soon to become a clerical caste—began to take shape, and ecclesial specialists distilled the various teaching manuals into lists of beliefs. Still, however, these varied widely from place to place, and as the fourth century began there was still no single creed. The scattered congregations were united by a common Spirit. A wide range of different theologies thrived. The turning point came when Emperor Constantine the Great (d. 387 CE) made his adroit decision to commandeer Christianity to bolster his ambitions for the empire. He decreed that the formerly outlawed new religion of the Galilean should now be legal, but he continued to reverence the sun god Helios alongside Jesus.

Constantine also imposed a muscular leadership over the churches, appointing and dismissing bishops, paying salaries, funding buildings, and distributing largesse. He and not the pope was the real head of the church. Whatever his motives, Constantine's policies and those of his successors, especially Emperor Theodosius (347–395 CE), crowned Christianity as the official religion of the Roman Empire. The emperors undoubtedly hoped this strategy would shore up their crumbling dominion, from which the old gods seemed to have fled. The tactic, however, did not save the empire from collapse. But for Christianity it proved to be a disaster: its enthronement actually degraded it. From an energetic movement of faith it coagulated into a phalanx of required beliefs, thereby laying the foundation for every succeeding Christian fundamentalism for centuries to come.

The ancient corporate merger triggered a titanic makeover. The empire became "Christian," and Christianity became imperial. Thousands of people scurried to join a church they had previously despised, but now bore the emperor's seal of approval. Bishops assumed quasi-imperial powers and began living like imperial elites. During the ensuing "Constantinian era," Christianity, at least in its official version, froze into a system of mandatory precepts that were codified into creeds and strictly monitored by a powerful hierarchy and imperial decrees. Heresy became treason, and treason became heresy.

The year 385 CE marked a particularly grim turning point. A synod of bishops condemned a man named Priscillian of Avila for heresy, and by order of the emperor Maximus he and six of his followers were beheaded in Treves. Christian fundamentalism had claimed its first victim. Today Priscillian's alleged theological errors hardly seem to warrant the death penalty. He urged his followers to avoid meat and wine, advocated the careful study of scripture, and allowed for what we would now recognize as "charismatic" praise. He believed that various writings that had been excluded from the biblical canon, although not "inspired," could nevertheless serve as useful guides to life. Still, Priscillian holds an important distinction. He was the first Christian to be executed by his fellow Christians for his religious views. But he was by no means the last. One historian estimates that in the two and a half centuries after Constantine, Christian imperial authorities put twenty-five thousand to death for their lack of creedal correctness.

The Constantinian era had begun in earnest. It was the epoch in which imperial Christianity came to dominate the cultural and political domains of Europe, and it endured throughout the medieval centuries, a time of both bane and blessing. It gave birth to both Chartres Cathedral and the Spanish Inquisition, both St. Francis of Assisi and Torquemada, both Dante's *Divine Comedy* and Boniface VIII's papal bull *Unam Sanctam*, which asserted the pope's authority over the temporal as well as the spiritual realm. Neither the Renaissance nor the Reformation did much to alter the underlying foundations of the Age of Belief, and the European expansion around the planet extended its sway over palm and pine. This middle era, the Age of Belief, was the one that prompted writer and historian Hilaire Belloc (1870–1953) to coin the phrase, "The faith is Europe, and Europe is the faith."

The Age of Belief lasted roughly fifteen hundred years, ebbing in fits and starts with the Enlightenment, the French Revolution, the secularization of Europe, and the anticolonial upheavals of the twentieth century. It was already comatose when the European Union chiseled the epitaph on its tombstone in 2005 by declining to mention the word "Christian" in its constitution.

Still, to think of this long middle era as nothing but a dark age is misleading. As we have seen, throughout those fifteen centuries Christian movements and personalities continued to live by faith and according to the Spirit. The vast majority of people were illiterate and, even if they heard the priests intoning creeds in the churches, did not understand the Latin. Confidence in Christ was their primary orientation, and hope for his Kingdom their motivating drive. Most people accepted the official belief codes of the church, albeit without much thought. Many simply ignored them while they thrived on the pageantry, the festivals, and the stories of the saints. Lollards, Hussites, and later thinkers like Italian philosopher Giordano Bruno (1548–1600) and many others explicitly rejected some of the church's dogmas. The medieval period, after all, was rife with what the officials called heresy and schism. The Age of Belief was also, for significant numbers of people, a spiritually vital "age of faith" as well.

Now we stand on the threshold of a new chapter in the Christian story. Despite dire forecasts of its decline, Christianity is growing faster than it ever has before, but mainly outside the West and in movements that accent spiritual experience, discipleship, and hope; pay scant attention to creeds; and flourish without hierarchies. We are now witnessing the beginning of a "post-Constantinian era." Christians on five continents are shaking off the residues of the second phase (the Age of Belief) and negotiating a bumpy transition into a fresh era for which a name has not yet been coined.

I would like to suggest we call it the "Age of the Spirit." The term is not without its problems. It was first coined in the thirteenth century when a Calabrian monk and mystic named Joachim of Fiore (ca. 1132–1202) began propounding an inventive doctrine of the Trinity. He taught that history, having passed through the ages of the Father (the Old Testament) and the Son (the Church), was about to enter an Age of the Spirit. In this new dispensation, Joachim declared, people would live in direct contact with God, so there would be little need for religious hierarchies. Universal love would reign, and infidels would unite with Christians.

Joachim died a pious Catholic, but some of his followers pressed his arguments further, declaring that the new age had already dawned and there was no further need for priests or sacraments. They also contended that this would be the last age and that the world would soon end. They even began setting dates. But the hierarchy did not look with favor on the prospect of a church without hierarchies. And the world continued to exist. Finally, some sixty years after Joachim's death, the church under Pope Alexander IV pronounced his ideas heretical.

Joachim of Fiore, and especially his followers, obviously got carried away, and scheduling the end of the world is always a risky proposition. Nonetheless, his idea of an Age of the Spirit, or something like it, has always fascinated people. There is an irrepressible visionary or utopian streak in almost everyone. In any case, I hope the new stage of Christianity we now seem to be entering is not the final one (there may be many, many more), but I still prefer to think of it as an "Age of the Spirit" for a number of reasons.

First, for centuries Christians have claimed that the Holy Spirit is just as divine as the other members of the Trinity. But, in reality, the Spirit has most often been ignored or else feared as too unpredictable. It "blows where it will," as the Gospel of John (3:8) says, and is therefore too mercurial to contain. But some of the liveliest Christian movements in the world today are precisely ones that celebrate this volatile expression of the divine. The Spirit's inherent resistance to ecclesial fetters still vexes the prelates. But it also inspires Christians in what used to be called the "third world," but is now termed the "global South" by those living there, to discern the presence of God in other religions. As women come into leadership positions in Christianity, many prefer "Spirit" as their preferred way of speaking of the divine. By far the fastest growth in Christianity, especially among the deprived and destitute, is occurring among people like Pentecostals, who stress a direct experience of the Spirit. It is almost as though the Spirit, muted and muffled for centuries, is breaking its silence and staging a delayed "return of the repressed."

Second, increasing numbers of people who might once have described themselves as "religious," but who want to distance themselves from the institutional or doctrinal demarcations of conventional religion, now refer to themselves as "spiritual." They often say, "I am a spiritual person, but I am not religious." But what does this mean? Often church leaders and theologians wince at the vagueness of the term "spirituality," which is burdened with a long history of ambiguity and controversy. Within the early Christian orbit people spoke of Jesus and then of themselves as being "filled with the Spirit." As decades passed, "spirituality" came to mean the subjective aspect of faith in distinction to the objective teachings. It described a way of life rather than a doctrinal structure. Later, in the Roman Catholic sphere, "spirituality" characterized the different manners in which those in religious orders practiced their faith. One could speak, for example, of a distinctly "Ignatian spirituality," as followed by the Jesuits, or of a "Carmelite" or "Franciscan" spirituality.

But the term "spiritual" also turned controversial at times, especially during the medieval period, when movements like those inspired by Joachim arose that accentuated the immediate experience of God or the Spirit without the necessity of the sacraments or the hierarchy. Some of them even vented explicit protests against the institutional church. Many, like the Beguines, were inspired by women. Some were led by clergy. Meister Eckhart (1260–1327), a Dominican priest, for example, taught that the soul is a spark of God that is to be nourished until the person attains full communion with the divine and is filled with love. He did not condemn churchly observances, but thought they were only of limited value. Shortly after his death Pope John XXII, who was pontiff from 1316 to 1334, declared his ideas heretical.

That did not, however, kill the ideas. Eckhart's student John Tauler (ca. 1300–1361), also a Dominican, took the next step and openly denounced reliance on external ceremonies. The "Spiritual Franciscans," who appeared shortly after the death of St. Francis, taught, as he did, that the Spirit could be found in nature, in "brother sun" and "sister moon," but they also preached against the wealth and power of the institutional church. Most were excommunicated, and some were burned at the stake. Centuries later Simone Weil found the institutional church more of an obstacle than a help in her spiritual quest. Pierre Teilhard de Chardin (1881–1955), the most farsighted Catholic theologian of the twentieth century, envisioned the entire sweep of cosmic history as a process of "spiritualization." And the German pastor Dietrich Bonhoeffer (1906–1945) wrote wistfully from a Gestapo cell of what he called a future "religionless Christianity," liberated from its dogmatic tethers. All of these figures were, in different ways, forerunners of today's dawning Age of the Spirit.[3]

---

3. See Kieran Flanagan and Peter C. Jupp, eds., *A Sociology of Spirituality* (Burlington, VT: Ashgate, 2007).

As in the past, today "spirituality" can mean a range of different things. At a minimum, it evokes an ambiguous self-reflection devoid of content. For some it can become mere navel gazing, a retreat from responsibility in a needy world. Sleek ads in glossy magazines promise a weekend of "spiritual renewal" in a luxurious spa where, for a price, one can reap the benefits of a sauna, a pedicure, and a guru who will help you cope with the stress of your demanding job. For others, however, "spirituality" can mean a disciplined practice of meditation, prayer, or yoga that can lead to deepened engagement in society. A researcher named Seth Wax recently gathered 105 interviews of self-described "spiritual" people in eight different professional fields. He found that what most of them thought of as their "spirituality" actually enhanced their sense of responsibility in their work and in society by giving them a larger goal or by helping them to concentrate on doing a good job.[4] It is evident that different forms of "spirituality" can lead to either self-indulgence or a deepened social engagement, but so can institutional religion.

Recent studies have shown that the conflict between the religious and the spiritual, even between the spiritual and the secular, are not as sharp as some have supposed. People today can move back and forth from one to the other with little sense of contradiction. They carry "spiritual" attitudes and practices into the congregations and religious values into the secular world. They develop what researchers call "repertoires" that include elements from all of these overlapping spheres and are able to negotiate continuously among them. Clerical leaders often object to what seems like the blurring of important distinctions, but the process is making the borders between the religious, the spiritual, and the secular more permeable.

How does the spectacular growth of megachurches like Saddleback and Willow Creek figure into this new picture? Entering Saddleback church, with its large TV screens, piped music, coffee bars, and choice of different music "tents," is more like strolling into a mall than stepping into a cathedral. Its architectural logic is horizontal, not vertical. The line between inside and outside is almost erased. There are now more than four hundred of these churches, with congregations of ten thousand or more. They are *not* fundamentalist. Their real secret is that they are honeycombs of small groups, hundreds of them, for

---

4. Seth Wax, "Placing God before Me: Spirituality and Responsibility at Work," in Howard Gardner, ed., *Responsibility at Work* (San Francisco: Jossey-Bass, 2007), 133-34.

study, prayer, and action. Sociologist Robert Wuthnow estimates that
40 percent of all adult Americans belong to one or another of a variety of small groups both in and out of churches, and that many join
them because they are searching for community and are "interested
in deepening their spirituality." He adds that these small groups are
"redefining the sacred . . . by replacing explicit creeds and doctrines
with *implicit* norms devised by the group." Although he expresses
some hesitation about this soft-peddling of theology, he nonetheless
concludes that many people who grew up in a religious tradition now
"feel the need for a group with whom they can discuss their religious
values. As a result . . . they feel closer to God, better able to pray . . . and
more confident that they are acting according to spiritual principles
that emphasize love, forgiveness, humility and self-acceptance."[5]

The recent rapid growth of charismatic congregations and the
appeal of Asian spiritual practices demonstrate that, as in the past
once again today, large numbers of people are drawn more to the experiential than to the doctrinal elements of religion. Once again, this
often worries religious leaders who have always fretted about mysticism. Echoing age-old suspicions, for example, the Vatican has warned
Catholics against the dangers of attending classes on yoga. Still, it is
important to notice that virtually all current "spiritual" movements
and practices are derived, either loosely or directly, from one of the
historic religious traditions. In addition, just as in the past offshoots
that the church condemned were eventually welcomed back into the
mother's household, the same is happening today. In India and Japan
Catholic monks sit crosslegged practicing Asian spiritual disciplines.
In America, people file into church basements for tai-chi classes. Challenged by the lure of Asian practices, Benedictine monks have begun
teaching laypeople "centering prayer," a contemplative discipline that
not so long ago church authorities viewed with distrust.

"Spirituality" can mean a host of things, but there are three reasons
why the term is in such wide use. First, it is still a form of tacit protest.
It reflects a widespread discontent with the preshrinking of "religion,"
Christianity in particular, into a package of theological propositions
by the religious corporations that box and distribute such packages.
Second, it represents an attempt to voice the awe and wonder before
the intricacy of nature that many feel is essential to human life without
stuffing them into ready-to-wear ecclesiastical patterns. Third, it recognizes the increasingly porous borders between the different traditions

---

5. Robert Wuthnow, *Sharing the Journey: Support Groups and America's New
Quest for Community* (New York: Free Press, 1994), 18-35.

and, like the early Christian movement, it looks more to the future than to the past. The question remains whether emerging new forms of spirituality will develop sufficient ardor for justice and enough cohesiveness to work for it effectively. Nonetheless, the use of the term "spirituality" constitutes a sign of the jarring transition through which we are now passing, from an expiring Age of Belief into a new but not yet fully realized Age of the Spirit.

This three-stage profile of Christianity helps us understand the often confusing religious turmoil going on around us today. It suggests that what some people dismiss as deviations or unwarranted innovations are often retrievals of elements that were once accepted features of Christianity, but were discarded somewhere along the way. It frees people who shape their faith in a wide spectrum of ways to understand themselves as authentically Christian, and it exposes fundamentalism for the distortion it is.

There is little to lament about the present decline of fundamentalism. The word itself was coined in the first decade of the twentieth century by Protestant Christians who compiled a list of theological beliefs on which there could be no compromise. Then they adamantly announced that they would defend these "fundamentals" against new patterns that were already emerging in Christianity. The conflict often became intense. In 1922 Reverend Harry Emerson Fosdick (1878–1969) preached a famous sermon entitled "Shall the Fundamentalists Win?" It seemed for a few decades that, indeed, they might. But now they are on the defensive. The old struggle continues, and their reduction of faith to beliefs persists. But since the emerging Age of the Spirit is more similar to the first Age of Faith than it is to the Age of Belief, the contest today goes on under different conditions. The atmosphere today is more like that of early Christianity than like what obtained during the intervening millennium and a half of the Christian empire.

The three-period way of envisioning Christian history holds a special resonance for me. Biologists say, "Ontogeny recapitulates phylogeny"; that is, the development of an individual repeats the evolution of the species as a whole. My own spiritual evolution traces the same profile. The first, my "age of faith," began in early childhood. Like many children reared in a Protestant Christian home, I first learned that being a Christian meant to be a "follower of Jesus." Admittedly, he was a tough act to follow, but at least the goal was clear. Since Baptists did not have creeds, I never heard about them until years later. At fourteen I was baptized and joined the church. As I had been coached, I told the congregation, while standing up to my waist in the baptismal pool, that I accepted Jesus as Lord and that I would endeavor to be his disciple. Then the minister gently plunged me under and pulled me up sputtering. Along with the other young people who had just "passed through Jordan," after being dried off by the deacons, I changed out of my sodden clothes in a Sunday school room and then rejoined the congregation to be welcomed as a full member. I did not know the phrase "rite of passage" at the time, but, as I look back, this was a memorable one. After that I thought of myself as someone who was trying, never all that successfully, to be a follower of Jesus, and this phase continued into my first semester in college.

Then things changed. A couple months into my freshman year at Penn I found myself involved in long conversations in the dorms. Some were with agnostics or skeptics. Others were with Catholics, Presbyterians, and Episcopalians, who, I found, had something called creeds. I also met conservative Protestant evangelicals and fundamentalists. When one of them asked me directly if I was a Christian, I told him yes, that I tried to follow Jesus. But he fixed me with a direct stare and asked, "But do you believe in the substitutionary atonement?" I was not sure what that was, and for a while I passed through a difficult period, worried that my faith might be fatally deficient. I began to think that maybe a "real Christian" had to believe a certain set of ideas about God, Jesus, and the Bible. This was my quasi-fundamentalist stage, which I will return to in a later chapter. For me it corresponds to Christianity's Age of Belief, which began in the third or fourth century, and, like the church with its historical period, I learned a lot from it and do not regret that it remains part of my life story. But eventually it had to be left behind.

Unlike the church's Age of Belief, mine did not go on for fifteen hundred years. It only lasted about two. In history classes I began reading about the endless debates over creeds and confessions that had roiled Christianity for so long, and I took a course in world religions, which made me see my own faith as one among many. I also became friends with several students who seemed to me to exemplify the Christian life better than some of the taut fundamentalists, although they were not particularly concerned with being doctrinally correct. By my senior year I had embarked on what was to become a lengthy transition into my third phase. But for a long while I remained confused over the vexed relationship between faith and belief.

Then, several years ago an acquaintance of mine described himself to me in a casual conversation as "a practicing Christian, not always a believing one." His remark puzzled me, but it also began to clarify some of the enigmas that had swirled within both my personal faith and my thinking about religion and theology. His remark suggested that the belief/nonbelief axis is a misleading way of describing Christianity. It misses the whole point of not only Christianity, but other religions as well. I have never heard this insight expressed more eloquently than I did one evening in Milan, Italy, where in 1995 Cardinal Carlo Maria Martini had invited me to give a talk at what he called his annual "Lectureship for Nonbelievers."

I had not known what to expect, but it turned out to be quite a glittering occasion. A large crowd draped in Armani and Prada had assembled in an ornate public hall, and I was already seated, when Martini, who stands well over six feet tall, entered in a scarlet cassock and black biretta, the full regalia of a prince of the church. He welcomed the audience and then went on to say that by calling this an event for "nonbelievers," he did not intend to imply anything about the people present. "The line between belief and unbelief," he said, "runs through the middle of each one of us, including myself, a bishop of the church."

To call oneself a practicing Christian, but not necessarily a believing one, acknowledges the variable admixture of certainties and uncertainties that mark the life of any religious person. In August of 2007 the *New York Times* reported that in her collection of letters, *Come Be My Light*, Mother Teresa (1910–1997) confessed that for years she had harbored troubling doubts about the existence of God, even as she worked ceaselessly to relieve the anguish of the sick and dying in Calcutta.[6] Her confession evoked a wave of criticism. Was she a hypocrite? Had she been faking it all along? But in the tumble of public comments that followed, a student named Krista E. Hughes made the most telling comment in a letter to the editor. "Mother Teresa's life," she wrote, "exemplifies the living aspect of faith, something sorely needed in a society where Christian identity is most often defined in terms of what a person believes rather than how he or she lives. Shouldn't it be the other way around?"[7]

Eliminating the spurious use of "belief" to define Christianity has another advantage. It recognizes that often people who call themselves "unbelievers" have episodic doubts about their unbelief. "Believers" go through similar swings. Beliefs come and go, change, fade, and mature. The pattern of beliefs one holds at ten are not identical with the ones one holds at fifty or seventy-five. To focus the Christian life on

---

6. Mother Teresa, *Come Be My Light* (New York: Doubleday, 2007).
7. *New York Times*, September 3, 2007, p. 16.

belief rather than on faith is simply a mistake. We have been misled for
many centuries by the theologians who taught that "faith" consisted in
dutifully believing the articles listed in one of the countless creeds they
have spun out. But it does not.

When I first realized this, it came as a welcome liberation. Starting
when I was quite young, I often had serious doubts about whether I
"believed" some church teaching or something I found in the Bible.
Did God really stop the sun so that Joshua could continue the battle?
Did Jesus really turn water into wine or walk on the sea? Was Mary
really a virgin? But I know now that even when I struggled with these
childhood doubts, I never "lost my faith." Somehow I sensed instinc-
tively that faith was something deeper than belief. Without knowing it,
I was beginning to tiptoe, almost unconsciously, toward my personal
"age of the spirit." Like any major change in one's life, this one did not
take place suddenly. It took a while, and it was only much later that I
began to apply this insight to my thinking about religious studies and
theology.

During my adult life various experiences continued to nudge me
along the path. My many encounters with the followers of other religions, especially Buddhists and Hindus, taught me that "beliefs," in
the way we use the word, were not part of their vocabularies. In fact
none of the other major world religions has a "creed." Even Islam, a
close cousin of Christianity, only expects its followers to affirm, "There
is no god but God, and Muhammad is his messenger" (the Shahada).
In all these traditions, religion means something quite different from
attaching credence to doctrines. My marriage to a Jewish woman, and
with it an unusual opportunity to participate as a "fellow traveler" in
the liturgies and holidays (and food) of her tradition, taught me things
I had never known about her faith, and things I had never realized
about my own (Jesus, after all, was a rabbi). Jews always say their religion is best understood not as a creed, but as a way of life. Slowly it
dawned on me that the same is true of my religion. The earliest term
used to describe it in the New Testament is "The Way."[8]

Once I realized that Christianity is not a creed and that faith is more
a matter of embodiment than of axioms, things changed. I began to
look at people I met in a new way. Some of the ones I admired most
were "believers" in the conventional sense, but others were not. For
example, the individuals with whom I marched and demonstrated and
even went to jail, during the civil rights movement and the Vietnam

---

8. See Paul Borgman, *The Way According to Luke* (Grand Rapids, MI: Eerdmans,
2006).

protests, included both "believers" and "nonbelievers." But we found ourselves looking out from behind the iron bars in the same jail cells. This suggested to me just how mistaken conventional belief-oriented Christianity is in the way it separates the sheep from the goats. But then according to the Gospel of Matthew (25:31-46) Jesus also rejects this predictable schema. What he said then no doubt shocked his listeners. He insisted that those who are welcomed into the Kingdom of God—those who were clothing the naked, feeding the hungry, and visiting the prisoners—were not "believers" and were not even aware that they had been practicing the faith he was teaching and exemplifying.

As Christianity moves awkwardly but irreversibly into a new phase in its history, those who are pushing into this frontier often look to the earliest period, the Age of Faith, rather than the intervening one, the Age of Belief, for inspiration and guidance. This should not be surprising. There are striking similarities between the first and the emerging third age. Creeds did not exist then; they are fading in importance now. Hierarchies had not yet appeared then; they are wobbling today. Faith as a way of life or a guiding compass has once again begun, as it did then, to identify what it means to be Christian. The experience *of* the divine is displacing theories *about* it. No wonder the atmosphere in the burgeoning Christian congregations of Asia and Africa feels more like that of first-century Corinth or Ephesus than it does like that of the Rome or Paris of a thousand years later. Early Christianity and today's emergent Christianity appear closely akin.

19

Why I Am Still a Christian (2009)

This chapter is taken from Arvind Sharma, ed., Why I Am a Believer: Personal Reflections on Nine World Religions *(New York: Penguin Books, 2009), 282-324.*

One of my favorite teachers at Yale was the late Professor Kenneth Scott Latourette. He not only possessed a truly sweeping command of the history of Christianity, but also a quick sly wit. Once after a lecture, a somewhat obstreperous student asked him a prickly question, "Given all the dismal things you know about Christianity, why do you remain a Christian?" "For three reasons," Latourette responded promptly, "birth, conviction and inertia."

I have little doubt that some admixture of Latourette's three ingredients also inform my continuation in the faith into which I was born, which I have retained through a series of shifting interpretations, and with which I am sure I will stay for as long as I live.

Beginnings

But let me begin at the beginning: how did I get to be a Christian? Like most people in the world, I inherited my faith from my family. But in my case it happened in a curious, inverse way. My ancestors on my father's side were Quakers who fled to Pennsylvania in the early 1700s to escape religious persecution and settled in Chester County, where I grew up. On my mother's side they were Rhineland Pietists. They were pacifists like the Quakers, but had arrived a bit later at William Penn's invitation, mainly to escape from military conscription. Neither my father nor my mother was a churchgoer during my childhood, and none of my grandparents were particularly devout either. Still, like many parents in America in the 1930s, mine sent my three siblings and me to the Baptist Sunday School next door. My story again differs from some others at this point: instead of resenting it and rebelling, I

334

actually liked it. I joined in the vigorous Gospel singing. I met many of my friends, at first boys but later—and more significantly—girls there. We enjoyed endless picnics and ever so many covered-dish suppers of steaming mashed potatoes, varieties of garden vegetables and bountiful pies. My Sunday school teachers were attentive and engaging, and some of them even knew something about Christianity. The main things I acquired in those early years were a fascination with the Bible stories, both the Old and the New Testaments, and a personal affection and admiration for Jesus. Although I understand both the Bible and Jesus differently now than I did then, what I learned during those early years remains with me many decades later.

As soon as I reached adolescence I began to "stay for church" when Sunday school was over. It seemed like the grown-up thing to do. Also I sang bass in the volunteer choir, and I came to look forward to that as well. Soon, my growing faith became a point of teen-age pride, something that lent me an edge over my indifferent parents. When I was baptized by immersion in the church's indoor pool at thirteen, while the congregation sang *Just as I am,* only my mother and grandmother from my family attended. But for me, the baptism became a real rite of passage. I know there are many jokes about Baptists dunking people, and to many the practice seems like an archaic holdover. But the people who pander these witticisms have never experienced the dramatic power of the ritual. Dressed all in white, I felt—as it had been interpreted to me—that I had died and been buried with Christ, and had risen again to a new life. I had entered a new phase of living, and so—since I had always been an inquisitive youngster—I began borrowing books from the minister, and reading not just about my religion but about others as well. I have never stopped.

Ever since those earliest years the feature of Jesus's life and teaching that has been most important to me is his message about the coming of the Kingdom of God. What I learned from the outset was that he was not talking about a kingdom that begins when this life is over, or about an era that starts when our present history ends. He clearly instructed his disciples in what we call "The Lord's Prayer" to pray for the coming of his Kingdom "on earth as it is in heaven." During my later years I heard a lot of preaching that ignored, postponed or misinterpreted this central keystone of Jesus's life. But the conviction that the "peaceable kingdom" was possible, at least provisionally and in part, never left me. I grew up determined that I was going to try to do something during my lifetime to realize some aspect of it. In retrospect, I can see that the pacifist, equalitarian and hopeful tone of my ancestors'

Quaker and Pietist traditions had probably made a mark on me after all. Maybe it is in the DNA.

After high school I sailed on a couple of merchant ships carrying horses, cows and other relief supplies to post-war Europe. The first ship I worked on docked in Gdynia, the port city near Gdansk (formerly Danzig), Poland. I will never forget what I found at the foot of the gangway. The charred wreckage of ruined buildings, the ragged hungry children who followed us through the streets, begging for chewing gum, and the pathetic teen-age prostitutes in grotesque mascara who accosted us, all further confirmed my earlier Christian conviction that the world did not have to be this way. Also, on one of those ships I shared crew quarters with a zealous fundamentalist, and on another I met a somewhat self-righteous Catholic. Both delighted in informing me how very wrong my understanding of Christianity was. I was also learning that within the tradition I called my own, there are lots of people I would prefer not to spend much time with. That is also still very much the case. I should add that as I have become older I have come to appreciate Catholics more but fundamentalists even less.

Given my interests and life goals, it was natural that I should feel "called," and decide to become a minister, a path that eventually led me to become a professor of religion and theology. I have never been sorry about my choice. I have had the advantage of a superb education at excellent institutions, including the universities of Pennsylvania, Yale and Harvard. But I can still report honestly that, if not all I know about Christianity, then the most essential elements, I learned in my youth. Some of it was in church and Sunday school. But like Herman Melville, who writes that the 'Pequod' was his Yale and his Harvard, much of it I learned on a Liberty ship called the SS *Robert Hart*. The rest was elaboration on the basics.

I never suffered through a wrenching "crisis of faith," though I know people who have, and I admire them. No one had ever told me that Christianity and the theory of evolution were irreconcilable, and I never noticed any real "warfare between science and religion" in my own life. When I got back from the seagoing days with a sharpened view of the cruelty and stubbornness of human beings, and some distinctly left-leaning political sympathies, reading Reinhold Niebuhr, who could write with equal verve about sin and redemption and also about imperialism—often on the same page—helped me hold it all together. On the contrary, my higher education mostly confirmed and amplified what I had absorbed earlier. For example, I discovered in my studies that the Christian figures I admired most had also believed that the Kingdom of God was the keystone of Jesus's life and ministry. It is the foundation stone of Walter Rauschenbusch's idea of the "Social Gospel." It was the subject of one of my teachers', Richard Niebuhr, earliest books. Even the European theologians I read, like Jürgen Molt- mann, who emphasize the passion and death of Christ, point out that it was because of his preaching and demonstrating this kingdom that he aroused such fierce opposition from the guardians of the status quo.

It is hard to avoid the conviction that if Jesus had concentrated only on the inner spiritual life, or on a strictly transcendental realm, his message would not have bothered anyone. He might have lived to a ripe old age as he does in the dream that comes to him on the cross in Nikos Kazantzakis's novel, *The Last Temptation of Christ*. But when he insisted that another kingdom was dawning, the ruling powers recognized that if this was true, their star was setting. In a real sense his message was indeed treasonous, and when Pilate sentenced him to crucifixion—a mode of capital punishment reserved for subversives and enemies of the *pax romana*—from the procurator's point of view, it was clearly the right thing to do. Jesus did indeed pose a threat. And he remains a threat today, to all regimes that arrogate absolute authority to themselves and that squeeze the life of the poor, the outcastes and the disinherited.

I must add immediately that, having spent a lifetime studying Chris- tianity, no one knows any better than I do just how badly this mes- sage of Jesus has been misread, manipulated and misused. It has been deployed to justify torture, brutality and injustices of every sort. These dreadful elements in the history of Christianity constitute one of the reasons why at times I have been seriously tempted to abandon ship. I know people who have and I respect their decision. I cannot even argue that "on balance" Christianity has done more good than harm. No one is in a position to weigh enough evidence to make that judgement, especially since so many compassionate and loving words and deeds go unrecorded in history, while the annalists seldom forget the massacres, pogroms and inquisitions. Every year I return to Dostoyevsky's "Grand Inquisitor" scene from *The Brothers Karamazov*, lest I forget the deep dark side of the faith I still hold to.

Reading that passage also reminds me of what I appreciate most about my own stream in the wider Christian river. It is the charac- teristically Protestant insight, what Paul Tillich called "the Protestant principle," that there will always be a tension between the faith and its historical realization. The reformers not only believed that Christian- ity had taken a drastically wrong turn and needed to be put back on track. Even more importantly, they also believed that, given human nature and perhaps even original sin, these wrong turns would continue to happen time and time again. Therefore, the church must be, as they put it, "*semper reformanda*," constantly renewing and reforming itself. For me this means that every religion should have a dependable and built-in mechanism for self-criticism and self-correction. As T. S. Eliot puts it in 'The Rock',

> And the Church must be forever building,
> and always decaying,
> and always restored.

I am not suggesting that other variants of Christianity, or other faiths, lack this self-critical capacity; and I have also come to appreciate what Tillich called the "catholic substance," that must always balance the Protestant principle. Still, I know of no other in which that principle has become the central pivot of a whole tradition, as it has in Protestantism. I also believe, however, that it is essential for individual persons and for whole societies. The ability to be aware of where we are and where we are headed, and the willingness to change direction when necessary are indispensable for survival. People who cannot change turn dry and rigid. History is strewn with the skeletons of civilizations that became too sclerotic to change.

The need for a source of reform and renewal in Christianity itself should not be surprising. From the beginning those who claim to follow Jesus have betrayed, denied and abandoned him. This pattern begins within the gospels themselves with Judas, Peter and the other disciples. It is an old, and sad, but true story. Those of us who profess to be Christian must live with it and recognize that it is still our story. But we can also be thankful that because of the Easter event, or the coming of the Holy Spirit, which lives within the community of faith (different theologies emphasize different parts of the story) renewal and repentance are always possible. We can always start over again.

Elements

I hope I am a follower of Jesus, maybe even a "friend" since that is what he asked his disciples to be. But I do not believe in trying to convert people to Christianity. This disinclination will surely distinguish me from many other Christians, and I understand and respect their perspective. I cannot deny that I have found something vital in Christianity that I do not believe I could have found anywhere else, and that I think many people might find the same benefits—if they wanted to. But that is the point. They must want to. I will never cajole, and I certainly would never coerce, especially since I believe a faith accepted by coercion is never an authentic one. If asked, I will make the best case I can for my own religion, but it will be my "testimony," and might or might not connect with someone else's life trajectory.

I do not believe that much is to be gained by arguments about matters of faith. They score some debating point, and as a former college debater, I am as skilled at that as any one. But they rarely help people to make a fundamental life decision. Rather, I would hope that the way I live my life might speak for itself, and—if asked—I would gladly explain as clearly as possible how my faith undergirds and guides my life. Still, if I were asked to make such a case, it is fair to ask, what would I say? In that connection I would mention two things. Both have to do with the centrality of Jesus in my understanding of Christianity. The first is what Christians, somewhat misleadingly at times, have historically called the "Incarnation." The second is the simple phrase "God is love."

1. In the simplest terms "Incarnation" means that God, as made manifest in Jesus, is present within the fiber and marrow of human life. God is not elsewhere, but here and now. God suffers and celebrates with human beings, and—in ways we cannot know much about—with the entire creation, animal, vegetable and mineral. This, may I point out, is not "pantheism." I do not believe that God is identical with all that is, but that God, having brought all that is into being, has chosen to be irretrievably present in that creation. God is "Emmanuel," which means "God-with-us."

The centrality of the Incarnation suggests that the way to learn about the incarnate God revealed in Jesus is primarily through one's own encounter with people who themselves have been touched or influenced by Jesus. In a faith in which God reveals Him/Herself primarily though a person, persons remain the main vehicles of truth. When I came to this conclusion a few years ago, I began to avoid teaching courses on systematic theology and to focus more and more on biographies. Life stories are the key, I believe, to understanding Christianity—and possibly other faiths as well, but that is not for me to judge. Since then I have steeped myself in the autobiographies, life stories and other similar accounts of an abounding succession of individuals for whom Jesus was a principal influence on their lives. My description of my own Christian faith, therefore, can best be told not by writing a credo. Although I know how important systematic statements of faith have been in Christian history, my credo would read more like a genealogy of spiritual forebears, whose example intersects with my own. None of them, of course, carried the fullness of God's love and presence as Jesus himself did. Still each displayed a facet of it with such radiance that I was illuminated by the glow.

I cannot possibly list all the names in my scrapbook of fathers and mothers in the faith. But a sampling will suggest a lot about where I place myself within the wide swath of Christian history, and how this history continues to inform my own life.

After the figures in the Bible itself, I like St. Augustine, but for reasons quite different from those that most of his admirers would mention. I appreciate the fact that he was an explorer. He tried a number of different philosophies, including Manichaeism, the stylish "new age" fusion of religion and science of his day, before he became a Christian. But I also like the fact that after his conversion he continued to integrate elements of his previous convictions into his voluminous writings. I appreciate St. Augustine as well because he was a theologian of culture and history. He looked around at the collapsing Roman Empire, the only world either he or most of the people of his era knew, and tried to discern what God was doing in what appeared to be a total catastrophe. Finally, I am thankful that St. Augustine not only looked out and looked around but also that he also looked back and looked within. His justly famous *Confessions* were written three decades after the events they recall and describe. Yet, in retrospect, he could see the hand of God at work in his life, even before he knew it was happening. The older I get, this habit of appreciative retrospection is one that I value more and more.

Of course there are many aspects of St. Augustine that annoy, embarrass, even anger me. His treatment of his mistress, with whom he had a child, was shabby. His later attitude toward sex and marriage has cast a long and debilitating shadow. His tendency to equate loyalty to the church with faith was a serious mistake. His willingness to use the power of the state to enforce orthodoxy was wrong. Still, warts and all, St. Augustine's portrait hangs in my spiritual parlor.

Perhaps my greatest favorite among the radiant spirits of the Christian past is St. Francis of Assisi. He stands at almost the opposite end of the spectrum of Christian possibility from St. Augustine. He was no intellectual. Starting out as a party boy and a ladies' man, he turned into a rebel, a songster, and a joker—God's troubadour. His style was antic and playful, but also serious and at times highly confrontational. He could lampoon the fatty excess of the church and get away with it. He slipped through the battle lines and debated with the sultan in a failed effort to bring the bloody crusades to an end. He included Sister moon and Brother fire in his songs and prayers. He died a disappointed man since fights over the succession had already broken out among his followers. But he identified with Jesus Christ so energetically that—so legend tells us—just before he died the prints of the nails—the "stigmata"—appeared on his hands.

St. Francis is truly everyone's favorite saint, far transcending the borders of the Catholic Church or even of Christianity. It was entirely appropriate that when Pope John Paul II called upon the leaders of other faiths to join him in a prayer meeting for peace, he suggested Assisi as the location, and they all came. No other spot on earth would have done it.

Next comes St. Teresa of Avila. She was a feisty, irascible lady, a mystic, an organizer of convents, a counsellor to bishops and princes, and a feminist *avant la lettre*. She lived most of her life just a few steps ahead of the ever-suspicious Inquisition to whom reports came of what appeared to some critics as excessive emotionalism and a clever capacity to evade the discipline of church authorities. But she never wavered from following the promptings of the Spirit, and her book, *The Interior Castle*, is one of the classics of Christian literature.

St. Teresa is important because she reminds me that Christianity is not just about ideas. It is also about emotions and feelings. But, at the same time St. Teresa, who contemporaries swear was sometimes actually lifted off the floor (levitated) by the sheer energy of her prayers, still recognized that emotion could sometimes mislead and deceive. She realized that just as ideas, when pursued too zealously, can push people down strange paths, unfastened emotions can do the same thing. I think it is important that despite her controversial career, the Catholic Church finally canonized her as a saint, thus legitimating the indispensable role of mysticism in Christianity.

I have only rarely had what I would call a mystical experience. But I cannot emphasize the importance of the mystical tradition too much. The clerical establishment and the theological fraternity are always suspicious of it. Mystics do not need hierarchies. They can do without elaborate theological systems. They appeal directly to the source. They are like shoppers who go to the original supplier and avoid the retailer. No wonder that the clerical retailers become apprehensive, and that mystics are often honored after they have been declared heretics, and canonized often long after they are safely dead (sometimes, like St. Joan of Arc, burnt at the stake). I am still a Christian today, despite all the legitimate criticisms of my tradition, in part because it sometimes has the sagacity, or perhaps the shrewdness, to honor its free spirits and deviants.

The repertory of the saints who shape my interpretation of Christianity includes many more men and women. Martin Luther is there, despite his disgusting descent into raging antisemitism in his old age. Roger Williams, sometimes thought of as the founder of the Baptists, at least in America, is there too. There are Sojourner Truth, Blaise Pascal, Feodor Dostoyevsky, Mahatma Gandhi, Dorothy Day, Martin Luther King, Jr., Pope John XXIII, Bishop Oscar Romero, and Dietrich Bonhoeffer. There are many more, but this sampling illustrates my point. Truth is found in incarnation.

When I think about this gallery of greats, the words of the *Epistle to the Hebrews* come to mind, which I quote here in the stately classical King James translation:

> Wherefore seeing we also are compassed about with so great a cloud of witnesses, let us set aside every weight, and the sin which doth so easily beset us, and let us run with patience the race that is set before us, looking unto Jesus, the author and finisher of our faith. (Hebrews 11:1, 2)

2. After the centrality of Incarnation, the second feature of Christianity I would point to is love: the entire narrative of Jesus's life as an assurance that the content of God's life is love. God, the Epistle of John says, "*is* love." God is not only *with* us but also *for* us, unconditionally. God's love has a special place for what Jesus called "the least of these," but it is utterly universal. It is in no sense restricted to Christians, or even—I would contend—only to human beings. In Psalm 148, one of my favorites, the frost and hail and storm winds, the cedars and mountains and all the reptiles and birds are pictured responding in praise of God's love.

When I was a theological student some of my professors were greatly enamored of a book by a Scandinavian theologian named Anders Nygren entitled *Agape and Eros*. In it the author draws a sharp distinction between the various types of love and warns that erotic love and *agape,* the love of God and of Christ, are very different and should not be confused. The late Norwegian-American theologian Nels Ferre, who was my hospitable colleague during my first teaching position at Andover-Newton Theological School, developed this theme further. But I did not accept this sharp distinction then, and I do not now. I believe that love is a continuum, with the various forms—*eros, philia, agape* (fleshly, fraternal and spiritual)—all shading into and mixing with each other. In *The Symposium*, Plato positioned these variants of love on a kind of ascending scale, but perhaps even that separates them too much.

As I will mention below in my discussion on the genius of Hinduism, I believe historically Christianity has done a great disservice in its negative and dismissive attitude toward erotic love. This is one of the reasons why I welcome some of the new documentary discoveries of the non-canonical gospels in which it becomes clear that Jesus's relationship to Mary Magdalene may not have been only a "platonic" one. But my own intimate experience with erotic love, although admittedly limited, has taught me that it is unwise and even impossible to separate it from the love of God expressed in Jesus.

It is said that Søren Kierkegaard, a great Christian thinker who, I admit, has never much appealed to me, broke his engagement to Regina Olsen because he did not believe he could fully love her and God at the same time. He asked that the only words engraved on his tombstone should be "The Single One." But Martin Buber, in his famous essay "To the Single One," wrote wisely and truthfully, that it is *through*, not *despite* the Regina Olsens of this world, that the love of God comes to us. I agree with Buber, and not with Kierkegaard, and when I talk about the "love of God," I mean love in its full range, not just one sub-species.

When one combines the Incarnation with God as love, it becomes clear that God has staked his very life, as it were, on the only universe and the only human race we know about. *This is it.*

Epiphanies

I suppose everyone who belongs to any religious tradition can recall specific moments when the meaning of that tradition became unusually clear. I am no exception. Some might call these moments "epiphanies." The word is now associated with the historic Christian holiday called "Epiphany" that marks the arrival of the wise men from the East in Bethlehem after the birth of the infant Jesus. But the term epiphany simply means to show or manifest. There are two such incidents in my own life I will describe here. Not surprisingly, given my particular "take" on Christianity, which I mentioned earlier, both resulted in deepening my appreciation for the *radical inclusiveness* of Jesus's teaching about the Kingdom of God.

The first took place in October 1963 when I found myself locked behind the steel bars of a southern jail for having taken place in a demonstration against racial segregation. I was hardly alone. With me were ten fellow ministers from in and around Boston and some forty young black demonstrators from the town in which we had been arrested, Williamston, North Carolina. All of us had been encouraged to take part in the march by Dr. Martin Luther King, Jr., and it took place under the auspices of the local chapter of the Southern Christian Leadership Conference, the organization he founded and led. The peaceful, non-violent march had been forbidden by the local sheriff as a threat to order, and he had succeeded in getting his decision backed up by an injunction from a superior court in the state.

For three days and evenings we had carefully prepared for the march, mainly in the local African Methodist Episcopal Church. We sang and prayed. We laughed and relaxed, even napped on the hard pews. But mainly we talked about our fears. Some of the young people who had marched previously described how at times the police had shoved, prodded, kicked and cursed them and even struck them with billy clubs. But there they were, ready to march again. And also ready to maintain non-violence, not just in their conduct but also in their attitude. Dr. King had frequently admonished them it was not enough to refuse to respond with violence. Every marcher had to look deep within and cast out any hateful, hostile or violent thought, or else stay away from the march.

We had been prepared to march in face of a local sheriff's edict, but when we heard about the action of the superior court we had to talk and pray again. Violating a sheriff's order can result in a fine or even a few days in jail. But if we had been found guilty of violating such an injunction it could result in a three to five year sentence in a state prison. This was not a cheerful prospect especially for a white outsider identified as a "nigger lover," and it was no less welcome a prospect for the young people who were preparing themselves for the march. Still, after hours of reflection, and a phone call with Dr. King, we decided we simply had to march. Anything else would have felt like a retreat.

We did march, two-by-two in a long winding line on a glorious, crisp autumn day. We started at the little church and made our way toward City Hall. Dozens of beefy state police literally lined the sidewalk where we walked, in part to protect us from an angry crowd that stood in knots behind them. Local officers arrested our entire group, nearly fifty of us, and we quickly found ourselves locked in segregated cell blocks. The clang of the closing of huge metal doors echoed ominously. After a brief moment of exaltation (since we had at least made it from the church to the jail without being beaten up), a nagging apprehensiveness began to seep into the "white" cells. How long would it be before those doors swung open? Would we be out in a reasonable length of time, or was this just the first way station on the road to a long, risky imprisonment? The thrill of danger subsided and a cloud of anxiety settled over us. Attempts to joke with each other about our uncertain situation began to sound limp. Silence crept through the bars as we sat glumly on our hard bunks.

But then we heard something. It was the black youngsters down the concrete hallway praying vociferously and singing hymns and freedom songs at the top of their lungs. The boys, of course, were separated from the girls. But some of the songs they belted out required responses and soon the two groups were answering each other.

"Are you ready everybody?"

"Oh, yes!"

"Are you ready for the journey?"

"Oh, yes!"

"Do you want your freedom?"

"Oh, yes!"

Then both groups would join lustily in the chorus, "We're gonna' march in the morning for our freedom, Lord."

Those of us in the "white" cells first listened. But then, hesitantly at first, then with more vigor, we joined in as well. Soon the entire jail was ringing with our music and with the soaring prayers of the young marchers.

It went on and on, for hours. We adults soon tired, but not they. A couple of times the warden tried to shush them, but finally gave up. He told us later he was a churchgoer himself and he hated to interrupt hymns and prayers.

After a couple of days three of my fellow white prisoners and I were transferred by police vehicle to another jail in a nearby town. It seems there had been more marches and more arrests, and the town jail's capacity was being severely strained. In the new prison there were no black demonstrators. It was quiet and dreary, with only the sound of traffic drifting in through the small, high, barred windows. Fortunately, after only a day or two there we were all released on bail to await trial. The members of the little black church had put their homes up for bail bond. A few days later a brilliant civil rights lawyer succeeded in getting the charges against us dropped by threatening a federal suit against the town for unlawfully depriving its citizens of their constitutional right to assemble. He told us that part of the arrangement was that we should leave town immediately and not come back. We complied, knowing that local black church people, and other members of the Southern Christian Leadership Conference, would continue the marches.

A few years ago I returned for the first time to the town where we had been arrested and to the brick jailhouse in which we had been locked. I had brought my sixteen-year-old son, Nichols, along for the trip. We found the building no longer in use as a prison, the paint on the window trim peeling and the doors locked. We could not get in. My son thought it was funny. "You mean when you were here before, you were locked in," he quipped, "and now you are locked out?" We both chuckled. But that dilapidated edifice will always remain the scene of my first epiphany.

The second personal epiphany that deepened my understanding of Jesus and his message actually took place in a church. It was summer, and I dropped in at a small Episcopal church on Martha's Vineyard where my family was vacationing. I knew that down the street from that church there was a camp for mentally retarded and emotionally disturbed young people. It was called "Camp Jabber Wocky," from Lewis Carroll's famous poem. I had also heard that sometimes the counsellors brought a contingent of the children to that church. That Sunday turned out to be one of those days. The children spanned the ages from nine or ten to about fourteen. There were twenty of them, and they were seated in a clump near the front. They seemed to be enjoying themselves. During the hymns they sang lustily even though they did not always appear to be singing the same tune, and they continued singing for a while after the hymn was over—until their counsellors gently quieted them. They seemed a little restless during the sermon, but then many people are, and the sermons at that church tended to be short and to the point.

But then I noticed a change in their mood. As the communion service—the Eucharist—began, they became quiet and alert. They even seemed reverent. When I asked about this later, one of the doctors who cared for them said that children like these often exhibited an unusually well-developed sensitivity to the subtle moods and feelings of the congregation. Maybe in this case they had picked up on the subtle shift of feelings among the people around them. When the appropriate moment came they tumbled out of the pews and knelt at the altar rail, eagerly accepting the wafers and the tiny sip of sacramental wine.

That was when my epiphany took place. I became blazingly aware that this was what the Eucharist, and the message of Jesus, was about. Christianity teaches that the communion service is a foreshadowing of the promised reigning of God Jesus announced, the "peaceful kingdom" now appearing in part and in promise. The Eucharist is sometimes described as the "aperitif" of the forthcoming feast, a preliminary taste that whets the appetite and suggests the good things to come. It dramatizes a utopian and counter-cultural vision, but one in which it is already possible to participate.

At that moment it became utterly clear to me that these children, who might still be called "handicapped" by some people, were equally valuable and precious to God as anyone else, *including myself.* In fact, given the evidence of the gospels, God seems to show a preference for those the society denigrates. It was clear that these children would probably never make a lot of money, never purchase trophy homes or luxury yachts. According to the standard most frequently deployed in America and most of the world today—money—they would not attain the goal of "success." I also realized they would not gain admission into prestigious colleges, write bestsellers, win Pulitzer or Nobel prizes. In fact, they might even be considered by some people to be an expensive burden, and if their condition could be detected in the fetal state, they might not be brought to birth at all.

Yet here we all were. I knew that, given the vacationers who can afford Martha's Vineyard in the summer, there were a considerable number of quite well-to-do people in the congregation that day. I also knew there were a couple of celebrities and some accomplished writers. But for a brief, luminous moment, none of that seemed to matter. The radically inclusive kingdom, the one Jesus told his followers to pray for, had been brilliantly present. Of course, after the coffee hour, we would all go back to our homes—or to the camp—and live our lives pretty much as we had lived them before. But not entirely, for once having sipped the aperitif, the appetite for more is whetted. One can never accept the present divisions and rankings we live with as forever fixed.

The German theologian, Wolfhart Pannenberg, has recently observed that the rediscovery of the Eucharist may be one of the most important events in the history of contemporary Christianity. I tend to agree. Having grown up in a tradition in which the Communion service was not at all central, I have found myself gradually edging toward a preference for the more liturgical, more symbolic, less cognitive and verbal dimensions of Christian worship, and especially for the Eucharist. I do not think I am alone. The same shift appears to be under way in other religious traditions, and in the culture at large. Metaphoric language and visual media play a larger role. Christians in the Western churches are beginning to appreciate the Eastern Orthodox love for icons. Even Luther once called the sacrament the *"verbum visibi-lum."* The fact that my second "epiphany" occurred at a Eucharistic service now seems to me not so surprising. After all, Jesus had said to his disciples at what we call the "Last Supper" to continue to "do this in remembrance of me."

I include these "epiphanies" here because they help illuminate the "why" in the title of this essay. They suggest reasons why, "in spite of all temptation," I still count myself a Christian. But what about the temptations?

Temptations

In defending their shipmate, Ralph Rakestraw, against accusations that in falling in love with his captain's daughter he had brazenly over-reached his humble station, his fellow tars sing a rousing shanty, insisting that "it is greatly to his credit that in spite of all temptations to belong to other nations, he remains an Englishman." The fact is that Ralph probably encountered very few such temptations. It is also true that during considerable stretches of human history, vast numbers of people have never been faced with the choice of changing religious loyalties. It is of course true that significant numbers of people have had to face the coercive pressures of one of the proselytizing religions like Christianity or Islam. For centuries people have converted to another faith for a wide variety of reasons. But, still in all, the opportunity to engage in a thoughtful and reflective assessment of the virtues of a faith other than one's own has generally been the experience of only a few.

That, of course, may now be changing. One of the many products of globalization is that hardly anyone anywhere on the globe can now escape the realization that there are indeed other religious paths than his or her own. Christianity, for example, is now no longer a "Western religion." In fact there are those who claim it never was, having arisen in the "East" and spread in all directions before becoming, after many centuries, the official religious ideology of Europe, which came to be called Christendom. Today, however, not just Christianity but Islam, Hinduism and Buddhism have each spread to every continent. Bookstores, magazine kiosks, films, music and the Internet all remind us daily of the unprecedented religious diversity of the world culture. I am one of those who came into adulthood just at the cusp of the death of "Christendom" and the emergence of this spiritually heterogeneous era. It has had a profound effect on my understanding of myself as a Christian. Unlike many generations of my Quaker and Baptist forebears, I have had to ask myself ask, not once but many times, why I remain one? Further, I have not just had to put this question to myself in the abstract, but in the living presence of genuine options. Here is how I responded, and continue to respond, to these "temptations."

The Jewish Temptation

Since my marriage some twenty years ago to a practicing Jewish woman, I have participated as a "fellow traveler" in a considerable amount of Jewish spiritual life and culture. I have found many elements of both exceedingly attractive. I appreciate the Jewish reluctance to engage in proselytism. I welcome the narrative, as opposed to the systematic approach to the content of the faith. I admire the uncanny capacity of the Jewish people to survive the buffetings and setbacks of a very tragic history. I look forward to our annual celebration of the Passover Seder, a festival of freedom, marking—I believe—that point in history when God's unwavering support for the oppressed and captive peoples of history became indelibly clear. I like the occasion that the "Days of Awe" between Rosh Hashanah and Yom Kippur provide us for deep reflection and the mending of our ways. I savor the antic spirit and zany clowning of Purim. The ancient, wise mourning rituals of shiva and the yahrzeit have often sustained our family in times of loss and sorrow. I also love the Jewish zest for argumentation.

But all of this I have written about at length in my book *Common Prayers: Faith, Family and a Christian's Journey through the Jewish Year*.[1] In fact, I talked about them with such heartfelt approval that one reader wrote to ask why I do not just convert to Judaism. My answer to him sums up why I have never succumbed to the "Jewish temptation." I said that I had indeed considered it, but that if I did so, I would have to "bring Jesus along." If I could have all the treasures of the Jewish faith and tradition plus the Nazareth rabbi, then I might indeed make the move. But I knew, even as I said it, that it was not a move the Jewish world would accept. Indeed, it has been tried. Today there are thousands of people who call themselves "Messianic Jews." They follow or accept Jesus (albeit in a variety of ways) but insist that they remain Jewish. I once visited a congregation of these Jews (at least "Jews" by their own designation) and felt quite at home. But I also know that most of the larger Jewish world rejects their claim categorically and insists they have cut themselves off from their own people. They respond, with

1. Harvey Cox, *Common Prayers: Faith, Family and a Christian's Journey through the Jewish Year* (New York: Houghton Mifflin, 2002).

considerable historical accuracy, that the very first followers of Jesus were all Jews, and that they are retrieving an old tradition, but their claim is dismissed, and they are often accused of a kind of dissimulation, of merely pretending to be Jews for the base purpose of snaring uninformed Jews into the Christian fold.

I have sometimes felt a bit bemused that most Jewish authorities insist one remains Jewish even if one takes up some alien philosophy or spiritual discipline. Thus I have met Jews who considered themselves to be Vaishnavite Hindus, Sufis or practitioners of Zen. But most interpreters of Jewish law still consider them to be Jews, albeit wayward ones. One can apparently even become an atheist and still be a member of the tribe. All of these unlikely categories of Jews are, according to the High Court of Israel, acceptable under the "Law of Return." But this principle of inclusion by which the child of a Jewish mother is ineradicably Jewish, seems decidedly not to apply to "Messianic Jews." Some of this has to do with the long and ongoing debate among Jews about whether they are a religion, a people, a culture or a little of each. But most of the seemingly illogical exception, the exclusion of followers of Jesus from the Jewish community, has historical, not theological, roots. It has to do with the brutal treatment Christians have meted out to Jews over the centuries. In any case, this practice closes the only door through with I could possibly have entered, although I am not at all sure that—even given an open door—I would have done so.

As it turns out, I can enjoy many of the benefits of Jewish faith and culture, the Jewish rituals—especially Sabbath meals—that we celebrate in our home because of my marriage and my subsequent inclusion in my wife's larger family. In all of these facets I feel warmly "included." Still, I remain a fellow-traveler, not a card-carrying member. I cooperate with my wife fully in raising our son Jewish. I helped him prepare for his bar mitzvah and I take real pride in his continuing association with his ancient faith. Judaism will continue to be part of my life, and it no longer really qualifies as a "temptation." It is, rather, a blessing.

The Hindu Temptation

In some ways what people in the West have come to call "Hinduism" stands at the opposite end of a spectrum from Judaism. How many million gods, goddesses, divine and semi-divine beings does it encompass, a far cry from, "Hear, O Israel, the Lord your God is One." Likewise, my "Hindu temptation" came in a very different way. It also provides an appropriate opportunity to talk about one important facet of interfaith communication, namely, what attracts an "outsider" to a tradition may be quite different from what the insiders consider to be important or vital. This may well be the case in my attraction, which, in any case, did not really rise to the level of a genuine temptation to the Hindu tradition.

Twenty-five years ago, I paid my first visit to the holy city of Vrindavan in north India. The name means "the forest of Vrinda," the bushy locale where Lord Krishna enjoyed his famous midnight revels with the gopis, or cowherd girls, whom he had lured from their beds (and from their husbands) with the magical melodies of his flute. Vrindavan is not a forest today. It is a pilgrimage city for thousands of devotees who reverence Krishna and his principal consort, Radha. It is crammed with temples. Someone told me there were a thousand, if one counts both the huge complexes, complete with courtyards, dining halls and dormitories, like the one I stayed in, as well as the tiny ones, the equivalent of storefront churches.[2]

Surrounding the city runs a circular path on its outskirts, which one follows from one small shrine to another in a series analogous to the Christian Via Dolorosa. In this case, however, rather than the passion and death of Christ, these temples all focus on one or another of the key moments in the tempestuous love affair between Krishna and Radha. It seems that Krishna was often absent and Radha often grew suspicious that he might be dallying with other ladies. Sometimes her jealously reached such a towering height that she refused to see him, forcing her lover to assume various disguises in order to gaze on her presence. Once he got into her salon by taking the form of a swan and swimming on her pond. One temple is entirely devoted to what is called "Radha's pique," the sour snit of irritation she sometimes fell into when she was at odds with Krishna. We all know what that feels like.

Each of these small jewel-like temples, replete with dozens of pictures, and always garlanded with fragrant flowers, is designed to call to the visitor's mind times when he or she has felt the same mood or disposition, and then to reflect on its spiritual meaning. For this is the whole point: disciples of Krishna see the love of a man for a woman, and vice versa, as no less than a vivid expression of the love God has for human beings, and that they should also express toward God. When I began to grasp this idea as I trudged from temple to temple in the blazing heat of Vrindavan, a powerful thought seized me: unlike in Christianity and Judaism, in which the erotic element of life has largely been

---

2. "Vrindavan," in *The Encyclopedia of Eastern Philosophy and Religion* (Boston: Shambala, 1989), 411.

repressed or sublimated, in the Vaishnavite tradition it is the principal symbol of the divine–human relationship.

The great Protestant theologian, Paul Tillich, who was my teacher at Harvard, once wrote that Christianity's shabby treatment of eros was one of its principal shortcomings. Not only had this negative attitude distorted and truncated the tradition itself, it had seeped into its environing cultures and wrought ruin in them as well. The result has been both Puritanism and pornography, both the hysterical denial of one of the most potent forces in human life and its inevitable bursting forth in destructive and degrading ways. What should have been honored and affirmed for its enormous spiritual potential has instead been derided and defamed. I am afraid he was right, at least in some measure.

It is hard to locate exactly where Christianity got off track on the question of the erotic. After all, Plato, the classical philosopher most honored by the church fathers, wrote—in *The Symposium*—one of the most eloquent tributes to eros ever composed. Also Christianity did grow out of ancient Judaism, and has retained within its canon the lovely and highly sensuous "Song of Songs," plainly a love ballad. But somewhere between St. Paul and St. Augustine the legitimate, indeed essential, role of erotic love in the human spiritual life was squeezed out. Virginity rather than marriage, with "a quiver full of children" as the Psalmist puts it, became preferred. I think we are still paying the price for this disastrous enforced divorce thrust on spirit and body, *eros* and *agape*. It is partially to blame for the sex-drenched way our capitalist economy markets its trinkets. As the French philosopher Michel Foucault wrote in *The History of Sexuality*, "What is peculiar to modern societies is not that they consigned sex to a shadow existence, but that they dedicated themselves to speaking of it ad infinitum, while exploiting it as *the* secret." I think he is right, and that this confused focus on sex inevitably elicits a corresponding kind of machismo, which in turn feeds militarism and often inspires vicious violence against women. But in Vrindavan I saw that it does not need to be this way.

I must admit here that when, on rare occasions, I have described my fascination with this particular facet of the measureless Hindu tradition to Hindus, they often seem a little discomfited. They quickly point out that the love between Radha and Krishna is "transcendental" affair, not one of flesh. They do not usually want to pursue the subject. Why? Has my distorted Western sensibility on these delicate matters imposed an already twisted version of sexuality on what I see in the temples and read in the texts? Perhaps it has. Other scholars, more familiar than I am with India, point out that all this fusion of sex and spirit on that subcontinent has not saved the country from male chauvinism, wife beating and its own type of militarism. I can agree with that as well. But still, I think it is infinitely better to welcome *Eros* into the religious tradition rather than to ban him. John Donne made a marvelous move in this direction for Christianity, and there have been others who have contributed to a reconciliation of spirit and body as well. But we have a very long way to go.

Two other features of the Hindu tradition also have a strong attraction for me. In shorthand, I will designate them "Gandhi" and "caring for the gods." Ever since I can remember I have been a consistent admirer of Mahatma Gandhi. It was his unconditional commitment to non-violence that drew me to him. Naturally, he was viewed with favor within the Quaker and pacifist-inclined religious circles in which I grew up. Although I remember a few jokes about what seemed in our small town to be his bizarre dress, nonetheless the respect was there. When he was assassinated, my father, in no sense a devout man, said to me soberly, "Well, they have killed the most Christ-like man on earth, and he wasn't even a Christian." Later I read Gandhi's *My Experiments with Truth* and biographies by Louis Fischer and Erik Erikson. The former tells of visiting Gandhi in the tiny cottage in which he lived in his ashram. The walls were bare, he reports, except for one picture. It was of Jesus, and under it was inscribed the words: "He is our peace." That sentence is from the second chapter of Paul's *Epistle to the Ephesians*, but I am not sure whether Fischer—or even Gandhi—knew that.

Gandhi, of course, was a relentless pursuer of religious synthesis. At his ashram he always asked for readings from the Qur'an and the Bible as well as from the Vedas and the Bhagavad Gita. His favorite religious song was "Lead, kindly Light," a Christian hymn with words by John Henry Cardinal Newman, an Anglican who embraced Roman Catholicism. Its first verse begins with:

> Lead, kindly Light, amid th' encircling gloom,
> Lead Thou me on!
> The night is dark, and I am far from home;
> Lead Thou me on!

Once when someone asked Gandhi why he was so fond of certain Christian prayers and hymns, "And you are not a Christian," the Mahatma answered, "Oh, but I am a Christian. And a Hindu and a Muslim and a Buddhist."

I am sure this answer was partly to throw the questioner off balance. Gandhi loved to do that. But part of it was also genuine. He never converted to or from anything, but simply incorporated into his own spiritual repertory elements he found sustaining and—especially for him—true. This is only one of the many ways in which Gandhi was in advance of his time. The most acute observers of contemporary religion, like the French scholar Danièlle Hervieu-Léger, tell us that more and more people today view the historic traditions not as discrete packages to be accepted or rejected in toto, but more as reservoirs of resources one can dip into selectively in order to assemble one's own collage.

Clerical establishments everywhere, of course, are shocked and horrified by this pick-and-choose tendency. They insist on the integrity of the whole package, and frequently inveigh against what they call "cafeteria religion." The Vatican has issued a stern caveat to Catholics about the danger of engaging in meditation practices derived from Asian spiritual traditions. Protestant preachers periodically voice similar warnings. But theirs is surely a losing cause, and historical evidence suggests that people have been doing more or less the same thing for centuries. The difference is that now there seems to be more to choose from.

I grant that "cafeteria religion" can be carried to excess, and some of the composites I have heard of seem quite wacky. But since I myself am something of a synthesizer, albeit always from what I am sure is a clear Christian point of reference, I am somewhat sympathetic. How can anyone like me who is constantly inspired by Gandhi's example, savors the stories of the Hasidic Rabbi Nachman of Bratslav (1772–1811) and often engages in a form of meditation taught me by a Tibetan lama complain? Further, I insist that not only am I not less of a Christian for all this, but—at least in my eyes—a better one.

The second element of the "Hindu temptation" is the one I call "caring for the gods." This is a concept that will sound utterly jarring to most Christians, and perhaps, to Jews and Muslims as well. Is not God the one who takes care of us? I had grown up with this idea and never questioned it. But then I witnessed a Hindu ceremony that made me think again. This also happened in Vrindavan, where I had encountered the amours of Krishna and Radha. In order to learn all I could during my short visit, I hoisted myself out of bed at a very early hour on the first morning and stumbled into the temple with my eyes still only half open to accompany my host for the opening puja (prayer service) of the day. When we entered I noticed that each of the statues of the deities had been covered for the night with a light semi-transparent white cloth. I also noticed that the devotees accompanying me were carrying small bowls of prasad, a mixture of wheat-flour, sugar and melted butter fat (ghee). Approaching the statues they chanted their prayers respectfully as they gently removed the covers. They were, they told me later, waking the deities up. Then, with a different set of prayers, they set the bowls in front of the deities. It was breakfast time. Later, they distributed the leftover prasad to everyone in the temple.

I thought about that ritual for most of the rest of the day. At first I just shook my head. But then I reconsidered. Was it really all that different from some of the Christian practices I knew? Do not Roman Catholic children garland statues of the Virgin Mary on special days? Do not all Christians offer bread and wine (". . . the fruits of your creation") to God at the beginning of the communion service? Does God need us as much as we are told we need Him or Her? There were certainly analogies.

Still, there was something quite different and worth noting. I could not help recalling the German philosopher Martin Heidegger. He wrote that the human race had begun to go astray into the perils of the modern world when we started thinking of creation as something we should study and control in order to master it. If religious rituals, as I believe, point to truths far beyond themselves, perhaps this gentle ancient Vaishnavite Hindu ritual had something terribly urgent to teach us moderns: we have a responsibility to care for the world, not just to analyze and use it. Here was a profound ecological insight, ensconced in a practice many Christians would find bewildering, possibly even offensive. I am not suggesting that this is the insight Hindus derive from the waking and feeding of the deities. That would be impossible for me to say. But it is what spoke to me, and is a further illustration that what might attract an "outsider" to a tradition is not necessarily what an "insider" would think.

Obviously the interest in the Hindu tradition that I have noted here hardly pushed me toward any kind of conversion. Indeed, it is hard to say just how anyone would "convert to" Hinduism, given its almost infinite capacity to enfold all the gods. Someone once pointed out that modern believers in any tradition, who see their own faith as in some measure a particular expression of a larger and more ample one, as those who talk about a "perennial philosophy" do for example, are in fact embracing "the Hindu solution." There is some truth to this, and although I am not a perennial philosophy devotee, I am sometimes tempted in that direction. Apparently, you do not have to be Jewish to eat rye bread, and you do not even have to use the word "Hindu" to be one.

The Buddhist Temptation

During my participation in the controversial campaign to end the war in Vietnam, like many other people, I had been moved to tears by the pictures of the Vietnamese monk who, to protest the destruction of his country, doused himself with gasoline, set himself on fire and then sat in the posture of prayer until he was consumed by the flames. Soon after that, when some of his fellow monks, like Thich Nhat Hanh, came to America to plead with us to end the awful devastation of their homeland, my admiration deepened. Naturally, I had also read some of the standard Buddhist texts during my theological training. I knew the charming stories of the Enlightened One's childhood, and his discovery of sickness, aging and death. But it was the example of those courageous monks that made Buddhism real to me. Still, I knew very little about Buddhism.

That began to change one day in the early 1970s when I met a truly extraordinary man named Chogyam Trungpa Rinpoche. He was one of the first of the exiled Tibetan lamas to reach America and begin teaching the Buddhist dharma in its typically Tibetan ("Vajrayana") form here.[3] We met shortly after his arrival in America and I arranged for him to give a talk at Harvard. I was impressed with his straightforward, simple but persuasive manner. We kept in touch, and when Trungpa invited me to teach a course on Christianity at the Naropa Institute in Boulder, Colorado, the first Buddhist college in America which he had founded, I happily accepted. For a couple of years during the 1970s I taught there during the summer term, sat in on a couple of classes, read several books and talked at length to the other instructors who were mainly Buddhists. I came to know Trungpa, and his brand of Buddhism, rather well.

Trungpa's goal, almost his obsession, was to "translate" the Buddhist dharma (its teaching) into some idiom that his growing following of mainly young American seekers could appreciate. He struggled arduously at what sometimes seemed to be an impossible task, since many Tibetan words are literally untranslatable into English. He seemed appreciative when I told him he reminded me at times of St. Paul trying to translate an essentially Hebrew message not only into Greek, but also into the categories of the Greco-Roman culture.

At Naropa, nearly all the courses (mine was an exception) were taught from a Vajrayana Buddhist perspective, informed by its prin-

---

3. See Chogyam Trungpa, *Cutting Through Spiritual Materialism* (Boston: Shambala, 1987).

ciples of attentiveness, non-aggression and nonintervention. In biology, the approach was to observe, not to dissect. The same was true in the art classes: just draw what is *there*. In the poetry workshops, led by the late and singular Alan Ginsburg, one was supposed to avoid romanticizing or metaphysical leaps, and write about everyday life as it comes to us. Every student and every faculty member was expected to "sit" at least an hour or two each day in the posture and style of meditation Trungpa and his close disciples taught. "Practice halls" and rooms were provided where one could "sit" with a quiet group for a whole day if desired, punctuated only by the ping of a tiny Tibetan bell announcing a brief ten-minute bathroom break every hour.

The whole scene at Naropa was new and exciting. It was exhilarating to be part of a college that was just coming to birth, especially after teaching at one that had been aging for 350 years. I decided after a few days that, since I was there, I might as well plunge in and experience the closest thing to Tibetan Buddhism available, short of a flight to Lhasa. In addition to attending classes and reading Buddhist literature, I began a "sitting practice" often seated on a balcony overlooking the abrupt ascent of the Rocky Mountains. It was the sight of those peaks which, it was reliably reported, was what had inspired Trungpa, homesick for the Himalayas, to establish the school in Boulder. I was especially touched by the "Lotus Sutra" and, for some reason, by the exquisite stories of Milarepa. I also listened carefully to Trungpa's biweekly dharma talks, which I found utterly fascinating, even though he spoke in a flat monotone and often went on for over an hour. But it was mainly my decision to take up the "practice," sitting cross-legged with my hands folded on my lap on a meditation cushion for one or two hours a day, that made the difference. During one weekend I even joined a group that "sat" for eight hours, with meals served to us while we remained on the cushions.

I learned an immense amount from Trungpa and my colleagues on the teaching staff. The "sitting practice" became a valuable part of my life, and I still engage in it, but with nothing like the rigor and regularity with which I did at Naropa. I met students and faculty in Boulder who had become so serious about the Vajrayana path that they had decided to "take refuge" (*kyabdro*), to embrace the dharma, the sangha (the spiritual community) and the Buddha. These elements are present in all the Buddhist traditions. I had heard that in the Tibetan variant, "the guru" is also added to the list, but I do not think that was the case at Naropa. I had a number of intriguing conversations with people I met there who had taken refuge, some of them formerly Christians but most of them Jews. It had obviously meant a lot to them. Like many conversion experiences into other traditions, for many it had been a life-changing event.

I could not see myself ever "taking refuge." But I clearly wanted to continue some of the practice, and to be informed and enlarged by the wisdom of the broader Buddhist tradition. Was I cheating or free-loading? I had an occasional talk with Trungpa, and—although I never described my dilemma to him explicitly—I could tell that he sensed it. Just before I left for home after my second summer at Naropa, he confided in me that he had never seen me as a candidate for conversion to Buddhism, that in fact he would have advised me against it. But, he added, I did need to find a stream of meditative practice in my own Christian tradition that would supplement the "sitting practice" I had learned in the foothills of the Rockies. He recommended the Benedictines. I should spend time regularly with them on retreats, he said. I thanked him, and as soon as I got home I signed up for a weekend at Glastonbury Abbey, an hour's drive from my home. I have been going there regularly ever since. When I once told the abbot why I had first signed up, he smiled wisely. Apparently, I was not the first Christian to have "passed over" into an Eastern practice, only to return to elements of my own that I had not previously appreciated.

Chogyam Trungpa Rinpoche died a few years after I stopped teaching at Naropa. He was immolated on the grounds of the practice house he had built near St. Johnsbury, Vermont. After his death sensational anecdotes and scandalous rumors, many of which I had already heard, began to circulate, including reports that he had been a drunkard and a womanizer. The stories may be true. But for me they do not detract from the fact that he was a gifted teacher and an eloquent interpreter of an ancient tradition. One learns in studying Buddhism that anyone who has learned anything of the dharma owes an eternal debt of gratitude to the teacher who introduced him to it. I take that instruction seriously. Consequently, I am grateful to the man who introduced me to a practice that has enriched my life, and also assured me that I did not have to abandon my own to benefit from it.

The Muslim Temptation

My exposure to Islam has been very limited, and has occurred under circumstances quite different from those under which I encountered the other world faiths. On a personal level it began twenty-five years ago when a young woman graduate student, a Muslim from Iran, came to my office. She was responding to a call I had issued for teaching assistants to lead discussion groups in a course I was beginning to offer on Jesus for undergraduates.[4] At first I was caught off guard: a Muslim helping teach a course on Jesus? But this young woman quickly outflanked me. She said she was willing to bet that she knew more about Jesus and Christianity than I did about the Prophet Muhammad and the Qur'an. After a few minutes of further conversation I could see she was right. I hired her, but before she left the office she handed me a list she had compiled of references to Jesus (all of them positive) in the Qur'an. She also asked me to look up and reread the gruesome opening lines of Canto XX in Dante's *Inferno*. I did that later, and was reminded of the ugly and vindictive picture the poet draws of Muhammad's eternal punishment, split from chin to anus (Muhammad was seen as a schismatic) so that his bowels gush out eternally. There is no comparable insult to Jesus anywhere in Muslim literature. I looked forward to an interesting semester working with my young guest, but that was not to happen. For some reason she had to return home before classes began, and I never heard from her again.

Since then, however, I have had a constant stream of Muslim students, men and women, in my classes. I have had a Muslim teaching assistant. I converse with helpful and sympathetic Muslim colleagues. I have made a decided effort to compensate for my past deficiencies by reading up on Islamic history and theology. As with some of the previous "temptations," I have never been motivated to convert, but I have found some powerfully attractive features in Islam, features that are not so well developed in Christianity, two of which I will mention here.

First, the theology of Islam generously provides an ample place for Judaism and Christianity as other "religions of the book." And now some Muslim scholars would like to enlarge this category to include any religion that has sacred texts. This provision is not just a dead letter. I have learned in the last few years, as I have spoken to several American interfaith organizations that, time after time, the local Muslim community often supplies a disproportionate share of the support and leadership for these groups. Muslims in America want to be part of our pluralistic religious culture.

It is not only unfortunate, it is tragic that in the tense years that have followed the attacks on the World Trade Center, the minority of Muslims who reject this premise have come to the fore, or at least been given the most publicity. Some scholars now even speak of a "war for

---

4. See Harvey Cox, *When Jesus Came to Harvard: Making Moral Choices Today* (New York: Houghton Mifflin, 2004).

the soul of Islam."[5] I cannot be sure if they are right, but, alas, as a Christian, I know about the kind of internal battles within a tradition that can breed animosity and hatred. I can only hope that somehow the generous and open tradition within Islam comes more to the fore. At least there is ample scriptural warrant for it in the Qur'an, while we have fewer such resources in the Bible, which brims with exclusivist language.

For the remainder of my lifetime I will undoubtedly live in a period where the two largest religions in the world, Christianity and Islam, must learn to come to terms with each other. The needed reconciliation will need to take place on many levels—historical, political and cultural. But it will also necessitate some thorough rethinking of inherited theological positions of both sides.

Christians, with some two billion adherents worldwide, and Muslims, with about one billion, represent the two largest religious groupings in the world. Both communities have much work to do in the next decades to avoid a spiral of violence, a "clash" that is wholly unnecessary and fully avoidable. As a Christian and a theologian, I think one of my tradition's most formidable challenges is to think anew about how Prophet Muhammad might find a place in our religious world view. I know that task is formidable, but it is not impossible. A half-century ago, the vast majority of Christians held the conviction that Christianity has displaced or "superseded" Judaism. In the past fifty years that belief has been officially disowned by the Roman Catholic Church and by most of the Protestant churches as well. A whole new and promising era in Jewish–Christian relations has begun. Could the same kind of things happen in relations between Christians and Muslims?

I am convinced that it could. Muslims already honor Jesus, but so far Christians have no language with which to honor the Prophet. This may be because churches have often been nervous about recognizing what might be called "post-canonical" prophets; that is, those who have appeared after the closing of the biblical canon. "Supercessionism" is the misbegotten theory that Christianity has displaced Judaism, and the church is the new "chosen people of God." But this idea, which seemed so firmly ensconced in the churches, has been rethought and discarded by many churches, including the Catholic Church in a relatively short time. This suggests that what might be called (to coin a

5. See Giles Kepel, *The War for Muslim Minds* (Cambridge, MA: Harvard University Press, 2004), and Tariq Ramadan, *Arabes et Musulmans face à la mondialisation: le défi du pluralisme* (Lyon: Tawhid, 2003).

term) "anti-post-canonicalism" could be rethought and eventually discarded as well.

There are some precedents to work with. Christians not only recognized and accepted the Hebrew prophets, but many also designated figures like Socrates and Plato as prophetic precursors of Jesus. But if God could use great teachers outside the church before Christ, would that not also be possible after him? Mahatma Gandhi has come extremely close to being recognized as a Christian saint. I have seen his image in more than one stained-glass window in Christian chapels. What a marvelous signal it would send if some future pope canonized him officially. This may not be just a utopian fantasy. But even if it did happen, it might be much harder to make a case for Prophet Muhammad.

Still, sainthood is not the only category that might give a status in Christian thought analogous to the position Jesus has in the Muslim spiritual tradition. In fact, Muslims might not like the use of "saint" at all for him. So why not "prophet"? In thinking about this issue I believe Christians in Western countries, in which until quite recently Islam seemed remote and ominous, have much to learn from the testimony of Christians who lived for centuries within the Islamic world, especially before the more recent eruptions of animosities arising mainly from political conflicts. In those areas Christians did often ponder the religious status of the prophet of Islam, and one Syrian bishop suggested that, if not a prophet in the sense of Isaiah or Jeremiah, Muhammad did "walk in the way of the prophets."

Islam does not qualify as an actual "temptation" for me, although I can understand how it does for many people, including thousands of black Americans. Its elegant simplicity, clear rules of living, straightforward doctrines and opulent history of stories, poems and legends have an undeniable appeal to many. No one who has read the Sufi poet Rumi or visited the Al-Hambra in Granada or the Dome of the Rock in Jerusalem can have missed the power of this attractiveness. But, for me today the main question posed by Islam is how my fellow Christians and I, myself, can understand and appreciate it, including the internal conflicts that are rending it, so that we can all live together on the one earth we share?

The Atheist Temptation

Is atheism a *religious* temptation? I think it is. The atheists I know (and I do know a few), unlike the agnostics (of whom I know a lot more), hold a view of reality that exhibits all the marks of a creed. Of course—

despite some fundamentalist Christian and some reductive pseudo-scientific claims to the contrary—there is no irrefutable evidence of whether there is or is not a God. One goes one way or another on this, possibly the most basic of all questions, without ever being fully certain. Faith always involves an element of risk and uncertainty. Further, any "a-theism" is always a denial of some particular idea of God/god. Atheism, as Paul Tillich wrote, is always the shadow or some form of theism. Show me what God you do not believe in; maybe we will discover that I do not believe in that "god" either.

Still, atheism is not just a religion, it is also a religious temptation. This is true at least for me, but I suspect it is also true of many Christians, and possibly of other religious believers as well. It probably announces itself in different ways. Some find the miserable record of Christianity and some other religions sufficient reason to discard any idea of God at all. But this has never seemed to me an intellectually justifiable decision. Whatever awful things have been done in God's name—and there have indeed been many—they do not logically affect the deeper question of the reality of God as such.

For me the "atheist temptation" comes in a different dress. It arrives with overtones of the famous words of Blaise Pascal who confessed that when he thought about the farthest reaches of space and time, ". . . the eternal silence of these infinite spaces terrifies me."

I began having these thoughts and fears when I was quite young, as soon as I learnt that our solar system is only one infinitesimal speck in a cosmos so immense it exceeds the range of normal numbers. It deepened when I learned that one day our planet would be burned to cinders by an exploding sun, which in turn would eventually disappear, along with all the memories and monuments of human life. There would remain only one vast, silent, empty void, with no one there even to observe it. Why would any God concern himself with anything so minute and so transient? Who, quite honestly, has not felt a moment of Pascal's terror in the presence of such vastness?

How have I overcome the atheist temptation? The truth is that I never have. It has become a permanent temptation, a possibility I live with as a man of faith. Those immense empty spaces do not provide an answer. They pose a question. They can bespeak either terror or awe, or probably both. I am convinced that a mature religious faith is one that keeps the questions open, against all attempts at premature foreclosure. If an element of doubt is always an ingredient of faith, as I think it is, I accept it. In one of his most eloquent passages, St. Paul writes: "Now hope that is seen is not hope. For who hopes for what he sees? But if we hope for what we do not see, we wait for it with patience" (*Romans* 8:24, 25).

It may sound paradoxical, but it is by allowing, even welcoming, an element of this "not seeing," of radical uncertainty, into my life, that I can face the terror Pascal spoke of without retreating either to a rigid religiosity that tries to expunge all uncertainty, or to an atheism that pretends to have sure and certain answers it cannot possibly have.

I have tried to catalogue these "temptations," but as I have done so it has become clear that the word temptation is probably misleading. What I have described are all alternative possibilities, different "takes" on a reality we must all ultimately confront and respond to. I do not consider them rivals, or opponents. They are fellow-travelers along the same path, and I welcome them, as I hope they welcome me.

Endings

It is important before concluding this sketch of why I remain a Christian to point out that I believe Christianity is not just a "religion." I do not agree with those theologians, like Karl Barth, who draw a sharp distinction between Christian faith and religion. Among other things, it is surely a religion, at least in this historical epoch. But I am still fascinated by those theologians, like Dietrich Bonhoeffer, who asked us to imagine what form the message of Jesus might assume if, in the long course of evolution, religion as we now define it did disappear. Could there be such a thing as what Bonhoeffer called "a nonreligious interpretation of the Gospel"? Is it possible that religion, as he also once wrote, might be the "outer garb" of the reality Jesus taught and demonstrated?

Bonhoeffer never had the opportunity to formulate an answer to his own questions. As a conspirator in the plot to assassinate Adolf Hitler which misfired so tragically on 20 July 1944, he was hanged by the Gestapo just hours before the concentration camp in which he was being held was liberated by the advancing American armies.

Now that we live in a time of what some see as "resurgent" religion, and secularization appears to be in decline, his query appears somewhat moot. Still, I have never been able to let go of his question. I am convinced that when Jesus spoke about the Kingdom of God, he had something far more ample and comprehensive than some alternative "religious" orientation in mind. He was referring to what Jews had called the *malkuth Yahweh,* the coming era of peace and plenty that includes the full sweep of liberated human living. He meant a utopia infinitely more far-reaching than any of the ones the "utopian" writers

like Thomas Campanella or Thomas More have tried to describe. The
Bible itself even hints at this reality-beyond-religion. There is no word
for "religion" in Old Testament Hebrew. In the New Testament, the
book of Revelation describes the heavenly city, which is to appear on
earth, as one in which ". . . there is no temple," presumably because,
as the same text says, the Spirit of God pervades everything so that no
separate "spiritual" or "religious" sphere is required.

I appreciate this insight for a number of reasons, but it attracts me
mainly because it means that in some important sense one does not
have to be "religious" in order to be a Christian, or to be a follower or
friend of Jesus. It also coheres well with my conviction that the words
"belief" and "believer" are ultimately of limited usefulness in matters
of faith. Bishop Jose-Maria Martini, the Roman Catholic Cardinal of
Milan, once invited me to address an annual meeting he sponsors,
designed especially for what Europeans call "non-believers," of whom
there are many in his highly style-conscious, sparkling and lavishly
prosperous city. But in welcoming the crowd that assembled for the
occasion in a large public hall, the bishop told them he felt the name
of the event was misleading. He said he did not think the world could
be divided between believers and non-believers, but that each of us is a
bit of each, including himself. It was a courageous avowal for a Roman
Catholic cardinal to make. But he was exactly right. I have already said
above that I think there must always be a place for an element of doubt
and uncertainty in faith. Otherwise it is not faith. And I know just too
many "non-believers" who have told me they often have doubts about
their non-belief.

We may be entering a new stage in Christian history. This admixture of belief and doubt is no longer an exception. It is becoming a
principal expression of faith in our time; I think of one of my favorite
writers, my fellow New Englander, Herman Melville, who both foresaw
this stage and personally embodied it. Nathaniel Hawthorne, his close
friend, once wrote about Melville in his notebook: "It is strange how
he persists—and has persisted ever since I have known him. And probably long before—in wandering to-and-fro over these deserts. . . . He
can neither believe, nor be comfortable in his unbelief; and he is too
honest and courageous to try to do one or the other."[6] The editor of
the writer of the essay from which the above quotation is taken goes
on to observe, "There can indeed be no Christian faith worthy of the
name (unless it be among the cherubim and seraphim) without this

---

6. See Randall Stewart, ed., *The English Notebooks by Nathaniel Hawthorne* (New
York: The Modern Language Association of America, 1941), 432-33.

struggle between belief and unbelief, and there can be no true human sympathy without it."[7]

Jack Miles, the widely respected Christian scholar and writer, once described himself as a "practicing Christian, but not necessarily a believing one." His statement, which may sound odd to some, makes perfect sense to me. Belief is not the same as faith. Belief hovers near the upper, cognitive stratum of the self. It can come and go. It can be strong one day, weak the next. But faith locates itself in a deeper dimension. It is really a matter of fundamental life orientation. The early Christians spoke of their faith as the "way." But in its journey through the Greco-Roman cultural landscape, Christianity became increasingly identified with a set of beliefs that were then organized into creeds. This happened because some Christians felt the need to distinguish themselves sharply from those around them and from those among them who—they thought—were getting the message wrong. But it did not have to happen that way, and it may well be that Christianity has emphasized "belief" entirely too much, and is now transmuting itself into a stage that is "beyond belief." The biblical text for this era might turn out to be the words spoken to Jesus by the distraught father of the young man possessed by the demon: "Lord, I believe; help thou my unbelief" (*Mark* 9:24).

It is here that the newly emerging conversation among the traditions may especially benefit mine. If historically Christianity has overemphasized "belief," it is a genuine strength of some of the other traditions that many of them do not. But this does not mean that we as Christians should merely discard our creeds. Rather, in future years we should understand them in a more mature way. We should appreciate them not as fences to separate us from other people, but as valiant attempts on the part of some Christians at certain specific moments in history to rethink their faith in the light of radically new cultural environments. However, we too now find ourselves in yet another new environment. We are entering an age of unprecedented religious interaction and a global world torn by hunger, injustice and the appalling threat of nuclear catastrophe. But it is also a world bursting with fresh promise and new possibilities. I cannot conceive of another epoch in which I would prefer to have lived.

---

7. See Nathan A. Scott, Jr., "The Vision of Evil in Hawthorne and Melville," in Nathan A. Scott, Jr., ed., *The Tragic Vision and the Christian Faith* (New York: Association Press, 1957), 241.

20

The Absence of God (2012)

Harvey Cox and Stephanie Paulsell contributed a volume on Lamentations and the Song of Songs to a multi-volume theological commentary on the Bible (Louisville: Westminster John Knox Press, 2012). Cox supplied the commentary on Lamentations, from which this chapter is taken.

> The Lord abandoned me to my sins,
> and in their grip I could not stand.
>   (1:14 REB)

What do I do when God abandons me? This question is one that
has a long and continuous history in the idiom of the Bible. Jesus
croaks it out on Golgotha while dying on the cross, and his words are
so charged that translators preserve the original Aramaic: "*Eli, Eli,
lema sabachthani,*" before they translate it, "My God, my God, why have
you forsaken me?" (Matt. 27:46). The deepest sorrow The Poet of Lamentations faces is that God is gone, or seems to be gone. She feels abandoned.

This wrenching sense of God's absence was once only the province
of the most daring of saints, like John of the Cross, or mystics, like the
anonymous writer of *The Cloud of Unknowing*. But what was once the
experience of a spiritually privileged few has in modern times become
much more general, if in a somewhat different key. The saints felt the
absence of God as a heart-stopping terror. Today many people sense
God's absence with a shrug of regret or indifference.

The "dark night of the soul" robbed John of the Cross of his sleep. It
bothers today's casual atheist or agnostic only occasionally. He or she
does not agonize over it.

Still, what both Lamentations and the writings of John of the Cross
reveal is that an acutely felt awareness of the absence of God can itself
be a religious experience. There is something awe-full about it, in the

sense of awe inspiring. For a significant number of people the question today is not *whether* one experiences the absence of God, but what one does in response to that experience. Like staring at the sun or contemplating one's own death, it is not an experience that invites one to stay with it for long. Consequently, for many people, the typical response is to pursue distraction. The result is the proliferation of instant communication devices. A recent study discovered one teenage girl who sends 2,700 text messages a month. But this is only one symptom of a culture-wide attention deficit disorder.

Still, as the twentieth century fades and the twenty-first rushes on, something else is happening. For more and more people the absence of God has sharpened into an awareness that something—it is not clear what—is missing from their lives. Surveys in the United States do not reveal any substantial growth in the number of atheists. They remain a small minority. But the surveys do reveal a steady growth in the number of people who declare that they are "spiritual but not religious." This self-designation means different things to different people. For most it implies that they have not forsaken some hope for a relationship to God, transcendence, or mystery. But they do not trust the institutional scaffolding or doctrinal wrapping in which the religious institutions they are familiar with teach or preach about this mystery. They do not want to accept something on someone else's authority, whether the authority is wearing a clerical collar or a white lab coat. They are "seekers." They want to find out for themselves, to test things out in the petri dishes of their own lives. The writer of Lamentations would understand them. She does not trust the sanctified representatives of her religion, and if there had been scientists in that time she would not have trusted them either:

> there is no direction from priests,
> and her prophets have received
> no vision from the Lord.
> (2:9 REB)

One of the most startling aspects of this often-overlooked biblical book is that the religious experience it describes replicates in an almost uncanny way the experience of both modern and postmodern humanity. For The Poet the awareness of God's remoteness is made more vivid by the stabbing recognition that it was not always this way.

> Why do you always forget us?
> Why do you forsake us so long?

Restore us to yourself, O Lord,
that we may return;
renew our days as of old
unless you have utterly rejected us
and are angry with us beyond measure.
                                        (5:20-22 NIV)

The big question here is, Has God rejected us, or have we rejected God?

I can still remember the shock I felt when I picked up *Time*'s April 8, 1966, edition and saw on its cover: "Is God Dead?" The article was an oversimplified and even sensationalized story about four then-current Protestant theologians, William Hamilton, Paul van Buren, Gabriel Vahanian, and Thomas Altizer. The four worked in very disparate ways. Hamilton derived much of his perspective from Dietrich Bonhoeffer's suggestion of a "religionless Christianity." Van Buren was influenced by analytic philosophy and by the dialectical theology of Karl Barth. Vahanian was steeped in European cultural history and linguistic studies but was also influenced by Barth. Altizer came to his position from a very different direction. A student of Asian religions, he was fascinated by the emphasis on "nothingness" in Buddhism and saw in it a connection to Western nihilism. All four found in Nietzsche's announcement of the death (or rather murder) of God in *Thus Spake Zarathustra* a powerful metaphor that seemed to bring their disparate thoughts into focus. The so-called death of God movement these men represented made a considerable splash for a time. But within a couple years it had faded away and was often even dismissed as a fad.

But rightly understood this movement was not just a vogue. What these thinkers were attempting to do was to respond to something that, at that time at least, appeared to be an indisputable fact. Whereas for centuries of Western history the reality of God had seemed to be a commonplace, increasingly this was no longer the case. In his massive study, *A Secular Age*, the Canadian philosopher Charles Taylor argues that our present spiritual situation is "historical." What he means is that we locate ourselves today as having "overcome a previous condition." This means that our past is contained within our present condition and that we do not understand ourselves or our present world unless we are clear about where we came from.

Taylor's insight is critical not just for understanding The Poet of Lamentations but for understanding our present spiritual situation, which he calls a "predicament." Who we are today spiritually does define itself in part by who we once were, and the meaning of that self-definition varies radically for different people. For some we are just leaving behind a past of superstition and obscurantism, if not fast enough. For others we are losing an invaluable heritage, and all too quickly. Those of us who try to make the message of the Bible available today must therefore talk to (at least) these two highly disparate audiences. There is also an emerging third public, constituted in part by the "spiritual but not religious" people mentioned above.

An important distinction must be drawn between "atheism" on the one hand and the "death" or "absence" of God on the other. For these theologians, although none of them expressed it explicitly, the late twentieth century was very much like the mood of The Poet of Lamentations. There had once been a God, or at least the widespread belief in God. Now, as The Poet of that book puts it:

> you have covered yourself with a cloud
> beyond reach of our prayers.
> (3:44 REB)

The stark difference between atheism and the loss or absence of God is that in atheism there is no sense of loss. It elicits a shrug or a smile or sometimes enormous anger against all theists. Even the somewhat hyperbolic phrase "death of God" suggests that there was once something that is now missing. How one responds to that empty space is, of course, the daunting question. For Nietzsche it was a kind of liberation, although even for him the "God" who had been killed was the "God" of Western, bourgeois piety. For others the emptiness was something that needed to be affirmed and embraced. For Altizer at least it meant accepting the utter self-emptying (*kenosis*) of God with all its radical implications.

While the brief "death of God" theology wave was cresting, some critics grouped me as one of the writers in this school (if it can be called a "school"). But I never was. I wrote the final chapter of *The Secular City* as a critique of the "death of God" theology. Although I appreciated what these theologians were trying to say, I thought they did not sufficiently grasp how much the "God" whose death they spoke of was a provincial, Western construction, an *idea* of God that was a product of their own somewhat narrow intellectual milieu.

Ironically, at the time they were writing, another powerful view of God was also coming to birth. Among Christians in what was then called the "Third World," now more commonly referred to as the "Global South," an understanding of God as the judge of Western imperial religiosity was coming to birth. The various liberation theologies, especially those that sprang up in Latin America, were saying to the death-of-God theologians, "So your God is dead! Well, good riddance. The God we trust is the vindicator of the poor, the one who casts down the mighty from their thrones and raises those of low degree." This theology of liberation not only seemed more biblical but resonated strongly with millions of destitute and struggling people outside the charmed circle of European and American illuminati.

In any case, although the death-of-God thinking seemed to sink out of sight for a few decades, it has recently made a bold new appearance, albeit under different auspices and with a different outcome. Now the discussion has been taken up by a congeries of younger philosophers and theologians. Some seem to be doing both these disciplines or cultivating the space in between them. Two of the key thinkers in this group are the American John Caputo and the Italian Gianni Vattimo. Caputo places himself in the "spiritual predicament" Charles Taylor describes, but he refuses to accept the either/or of atheism or traditional theism. He does not see our postmodern era as either a brave new world of human emancipation (there are still too many forms of bondage around us) or as a plunge into degeneration. Like Vattimo he rejects the words *desecularization* or *resacralization* because they seem merely to be reversing previous patterns.

With reference to current debates between atheists and theists, Caputo draws on his Catholic background. He recalls that Thomas Aquinas taught that God cannot be described either as "existing" or "not existing" since God transcends both these human categories. Caputo also insists on a sharp distinction between Christendom and Christianity, the first being a territorial designation from what was indeed another era, the second being the name of a movement that is still very much on the move. He also cites favorably Søren Kierkegaard's trenchant *Attack upon "Christendom"* and Bonhoeffer's "religionless Christianity" for a "world come of age," which the German pastor and martyr alludes to cryptically in *Letters and Papers from Prison.* Caputo believes that with the death of Christendom, Christianity can now shed much of the institutional and doctrinal baggage it carried for centuries, and that it has a vital message to demonstrate and to preach in this new "spiritual situation." He describes this situation as one in which growing numbers of people have lost confidence in both what he calls "scientific positivism" and "transcendent authority." His analysis may sound overly intellectual to some, but he puts his finger on a sentiment that is also widespread among young people today. It was hit upon well in "If I Ever Lose My Faith in You," a song made popular almost two decades ago by Sting: "I lost my faith in science and progress . . . I lost my belief in the holy church."

This is a kind of pop postmodernism, but Caputo would agree. He believes postmodernism has cut the ground from under both traditional theism and atheism since the attacks on God by the deconstructionist critics have now boomeranged back on those critics. It has also undermined the serene confidence some modern people once had in the capacity of science to fashion a brave new world. The postmodern sword cuts many ways. What we see now he says, in a gnomic phrase, is something like "the death of the death of God."

Caputo also believes that Christians have nothing to fear from this seemingly radical, even blasphemous language. The God of the Christian gospel is the one who laid aside his divinity to become man and experience a human death. This is the core of Paul's *kenosis* passage in Philippians 2. God's power, Caputo asserts, echoing Paul again, is a weakness that is stronger than the strength of any human. God's sovereignty is not a matter of grandiose omnipotence but of self-emptying love.

I cannot help feeling that The Poet of Lamentations might find some kinship with these twenty-first-century thinkers. Otherwise how could he or she have combined in a few short verses at the end of the book phrases like, "Lord, your reign is for ever, your throne endures from age to age" with "Why do you forget us?" and "you have utterly rejected us" (5:19, 20, 22 REB)? Could it be that there is a strange kinship between an intense awareness of the absence of God and an intense appreciation of God's reality?

21

The Baptist Motif (2012)

This lecture was delivered at Wake Forest Divinity School on January 14, 2012, for the inauguration of the first Chair of Baptist Studies.

My great theological teacher Paul Tillich coined the term "Protestant Principle," the prophetic-critical perspective, which he said must be held in tension with what he called the "Catholic Substance." He argued that although the Protestant Principle, the capacity for constructive critique, had first appeared with the Hebrew prophets, it had been most clearly expressed during the sixteenth-century Protestant Reformation. He contended further that the Protestant Principle had virtually disappeared from institutional Protestantism by the twentieth century, but had immigrated into other historical movements.

Echoing Tillich, when I speak about the "Baptist Motif," I prefer the term "motif" rather than "principle." A motif is defined as "a distinctive feature or theme," usually in an artistic, musical or literary work. I apply it here to the religious and social history of Baptists in which I will highlight two distinctive features. The first has been called "*soul liberty*" or "freedom of conscience," with its logical consequence that the state has no jurisdiction over matters of faith. It was Roger Williams, the founder of the Baptist movement in America, who staked out this element in the Baptist motif. The second is "*the beloved community*," the vision of a just and peaceful commonwealth which Baptists are called to help shape. This element was best articulated by another American Baptist, Martin Luther King, Jr. These two components of the Baptist motif were intended to work together and to complement each other.

I prefer the word "motif" because "principle" can sometimes sound too rigid, whereas in Baptist history this motif appears, like a musical figure, in several varied and nuanced expressions. Once stated, it is subject to expansion and enlargement, appearing, as it does in music, in different keys and harmonic variations, but always identifiable. It also surfaces mightily in certain individuals, often to be lost or obscured by what follows. Finally I wish to echo Tillich in contending that, alas, although historically Baptists gave birth to and nourished this motif, we have no monopoly on it, and we stand today in grave danger of losing it.

Roger Williams

As a New Englander and a Baptist I have for years taken special pride in the founder of our movement, namely Roger Williams. Williams was born in England around 1603 (he died in 1683), but lived most of his adult life in my own neighborhood. A Puritan dissident, he fled to the Massachusetts Bay Colony in 1631. A graduate of Cambridge University, he had learned Greek, Latin, Hebrew, Dutch, and French. When he arrived in America he was determined to learn the language of the indigenous people and was one of the first to prepare a grammar of it. A brilliant scholar and gifted preacher, he was called to minister to the Boston church, a singular honor. But Williams refused. That congregation, he contended, had not formally separated itself from the Church of England. Instead he became the minister in Plymouth, a separatist congregation. But within a short time he took another step that evoked a sharp negative response from the Puritan powers-that-be. He denied that the civil authorities had any right to enforce "the first table of the Law" since it involved relations between the individual and God, matters in which the civil powers had no authority. He granted that these authorities could enforce the Second Table, on stealing, adultery, and murder, but also insisted they could not require non-believers to swear an oath in God's name, which seemed to him an act of hypocrisy.

At first the Puritan colonial authorities considered Williams something between a bother and a pest. But they shrugged and decided that his behavior, however unseemly, was something that might, with forbearance, be overlooked. But then he stepped over the line. In a series of sermons he denied the validity of the Royal Charter that was the colony's basis for legal existence. What right did the king have, Williams asked, to expropriate the lands of the indigenous people and hand them to someone else? Every square inch of land, he contended, must be purchased from the Indians at a fair price. With this bold move, Williams had veered beyond ecclesiastical disputes, however important to the rulers, and undercut the very foundation stone of the Bay Colony's claim to legitimacy. He had gone too far. In 1635 the

Great and General Court of Massachusetts Bay ordered him to leave
the colony forthwith.

Williams, however, showed no indication that he was packing. The
officials lost patience. Then, warned by friends that an armed posse
was on the way to apprehend him and ship him back to England, where
he would probably have been executed, Williams fled into the thick
forests in the face of a fierce blizzard. Fortunately, his advocacy for
indigenous rights and his patient study of the Indian language had
won him many friends among the Narragansett, so eventually they
sheltered him until he was outside the colony's jurisdiction. Once he
was safely camped he founded a town he called "Providence" to honor
the divine guidance he believed had led him safely through his hazard.
Then he started a new colony that came to be called Rhode Island.
There he insisted not just on "tolerance," but on total soul liberty. Williams was utterly serious that Rhode Island should welcome all peoples
without reference to their religious convictions. The colony became
a refuge with the Puritan "heretic," Anne Hutchison, moving there,
joined by many other dissidents. The Bay State Puritans sneered on
it as "the cesspool of New England," but its reputation for freedom
of religion also attracted Jews and later Roman Catholics. In Sidney
Mead's magisterial *Religious History of the American People,* he writes
of Rhode Island, "Conceived in Puritan 'heresy,' and maturing as a
remarkable seat of religious pluralism, it provides both an invaluable
insight into the 'left wing' of the Puritan movement and an important
anticipation of American problems and solutions." Furthermore, one
might add, the Baptists started the whole thing.

Where did Williams' deep commitment to "soul liberty" come from?
It appeared early at both the intellectual and personal levels. He read
and absorbed John Milton's "Areopagetica." But more importantly he
once witnessed the branding of "S.S." standing for "sower of sedition"
on the cheek of a dissenter by English officials. The seared scar left its
mark on Williams as well. There is a common thread, a motif, running
through his youthful career. The idea of either church or civil magistrates either enforcing or banning a religious belief or behavior on
anyone evoked his deep revulsion—on biblical grounds—to any interference in the sanctuary of the soul (later he would call it "soul rape").

The new Rhode Island colony had a rocky beginning. The leaders
of the Massachusetts Bay, concerned with Williams and his heretical
ideas just across the border, tried to annex it. But Williams fought
back, and even travelled to England to secure a separate charter for
the new settlement, the land for which he had purchased from the

Narragansett Indians. The charter was eventually granted, and became immediately one of the most powerful and influential documents in the history of religious liberty. It declared that people of all spiritual persuasions—bar none—were to enjoy complete religious liberty in that realm. It explicitly included "papists, Jews, Protestants and Turks." The charter has been called the "Magna Charta of religious freedom." It is not surprising that the first Jewish immigrants to America came to Rhode Island, or that the oldest synagogue in America is there. But the mention of "Turks" may be for us today even more arresting. "Turks" was the word then used for all Muslims. Here Williams is following Thomas Helwys, found of the Baptist movement in England, who also explicitly mentioned "Turks" as among those who should be granted "soul freedom." Helwys is vital to the Baptist motif as a bridge between soul liberty and the beloved community because it was in his time that early Baptists took a decisive step. They disagreed with Mennonites and some other Anabaptists and taught that Baptists could and should participate in civil society and even become magistrates. Soul liberty should enable people to contribute to a beloved community.

It was not long after the charter that Williams decided christening children "did not a Christian make," and declared himself a Baptist. His reasoning was consistent. Was not baptizing infants in fact a form of religious coercion since the babies were unable to give consent? He then founded, in Providence, what was and still is called "The First Baptist Church of America." Not long after, however, he felt too confined even in the Baptist fold and began to style himself a "seeker." He might even be comfortable today with some of the people who call themselves "spiritual but not religious."

These are all things for which Williams is well known. But his teaching included other elements that are not so widely recognized. When he resided in Massachusetts, for example, he bridled under the governor's practice of handing out large land grants to men who already had considerable wealth and standing. Therefore, when he founded the new Rhode Island colony and then ruled as chief administrator his policy was first to purchase the land from the Indians and then to make grants to anyone who arrived, regardless of their existing wealth or social position. At that time land was the principal source of wealth, so this amounted to a radical redistributive policy. Rhode Island was also the first colony in America to make slavery illegal. Here Williams exhibits the link between soul liberty and the beloved community.

One can easily see why someone might become an admirer of Roger Williams. Recently, the University of Chicago law professor Martha

Nussbaum says she has "rediscovered" him and claims that he is even more important than John Locke as the philosopher of liberty and freedom of conscience. John M. Barry has just published a dazzling biography entitled *Roger Williams and the Creation of the American Soul: Church, State, and the Birth of Liberty.* One might even say that now in the early years of the twenty-first century we are witnessing a Roger Williams boom.

As important as the insights of Williams and the early Baptists are I believe their theological thinking also contained anticipations that would only come to fruition years later in our own time. I will mention two.

First, imbedded deep in the idea of separation of church and state is the recognition that in order to bring a constructive critique to bear on any society, *one must be rooted in a community that is not enclosed in that society.* As Robert Bellah has reminded us in his monumental *Religion in Human Evolution,* previous to the Hebrew prophets (and their analogs in some other cultures) the king was divine and the priest was king. There was as yet no differentiation. God spoke to the people through the king. But in the Bible we witness something new: a constant tension between the prophets and the kings. The prophets insisted that the people were grounded in a covenant with God that transcended the royal order. Only when this differentiation appeared in human history was there the vital point of leverage for bringing an ethical demand to bear on the culture as a whole. Thus whenever the priest/prophet tries to usurp the king's role, or the king the prophet's, the culture is in danger of relapsing into an undifferentiated tribal cult lacking a capacity for self-criticism.

The history of Israel is a saga of this drama. Samuel confronts Saul; Nathan confronts David; a series of later prophets confront a series of kings. The story culminates, but does not end, with Jesus, the heir of the prophetic movement, confronting Pilate, the embodiment of the regime of divine Caesar. We do not have many kings today, but we still nurture a vital differentiation between the secular and the spiritual. The reason for this "separation" is not, however, so that the two inhabit separate realms, but so that the spiritual can "speak truth to power" from a perspective to which the secular powers as such have no access. When Jesus says, "My kingdom is not of this world," he does not mean his kingdom has nothing to do with this world. He means that the community he embodies and speaks for cannot be enclosed in "this world." This is one underlying theological premise of the separation of church and state.

There is a second insight just beneath the surface of this Baptist motif, one that is especially important in our era of increasing religious diversity. The Anabaptists refused to force any religious practice on anyone, and some even refused to use force for any reason because they believed that all people are created in the image of God. As the Quakers, early cousins of the Baptists, put it, "there is that of God in every man." When Williams eventually left the Baptist fold and styled himself a "seeker," he suggested that God might indeed speak to him through people with diverse religious views. To welcome "papists and Turks" to the colony was to recognize that God's truth cannot be exclusively contained in any one person or belief. Roger Williams is rightly credited with introducing universal religious tolerance into America, and thus into the world. But as his ideas matured, he went far beyond mere tolerance. He not only permitted religious diversity, he welcomed, indeed invited it.

Are Baptists today in danger of losing the heritage of soul liberty and the beloved community? Have we sometimes overemphasized the "soul" and lost sight of the larger community? Hyper-individualism has long been the Baptist's Achilles' heel. Harold Bloom in his often quite unsatisfactory book *The American Religion* devotes a chapter to E. Y. Mullins, who must be credited with vigorously carrying forward Williams' "soul liberty." But Bloom also writes something that is just close enough to the truth to be painful. The ideal of American Christianity, of which Baptists are the most typical, is to "be alone in the garden with Jesus." It is a religion, he contends, that can easily evaporate into a kind of Gnosticism, in which the world simply disappears into a mist.

I use the word "painful" to describe Bloom's assertion because he knows this Baptist weakness. Take for example a song we all sang in Sunday School, "In the Garden." Although it is frowned upon in most circles today, many of us could probably sing all the verses from memory.

> *I* come to the garden *alone*, while the dew is still on the
> roses,
> And the voice I hear falling on my ear, the Son of God
> discloses.
> And He walks with *me* and He talks with *me*,
> And He tells *me* I am His own . . . (italics all mine)

There is in fact an individualistic, even narcissistic, strain on our faith that often dilutes the fullness of the biblical tradition. What, we might ask, was Jesus *doing* in the garden in the first place? He was there because he knew he was the object of a search party organized by the priestly elite through whom the Romans were tyrannizing his people. They were enraged by his behavior in confronting the corruption of the Temple. Jesus was there to seek God's guidance and strength in order to go forward into his next confrontation with imperial power. He was not alone in the garden for long. He was soon accosted by a posse brandishing spears and clubs. The dew on the roses was soon trampled by leather boots. Roger Williams started with soul liberty and reached toward the beloved community. It required another Baptist preacher who lived 300 years after Williams to take the next decisive step.

Martin Luther King, Jr.

As I turn to Martin Luther King, Jr., my remarks will take on a more personal tone. This is because despite my apparent antiquity, I never knew Roger Williams. But I did know Martin Luther King rather well. I first met him in the summer of 1956 during the Montgomery bus boycott. We shared a common interest as Baptist ministers and students of Paul Tillich's theology. Later, at his request I helped organize the Boston chapter of the Southern Christian Leadership Conference and then participated in several demonstrations under his guidance. In 1966 he invited me to deliver a principal address to the annual meeting of the SCLC. What can be said about Martin Luther King, one of the towering figures of the twentieth-century American landscape, that has not already been said?

This: that he was not just a "civil rights leader" or even a Nobel Prize winner. His life is inexplicable unless we begin with the fact that he was born and bred, and born again, and lived and died a Baptist, and indeed a Baptist minister. Hardly any of the many biographies or the documentaries that are rolled out on the holiday named for him gives this salient fact—that he was a Baptist minister—the weight it deserves. The oversight is sometimes almost absurd. On the night of the day he was assassinated I watched a TV news program with its cameras trained on Abyssinian Baptist Church in Harlem where a service of mourning was in progress. "It is not surprising that they should be having a service in this church," the clueless TV commentator mumbled, "because after all Dr. King's father was a Baptist minister." "His father," I yelled at the screen, and thought "you will never understand this complex and courageous man unless you recognize that not only was he *himself* a Baptist minister, but that he considered his entire life a ministry.

I have even heard it said that Martin Luther King "left his pulpit" to lead the civil rights movement. But King never left his pulpit. His pulpit went with him wherever he went. He preached and enacted the Gospel of Jesus Christ in churches and on picket lines and in jail cells, in decaying urban slums and in the marble halls of governance. His life was a personification of the love that God demonstrated in coming as a healer into this broken world in Jesus Christ, and his lifelong goal was what he liked to call "the Beloved Community," another way of saying, "the Kingdom of God." He was a living embodiment of the Spirit of God which mends broken hearts, challenges the arrogant misuse of power, and inspires us to seek a city in which justice and mercy rule. On this day, when we inaugurate the first ever Chair of Baptist Studies, I contend that any portrait of Martin Luther King that overlooks or short circuits his being a Baptist Christian minister is incomplete at best and misleading at worst. But why is this mistake so often made?

There are, I fear, a number of reasons. The first is that most of the people who write the biographies and make the documentaries know precious little about Baptists or Baptist history. This is not surprising since we Baptists ourselves know very little of our own history. The other reason, one must sadly admit, is that during his short ministry, cut off by a bullet in Memphis, many if not most of the Baptists in America, North and South, conspicuously disapproved of what he was doing. He was viewed as a troublemaker and rabble-rouser who was "pushing too hard," or "going too fast." His own fellow clergy often turned against him, just as the religious establishment had opposed the rabble-rousing rabbi from Galilee. His "Letter from a Birmingham Jail," remember, was written to the *clergy* of that city. When he spoke from the Lincoln Memorial in August 1963, can anyone deny his quotations from Isaiah and Amos represented a powerful *sermon?* What kept him going despite constant death threats, divisions in his own ranks, and the opposition that rose up furiously against him when from the pulpit of that historic Baptist Church on Riverside Drive in New York City he risked losing supporters by taking a firm stand against the Vietnam War?

What sustained him, according to his own testimony, was that while seated at his kitchen table after yet another bombing, God had promised him that He would "never, no never, leave me alone." I have seen that line cited many times, but few of those who cite it know that it is a quotation from the Gospel of John (11:28) or that it is a line from the hymn "Oh Lord God Almighty," that King must have sung many times throughout his life. What sustained him, he said, was a serene confidence that he had "cosmic allies," and that love throbbed at the heart of a universe that was "bent toward justice."

So here we have two great practitioners of the Baptist motif, and they share some striking similarities. If Williams' early years were marked by the persecution of dissidents in the pre-commonwealth England of James I, King's early years were lived in the segregated world of pre–civil rights America. Each in his own way witnessed and tasted the pain of a discrimination that robbed people of dignity, that was enforced by both church and state, and that was ultimately backed up by the threat of imprisonment or death. Of course, just as Williams had immersed himself in the classics as well as the Bible, King pondered Reinhold Niebuhr and wrote his dissertation on Paul Tillich and Henry Nelson Wieman. But King was always the son of the Black Church. Both Williams and King nurtured visions of a free and radically equalitarian church in a society that reflected these values.

Yes, there are some differences between these two prophets of the Baptist motif. If Williams emphasized individual and personal "soul liberty," King's emphasis was on what he called "the beloved community." But Williams also insisted that property in Rhode Island, his century's source of wealth, be equally distributed, and that slavery be outlawed. He believed not only that love constituted the inner core of each person, but that love was the force that bound the constellations together. Love throbbed at the heart of the universe itself, and although there would be defeats and setbacks, the overall direction of the cosmos was bending toward justice, the structural expression of love.

King's unwavering insistence on nonviolence was not just a strategy. He believed that in the end love was more powerful than hatred and division. He insisted that anyone participating in a march he led should not only act nonviolently, but must root out all hatred from his heart. Otherwise he told them in no uncertain terms: "Don't march."

King's vision of the beloved community was thoroughly holistic. Body, mind, and spirit were all included. In the speech he gave in Oslo in 1963 upon accepting the Nobel Peace Prize he said, "I have the audacity to believe that peoples everywhere can have three meals a day for their bodies, education and culture for their minds, and dignity, equality, and freedom for their spirits." Martin Luther King picked up where Williams had left off. He knew, from experience, that tyranny in the political and economic realms could poison and distort souls. He knew the two could not be separated.

So, how are we as Baptists doing with the "Baptist motif"? The record, I fear, is a mixed one. We can be thankful that Baptist leaders and thinkers in the twentieth century like Walter Rauschenbusch, James Dunn, Bill Leonard, and Bill Moyers have combined the visions of Williams and Martin Luther King. They have taught us that the prophetic tradition, the Protestant principle, and the Baptist motif not only permit, they *require* Christians to plunge into the civic realm to promote justice and peacemaking. Inspired by their example, we have decided not to tarry in the garden forever but to step out into the arena "where cross the crowded ways of life." In doing so, we have learned to be very careful about how we understand the phrase "separation of church and state." For Williams, the intent of this notion was to protect religion from state interference. The intent of King was to bring the prophetic voice of this religion to bear on the injustice and inequality of the society at large. But today the idea of "separation of church and state" is often misused to pillory Christians who strive, as Williams and King did, for peace and justice in a world of wars and inequity. It was often brandished against Martin Luther King, and its meaning is twisted so as to oppose any actions by Christians or other religiously committed people in the public arena.

For Williams and later Jefferson the phrase meant that the state has no authority to impose or to prohibit any religious belief or practice. It does not mean that it can protect *my* religion but I can call upon it to limit *yours*. It does not mean that the government can favor mine but not yours. Still there are some Baptists today who want the government to impose or sanction a prayer for public school children. But we want it to be *our* prayer, not *their* prayer. Some want these children to be required to listen to a Bible reading, but it must be *our* Bible, not *their* Bible.

Who should be welcomed into the public square? Roger Williams quickly had to face this test. Williams could not stand Quakers. A man of resolute faith himself, he strongly disagreed with their beliefs and was exasperated by their often noisy and disruptive practices. The other colonies all urged him to join them in banning Quaker immigration. But he refused. Quakers, as distasteful as they were to him, would be welcomed into Rhode Island as long as they abided by the civil law like everyone else. In recent years, people who still want to use state power to enforce or delimit religion have sometimes used the tactic of insisting that someone's religious practice is "not a real religion," but only a "cult."

So what is a cult? We should remember that there was a time when nearly everyone considered Baptists a cult, and a dangerous one at that. We were hounded, burned, and drowned by Lutherans, Catholics, and Calvinists. Let us be careful about deploying the word "cult." Some years ago I found myself in a court as an expert witness in a case about whether the Society for Krishna Consciousness was a "real religion" and thus deserved First Amendment protection. I have little sympathy for this religious movement. But I am a staunch defender of "soul liberty." I started by telling the judge and jury that the worship of Krishna antedated Christianity by centuries and that it claimed millions of people in India and around the world. But as the cross examiner pressed me relentlessly I changed my approach. I told the court I would not continue to testify because the court had no authority to decide what was or was not a "real religion." In saying this, I thought I saw Roger Williams smiling down on me.

For us in the United States today Williams' welcoming of "papists and Turks" is the key. "Papists" was the term used for Roman Catholics. "Turks" was the term then applied to all Muslims no matter where they were from. Today in America Catholics enjoy all the privileges of citizenship and have been elected to the highest office. It is hard to remember that when Williams insisted they should be welcomed to his new colony, Catholics were viewed by many as the religiously inspired terrorists of the day, and not without reason. It had been less than fifty years earlier, in 1588, that the mighty Spanish armada at the orders of Catholic Philip II had been sent to overthrow Protestant Queen Elizabeth. If the armada's mission had been successful Philip would have deposed Elizabeth. The armada was a hugely expensive failure. But it came close enough to victory to leave a sense of bitter hatred and suspicion of "papists" roiling in English hearts. Then in 1605, less than twenty years later, English officials uncovered a plot involving one Guy Fawkes to blow up the building of Parliament and to assassinate King James I. Most English people therefore viewed papists not only as religiously motivated zealots but as fanatics, intent on destroying the English state. They were the "international terrorists" of the day. Though they were banned from all the colonies, Williams insisted on giving them equal rights with everyone else in Rhode Island.

Today we no longer view Catholics as international terrorists. But many people, here and in Europe, would like to delimit the religious freedom of Muslims or ban them from immigration. Switzerland has outlawed the building of minarets anywhere in the country. France has banned the wearing of head scarves in school. One leading politician in Holland wants to outlaw the Qur'an. The people of Murfrees-boro, Tennessee, have succeeded so far in preventing a mosque from being built in their town. And in Gainesville, Florida, one minister, Rev. Terry Jones, announced he would burn 200 Qur'ans and wanted to initiate a national "Burn a Qur'an" day. It is clear where Roger Williams with his steadfast advocacy of soul liberty, and Martin Luther King, who not only eschewed overt acts of violence but also the hatred that poisons the heart, would stand on all this.

How should those of us who today are still motivated by the Baptist motif respond to this upsurge of bigotry? The answer seems self-evident: the test of soul liberty is not whether we insist on it for ourselves, but whether we insist on it for everyone, especially (as was the case of Williams regarding the Quakers and Papists) for those with whom we disagree. Also, while thanking God for Roger Williams and his successor defenders of soul freedom, and Martin Luther King for enlarging the Baptist motif to include a vision of "the blessed community," we must be ready for further variations on the theme, for the enlargement and deepening of the motif. Who will be the next Roger Williams or Martin Luther King? Where will he or she be prepared to minister? I welcome the launching of this chair of Baptist Studies, and I pray that it be not only historical, pastoral, and theological, but prophetic and visionary.

22

The Courage to Be (2014)

This was written as an introduction to the Third Edition of Paul Tillich's The Courage to Be *(New Haven: Yale University Press, 2014).*

It seems like only yesterday that I walked out the door of 16 Chauncey St. in Cambridge after attending my last meeting as a student in Professor Paul Tillich's famous "home seminar." We had gathered every two weeks in the ample living room of his apartment under his huge print of Picasso's "Guernica," which he called "the greatest religious painting of the twentieth century." Doctoral students from several different divisions of the university were always included. We sat in a circle with Tillich seated like a benevolent uncle in an armchair at one end. Cans of beer and soft drinks were available. Each time we met one of us gave a thirty-minute summary (not a second more) of the thesis we were working on. First, Tillich would comment on it, always perceptively and constructively. Then he would lead a general discussion. His objective was to help us to appreciate different disciplines and various ways of thinking. The home seminar was one of my most valuable educational experiences. But when I walked out the door that day in 1962 I was a bit depressed. Tillich and I were both leaving soon, he to move to the University of Chicago and I, having finished my dissertation, to look for a job.

Tillich had been a teacher and a model for me, both personally and intellectually. It started when, in 1952, I first read *The Courage to Be* and decided immediately that someday I wanted to study with him. But his influence flowered during the time we were both at Harvard, he as a University Professor and I as a doctoral candidate. True, I voiced some criticism of him in my book *The Secular City* (1965), but I often assigned his books in the courses I taught. Nonetheless, when I began to re-read *The Courage to Be* in 2012, I opened it with some misgivings. What if it no longer carried the impact that had enchanted me sixty

384

years before? What if the Tillich I so admired now turned out to be dated—as my students might say—"so yesterday"?

One of the benefits of studying with Tillich was that he so evidently loved being at Harvard, a sentiment his students sometimes did not always feel as intensely during the grim slog through general exams and dissertations. A couple months after he moved to Cambridge in 1955 from Union Theological Seminary, someone asked Tillich how he was liking it. He answered emphatically, "Very much, at last I am back in a *university*." His response no doubt echoed the years he had spent both as a student and then as a faculty member at the universities of Berlin, Tübingen, and Frankfurt. He loved being at a university because its sheer diversity provided the scope he needed to pursue his lifelong intellectual project: crossing boundaries to bring back together that which had been wrongly torn asunder. He longed, as he often said, to restore the "uni" to the university. But as I picked up *The Courage to Be* again and thought of all that has changed since 1952, my uneasiness quickened. How would Tillich fare today?

I discovered that Tillich does indeed hold up. And of all his myriad writings, *The Courage to Be* best epitomizes his passion to cross boundaries. The book grew out of the Terry Lectures which Tillich delivered at Yale in 1950. The terms set by the foundation for these lectures state explicitly that they should examine "religion in the light of science and philosophy." For Tillich this was a perfect formula, exactly what he always wanted to do, with perhaps one qualification. Ever the dialectician, he also wanted to talk about science and philosophy *in the light of religion*.

Today *The Courage to Be* remains a *tour de force*. Like a triumphal arch it spans the centuries from Plato to Heidegger, and includes the Stoics, Augustine, the Renaissance and Reformation, Spinoza and Nietzsche. It touches on Sartre, Camus, Arthur Miller's *Death of a Salesman* and Tennessee Williams' *A Streetcar Named Desire*. But why, one might ask, should Tillich select such a seemingly unlikely keystone as "courage" to support this arch? The Greek word for courage is *thorros* which suggests boldness or confidence. Achilles is perhaps the classical embodiment. But except for self-sacrificing fire fighters or heroic Navy Seals, courage is not a virtue we talk about much nowadays. It rings just a little archaic.

Still, Tillich knew what he was doing. He begins *The Courage to Be* with a discussion of Plato's dialogue *Laches* in which Socrates and his companions try to define courage. They fail. But for Tillich, the failure is significant. They fail for a good reason: because "courage" is *not one virtue among others: it is the central virtue* on which all the others depend. Nor is it just a moral virtue; it is also what he calls an "ontological" virtue. It is the courage "to be." Spinoza, who might qualify as one of Tillich's favorite philosophers, advances in Part III of his *Ethics* a similar idea in his description of what he called "conatus": *"The effort by which each thing endeavors to persevere in its own being is nothing but the actual essence of the thing itself." [Proposition 7].*

Spinoza's *conatus* is the near equivalent of Tillich's courage to be. Being is not something that just *is*; it must constantly strive to affirm itself against the threats posed by nonbeing. For both Spinoza and for Tillich, this continuous affirmation of being is also the essence of each individual person. It is related to both Augustine's "restlessness" and Nietzsche's "will to power." From the tiniest insect to the entire cosmos that which *is* must strive to maintain itself in being. For Tillich, this endless struggle is not something to be lamented. Without it life would be inert, not real life at all. Hamlet's "To be or not to be" is indeed *the* question. It is everyone's question, and it is also the one that underlies all the questions asked by the various academic specialties. This explains why Tillich believed that an analysis of courage could help bridge the gaps between philosophy, science, literature and theology.

To today's reader, however, who rarely worries about bridging the chasm between disciplines, but does muse, at least on occasion, about his own existence, this may all sound quaintly theoretical. For Tillich it is not. When he recalls that the word "courage" derives from the French word for heart, he also reminds the reader that the "heart" symbolizes far more than just the seat of emotions. It has meant, and still means, the vital center of reality, including human reality. Courage is the capacity to affirm oneself in spite of death, finitude, and anxiety which are constantly arrayed against it. No one is ever an outsider to this struggle.

Here one of the first big question marks about Tillich's relevance for the twenty-first century crossed my mind. Today developing one's "human potential" has burgeoned into a lucrative cottage industry. Airport kiosks bulge with books on confidence building. People pay good money to attend weekend conferences on "assertiveness training." What, if anything, does all this have to do with Tillich's "courage to be"?

Tillich was writing this book in 1950, before the full blossoming of the "me generation," or the human potential movement. Consequently, he never confronts the mass producing of self-assertion. But when he comes close, he is more positive than might be expected. He censures theology for criticizing "anything that seems to affirm the self." But, in his characteristic fashion, he delves deeper. He locates the threat to the self at levels that cannot be swept away by positive thinking or self-help manuals. This threat he calls simply "anxiety." It is "existen-

tial." It arises because the self as a participant in "being" constantly
faces the menace of nonbeing as its price for staying alive. Anxiety is
different from fear. With fear there is always an object. We fear *some-thing*. But since anxiety results from the threat of nonbeing, there is no
object. Anxiety is the sheer, naked terror of nonbeing, which Tillich
finds hinted at in such diverse sources as Durer's "Knight, Death and
the Devil," and in Sartre's "No Exit." But the artists and poets are never
fully successful in depicting anxiety because it has no name or face.

At the core of this book is Tillich's famous phenomenology of three
types of anxiety: of fate and death; of guilt and condemnation; and
of emptiness and meaninglessness. These phantoms have all surfaced
as the principal form of anxiety in successive periods of Western his-tory. For the ancients it was the anxiety of fate, which—in the end—no
one could escape, as the House of Atreus discovered. In the medieval
period it was guilt, which the Catholic Church sought to confront with
the confessional and the sacraments. At the Reformation the Protes-tant churches responded with the preaching of justification by grace
through faith. But in our time it is the threat of meaninglessness that
is the most devastating expression of anxiety. For Tillich we no longer
live in the fate-haunted era of *The Iliad* or the guilt and condemnation
tormented age of *The Inferno*. We wander in T. S. Eliot's "Wasteland"
among works by Picasso, Dali, and Jackson Pollock in which space and
time have imploded.

But, the question persists: do people today still experience this gut-numbing anxiety? Tillich thought they do, as the demons that come to
light in psychotherapy and psychoanalysis show. He draws a sharp dis-tinction between what he calls "pathological" or neurotic anxiety and
"existential anxiety." The fact that "talk therapy," which was flourish-ing during Tillich's lifetime, has now faded, and pharmaceuticals are
the preferred treatment does not change his analysis. Psychotherapy,
whatever its form, may treat neurotic anxiety, but it cannot and should
not try to eradicate existential anxiety, which is integral to being alive.
Still, the question remains: do people today experience the anxiety
Tillich describes?

The British Tillich scholar Russell Le Manning has remarked that
many people today are so engulfed by the distracting tsunami of mar-ket consumer culture that no existential threats can penetrate the
relentless buzz and glitz. We are dazed and numbed by a daily barrage
of tweets and ads. We lose the capacity for reflection, and are insu-lated by the endless chatter from being aware of any existential peril.

If asked what their characteristic form of anxiety is today many people might check "none of the above."

I think Le Manning is right, up to a point. Researchers who observe how young people rely on their iPads, Facebook pages, and cell phones have noticed a certain jittery anxiety in their behavior. Some send and receive up to 400 messages a day. Why? Many cannot go for more than a few minutes without checking on whether they have received a message. Many insist on using the devices while driving, despite laws against it in several states. Videos of such young people indicate if they have to stop using them even for a short time they grow tense and fidgety. Have they missed a call or message? Should they send a text, however trivial, to someone, anyone? Have we bypassed Descartes and landed in the age of "I text, therefore I am"? In an age of massive "attention deficit disorder" it appears that what they are actually seeking is not *distraction*, but *connection*, something—anything—that will help them avoid facing the precariousness of their own being.

I have sometimes raised the question of whether anxiety still intrudes into their lives with students in my classes, mostly young people between 18 and 25. First I describe what I call my own "three o'clock in the morning syndrome." It occurs when, with a touch of insomnia, I wake up and climb out of bed. The house is dark. Everyone else is asleep. The normal markers of my everyday life, the books and furniture, seem somehow inert and slightly unreal. If I resist the temptation to switch on the TV or computer I catch a glimpse of what Tillich is talking about. And I understand why no one can endure it for very long. Like contemplating one's own death, or staring into the sun, one quickly turns away. We need to recreate those markers, do something to reduce the menace of nonbeing (anxiety) to something we can merely fear so it becomes manageable.

One of the signal strengths of *The Courage to Be* is that it does not stop at the personal level. Tillich believed that whole cultures can fall into pathologies as they desperately try to fend off collective anxiety. His famous distinction between "the courage to be as a part" and the "courage to be as oneself" leads into an analysis of the politics of modern societies. His examples of the courage to be as a part are the collectivisms of the twentieth century. Tillich knew both Communism and Nazism painfully and at first hand. His description of them as systems in which people surrendered their individual selfhood for the false security of a sheltering but stifling corporate identity rings true. He fought against both in Weimar Germany by helping to organize the religious socialist movement. Nazism collapsed with the defeat of Germany in 1945, but Communism continued as a vigorous worldwide movement for nearly half a century. China, the most populous country in the world, had just fallen to the Maoists the year the Terry Lectures were delivered. One wonders what Tillich might say about the stunning transformation of whole nations like China and the USSR from Communism into ruthless state capitalism.

But what about America? In some ways Tillich's description of his own adopted country, as an example of "democratic conformism," another expression of the "courage to be as a part," reveals him at his most discerning. Unlike the dismissive rants of some critics of mass society, Tillich's view is more nuanced. He rightly notes that for Americans "productivity" is the key. We, or at least most of us, stake our lives on our work, in participating—in Tillich's words—in the process by which the cosmos constantly creates and recreates itself. Work is sacred, and this is a quality shared by the Greenwich Village artist, the "productive" writer or scholar, and the welder on the Detroit assembly line. Productivity in this sense also underlies our typical American philosophies like pragmatism and process thought. This also explains why the crisis of joblessness is far more than an economic one. To be without work is to be deprived of a role in the life process itself. It is the modern equivalent of being banished from the polis or excommunicated from the church.

What would Tillich make of the current spiritual climate in America, such as the resurgence of fundamentalisms? He thought that the main challenge to making the Christian message known in the modern world would be secularism and scientific skepticism. We do have a few well-publicized atheists today, but secularism appears to be in retreat. The most prominent feature of our religious situation, besides fundamentalism, is its opposite: a vague spirituality, the merchandizing of shallow religiosity, and a kind of "whatever" indifference. Wired into a pulsing global web of information, "distracted from distraction by distraction . . ." as T. S. Eliot writes, our culture only rarely rises to the level of being aware of the threat of meaninglessness. Still I am convinced that anxiety remains present and only needs to be acknowledged, named, and answered.

Tillich closes *The Courage to Be* by turning to existentialism, his example of the "courage to be as oneself." He believed it was the signature philosophy of our time. It may have been in his time, but is it today? When I was a college student, existentialism was *le dernier cri*. We didn't know much about it but it sounded intense and cool, and we all had our well-thumbed editions of Camus's *The Stranger*. When I visited Paris one summer with a tour group in 1957 I quickly made my way to the St.-Germain-des-Prés and bought a glass of *chianti* at the

Café les Deux Magots. I wanted to see where Sartre and Simone de Beauvoir wrote, and perhaps catch a glimpse of some current existentialists. I don't think I saw any, but when Tillich wrote this book, existentialism was still a formidable presence. Now, half a century later, it is an endangered species.

Tillich distinguished between what he calls the "existentialist *attitude*" (we can only know what radically concerns us by a radical personal involvement in our knowing), and the "*philosophy* of existentialism." The latter he traced back to Nietzsche and Kierkegaard. For Tillich, existentialism was principally a philosophy of protest, a dissent from the objectifying impersonality of modern society. It insisted that human beings have no previous given essence, that we must generate our own. In Sartre's famous dictum, "the essence of man *is* his existence." Tillich believed the existentialists made a vital contribution: "They tried to indicate a way for the courage to be as oneself under conditions which annihilate the self and replace it with the thing."

Tillich warmly embraced the existentialist *attitude*, but was cautious about the *philosophy*. He liked to point out that we all live in the polarity between self and world. The collectivists subsume individuals into a closed "world," which vacates the self. Its danger is totalism. But the existentialist fixation on self-formation eclipses the world. Its danger is solipsism.

As far as I know there are no more existentialist philosophers sipping Pernod at Parisian cafes (or anywhere else), so I am glad Tillich did not wed his theology too tightly to them. But that prompts another question. If existentialism is no longer, as it once was, the characteristic philosophy of our time, then what is? Is there a philosophy that has displaced it?

I think the answer is that we have no single characteristic philosophy today. There is an understandable reason for this absence. By Tillich's own account both the existentialist attitude and the philosophy grew out of the preoccupations of Western civilization. They were a response to its crisis. But today we are no longer so clearly defined by that Western tradition. The advent of a global civilization and the unexpected resurgence of world religions have dramatically de-centered our sense of living out the narrative of the old Greeks-to-Romans-to-Europeans narrative of "Western Civ." Western culture is hardly dead, but it is now one voice in a larger polyphonic chorus. There is no single "attitude" or philosophy that focuses the temper of our times. Tillich styled his work as "answering theology," addressing the deeper questions posed by the culture and showing "how the symbols of faith" respond to these questions. But what are those questions today? *Whose* questions are they? And in a world of multiplying religious pluralism, *what* are those symbols of faith? And *which* faith are we talking about?

Only toward the end of his life did Tillich struggle to come to terms with the religious and cultural diversity that is now so evident. His trip to Japan in May–July of 1960 and his encounter with Buddhist scholars at Kyoto obviously shook him. There he met thinkers who were not focused on Being but on Nothingness. Still, Tillich remained a boundary-crosser into his last years. Perhaps the mystical current in his theology, his fascination with the Pseudo-Dionysius and Jacob Boehme and the mystical stream in Christianity might have helped him cross this boundary as well.

Tillich's answer to the challenge of living in the self–world polarity, avoiding the false solutions of the "courage to be as a part" or as oneself was what he calls "absolute faith," which is not an opinion or a theoretical affirmation of something uncertain. It is "a state of being grasped by the power of being. . . . He who is grasped by this power is able to affirm himself because he knows that he is affirmed by the power of being itself." Absolute faith does not destroy anxiety, but takes it into itself. Tillich saw this as a contemporary expression of the "dark night of the soul," known by the classical saints and mystics. But Tillich knew in his own life about this dark night. He knew the demons of doubt. He states in *The Courage to Be* that just as in classical Protestant theology we are forgiven by God even though we are sinners, so we are accepted by God even though we doubt his existence. For Tillich, doubt is not something to be scorned or denied; it is a vital component in any genuine faith. Perhaps the most famous sentence he ever wrote is the final sentence in this book. I am sure he himself realized it was foundational because he put it in italics: *"The courage to be,"* he wrote, *"is rooted in the God who appears when God has disappeared in the anxiety of doubt."*

Tillich was widely admired by scholars in many fields, including the Harvard physicist and fellow refugee from the Nazis, Gerald Holton, who compared him with Albert Einstein as a man in search of the unity of the universe. He was also held in esteem by some philosophers. He was elected to membership in the Columbia University Philosophy Club, whose early members had included Bertrand Russell and William James. But he was not universally admired. He did not escape biting attacks both from inside the theological guild and from outside. Some modern philosophers, especially those inclined to positivism or linguistic analysis, did not see his work as a bridge at all. They dismissed it as a phalanx of planks from a ponderous German philosophical past. There were other criticisms. "Courage?" scoffed one classical scholar, "courage is a pagan virtue, not a Christian virtue." Another wrote, "What is this 'God above God'? Isn't this just thinly disguised atheism?" Tillich handled these criticisms with tact. He listened carefully. He responded with respect. He rarely wrote a polemical phrase. He had, one might say, both the courage of his convictions and the courage to change. He never stopped re-writing and re-thinking.

For Paul Tillich courage was not just an essential intellectual category. It was profoundly personal. *The Courage to Be* is in some ways an autobiographical portrait of the author himself. What inspired me most about Tillich when I was a young theologian was not first of all his stunning command of the history of philosophy and theology, but his own human courage: his willingness to stare the withering challenge of modernity in the face without retreating to either a safe orthodoxy or a cynical skepticism. It was his courage to confront and accept his own doubts and his own anxiety.

There is a quality of daring in Tillich's thinking. He took risks, and he dared us to do the same, something a novice scholar in almost any field is rarely encouraged to do. One of the risks he ran was to abandon any fetishism of particular words. He knew, both from his keen observation of modern culture and through his own spiritual struggles, that the words "grace" and "faith" and even "God" had not only lost much of their original power, but had also been so distorted that they had often been evacuated of meaning. So he boldly experimented with a new vocabulary. If the word "God" no longer speaks to you, he once wrote, say "depth." Instead of "sin," say "separation." Instead of "forgiveness," say "acceptance." Tillich was sometimes called "the theologians' theologian"; still, many of these audacious experiments in a new religious language appear not in his formal theology, but in his sermons, collected in books like *The Shaking of the Foundations*.

Yes, Tillich still speaks to the current generation. Even though the challenges to faith may be different ones, his fearless way of facing the challenges in his day still provides a compelling example. One of the reasons we who were just entering the theological guild admired Tillich was that he could speak so eloquently to those outside, and we all wanted to be able to do that too. He still does. I welcome this sixtieth anniversary edition of *The Courage to Be*. It is not just for religion scholars but for anyone concerned to live today with both unblinking realism and genuine faith. As any reader will discover, it is not an easy book to read. It is demanding, but absorbing, and is still infinitely rewarding.

23

The Babylonian Captivity
of Theology (2015)

This address was delivered on August 31, 2015, for a Convocation marking the 200th anniversary of Harvard Divinity School. It also marked Harvey Cox's fifty years—or, as he noted, 100 semesters!—on the faculty of HDS.

Yes, it is true. It was fifty years ago that a rookie professor nervously faced his first class here at Harvard Divinity School. And yes, it is true that two hundred years ago the Harvard Corporation took an action that we refer to as the founding of the HDS.

It is also true that 3,456 years ago the Israelites escaped from their enslavement in Egypt in an event we call the "exodus."

And it was 2,650 years ago that the Israelites were driven by Nebuchadnezzar into their seventy years of captivity in Babylon, which we call the "exile."

My question for us today is this: was the founding of HDS an exodus or was it an exile?

A Troublesome Subject

At the first meeting of a committee he organized last fall to think about how to mark our bicentennial, Dean Hempton commented that the founding of HDS could be viewed as a tactic by the anti-clerical wing of the Enlightenment to remove religion from the place it once held both in the public sphere and in the academy, a place it had occupied from the time of the ancients, through the medieval era, and indeed up through first two centuries of Harvard's history. It could be seen as an attempt to privatize theology, to consign it to its own little realm.

In his magisterial three-volume work on the history of religion at Harvard, the late George Hunston Williams agrees with this "exile" interpretation. He describes the beginning of HDS in a section he

entitles "A Tendency to Distance Divinity," then quotes an announcement made by the Corporation of the University on May 13, 1824,
which reads as follows: "The purpose of the Theological Institution
will be more effectively served by separating it from the University. . . ."
This distancing was carried further with the construction of Divinity Hall a decade after the founding of HDS. It was the first Harvard
building to be located outside Harvard Yard.

Professor Williams then quotes an address delivered one hundred
years later in 1915 by Francis Greenwood Peabody, then the dean of
HDS, in which he states that the erection of the red brick building was
not really to maintain a school of theology, "but on the contrary to
remove the troublesome subject of theology from among the responsi-
bilities of the university." Peabody then points to a revealing sentence
in the original announcement which suggests that the advantage of
this banishment of theology to its own separate location would also
be a relief to those officials charged with tending to the "important
concerns of the University"— theology and religion obviously not being
among them.

What, we may wonder, was so "troublesome" about theology?
Undoubtedly the squabble over Unitarianism going on at the time was
irksome. But, truth be told, theology by its very nature is, or should be,
troublesome. If theology is doing its job, applying the teachings of the
prophets from Jeremiah to Jesus to current issues, it will inevitably vex
the guardians of the status quo. It is part of theology's job description.
But what, we might ask, was the particular trouble theology was stirring up in the early 1800s?

One scholar has suggested it might well have been the college's concern about the involvement of its students in the movement to abol-
ish slavery. The idea is intriguing. In the decades after the Divinity
School's dismissal from the Yard it was the churches, especially in
New England, led by voices like those of Wendell Phillips and William
Ellery Channing, that became the epicenter of abolitionism. Lucretia
Mott, both a feminist and an abolitionist, wrote that her inspiration
had come from the words we heard in today's reading from the Bible
about the "release of the captives." But Harvard College, along with its
Ivy sisters, did not support the movement that many of its graduates
were leading, suspecting abolitionism of being impulsive, hasty, and ill-
considered. Rather it was a small college in Ohio called Oberlin that,
under the leadership of revivalist preacher Charles Granison Finney,
linked abolitionism to Christian discipleship, and was the first to admit
African Americans and women into its student body.

Successive generations of Harvard administrators have continued to have trouble with this "troublesome subject," particularly with its political aspects. During the ruinous Vietnam War once again voices from the religious community, such as Fr. Daniel Berrigan, Rev. William Sloan Coffin, and Rev. Dr. Martin Luther King, Jr., gave clear voice to the anti-war movement. When in 1969 many Harvard students and faculty called for a non-violent strike to end the university's collaboration with the bombing and napalming, college officials were not happy. And one administrator said he was particularly distressed to learn that Divinity School students and faculty were among the protesters.

Today, according to Pope Francis's eloquent new encyclical *Laudato Si*, it is the earth itself that we have enslaved, and the air and the seas with which we are at war. And now once again students and faculty are demonstrating, this time to ask that the university withdraw its support from these new forms of war and slavery by divesting from the industries that are making billions of dollars by extracting carbon fuels and pumping them into our atmosphere, pushing us ever further into a climate catastrophe that has already begun. And once again it is a voice from the religious community, none other than the bishop of Rome, who has issued the clarion call. Yes, theology continues, to be, in Peabody's words, a "troublesome subject," in more ways than one.

The Deification of the Market

Paradoxically, just as theology was being politely ushered out the back door of the university, another religion, although we rarely call it that, was coming in through the front. The latter part of the nineteenth century in America became the period when what might be called the "market worldview" was beginning to affect every aspect of national life, including that of the university.

How did it happen? It is useful to glimpse at how this pecuniary mentality, the religion of Mammon, first crept into and eventually saturated the ethos of the modern university, including Harvard. Remember that here at Harvard we are all children of the Puritans. Despite Harvard's relegation of theology to the periphery, the influence of a secularizing Calvinism inherited from our founders still shaped the university's thinking. It might also be recalled that after centuries in which theologians deplored avarice as one of the seven deadly sins, and the church placed usurers (those who lend money at interest) among the worst of sinners, it was John Calvin who in the sixteenth century had permitted moderate interest to be charged in the ultra-Reformed city state of Geneva. But while the "permitted" part of his doctrine was quickly accepted, the "moderation" part was soon neglected. In England, the Puritan descendants of Calvin seized on the "moderate interest" idea and ran with it. The first step in the rise of the market culture social imaginary had been taken.

Not everyone accepted this retreat of religion from the growing cultural power of the market. In 1552 in Scotland the newly Reformed Church issued a catechism that condemned usurers along with covetous merchants, masters who withhold wages, and landlords who grind their tenants. But though they often tried, neither Protestants nor Catholics could hold out for long against the commercial flood. As the ring of the cash register grew louder it all but drowned out the exhortations of preachers and moralists. Theologians began raising the white flag. A widely read treatise by Thomas Wilson entitled "Discourse on Usury" advised merchants that they "must not be overthwarted by preachers and others that cannot skill their doings." In twenty-first-century English this simply means: Don't pay any attention to these religious busybodies and their harping about greed; they don't know what they are talking about. The dismissive tone may sound familiar. It is the same one used today by such Catholic politicians as Marco Rubio and Rick Santorum to explain why they can simply ignore the words of Pope Francis when he talks about global economic inequality or climate change. But notice that it is not just some particular teaching that is dismissed by this sentiment; it is the very idea of theologians meddling in the sacred marketplace.

The momentum continued. We were instructed that the market needs no restraints from church or state because it is self-regulating; it has its own infallibility. Finally, in the seventeenth century, a symbolic climax occurred in the millennia-long dispute when a certain Rev. David Jones decided to preach a sermon against usury in St. Mary Woolmoth on Lombard Street on the text, "The Pharisees who were covetous heard all these things and they derided Christ." The preacher was summarily dismissed from his post. The market religion could not permit such brazen heresy.

As the nineteenth century unfolded it sometimes seemed that the cultural power of the market was achieving monopoly, its own kind of omnipresence and omnipotence. But during the same period, history witnessed some impressive, if ultimately unsuccessful efforts to challenge the growing hegemony of what Walter Benjamin has called the "arcade culture" and its religion. Pope Leo XIII's historic encyclical *Rerum Novarum* (1891) insisted on the rights of labor. In the first decades of the twentieth century, a Baptist minister, Walter Rauschenbusch, advocated what he termed the "Social Gospel," which called for the application of Christian principles to the economy. Distinguished Protestant theologians like Paul Tillich and Reinhold Niebuhr have written scathing critiques of the excesses of capitalism, and both were active socialists early in their lives. In the 1960s a movement called "liberation theology" appeared in Latin America and contested the Catholic Church's long alliance with the ruling elites. Its watchword was a "preferential option for the poor." It thrived for some years and spread to Asia and Africa, even as Rome strove to contain it. Recently, however, liberation theology has staged a remarkable comeback as Pope Francis emphasizes its central themes in his teachings and publicly endorses some of its key figures, such as Fr. Gustavo Gutiérrez of Peru, sometimes deemed the movement's founding theologian, and the martyred Archbishop Oscar Romero of El Salvador, one of its most revered spokesmen. Clearly, the continuous surfacing of movements like these suggests that the protracted cold war between prophetic biblical faith and the pecuniary values of a consumer lifestyle is not entirely over.

At Harvard, however, during the two hundred years after the exile of the Divinity School, the religion of the market, albeit still unrecognized as a religion, was extending its sway. Harvard, Protestant to its marrow, and individualist by temperament, took little notice of papal pronouncements. Even Dean Francis Greenwood Peabody's version of the social gospel fell under its sway. In his *Jesus and the Social Question* (1900), he stressed the need for labor rights and prison reform, but he did so by portraying the figure of Jesus as one who "sought to transform the world by transforming the individual and human motivations."

The kind of theology that did achieve recognition at Harvard was of the strictly inward variety. In other words religion was being subjected not only to external deportation but also to internal deformation, or shrinkage. By 1902 William James in his Gifford Lectures which became *The Varieties of Religious Experience* begins with these sentences: "Now in these lectures I propose to ignore the institutional branch entirely, to say nothing of the ecclesiastical organization, to consider as little as possible the systematic theology and the ideas about the gods themselves, and to confine myself to religion pure and simple."

One might well wonder what, if anything, is left of religion after both its corporate expression and its intellectual substance are so summarily discarded. The answer for James, and then for legions of his epigones, was, as James put it, ". . . the feelings, acts and experiences of individual men in their solitude, so far as they apprehend themselves to stand in relation to whatever they may consider the divine." As for the Market Religion, James did not escape it either. He began referring to the truth of any claim as its "cash value."

James's accent on personal virtue and individual piety persisted, and was picked up by a later Harvard philosopher, Alfred North Whitehead. In his Lowell Institute Lecture in 1926, published in his *Religion in the Making*, the man who is often credited as the inspiration of process theology defined "religion" as what "the individual does with his own solitariness." Thus held at a long arm's length topographically and reduced to internal spirituality, theology could do little to question the rising tide of the market faith, especially when few people could see it as a faith, indeed, as by far the world's most powerful arbiter of meaning and values. So where do we stand today in this contest of worldviews at the beginning of HDS's third century?

The Battles of the Gods

We may be living today at the apex of the market worldview's power, even in the university. In his eye-opening book *Universities in the Marketplace*, our highly esteemed former president Derek Bok asks, "Is everything in a university for sale if the price is right?" Bok cautions that the answer is all too often "yes." Deeply troubled by the growing commercialization of our academic institutions, he probes the efforts on campus to profit financially not only from athletics but, increasingly, from education and research as well. He shows how such ventures are undermining core academic values. He finds that ". . . a brave new world has now emerged in which university presidents, enterprising professors, and even administrative staff can all find seductive opportunities to turn specialized knowledge into profit." But, Bok argues, universities, faced with these temptations, are jeopardizing their fundamental mission in their eagerness to make money by agreeing to more and more compromises with their historic purpose.

Bok wrote his book a full decade before the ominous legislation now being proposed in Wisconsin whereby, if it becomes a national model, professors could be sacked if enrollments in their courses drop below a certain number. This would amount to a large step in the further marketization of higher education. Imagine instructors desperately trying to drum up enrollments by parading around the campuses carrying sandwich boards peddling their seminars.

Harvard philosopher Michael Sandel has written that we once had a market economy, but now we have a market society. I have suggested that if we think of religion as a bundle of narratives and rituals that inform our values and endow life with meaning, then we also have a market religion, dispatching its zealous missionaries to every corner of the globe, converting people of all nations and tongues into customers, and spreading its version of the Golden Rule, in the form of cost–benefit analysis. Further, this is a religion that is all the more dominant because it is rarely recognized as such, even though those of us who study the phenomenology of religion know one when we see one.

Has that troublesome subject, theology, then, been successfully banished from the ivory tower?

Not quite. I am thankful that when I began doctoral studies here in 1958, it was in a program, "The Study of Religion," offered jointly by both the Graduate School of Arts and Sciences and HDS. And if the social-political dimension of religion had been diminished if not eliminated by the GSAS, this was decidedly not the case in the Divinity School. I continue to be grateful that my teachers—Paul Lehmann, Robert Bellah, James Luther Adams, and Paul Tillich—all focused on the cultural and structural aspects of religion. I was especially blessed that my principal advisor was Jim Adams, whose central conviction was that the essence of any religious movement becomes clearest in its institutional embodiment. Nor has our exile been complete. Our professors have taught in several other divisions of the university and bridge-building efforts continue.

The introduction of teaching in Religion at Harvard College in 1974 opened classrooms there for our faculty. It is fair to say that for decades Harvard College did not offer much support for undergraduates who wanted to pursue the serious study of religion. When, in the early 1980s, I was asked by the faculty of the College to teach a course on Jesus in the Moral Reasoning program, I looked through old catalogs to find when the last time a course with "Jesus" in the title appeared. That turned out to be 1913, in a course offered by George Santayana! In the meantime undergraduates who wanted to study religion had to find their way to the Divinity School, not always an easy task. But some venturesome souls did. The renowned *Washington Post* columnist E. J. Dione was one. Hearing about a course here that he thought he would like to take he asked his house master where the Divinity School was, and was promptly directed down Brattle Street to the Episcopal Divinity School.

But the initiation of a "Study of Religion" concentration did not qualify as a full-fledged return of theology. What many of the college faculty who approved of the new concentration seemed to want was the comparative, historical and "wissenschaftliche" teaching not *of*

religion but *about* religion. Some continued to be suspicious of "theology" as unduly particularistic, even confessional, not sufficiently objective. Consequently many of us who taught in the program sometimes
bent over backward to avoid what might be viewed as advocacy. We did
not want to be viewed as troublesome.

Return from Exile

The good news today is that the expatriation of theology may be coming to an end. One reason is that, for bane or for blessing, religions
and theologies are beginning to play a larger role in public life here
and abroad, and we cannot afford to ignore them. Martin Luther King
taught us all that theology has a vital contribution to make to public
life. Now Pope Francis continues that example by trying to inch his
church away from its obsession with bedroom issues toward addressing economic injustice and the climate breakdown. In the university
there is a growing feeling that some of the conditions that obtained in
the early nineteenth or even the twentieth century no longer do.

A more generous reading of the Divinity School's deportation in
1815 is that it was simply a part of the segmentation and specializa-
tion of the time, a fragmentation that in recent years has sometimes
reached an absurd extreme. When Paul Tillich, who had taught at Mar-
burg and Frankfurt, first arrived here in 1955 from Union Seminary he
exclaimed that he was delighted to be at last "back in a university." But
after a year or two, Tillich remarked that he hoped one thing he might
do here was to help "restore the lost 'uni' to the university."

That "uni" remains elusive, but our colleagues in the various disparate sectors of the university are noticing that our ever narrowing specializations are reaching a dead end. From medicine to law to public
health, physics, economics and across the board, issues have arisen that
cannot be reasonably tackled within the constricted borders of their
own disciplines. To take the most glaring example, the lethal threat
of catastrophic climate break-down demands the devoted attention
of geology, political science, psychology, law, education, public health
and . . . yes, religious studies. And it requires us to work together in
ways for which our training has not always best prepared us.

Another healthy change is that the old distinction between theology and religion is much less useful. The myth of total objectivity
in teaching is being left behind as unattainable and probably misbegotten. As teachers we are human beings incarnate in history, not
detached observers. We cannot, and should not, shed our skins as we
enter the classroom door. Our living commitments inevitably reveal

themselves in what we choose to teach, what we include or leave out, how we present the material, even in our body language and tone of voice. What we need to do is to be sharply aware, as the students say, of "where we are coming from." We need to be conscious of what shapes our thinking, and make very sure that other perspectives get equal time. The hoary idea that theology is incurably subjective and the study of religion is objective no longer describes the intellectual horizon within which we work.

All this means that as the Divinity School begins the 201st year of our life, we must ponder carefully the meaning of our initial "distancing" from the university. Let us remember, for example, that Israel's captivity was not a total loss. The faith of the covenant people deepened and broadened during those decades of exile. The years in Babylon produced two of the greatest prophets, Ezekiel and Deutero-Isaiah. The great Babylonian Talmud was composed. When the Israelites did return they had a richer gift to offer as a light to the nations.

Now the time may be ripe for the Divinity School's return, a return that, as I have suggested, may already be under way. Clearly, the Divinity School and the other parts of our university need each other. As Pope Francis has recently written, when theology does not engage the burning concerns of the age, it becomes trivial and sterile. But if the university is truly committed to shedding the light of Veritas, not just within its own precincts, the Divinity School has a couple gifts to bring to the table.

First, we have learned how to tap into many traditions to uncover the language human beings have used to struggle with those questions of meaning and value that keep recurring in different forms.

Second, if the university wants to reach outside its gates, the Divinity School has something unique to offer, namely congregations. Lawyers have clients, doctors have patients; even educators deal with students who are under their influence only for a limited span. But the ministers and other leaders of the faith communities we prepare often serve their congregants over extended periods of time. We have an unparalleled constituency that encompasses people of a vast variety of classes and colors.

But we need to be cautious. Clearly the role we once tried to play in the classical university, when some still referred to theology as the "Queen of the Sciences," should be left behind. A much more appropriate role is that of servant. Can the Divinity School forgo the lure of seeking privilege and recognition for itself and instead seek to provide the welcoming space where a variety of fields and disciplines struggle together to confront what Tillich called the "ultimate concerns" their work has uncovered, and for which neither they nor we have all the answers? And at the same time can we continue our calling as the "troublesome subject," quietly challenging any ideology or worldview, including the market culture, that insists on its own picture of reality as the singular and ultimate one? I hope we can. Let us all gather here again in one hundred years and see how well we have done.

"Just as I Am" (1983)

This text is adapted from the final chapter of Just as I Am *(Nashville: Abingdon Press, 1988).*

Readers who grew up as I did in an evangelical Baptist church will not need to have the title of this book explained to them. It is the name of the hymn that is often sung during revival services, after the sermon, when a life without God and hell's terrors have been vividly painted and the doors are opened to accept Christ and be saved. The "invitation" is given. And now "with every head bowed and every eye closed" the preacher or the visiting evangelist urges those in the congregation who have not yet made their decision for Christ to come forward. The organ or piano plays "Just as I Am." The choir, often with the congregation humming along, sings too . . . "without one plea, / But that thy blood was shed for me."

Though the words may sound lachrymose to many, for me they still convey a sense of comfort and assurance. Was I really acceptable to God "just as I am"? Was it really true that I needed no improvements, no alterations, that I could enter the presence of the Most High, the terrifying *mysterium tremendum* (as I later learned to say) *just* as I am? If true, that was very good news to an adolescent who was always being reminded—or so it seemed to me—of my shortcomings and defects. I was never good at football or basketball. Someone else played the saxophone sweeter than I did. Most of the girls seemed to prefer other guys for dates. Although I did fairly well in my classes there was always someone, usually one of the girls, who got a higher score on the exam. Both my parents seemed to love me unconditionally but, like all kids, I sensed behind their expressions of affection a lot of hopes and expectations I was not sure I could live up to.

But God accepted me just as I am?

That was not judgment but good news. Years later, when I read Paul Tillich's famous sermon entitled "You Are Accepted," I knew exactly what it meant, and I could hear the melody of the old hymn still humming on in the back of my mind.

Now the time has come to close this book about my faith journey and, once again, the perfectionist pressures instilled in me by a productivity-driven culture war within me against the assurance that I am accepted "just as I am" and that this book will have to be ended "just as it is."

Ending a book about my faith journey is no easier than beginning it. The book must end. The journey lurches on. . . .

As I reread the pages I have written here in an effort to bring them to a close what impressed me most of all is that my faith journey has been inextricably bound up with passing the faith on: not just my passing it on to others, but the others who passed it on to me. . . . Biblical faith is a generational phenomenon. It comes alive as it is lived out and passed on. My own faith grows and deepens—if and when it does—mostly when I act on it and when I try to give it to someone else, usually my children but also to my students. What is real and what is ersatz, what I believe and what I think I believe (or would like to believe), sort themselves out when I face that generational bridge-and-barrier, that awful obligation we have to help the next cadre of human beings make sense out of the senseless. This taxing test has taught me that faith is not just something Abraham, Isaac, and Jacob shared (as did Sarah, Rebekah, and Rachel) but something which *came into being as it was passed along.* . . .

Some contemporary philosophers believe that human beings think by putting things in words, that if we believe we have an idea but cannot express it, we do not really have it yet. This may not be true for other people, but it is true for me. I often find myself saying something, or writing something, I had just not thought of before I expressed it. Only when it comes to speech—silent, written, or spoken—does a thought attain any reality for me. Consequently this rambling and disjoined account has not just been a description of my faith journey or a resumé of the process of passing it on. It has been a part of the journey and of the passing it on. My fondest hope is that those who have stayed with me this far have also done some journeying and some passing it on while they have been reading. And as I end I take some satisfaction in knowing that just as the journey began long before I appeared, it will continue after I am gone.

Index

405